ROUGH AND REGULAR

A History of Philadelphia's 119th Regiment of Pennsylvania Volunteer Infantry, The Gray Reserves

Larry B. Maier

This Burd Street Press publication
was printed by
Beidel Printing House, Inc.
63 West Burd Street
Shippensburg, PA 17257-0152 USA

In respect for the scholarship contained herein, the acid-free paper used in this book meets the guidelines for permanence and durability of the Committee on Production Guidelines for Book Longevity of the Council on Library Resources.

For a complete list of available publications
please write
Burd Street Press
Division of White Mane Publishing Company, Inc.
P.O. Box 152
Shippensburg, PA 17257-0152 USA

Library of Congress Cataloging-in-Publication Data

Maier, Larry B., 1949–
Rough and regular : a history of Philadelphia's 119th Regiment of Pennsylvania Volunteer Infantry, the Gray Reserves / Larry B. Maier.
p. cm.
Includes bibliographical references and index.
ISBN 1-57249-082-9 (alk. paper)
1. United States. Army. Pennsylvania Infantry Regiment, 119th (1862–1865) 2. Pennsylvania--History--Civil War, 1861–1865--Regimental histories. 3. United States--History--Civil War, 1861–1865--Regimental histories. I. Title.
E527.5 119th.M34 1997
973.7'448--dc21 97-25357
CIP

PRINTED IN THE UNITED STATES OF AMERICA

This effort is dedicated to all those who discover that an ancestor served in the 119th Regiment of Pennsylvania Volunteer Infantry, and who wish to gain some idea of what price that ancestor paid so that the Union could be preserved for his descendants.

TABLE OF CONTENTS

List of Graphics

List of Maps

PREFACE

Upon being advised by a well-intentioned historian at the Fredericksburg National Park that, "there isn't much written about the 119th Pennsylvania, they were just another regiment out of Philadelphia," my personal research into the history of an ancestor was converted into a mission. I was suddenly no longer content solely with discovering the story of the tall, pensive young Union soldier pictured in a long hidden tin-type, which was discovered one Christmas morning behind a photograph of my father and grandfather standing side by side in their 80th Division uniforms. After hearing the historian's comment, the challenge became to rectify his accurate observation concerning the lack of a thorough history of the regiment in which my great-great-grandfather and his cousin were serving when they gave their "last full measure."[1]

At the time, I was not a Civil War enthusiast, and I had only the most rudimentary mental imagery of that war; blue-coated lines marching heroically into the face of fire-belching cannons with flags flying and bayonets gleaming; the Civil War as fought by John Wayne. I had no personal experience with war, having been blessed with a lottery number that was high enough to permit me to opt out of a conflict that was regularly portrayed as immoral and which appeared doomed to failure. Perhaps a certain amount of guilt and regret amplified my urge to memorialize what that sad-looking youth in the tin-type, and his comrades-in-arms in the 119th, experienced during their war.

What I learned over the next two and a half years while researching and writing this history added something to my life which had been sadly lacking; I gained a hero, or more correctly, thousands and thousands of heroes. The participants in the Civil War were heroes

---

[1]John E. Faust of H Company was the author's great-great-grandfather pictured in the tin-type. The author was also more distantly related to two other members of the 119th, Aaron Faust and Daniel Bardman.

only partially because of their willingness to march forward, time after time, into the face of often hideous death or disfigurement. What truly defined those men as heroes was the days before and after the great battles, when the adrenaline wasn't pumping, and the landscape was not tinted red from the rage of combat.

Day after arduous day, the soldiers of the Civil War did their duty: they marched mile after crushing mile in heat, cold, and rain; up mountains, through swamps, while sometimes choking on dust, as ill fitting or worn shoes tortured their aching feet and as pack straps and rifle slings grounded coarse woolen clothing into their shoulders like sandpaper. They did their duty despite exhaustion induced by late bivouacs and pre-dawn marches, or perhaps from marching all night, often with nervous systems fried by stress and adrenaline burn-out from the previous day's combat. They routinely performed those feats of physical endurance on stomachs that were either empty, or partially filled with stuff that today would not be fed to a household pet; wormy bread, rancid bacon, fetid water, spoiled vegetables, and when even that was not available, with green apples or green corn. They did their duty with diarrhea, fevers, cramps, coughs, rashes, sprains, strains, blisters, and partially healed wounds, all without the benefit of even the most basic medications which every household now has in its medicine cabinet in the bathroom. As the men persevered through all the hardship, they did so with full knowledge that the next day might bring the same fate which they had witnessed being inflicted upon others on the battlefield; bodies ripped and torn by lead or iron, excruciating pain, gross and gut-wrenching disfigurement, or perhaps instant death without a moment to ask God for forgiveness; and then an unmarked grave.

There were certainly many reasons why most Civil War soldiers chose to ignore the high probability of a successful desertion and to accept that hardship; pride, loyalty to their unit or the friends and family who served by their side, or perhaps hatred of the enemy, and for the Confederates, the defense of home. It would seem that the predominant motivating factor for both sides, but especially for the North, was ideology and patriotism. Not all the Yankees shared all the same ideals, some fought to free the slaves, including the tens of thousands of black Americans who took up arms in a more personal crusade against slavery, while many couldn't have cared less about the fate of those held in bondage. Most however, had an abiding faith that the United States was a unique achievement in the history of mankind, and that its preservation justified any sacrifice which they might be called upon to make. Although the Southerners were not interested in the Union, their devotion to most of the concepts of democracy as they understood it was not entirely discredited by the issue of slavery. Now, in a time and country desperately in need of heroes, no better source can be found than in the men who fought in the Civil War.

The soldiers who comprised the 119th Regiment of Pennsylvania Volunteer Infantry were never placed at the pivot point between the success and failure of the Union cause as were a few other celebrated Federal regiments. There were, however, few regiments in the Army of the Potomac that could claim to have participated in more successes and endured more hardship in the cause of the preservation of the Union than the 119th. This history is offered as a tribute, in appreciation for the sacrifices made by the members of the 119th.

ACKNOWLEDGMENTS

A famous saying allows that any project worth doing is built upon ten percent inspiration and ninety percent perspiration. I have been blessed with ample assistance in both categories. Foremost in the inspiration department has been my teenage son, Eric. At this point in his young life he has little interest in his heritage. It has been my goal to prepare a work that will allow him, when that issue does become significant, to be able to fully appreciate the sacrifices his ancestors made to assure that this country could achieve its potential for greatness and goodness. If my son provided the carrot, then Historian Ray Brown from the Fredericksburg National Battlefield park, with his well-intended comment that there was not much written about the 119th Pennsylvania because they "... were just another regiment out of Philadelphia ..." provided the stick. Finally, my father, Clarence P. Maier, through his enthusiastic reception of each new chapter upon its completion, provided a fresh impetus for another.

Much of my perspiration was the result of worry over the visual content of the work, because obtaining appropriate photographs and the production of acceptable maps were matters beyond my direct control. There were many people who lent help to alleviate my anxiety in this regard. The staff at the United States Military History Institute in Carlisle, Pennsylvania were extremely helpful; and when it came to my rather inept efforts at photography in the image archives branch, they were extremely tolerant, as well. Kenneth Turner was kind enough to allow me access to the images of members of the 119th in his private collection, and then took valuable time from a busy schedule at a Gettysburg artifacts show to allow me to obtain reproductions of same through the assistance of *Military Images* magazine.

Most of the balance of the images contained in the work were obtained through the courtesy of the First Regiment Corp. and the 103rd Engineer Battalion museum in Philadelphia. I could not have asked for more help than was graciously provided by Colonel J. Craig Nannos and

Michael Benson. They, along with Joseph Harrison, allowed me full research access to the 103rd Engineer Battalion museum (a small gem of a museum containing hundreds of artifacts of the 103rd and its predecessor units from the Revolutionary War to Viet Nam), at the cost of significant contributions of their own time and travel. Further, Colonel Nannos not only provided exceptional efforts to secure the photographs of the officer's and enlisted man's kepis which appear in the work, but he also arranged for the services of Major John Miatta. The major was kind enough to photograph images of members of the Regiment, various artifacts from the First Regiment N. G. P. and the 119th, and various items of my own material, all free of charge. Finally, the First Regiment Corp. offered a significant financial contribution to help defray the expenses which I incurred in obtaining graphics and performing research.

Perhaps the issue which generated my most apprehension concerned battle maps. I was very fortunate to locate Don Barrett, with the local engineering firm of Rettew & Associates, who enthusiastically took on the task of transforming my crude sketches into a presentable format. The time and effort which he expended had a value far beyond what he charged, and I believe the end product, especially considering what I gave him to work with, is a highlight of the work.

I was also fortunate to receive invaluable assistance in the production of the text of the work. Several good friends, especially Barry Kintzer, were kind enough to proofread early drafts, and provided much welcomed constructive criticism. The most important assistance of all that I received was from the office computer wizard, Brenda McDonald. Without her effort and expertise, which ran the gamut from proofreading to setting up macros, the table for the roster, and graphics locations, this project would have taken ten, instead of three, years to complete -- if it would have been completed at all.

"Boys, it's rough, but I tell you it's regular."
Henry _____, pre-dawn hours, July 2, 1863,
Baltimore pike near the Pennsylvania border.

1

JOINING THE ARMY

For the first time in months, the Army of the Potomac was going to attempt an all-out assault on the Confederate trenches protecting Petersburg, in hopes of penetrating the enemy lines, capturing the rail center which supplied Richmond, and perhaps ending the war. Not since the very beginning of the siege in the summer of 1864 had the prospects for such an assault been brighter. For weeks the Southern lines had been hemorrhaging deserters, many of whom were boys or old men, and most of whom were tired, emaciated, and threadbare. On the previous day, April 1, 1865, Union Major General Philip H. Sheridan and the Fifth Corps had crushed Major General George E. Pickett's division and captured the key intersection of Five Forks on the Rebels' right flank. The rebellion was clearly tottering on the brink of collapse.

Despite those positive developments, there was surely not one member of the 119th Regiment of Pennsylvania Volunteer Infantry who expected anything but a bloody and desperate struggle. Only days before, Major General Horatio Wright, commander of the Sixth Corps of which the 119th was a part, had personally reconnoitered the Confederate emplacements which he described as an "... extraordinarily strong line of rifle-pits [trenches], with deep ditches and high relief, preceded by one or two lines of abatis[1] ... unusually well constructed ... [with] a line of very strong fraise[2] ... between them ... [and along

[1]Abatis consisted of trees felled in the direction of the enemy, creating a barrier of intertwined and tangled tree branches which would slow an attacking force so as to allow greater exposure to the fire from the defenders.

[2]Fraise [Chevaux-de-Frise] consisted of sharp stakes pointed toward the enemy, often run through a center log in an X fashion.

every] few hundred yards of this line were forts or batteries well supplied with artillery."[3] Having studied the enemy emplacements for weeks while manning the forward trenches, the veterans from Philadelphia could not help but compare their prospects for survival in the approaching action against memories of the assaults at Spotsylvania and Cold Harbor, and such comparisons were not reassuring.

At least there was one positive comparison to those earlier bloody conflicts -- the pre-dawn hours of April 2, 1865, were clear and cool, without the torrential rains of Spotsylvania or the scorching heat of Cold Harbor. In contrast to the tranquility above, however, the ground shook under nearly continuous concussions from the Federal artillery which began pounding the Confederate emplacements hours earlier in preparation for the assault. Commencing at around 10:30 p.m. on the first, the men of the 119th, and their comrades, were moved into the no-man's land between the lines under cover of the Federal barrage, and once there began the time-consuming and dangerous process of forming into battle lines, hopefully without alerting the enemy to their presence. The precious element of surprise was almost lost, however, when several Union pickets inexplicably fired their muskets, drawing a savage volley from the enemy trenches. Despite taking numerous casualties, the Federals stoically withheld further fire, and at least for the moment the enemy remained ignorant of the true extent of the threat gathering in front of the Union lines.[4]

When the formation was completed, the blue-coated soldiers had nothing to do but wait for the order to advance. Many of the battle-hardened veterans who had learned the hard way never to squander an opportunity to sleep, no matter what the circumstances, quickly dropped off into a fitful slumber. For those men unfortunately unable to sleep through the din of the artillery, there were still hours to wait and think. Some relived memories of happier times with lovers or wives and children; some prayed; some passed the time gaping at the perverse beauty of the shells which flew overhead like yellow comets and then burst in the west like Fourth of July rockets; while a few probably

---

[3]Official Record, series 1, vol. 46, part 1, p. 903, Wright [hereafter cited as O.R.-1-46-1-903].

[4]O.R.-1-46-1-903.

pondered the chain of events which brought them to a muddy hole on a scorched and barren Virginia field, facing the very real possibility of being one of the last casualties of the war.

* * *

At no time during the Civil War were the prospects for preserving the Union bleaker than in the summer of 1862, when almost every other week brought news to the North of another military reverse. During the months of May and June, Confederate Major General Thomas J. "Stonewall" Jackson pummeled the Union forces all over the Shenandoah Valley of Virginia, and on August 9 Jackson's men defeated Major General Nathaniel Banks at the battle of Cedar Mountain. At the other end of Virginia, in the latter part of June, the Army of the Potomac was engaged in a number of battles collectively known as the "Seven Days" portion of the Peninsular Campaign, the culmination of Major General George B. McClellan's attempt to capture Richmond. Although in several of the battles the Confederates suffered considerably higher casualties than their foes, each battle ended with a retreat by the Union army. By the beginning of July, it was commonly accepted in both the North and South that McClellan's army had been defeated; and in mid-August, as if in confirmation of defeat, the Army of the Potomac was evacuated from the Peninsula.

Union Major General John Pope, who had been brought in from the West on the boast that his troops never showed their backs to the enemy, contributed to the pervasive sense of gloom which infected the North that summer by demonstrating the lack of substance which lay behind his bragging. Rather than providing the trumpeted victories, Pope spent much of that August floundering around northern Virginia with his Army of Virginia, trying to locate and hopefully destroy Stonewall Jackson's elusive "foot cavalry." Finally, Pope's inept effort ended in what was arguably the worst defeat suffered by the United States military during the entire war, when his forces were routed at the Battle of 2nd Manassas at the end of August. For a short time thereafter, there was a very real possibility that the capital of the United States might be captured by the Rebels.

There seemed to be no respite from the weight of disheartening news which continued to accumulate. At about the same time that

McClellan was being pushed off the Peninsula, the Rebels in the West began a two-pronged invasion which made such progress throughout the month of August that the Union appeared to be threatened with the loss to the Confederacy of both Tennessee and Kentucky. There were even fears that Ohio might be the eventual target of the Confederate marauders. Noted diarist George Templeton Strong captured the despairing mood of the country in an entry in his journal at the beginning of September. "The nation is rapidly sinking just now ... Stonewall Jackson (our national bugaboo) about to invade Maryland, 40,000 strong. General advance of the rebel line threatening our hold on Missouri and Kentucky. Cincinnati in danger ... Disgust with our present government is certainly universal."[5] Hopes for the restoration of the Union had reached a nadir.

It was during this dark time that the 119th Regiment of Pennsylvania Volunteers was created. However, unlike most of the Pennsylvania volunteer regiments raised during the Civil War, the 119th was created by, and partly staffed with, members of the social, political, and economic elite of Philadelphia society who had already been active participants in the state militia system for years as members of the "Artillery Corps, Washington Grays," or sister commands. Although not always known by that name, the unit to which those gentlemen belonged was founded in May of 1813 in response to the growing conflict with England, by Captain Condy Raquet, who formed a company which bore his name and the designation of the "Washington Guards." Although it saw no combat, the new unit was expanded to three companies in 1814, and was redesignated as the "Washington Guards, First Pennsylvania Volunteers." In 1827 the unit received another title and a new role, becoming the "Light Artillery Corps, Washington Grays." The designation as an artillery corps may have resulted more from hope than fact, however, since it is not clear that the Washington Grays possessed any artillery at that time, other than two small bronze guns salvaged from one of the prize ships captured by the U.S. *Constitution*. It is doubtful that any of the Washington Grays were particularly distressed by the deficit of ordnance however, because during the years between wars the unit, in common with most such volunteer

[5]Strong, *Diary*; as cited in McPherson, pp. 532-533.

militia organizations of the time, actually more closely resembled an exclusive men's club, with uniforms, than a military force.

In any case, the following year the unit was assigned, along with five other similar companies, to the "1st Artillery Regiment, Pennsylvania Militia," which traced its origins to the "Associator Artillery of Philadelphia." The latter unit was one of the "Battalions of Associators" organized by Benjamin Franklin in 1747, and which boasted participation with the Continental Army in the battles of Trenton, Princeton, Brandywine, and Germantown. Despite a name change in 1843 to "Artillery Corps, Washington Grays," the company remained a component of the "1st Artillery Regiment" until the commencement of the Civil War.[6]

At the beginning of the Civil War everyone, including the members of the Washington Grays, naively believed that the conflict would be very short, and as a result the volunteers for the early state regiments signed on for only three-month terms. Companies A and F of the 17th Regiment of Pennsylvania Volunteers, one of those early three-month regiments raised in Philadelphia, were comprised of men from the Washington Grays.[7]

At about the same time that the 17th Regiment was filling its rolls with volunteers, a group of older members of the Washington Grays gathered together to reorganize, revitalize, and enlarge the "1st Artillery Regiment" into a reliable home guard unit for the defense of the city. On April 19, 1861, Peter C. Ellmaker, a crusty 6-foot, 2-1/2-inch tall, forty-nine-year-old attorney, who for the previous twenty-eight years had been a member of the Washington Grays, began to advertise for volunteers for the home guard unit.[8] The official designation for the reorganized regiment formed in response to Ellmaker's call became the "First Regiment Infantry, Gray Reserves, Reserve Brigade of the City of Philadelphia," and all but one of its officers were members of the Washington Grays.[9] [See Appendix B for Historical Outline of First Regiment.]

---

[6]Nannos, pp. 1-3; Benson, pp. 1-12; Pa. Dept. of Military Affairs, pp. 2-3.

[7]Taylor, pp. 18, 21.

[8]Bates, *Martial Deeds*, p. 935.

[9]Taylor, pp. 18, 22.

Peter C. Ellmaker (tallest standing officer)
with First Regiment, Gray Reserves

(First Regiment Corp., 103rd Engineers Museum)

Almost immediately after the reorganization of the unit was completed, and the recruiting had ended, the members of the First Regiment began to meet and drill on a regular basis with their old, smooth-bore muskets and such other odds and ends of equipment as they were able to accumulate. Because the regiment was not totally funded by either the state or the city, obtaining the rest of the equipment necessary to outfit the unit and permit proper training was neither simple nor automatic. In January of 1862 it was even necessary for the men to resort to a fund raiser to facilitate the purchase of overcoats so drilling could continue over the winter.

Finding a location to meet, train, and store their equipment also proved to be a challenge. Initially, the headquarters for the First Regiment was Ellmaker's home at 1637 Race Street in Philadelphia, but the regiment soon swelled to such a size that in April of 1862, Ellmaker's request for authority to build an armory to house the new regiment was quickly granted.[10]

---

[10]Latta, *History of the First Regiment...*, p. 34.

One of the recruits who joined the First Regiment Gray Reserves and participated in the drilling was a young Philadelphia lawyer named James W. Latta. Latta was born in 1839 to a prominent Presbyterian family (his great-grandfather was a member of the first class to graduate from the University of Pennsylvania in 1757). Admitted to the Pennsylvania Bar in 1860, Latta, like many young men of his class, responded to the concerns about the future of his city and country in a manner that would not unduly interrupt his blossoming career if the war turned out to be as brief as everyone expected.[11] Standing before the Bar, however, did not prepare a young gentleman for soldiering. As a result, Latta suffered what was probably the first and most embarrassing war-related wound for a member of the 119th (Latta would leave the First Regiment and enlist in the 119th on September 1, 1862, as a 1st lieutenant), when the young lawyer managed to gouge off a portion of his little finger while ramming a ball down the barrel of his bayonetted musket during one of the early drills.

James W. Latta

(USAMHI)

Certainly worried by the events in Virginia and Kentucky, and perhaps inspired by the dedication and efforts of recruits such as James Latta, Ellmaker and his fellow officers in the First Regiment began to question whether a home guard regiment was an adequate response to the crisis facing the Union cause -- a question given special urgency by the president's call in July of 1862 for 300,000 more troops, which order was to be enforced by a type of draft. Concluding that more was

[11] *Philadelphia North American*, 3/27/1922.

required from true patriots, the elders of the First Regiment Gray Reserves resolved to raise forces for field operations.

On the steamy evening of July 29, "... a large meeting of the friends of the Gray Reserves was held ... at Sansom Street Hall for the purpose of devising measures to form a regiment to be commanded by Col. Peter C. Ellmaker."[12] Various local dignitaries were called forward to give their best efforts at stemwinding patriotic speeches, and then the rally was capped off by a short address by Ellmaker, who pledged "... himself to do his duty by the men enlisting in the Regiment ..." and urged action by the young men in attendance.[13] The speeches, with the assistance of a $100 bonus paid on the spot, resulted in a number of enlistments on the floor of the hall.

The next day the *Public Ledger* included its own exhortation for enlistment, along with an account of the rally: "The meeting was very enthusiastic. There were present among the number in the hall at least 1000 able-bodied young men who as members of the Reserve Brigade, are familiar with drill ... Let every member of the Brigade who can by any possibility go, enroll himself *today*. A regiment of Reserves within ten days would be worth a dozen regiments three days hence."[14]

However, Ellmaker did not have exclusive access to the manpower pool of the First Regiment. At about the same time that the recruiting drive commenced for Ellmaker's regiment,

RECRUITS WANTED.—PHILADELPHIA GRAYS, attached to the Seventeenth Penna. Regt., Col. GIDEON CLARK, are now recruiting. All bounties guaranteed by the City, State and General Government, will be paid on mustering into service. Recruiting Stations:—
No. 808 MARKET Street, third story.
METAMORA HALL, corner of Second and New.
TERPSICHOREAN HALL, Sixteenth st., above Callowhill.
P. W. RODGERS, Captain.
EDWIN NELSON, 1st Lieutenant.
ENOCH McCABE, 2d do. jy29-3t*364

ZOUAVES D'AFRIQUE.—$150 BOUNTY.—ONE MONTH'S PAY IN ADVANCE. *Recruits Uniformed and sent to "Camp Banks" at Once*.—A splendid opportunity is now offered to young Men anxious to serve their country to join Company B of this favorite Regiment. Apply at the "Hotel des Zouaves D'Afrique," THIRD and GASKILL Streets.
Captain, E. R. BOWEN.
First Lieut., C. B. SLOAN.
Second Lieut., GEO. J. SCHWARTZ, of the original Company of Zouaves D'Afrique. jy29-6t*572

CORN EXCHANGE REGIMENT, CHAS. M. PREVOST, Colonel.—$160 BOUNTY.—*ONE MONTH'S PAY IN ADVANCE*.—Wanted, steady, able bodied MEN for this Regiment. Enlisted at No. 513 South SECOND Street.
C. M. O'CALLAHAN, Captain.
A. N. WETHERILL, 1st Lieut.
FRANK McCUTCHEN, 2d Lieut.
Recruits mustered in at once. jy28 6t*789

RECRUITS WANTED—CORN EXCHANGE REGIMENT—Col. Chas. M. Prevost; $160 bounty; $10 on being sworn in; $75 and one month's pay when the Company is mustered in. Apply at Recruiting Station, 241 RACE Street.
JOS. W. RICKETTS, Captain.

Recruiting Advertisements

(Philadelphia Public Ledger)

[12]*Philadelphia Public Ledger*, 7/30/1862.
[13]*Philadelphia Public Ledger*, 7/30/1862.
[14]*Philadelphia Public Ledger*, 7/30/1862.

119th REG. P. V.

For THREE YEARS or THE WAR.

UNDER THE AUSPICES OF THE

GRAY RESERVES

COLONEL P. C. ELLMAKER.

$162 BOUNTY

Active, Able-Bodied Young Men Wanted for this Regiment, at

1805 RIDGE AVENUE

EACH MAN WILL RECEIVE $100 IN CASH

BEFORE LEAVING FOR THE SEAT OF WAR.

Captain PETER W. RODGERS.

1st Lieut. C. M. HODGSON. 2d Lieut. EDWIN NELSON.

119th Recruiting Poster

which would soon be designated as the 119th, two other members of both the Washington Grays and the First Regiment also made overtures to potential recruits from the home guard regiment. Gideon Clark began to advertise for enlistees to resurrect the 17th Pennsylvania Regiment, which had supplied ninety-day troops in 1861, and Charles M. Prevost campaigned for men to join his 118th Regiment. Prevost, with the assistance of the Philadelphia Corn Exchange, which provided funding for equipment and probably bounties, successfully filled his regiment a few days before Ellmaker, but for unknown reasons Clark's efforts ended in failure.[15] By the end of August, 125 members of the First Regiment Gray Reserves had enlisted in either the 118th or 119th.[16]

Colonel Peter C. Ellmaker

(First Regiment Corp., 103rd Engineer Museum)

As the enlistment drive gathered momentum, a number of the officers from the First Regiment resigned in early August 1862 so as to be available for field commissions in the 119th. Ellmaker officially retired from the First Regiment on August 14, and immediately assumed command of the fledgling 119th. Perhaps in a move intended to bring in such recruits as he had managed to gather, Ellmaker appointed as his second in command 40-year-old Lieutenant Colonel Gideon Clark, who

---

[15]Gordon, p.40; *Philadelphia Public Ledger*, 7/31/1862.

[16]Latta, *History of the First Regiment...*, p. 36. In addition to a comprehensive history of the First Regiment which included some information about the 119th, Latta would also provide the 119th's oration at the dedication of its monument at Gettysburg, and a diary. That diary, which is now in the possession of the Library of Congress, provided the only detailed history of the 119th which is known to this author, and as such provided the core information for this history.

Lt. Colonel Gideon Clark

(USAMHI)

had been Ellmaker's comrade in the Washington Grays since 1843.[17] When Clark mustered into the 119th on September 1, 1862, he brought not only recruits and years of quasi-military experience, but also a certain amount of ill-will which in time would have serious consequences for himself and his new regiment.[18]

The 119th not only obtained the core of its officer staff from the First Regiment, but it also received the name of the parent unit, the "Gray Reserves" [The 119th will often be referred to as the Grays, and occasionally as the Philadelphians hereafter]. What the new regiment did not receive was enough recruits from the parent First Regiment to fill its expected complement of approximately 1,000 men. To offset the fierce competition for the city's able-bodied young men, the Grays' recruiters were assisted in their efforts by the fact that the population in the North still held strong feelings of patriotism, which feelings were heightened by the sense of urgency stemming from the recent military disasters, and the growing fear that Lee intended to invade the North. The Regiment's complement was filled in a little over thirty days.

It can be assumed that most of the original members of the First who joined the 119th did so primarily out of a sense of patriotism, since they could have chosen to remain in their original safe and secure positions, rather than risk life or limb. Men like Colonel Ellmaker and Lt. Colonel Clark were already prominent citizens of the city, with military positions sufficiently impressive so as to eliminate any question

---

[17]Bates, *Martial Deeds*, p. 785.

[18]Bates, *History of the Pennsylvania Volunteers*, vol. 4, 119th.

about whether their enlistment might have been merely the result of ambition, pride, or flamboyance.

Patriotism was also the most likely factor motivating the many members of the 119th who left families behind when they signed on to serve their country. For example, Charles P. Warner, captain of Company K, left behind five young children and his wife Emma, whom he had married in 1847; while Peter W. Rodgers, captain of Company B, left his wife of eight years, Margaret, and three minor children.[19] Most of the men like Warner and Rodgers, who were granted commissions by the Governor of Pennsylvania, were substantial enough citizens to have found a way to have avoided field service had they so chosen, even if it meant buying a substitute for $300.

John R. Laurens, however, set the standard amongst the Grays for patriotic motivation. Originally from South Carolina, Laurens ignored his Southern heritage and joined the Union army early in the war, and was soon afterwards taken prisoner during the first battle at Bull Run. While in prison in Richmond, his influential Confederate family arranged for the boy to be offered immediate release and a significant position in the Southern army, if only he would come to his senses. He refused. Shortly after being exchanged, Laurens signed up with the fledgling 119th, and in recognition of his combat experience was immediately mustered in as a 1st sergeant in C Company.[20] Close behind Laurens in the devotion to country category, was James Brison, who at the very mature age of forty-five, was the oldest man willing to volunteer for the rigorous life of a private soldier in the Regiment.[21]

Patriotism was not limited to the ranks of the commissioned and noncommissioned officers. George C. Booze enlisted as a private at the age of 22, out of a fierce sense of loyalty to the Union, although his decision to serve as a nurse in the Regimental hospital would indicate that his personality was more gentle than belligerent.[22] Lewis (Gillis) J. Dunlap apparently wanted to serve his country so desperately that not only did he travel all the way to Philadelphia from Indiana County (near

---

[19]National Archives, Pension Records for Warner & Rodgers.

[20]Pennsylvania Archives, correspondence.

[21]Pennsylvania Archives, Muster-In Rolls.

[22]National Archives, Military and Pension Records for George C. Booze.

Henry P. Truefitt

John D. Mercer

William W. Wagner

Benjamin Saylor

Officers of the 119th wearing First Regiment Uniforms
(First Regiment Corp., 103rd Engineer Museum)

Pittsburgh) Pennsylvania, but once there, he lied about his age and enlisted when only 16 years old.[23] The Millard brothers, John H. and James B., signed up because it seems they had patriotism in their genes. The brothers' grandfather, Thomas Millard, was an officer in the Revolutionary War who served from Lexington to Yorktown. Their father enlisted to serve, although he did not fight, in the War of 1812, and their uncle served in Mexico in 1848. Even the youngest Millard brother would have joined, but his mother would not grant her consent.[24]

For others, there were additional significant considerations besides the demands of patriotism. A relatively new concept, the president's call for an additional 300,000 men to be obtained by the draft into nine-month regiments if enough volunteers could not be obtained, was viewed very negatively by both local governments and the prospective draftees.[25] In order for the city of Philadelphia and the Commonwealth of Pennsylvania to meet the assigned quotas of soldiers without having to resort to the draft, the state and city governments, with the assistance of public contributions, offered recruits a cash bonus for enlistment; $162 in the case of the 119th. In 1862, $162, including $100 cash paid on enlistment and the balance at mustering out, was an inducement which warranted serious consideration. It may be safely assumed that many men, who might not otherwise have enlisted, knew that they faced a strong possibility of being drafted, and decided that if going to war was likely, it was better to do so with a pocket full of bounty money.

Two recruits, John E. Faust and his cousin, Aaron Faust, both from Frederick Township, Montgomery County, Pennsylvania, and both in their early twenties, probably joined for a combination of reasons including patriotism, the $162 bounty, and the prospects of a steady income to meet financial responsibilities for their families. John's father seems to have had a well-established reputation as a ruptured, dissipated drunkard who frequently left his wife without support for substantial periods of time, and when home, spent recklessly what little money the couple did have.[26]

---

[23]National Archives, Military & Pension Records for Lewis J. Dunlap.

[24]*Philadelphia Sunday Press*, 12/28/1890.

[25]McPherson, p. 492.

[26]National Archives, Pension Records for John E. Faust.

John had apparently assumed at least partial financial responsibility for his mother both before the war and after he enlisted. Just before he departed for the army, John left his horse to be sold so that his mother would have the proceeds to live on until he could send her some of his first pay. After he was gone, his mother's situation became so desperate that she was forced to beg a neighbor to rent a house for her, with the promise that John would pay back the money. He did, and thereafter he continued to forward to his mother regular portions of his army pay.[27]

Aaron seems to have joined the Regiment for much the same reasons as his cousin. Aaron's father died in 1861, and while no date of birth is available for his mother, Sarah, by 1877 she was described as old and crippled with rheumatism. Also like his cousin, Aaron came from an impoverished background. His father died owning a 20-acre farm, but it was sold for $1,850 to settle his estate, and his widow, Sarah, received only about $150 worth of personal property as her distributive share.[28]

From the time of his father's death, it appears that Aaron also assumed financial responsibility for his mother. He worked for her during the day and occasionally did outside day work, contributing a portion of his pay toward her welfare. Before going off to the recruiter, Aaron and his mother had a conversation which was probably similar to that held by many other young members of the 119th: "... She said to him when he was about to leave 'how shall I live if you go to war'. He said 'Mother if I go to war I can do more towards your support than at home, every time I get my pay I will send the money and you can use as much as you need ... if it takes [it] all ...'"[29]

Although the tendency now is to assume that the Civil War was fought primarily by men motivated by patriotism, for these two young men enlistment was viewed at least in part as hiring on for a job, albeit for the commendable purpose of helping to support their mothers. They probably had no idea how hard and dangerous the profession of soldiering would turn out to be.

---

[27]National Archives, Pension Records for John E. Faust.

[28]National Archives, Pension Records for Aaron Faust.

[29]National Archives, Pension Records for Aaron Faust.

It was not, however, only poor farm boys who signed up to provide security for a widowed mother. At age twelve, William C. Moss was apprenticed to a local lawyer to learn the legal profession, and by the start of the war Moss was actively, although not very profitably, engaged in the practice of law. Of the six dollars per week that he managed to wring from that practice, he contributed five to the support of his mother. Apparently well-connected if not well-paid, Moss secured a commission as captain of Company D of the 119th; and thereafter his mother's economic situation markedly improved, because Moss kept only $10 of his $70 monthly pay and sent the rest home to her.[30]

For whatever reasons, 971 men mustered into the Regiment during the month of August and into early September 1862. The first eight to join, six officers and two privates, signed up on August 4. They were: Company B - Private William H. Christ and Private Amos M. Chandler; Company F - Captain William Wagner and Captain W. A. Wiedersheim; Company G - 1st Lieutenant Francis R. Faust; Company H - Captain Benjamin Saylor and 2nd Lieutenant G. W. Zimmerman; and Company K - Captain Charles P. Warner. The last to enlist that year was James C. Hughes, on September 28.[31]

Unidentified

(First Regiment Corp., 103rd Engineers Museum)

The first camp for the 119th was located at the corner of 2nd St. and Fisher Lane, which at that time was about five miles

[30]National Archives, Pension Records for William C. Moss; Pennsylvania Archives, Payment vouchers.

[31]Bates, *History...*, vol. 4, 119th Pa.

outside the city limits.[32] Once mustered and settled into camp, the recruits were issued equipment and Bridesburg contract rifled muskets, which had been locally manufactured by the firm of Alfred Jenks & Sons.[33] Although a month's worth of drilling with glistening rifles and flashing bayonets, while resplendent in their new uniforms, probably had the young men feeling like warriors, the Grays' career as real soldiers began when, after "suddenly" receiving orders that the Regiment was transferred to Washington, the men were marched off to the train station in a pouring rain. In time, the discomfort of such a march would become depressingly routine, but at this point, it was worthy of comment in a letter home to the local newspaper: "... a delightful march it was -- for owing to the dry weather of the previous week, the dust had become very deep, and was now, by the falling rain, formed into a bed something like mortar, about four inches deep."[34]

The journey to Washington commenced on September 5 in train cars "... used in time of peace to convey cattle, sheep and hogs to market ...", and was completed in two stages, with the first stop in Baltimore, where the men ate at the "Refreshment Saloon" and then spent the night trying to get some sleep on the train platform. The Regiment arrived in Washington the next day in time for the noon meal at the "Washington Retreat," which in the opinion of at least one member of the 119th was a decidedly unpleasant experience: "I was astonished that the meat, which might have once been clean and fresh, but which must have sadly felt the effects of the 'hand of time' would be set before a soldier within sight of the Capitol. It was fairly offensive." Apparently the ambiance matched the food, because the floor of the establishment was so covered with decaying table scraps that the management was forced to spread "chloride of lime" to keep the odor under control.[35] After finishing at the "Retreat," the Grays marched to the Washington Arsenal where, for the next two weeks, their days were filled with training and drilling in earnest.[36]

---

[32]Stapler, T. W., *Bucks County Intelligencer*, 10/14/1862.
[33]Flayderman, p. 452.
[34]Stapler, T. W., *Bucks County Intelligencer*, 9/30/1862.
[35]*The Press*, Philadelphia, 10/9/1862; Latta diary.
[36]Stapler, T. W., *Bucks County Intelligencer*, 10/14/1862.

On September 19, orders were received transferring the Philadelphians to Tennallytown, Maryland for fatigue duty constructing fortifications for the defense of the capital, rather than to the front as expected.[37] We may assume that since the unit was recruited mostly from the city of Philadelphia, many if not most of the recruits had previously held jobs that were not extremely physical in nature as, for example, the 13 newspaper "compositors" in Company F; and undoubtedly the Regiment contained a large contingent of "Yankee shop-keepers," a derisive Southern description of Northern soldiers. According to a letter to Philadelphia's *The Press*, many of the men were inexperienced in the use of pick and shovel, but labored "manfully" nonetheless and despite the unaccustomed and unanticipated manual labor, probably benefitted from the exercise much like athletes training in pre-season camp. The unnamed author of the letter to *The Press* also reported that during this period, despite the heavy physical exertion, the men's health and attitude were excellent. For one recruit, life at Camp "Addicks" was not so benign. On October 5, 1862, Private Edward H. Blakey, one of four Blakeys in Company B, became the first Gray to die, presumably from disease.[38] Private Blakey received a military funeral, a ceremony which would soon be discarded as an impossible luxury.

Although Ellmaker and his staff were probably disappointed in August that Prevost was the first to obtain his complement of recruits for the 118th, that opinion may have changed when news began to trickle into their camp about the battle of Antietam, which was fought on September 17, 1862, approximately fifty miles west of where the Grays were stationed. The news certainly evoked mixed feelings among the men of the 119th, because even though they had avoided what would prove to be the single most bloody day of the War, they also learned about the fate of the 118th which held many friends and acquaintances. Although the Corn Exchange Regiment [as the 118th had come to be named] escaped serious action on the seventeenth, that regiment was included in a small force dispatched on a reconnaissance mission across the Potomac on September 20. The entire force was routed by a much larger contingent of Rebels, costing the 118th 282 casualties out of an

---

[37]Latta diary.

[38]Latta diary; Bates, *History...*, vol. 4, 119th.

active force of 800 men. If Ellmaker's men also learned of the fact that many of the casualties suffered by their sister regiment resulted from gunshot wounds to the back, inflicted as the men were attempting to recross the river, many grudges were undoubtedly formed against the Confederates even before the Regiment faced its first hostile fire.[39]

Providing at least some relief from anxiety over the fate of friends, on September 24 a group of officers appeared with the city bounty, which was sufficiently generous to allow the men of the Regiment to send $26,000 home to loved ones. Then, on the following day, morale received another boost when, "... a fine body of men ...," the transferees from Colonel Adams' Philadelphia regiment, arrived in camp and became the Regiment's new Company H.[40]

The exact origins of H Company is a mystery, especially so because of a rather cryptic letter concerning the company sent to Pennsylvania's Governor Curtin by Colonel Ellmaker. In that letter, Ellmaker mentioned that several disreputable men appeared at the Regiment's camp and claimed some sort of reward or position for having brought in a small contingent of recruits who had been protesting in Harrisburg about their transfer to the 119th. Why Ellmaker found the deliverers so disagreeable or why the men were so opposed to joining the 119th was not made clear, but the Grays' colonel stated in no uncertain terms that he threw the deliverers out of camp practically on their ears.[41]

Several weeks later, on October 16, 1862, the Regiment was ordered to move to Frederick, Maryland on the first leg of its journey to join the Army of the Potomac. The unit arrived in Frederick, Maryland on the nineteenth after two days of marching, the first day of which left the "... Men in [a] horrible state of demoralization -- on [the] road all night ...," and the second found the men marching for 22 straight hours.[42] For the next 15 days, the Regiment marched through Western Maryland and Northern Virginia trying to catch up with the Army of the Potomac, under circumstances that can best be described as arduous.

---

[39]Allen, pp. 446-447.

[40]*The Press*, Philadelphia, 10/9/1862.

[41]Pennsylvania Archives, Correspondence.

[42]Latta diary, 10/17/1862, 10/19/1862.

One day's march covered eighteen or nineteen miles,[43] but the average length of a day's march seems to have been about ten miles per day, about double what the main body of the army accomplished per day under General McClellan. Such distances may not seem very impressive until it is recalled that the men were new to this regimen, and carried forty to fifty pounds of equipment, as well as a ten-pound rifle. As if the length of march and the weight of equipment were not enough, the elements also tested the Grays, who spent several days marching in the cold and rain, and one night camped in a swamp.[44]

During the journey, the Regiment did not engage in any combat, but their exposure to the remains of combat must have certainly given them all dark thoughts to ponder as they marched toward the front. On November 1, after a week's bivouac, the Grays passed through Crampton's Gap, one of the passes through South Mountain on the eastern side of the town of Sharpsburg.[45] This pass was one of the locations where a preliminary engagement leading to the battle of Antietam was fought, as the Union army was forced to overcome spirited opposition in order to force its way through the gap to get at the Confederates at Sharpsburg. General accounts indicate that for months after a battle the wreckage and carnage of war remained on the battlefield. Often, the dead soldiers were hastily buried in shallow graves, and unfortunately some of the corpses shortly thereafter became partially uncovered by erosion or animals, and it usually took weeks, if ever, before all of the dead horses and amputated body parts were buried. It can be assumed that when the Regiment passed through the area of the battlefield, all were exposed to a grisly display of the horrors of war.

The Regiment, perhaps sobered by the experience at Crampton's Gap, finally joined the main body of the army on November 4, where it was assigned to Pratt's Brigade of Brigadier General William B. Franklin's Sixth Corps.[46] Unlike many of the volunteer regiments that fought in the Civil War, the Grays were permitted a rather gradual introduction into the thing called war, and this gratuity continued for

---

[43]Latta diary, 11/1/1862.

[44]Latta diary.

[45]Latta diary.

[46]Latta diary.

another month. During the balance of November and into mid-December, the unit's only conflict would be with nature, which offered rain, snow, lightning, wind, cold, and mud as the Regiment marched and camped across Northern Virginia on a journey leading towards the town of Fredericksburg and the waiting Robert E. Lee.[47]

---

[47]Latta diary.

2

FREDERICKSBURG

Three days after the Grays merged with the main body of the army, George McClellan was again relieved from his position as commander of the Army of the Potomac by President Lincoln, because the "Young Napoleon" had failed to aggressively pursue the weakened Confederate force as it fled from Antietam.[1] The new commander of the eastern army became Major General E. Ambrose Burnside, a general more noted at the time for the cavalry carbine which he invented and his huge "mutton chop" sideburns, than for any military accomplishments. The appointment came in spite of his limited stature in the army, which had just recently been somewhat diminished at Antietam, because the forces under his control, although displaying great personal bravery, wasted hours making repeated assaults over the now famous "Burnside's Bridge," when the position could probably have been taken more quickly had the troops simply forded the creek. Fully appreciating the implications of the termination of his predecessor for perceived timidity, and the recent smudge on his own reputation, Burnside immediately formulated a bold plan to flank the Confederate army by an attack across the Rappahannock River at the town of Fredericksburg. The plan was sound, and in early December it appeared to have promise as the Union forces moved into position across from Fredericksburg ahead of the main body of Lee's army.

It took the army several uncomfortable days, marching in bitter cold, over roads thick and slippery with mud, to reach the staging area several miles north of the intended crossing point.[2] Unfortunately for

---

[1]Stackpole, *Fredericksburg*, p. 4.
[2]Latta diary, 12/4-10/1862.

the Union forces, events conspired against their leader as the pontoon boats necessary to get the army across the river arrived days after the troops, allowing General Lee and his army to catch up. While the Federals marked time waiting for the pontoons, they spent much of the time standing and shivering around "immense campfires" of green wood which generated so much smoke that numerous soldiers developed vision problems.[3] The Southerners put the extra time to better use, occupying a ridge line known as Marye's Heights, located immediately behind and to the south of Fredericksburg, which was quickly converted into an impregnable fortress. When the pontoons finally arrived, Burnside pressed ahead with his plan without the element of surprise, and seemingly oblivious to the implications of the Rebels' incredibly strong defensive position.

On December 9, after cooking three days' rations and receiving twenty rounds of ammunition, usually a portent of imminent battle, the Philadelphians steeled themselves for their first opportunity to "see the elephant" [the phrase the soldiers often used early in the war to refer to experiencing combat], but still the order to cross the river did not arrive.[4] Finally, at 4:30 a.m. on the eleventh, the Grays' Sixth Corps commenced a movement down to the river to a point known as Deep Run, which was located about one mile below the east end of the town. Once there, Ellmaker's men, who had been assigned the duty to guard the laying of the pontoons across the river, had little to do other than watch the gunners sweat over their pieces, and observe for the first time the awesome spectacle of the exploding shells which kept the Confederates at bay while the engineers completed their assignment.[5] When it was finally completed around sunset, the Regiment and the balance of the brigade followed the rest of their corps over the bridge, which by then was nearly covered with thousands of playing cards which had been discarded by soldiers fearful of being killed with those devil's tools in their possession.[6] Fortunately, the day's action, which could have been

---

[3]Latta diary, 12/7/1862.

[4]Latta diary.

[5]Latta diary.

[6]Best, p. 41.

quite bloody if the Southerners had contested the crossing, resulted in only one minor wound to a private in the Regiment.[7]

The river crossing did not go as smoothly for the men of Burnside's right wing, who were sent across the Rappahannock directly in front of Fredericksburg. There, engineers suffered numerous casualties as they struggled to piece together the bridges practically within a stone's throw of the Confederate snipers. The bridging was only completed after an artillery barrage had laid to waste large portions of the previously handsome old town.

The next morning the Philadelphians moved into position along the Richmond Stage Road, where they remained under sporadic musket fire in a field near the Bennett Mansion for the rest of the day.[8] While the Regiment manned its position, the men had their first opportunity to observe Rebel pickets up close, and watched with some curiosity as a large force of the enemy, in the "hundreds," moved into position -- an event then worthy of note in the diary of the still inexperienced Lieutenant Latta. During the night the skittish pickets for both sides continued to bang away at each other, making it doubtful that anyone got much sleep.[9]

The Grays, who were positioned to the east of town, in an area broken with woods and gullies which provided plenty of cover, were spared direct involvement in one of the most pathetic, as well as heroic, episodes of the Civil War. Burnside deluded himself into believing that the best course of action was to attack with his right wing in the center of the Confederate line behind the town, theorizing that the Southerners would be surprised by, and unprepared for, an audacious attack at the strongest point of their defensive line. At the same time, he all but ignored the potential benefits of a concerted attack by his left flank, which included the 119th. The Butternuts were probably surprised by the attack against the Heights, but mostly by the stupidity of the Union commander.[10]

---

[7]Latta diary.

[8]Latta diary, 12/12/1862.

[9]Latta diary.

[10]The term "Butternut" was a nickname applied to Confederate soldiers which was derived from the yellowish brown color of many of their field uniforms. The color resulted from the application of a dye made from copperas and walnut shells. Faust, p. 101.

All during that cold and bleak thirteenth day of December, wave after wave of blue-coated soldiers marched up the barren hillside toward the Confederates on Marye's Heights, who were packed in a sunken road behind a stone fence. The defender's artillery and massed musket fire shredded each successive Union line of attack, and not one Yankee actually reached the wall, except perhaps as an invalid or a prisoner. When each assault lost its momentum, the men who were not knocked down went to ground knowing that it was equally as dangerous to flee as to advance. Many Federals that day owed their survival to the corpse of a comrade employed as the only cover available on that awful slope. By the end of the day, the field was strewn with blue-clad bodies, many dead, some in agony, and others stiff with fear and cold.

Although the Regiment was spared involvement in the senseless slaughter on Marye's Heights, the Grays' stay across the river was not without its anxious moments, as the Philadelphians spent most of the thirteenth on the front line. Latta, trying to sound like a veteran, recorded that the, "Ball opens at 9 a.m. under heavy firing of shells until 10:30 - Major Knight wounded - Shell, grape and canister were thrown on and off all day - advanced up the hill at sunset under quite a fire - Rebs within 50 yards - remained in line of fire all night again."[11]

For the rookies of the 119th, "seeing the elephant" on the thirteenth must have been nearly as harrowing as a full-fledged attack would have been. From the Southern side, the men received a steady dose of shrieking shells, followed by bursts of hot iron fragments, as well as the whine of canister and bullets passing over their heads or thumping into the dirt in front of them. Veterans knew which sounds meant trouble and which were not to be feared, but it must have seemed to every Philadelphian that the whistle of each approaching missile was a harbinger of his own death or disfigurement.

As if that were not bad enough, there was also "friendly fire" with which to contend. Union batteries on a bluff on the north side of the river pounded away at the Southern lines over the heads of the Federals, including the 119th, who were caught in the lowlands in between. Unfortunately, the technology of the time was not quite up to the task, and many of the shells exploded early, either from defects or

---

[11]Latta diary, 12/13/1862; *The Press*, 12/27/1862.

because the gunners had misjudged the length of the fuses necessary to allow the shells to reach the enemy lines. All of the security from Confederate fire gained by hiding behind a thick tree, a rock, or a pile of dirt, disappeared when a shell came from the rear.

At one point later in the day it appeared that the Grays' involvement in the battle was about to change from passive to extremely active, when the Rebels began forming for a charge, and the order was given for the Regiment to prepare to repel the attack. In the commotion, Colonel Ellmaker, the commander of the 119th, was unhorsed; and because his mount had to be taken to the rear, the colonel was forced to take his position at the head of the Regiment on foot. On Ellmaker's command the men rose and fixed bayonets in preparation for what they expected would be a bloody countercharge into the guns of the enemy. Apparently, however, the Southerners could not stand both the Union artillery and the prospects of a counterattack, because they broke and ran, eliminating the need for the bayonet charge.[12]

The Grays spent two more days on the Confederate side of the Rappahannock, as concisely described by Lieutenant Latta:

"12/14 - Ball opens before sunrise - grape and canister again hurled at us, skirmished along left ... [and] ... our front all day until 3 p.m. - shelling from Rebs ceased about 9. Result of yesterday's fight a draw game. Private [George S.] Smith of our Co. wounded in wrist by a minnie ball."

"12/15 - Moved our position at 4:30 a.m. 300 yards to right & rear - remained in line of battle all day. At 7:30 p.m. moved in silence across the river again - looks like a skedaddle, rained terribly at night."[13]

Even though the Grays had not faced the ultimate test of courage, as had their comrades on Marye's Heights, they must have been satisfied with their first performance under fire. The commander of the Regiment performed satisfactorily, although perhaps not as magnificently as described in a florid letter published as a newspaper article back home: "Our worthy colonel, Peter C. Ellmaker, has won for himself laurels by his heroism and bravery. Officers and men are loud in their praises as

---

[12] *Philadelphia Inquirer*, 12/27/1862.
[13] Latta diary.

to his conduct under fire."[14] For a first fight, however, the most important fact was that the unit stayed together; and despite prolonged artillery fire and the prospects of a bloody bayonet charge, nobody ran.

The good fortune of having avoided the heavy casualties suffered by other Federal units was probably adequate compensation for the privations Ellmaker's men endured after crossing back over the river. Again quoting from the Latta diary: "Remained all crowded together in woods - rumors of the losses and tales of survivors floating around but no authenticated information yet as to actual, skedaddle complete, pontoons removed 4 a.m. - slight cannonading."[15]

The worst was not over. Organization had been lost, and what amounted to little more than a mob huddled in the "intense and severe" December cold waiting for something to happen or someone to take charge of the situation. The 119th remained at the same spot, without tents and apparently with little to eat, from the evening of the fifteenth until sometime on the eighteenth, when late in the day the Regiment's baggage finally arrived. It was not until the nineteenth of December that the Regiment finally trudged back to its base camp in a state of what must have been nearly overwhelming despondency.[16]

The conclusion of the retreat from Fredericksburg marked the end of the campaigning season, and the Sixth Corps was allowed to settle in to what would become its winter camp and base of operations, Camp Wray near White Oak Chapel, Virginia. The following is a description of that camp which was written by 1st Lieutenant Latta and published in the March 14, 1863, edition of the *Philadelphia Inquirer*: "The camp is pitched on the slope of a gentle hill, the log huts of the men extending from the base to the brow. They are built with much regularity and neatness, each company having a separate avenue which is generally named in honor of their respective Captains. The log houses of the company officers are situated at the head of their respective company streets on the brow of the hill with a plaza in front of each and each surrounded by choice green pine and cypress trees, selected and replanted with much care so that on a clear balmy day you may almost

---

[14]*The Philadelphia Inquirer*, 12/27/1862.
[15]Latta diary, 12/16/1862.
[16]Latta diary.

119th Winter Hut

Leslie's Illustrated Newspaper

imagine yourself wandering amid some of our cozy lanes near Germantown, or on the banks of the Wissahickon. I omitted to mention that the men of our regiment have also displayed much good taste in having cut and planted evergreens, one at each corner of their huts almost hiding them from view .... Each hut has a chimney, formed of small pine logs plastered inside and out with the best quality of Virginia mud."[17] The bucolic scene described by Lieutenant Latta seems to have had a beneficial effect on the men of the Regiment; "The health of this regiment has been good, owing no doubt to the efforts of our gallant commander (P. C. Ellmaker), being very careful to select the most healthy positions for camping."[18]

The Grays' four months of relative ease at Camp Wray was to be interrupted by one extremely unpleasant and humiliating exercise in futility, now known as "Burnside's Mud March." In January 1863, General Burnside, still trying to avoid the stigma attached to his predecessor and satisfy the demands of the administration, decided to

---

[17]For the higher staff officers of the Regiment there was another factor, in addition to the comfortable location, which added to their winter of contentment, namely the assistance of servants paid for by the government. Colonel Ellmaker and Surgeon Leidy each had two servants, while each captain in the Regiment was permitted one servant. Payment Vouchers, Pennsylvania Archives.

[18]W., T. B., *Bucks County Intelligencer*, 3/31/1863.

make an attempt to turn the Confederate left flank, this time with a movement upstream (westward) from Fredericksburg. At the beginning of the campaign, the prospects appeared favorable because the weather was unusually warm and dry, and the movement in the dead of winter caught the Southerners by surprise. As so often happened during the Civil War, however, nature stymied the best-laid plans.

Almost as if nature had sided with the Secessionists, the Yankees were permitted to get their entire army on the march; but almost immediately thereafter a storm of cold driving rain, which continued for three days, broke over their heads. Wagons and artillery pieces repeatedly sank to their axles in the mud, and there were even reports that horses drowned in the mud while still in their traces. Lieutenant Latta recorded in his diary that "32 horses cannot move a caisson ...", and that the mud was of a "... soapy & clammy nature -- officers had to be pulled out," leaving the "Army of the Potomac stuck in the mud."[19] Many of the men collapsed from exhaustion caused by marching in knee-deep mud or from muscling cannons from one slough to another, while others succumbed to the diseases that naturally accompany exposure to the cold and rain without the opportunity to dry off and warm up. After three days, the attempt was abandoned and the sodden army returned to its camps. Perhaps not coincidentally, two of Ellmaker's officers, Captain Andrew A.

Captain Andrew A. Ripka
(Courtesy K. Turner Collection)

[19]Latta diary, 1/23/1863.

Ripka and Captain William W. Wagner, were discharged on Surgeon's certificates only a month after the march. With gallows humor, one participant (probably not one of those officers) described the ordeal in a poem:

> Now I lay me down to sleep
> In mud that's many fathoms deep;
> If I'm not here when you awake,
> Just hunt me up with an oyster rake.[20]

The debacle of the mud march proved to be the last straw for Burnside as far as the administration was concerned, and Major General Joseph Hooker became the new commander of the Army of the Potomac. As had by then become standard operating procedure after a change of command, Hooker instituted a series of reforms and reorganizations, including a shake-up in the command structure and a much-needed improvement in the method by which intelligence was to be gathered. Of greatest psychological significance was his adoption of geometric emblems for each of the corps, which were to be worn on a soldier's uniform or on the top of a kepi, in order to facilitate rapid identification and reorganization during battle. The emblems quickly generated an additional and unexpected benefit when the men developed pride in, and identification with, their particular badge; a situation which significantly added to unit cohesion and "esprit de corps."

Captain William W. Wagner

(USAMHI)

[20] Billings, p. 72.

1st Lt. Walter K. Ludwig

(USAMHI)

The emblem system was rather simple. Each soldier's corps emblem was to be of a different color depending on the division; the color for the first division was red, the second division white, the third blue, and in the rare case of a fourth division, green. The corps emblems were as follows: First Corps a round dot; Second Corps a club (trefoil); Third Corps a diamond; Fourth Corps a triangle; Fifth Corps a Maltese cross; the Grays' Sixth Corps a Greek cross; Eighth Corps a six-sided star; Ninth Corps a shield with crossed anchor and cannon barrel; Eleventh Corps a crescent moon; and the Twelfth Corps a five-pointed star.[21] From the spring of 1863 until the end of the war, the men of the 119th would proudly display a red Greek cross on the top of their kepis, and would rally to the new 3rd Brigade pennant, a white triangle with a blue border, bearing a red Greek cross in the center.[22]

Although Hooker never achieved the adoration that the men accorded to McClellan, and despite his own personal unsavory reputation, his ascendancy to command of the Army of the Potomac seemed to have had a positive effect on the troops. Whereas the morale of the army after Fredericksburg and the Mud March was at a nadir, a Union officer reported that after the changes initiated by Hooker, "I have never known men to change from a condition of the lowest depression to that of a healthy fighting state in so short a time."[23]

---

[21]Billings, plates I-III.
[22]Billings, plate VI.
[23]Couch, Darius N., *Sumner's Right Grand Division*, as cited in McPherson, p. 585.

Major General John Sedgwick
(USAMHI - MOLLUS)

One of the command changes which Hooker made would prove to have a significantly positive effect on the 119th and their comrades in the Sixth Corps. Major General John Sedgwick, who was fondly referred to by his men as "Uncle John" in appreciation of his common touch and his obvious regard for their lives, became the new commander of the Sixth Corps. Despite the change at the top of the Corps, the rest of the chain of command affecting the 119th stayed the same; the Regiment remained in the First Division under Brigadier General William T. H. Brooks, and in the Third Brigade under the command of Brigadier General David A. Russell. Russell's Third Brigade, as the army began to rouse itself for the spring campaign, consisted of the 18th New York, 32nd New York, 49th Pennsylvania, 95th Pennsylvania, and 119th Pennsylvania.

The Grays all understood that there was a serious purpose behind all of the staff shuffling, and also that with the spring foliage and warmer weather came the campaigning season. No definite plans had yet been released by the compulsively secretive commander of the Union army, but anticipation of an impending campaign began to build in the camp nevertheless. Perhaps as an omen of things to come, on March 31, 1863, the 119th received four wagonloads of supplies donated by citizens of Philadelphia intended for the Regimental hospital. The shipment included a few "delicacies," but the wagons were mostly packed with drugs and medicines. According to the *Philadelphia Inquirer* of May 10, 1863, this was such a significant event that a small parade was held, a resolution of thanks passed, and the colonel gave a speech. Unless Ellmaker's speech was very short, there were undoubtedly Grays standing in the ranks daydreaming about whether they would become direct beneficiaries of the supplies from home.

3

SECOND FREDERICKSBURG

The Confederates did not waste the respite granted to them by the winter of 1862-1863, having erected a formidable defensive line on the south bank of the Rappahannock River in the immediate vicinity of, and especially along the heights behind, Fredericksburg. By mid-April, however, the new commander of the Army of the Potomac had evolved what he considered to be a near flawless plan which would, in theory at least: overcome the Confederate defenses without a repetition of the senseless slaughter which occurred in December; shield Washington from possible attack; and crush the Confederate army. In essence, the Union commander borrowed both plans attempted by his predecessor -- a flank march with a river crossing to the northwest of Fredericksburg, like that planned for the failed "Mud March"; and also a direct assault across the river against the town of Fredericksburg itself. Hooker's contribution to the earlier schemes was to be speed, stealth, and a larger and fresher army that could perform both maneuvers simultaneously.

As Hooker visualized the scenario, there could be only three possible outcomes. If the assault on Fredericksburg froze the Rebels in place, then his right flanking column would smash the Army of Virginia by pouncing on its left flank and rear behind the town; but if Lee shifted his forces to the west, the Union left would perform the same function from the opposite side. Hooker really expected, however, that Lee would make the only reasonable decision and retreat toward Richmond.

Although in his mind the Rebels were as good as routed, Hooker still had to perform the mundane tasks of arranging and executing his campaign. He divided the Army of the Potomac into two roughly equal segments -- the Second, Fifth, Eleventh Corps and Twelfth Corps were assigned to the right flanking column, and the First, Third Corps and

Sixth Corps were assigned to the left column under the command of General Sedgwick. The left wing was instructed to make a crossing just below the town, hold the enemy in place with a convincing demonstration, and then to pursue the inevitable retreat.[1]

Before Sedgwick could begin either the demonstration or the pursuit he had to get his men across the river, an operation which was at best a perilous undertaking. Rather than repeat December's method of crossing the Rappahannock, where many engineers lost their lives to Confederate snipers while building a pontoon bridge in broad daylight, toward a shore line held by the enemy, it was decided that an amphibious assault should be attempted in the pre-dawn darkness of April 29. After a bridgehead was secured, the necessary bridges could then be built for the rest of the army in relative safety. To secure such a bridgehead, however, a group of men would have to cross a significant river and land in hostile territory under the guns of a well-emplaced enemy. The men of General Russell's Third Brigade, of which the 119th was a part, were assigned to that duty.[2]

The Third Brigade marched to its jump-off point, where it arrived at 11:00 p.m. on the evening of April 28. "The night being close and sultry, there was a very heavy fog along the river," a Stygian scene which, given the prospects for the coming morning, probably matched the expectation which many of the men held for their immediate future.[3] The order to cross arrived from headquarters at midnight, but the crossing did not begin immediately because the pontoon boats were delayed and then had to be arranged in some semblance of order. To further complicate and delay the assault, only twenty-three boats initially arrived at the scene; and then there was a protracted disagreement between General Russell and Brigadier General Henry W. Benham, the engineering officer in charge of the bridge construction.[4]

The boats were in the water and ready by around 1:30 a.m., but because Russell did not believe the amphibious assault could be successfully made in the dark, he delayed the launch despite Benham's

---

[1]Furgurson, p. 97.
[2]Furgurson, pp. 97-98.
[3]Westbrook, p. 143.
[4]Slade, p. 122.

orders to launch immediately. The two officers argued, and even though Benham asserted his rank, Russell remained adamant. Russell was the type of officer who was perfectly capable of taking a hard-nosed position when it came to the welfare of his men, but his refusal probably had as much to do with his observations of the officer issuing the orders as the tactical situation. Lieutenant Stephen M. Weld of Benham's own staff described his commander that morning as, "...drunk as could be, with a bloody cut over his left eye...," which he received from a fall. Repeating the performance that resulted in the cut, Benham later, "... reeled in his saddle and in trying to shake hands with General Pratt, he fell right off his horse on to the ground."[5]

When orders and threats failed, Benham placed Russell under arrest. Russell still refused to act, so Benham took the matter to General Brooks, Russell's First Division commander, but Brooks backed his brigade commander, a decision which may have been influenced in part by Brooks' own assessment of Benham's condition. At that point Benham apparently decided that discretion was more important than pride, because he acquiesced to Russell's position and let the arrest fade away with no charges being pressed to a court-martial.[6] Lieutenant Latta of the 119th may have also been a witness to some or all of the confrontation between his brigade commander and the tipsy engineer, because he described the preparation for the crossing as "A night of activity and suspense ... the whole appeared to be badly managed and everyone anticipated a signal failure."[7]

Finally, the 119th, 95th Pennsylvania, 49th Pennsylvania, and a small portion of the 32nd New York, began to make final preparations for the crossing. Private Galloway of the 95th Pennsylvania described the approach of the landing party to the boats: "Feeling our way in silence down the rugged hillside in the gloom of a drizzly, rainy night, we joined the pontooniers ..."[8] The pontoon boats, by then forty in number, were each carefully and quietly filled with one company of forty to forty-five infantrymen, and four oarsmen from the 15th New York

---

[5]Weld, *War Diary and Letters*, as cited in Sears, *Chancellorsville*, p. 154.
[6]Winslow, p. 122.
[7]Latta diary, 4/28/1863.
[8]Galloway, p. 15.

Engineers.[9] Despite any misgivings they may have harbored, approximately 719 Grays boarded the boats and shoved off as the lead regiment in the crossing of the river and the intended assault on the Confederate positions on the south bank, with the men of the 95th Pennsylvania close behind them.[10]

The crossing commenced at 4:20 a.m., in the palest light of predawn, cloaked in a fog which partially concealed the boats and helped to deaden the sounds of the oarsmen. "... As the boats moved out from the dark waters and felt the affect of the current, they drifted together in great confusion."[11] The boatmen struggled to restore order while the Grays struggled to maintain silence and the precious element of surprise. No one spoke, but nerves screamed with fear -- partly from the effort to maintain balance in the crowded rocking boats; partly from the expectation that the expedition would be discovered in its helpless and exposed position in the middle of the river, provoking a dreadful blast of rifle fire and canister which would sweep the bloody remains of the men into the water; and also from the certainty that even if the boats reached the opposite shore, that the rumors of lights having been spotted on the far side of the river would prove to be true, and that the men were about to be delivered into a death trap.[12]

Fortunately, no noise sufficient to alert the enemy was made until the Federals began to splash onto the southern shore. Then, "There was a crack of a rifle followed by a ringing voice of a confederate picket as he called 'Corporal of the Guard double quick!'"[13] Discovered, the 119th and the 95th made a "... fierce scramble up the steep and slippery banks made doubly so by the rain."[14] The Rebels were completely surprised however, and could manage only one volley from the top of the bluff, which mostly passed over the heads of the landing party, claiming only a few blue-coated victims.[15] The rout was so complete

---

[9]O.R.-1-25-1-566, 591; Westbrook, p. 143.

[10]Anonymous, *The Press*, May 5, 1863; Regimental Muster Roll for April 30, 1863, Pennsylvania Archives.

[11]Galloway, p. 15.

[12]Slade, p. 122.

[13]Galloway, p. 16.

[14]Galloway, p. 16.

[15]Latta diary, 4/28/1863.

119th and 95th Pennsylvania Crossing the Rappahannock
April 29, 1863 - *Harper's Weekly*

that during the pursuit the Yankees were able to capture a Confederate lieutenant in his bed.[16] Russell's entire brigade suffered only eleven casualties during the operation, with the 119th's share of those losses totaling one enlisted man killed and three enlisted men wounded.[17]

The Grays and their comrades were not the only Yankee soldiers required to make a river crossing that morning. Downstream about two miles, troops from Major General John F. Reynolds' First Corps were discovered making preparations for their attempt, which promptly drew a withering fire from across the river. Soon, however, with the aid of a barrage from thirty-four Federal cannons located on high ground on the north bank, and some enthusiastic paddling by the men in the pontoons, the Iron Brigade quickly established their own bridgehead in Southern territory.[18]

While Reynolds' men were still waiting for their artillery to complete its work, the Grays' brigade became involved in a running gunfight as the skirmish line pressed ahead to expand the Union beachhead. By 10:00 a.m. the Third Brigade had seized a position on the right flank of the Union incursion, near the Bernard house, where an amazing transformation occurred.[19] "... The Rebels ceased popping at us and at once showed a disposition to be in good terms trying to drive a bargain on papers, tobacco and coffee, but General Russell 'sat upon' our commerce quite right lively."[20]

For the next several days Sedgwick's forces did little more than wait, gaze at Thaddeus Lowe's hot air observation balloons which lazily hovered over Falmouth, across the river from Fredericksburg, and hold their positions on the South bank of the river. Meanwhile, at Chancellorsville, ten miles to the west, things were not so peaceful for General Hooker. On May 2, due to some incredibly poor leadership, Stonewall Jackson's men were able to surprise and crush the right flank of the Union forces. Faced with a desperate situation, Hooker ordered the First and Third Corps to leave Fredericksburg and join him at Chancellorsville by way of the roads north of the Rappahannock. At

---

[16]O.R.-1-25-1-591.
[17]O.R.-1-25-1-172.
[18]Sears, *Chancellorsville*, pp. 157-158.
[19]O.R.-1-25-1-566.
[20]Galloway, p. 16.

almost the same time, he demanded that Sedgwick use the Sixth Corps to storm the Southern defenses behind the town and come to his rescue by way of the Orange Plank Road, which ran between Fredericksburg and Chancellorsville on the south side of the river.

While the Union Eleventh Corps on the far right flank was being crushed and the rest of the right wing was fighting for its life, Ellmaker's men were experiencing only limited activity. Latta's diary contains this account of the day: "Artillery firing commenced about 8 [a.m.] along whole line, nearest on extreme right - Regiment formed in close column by wing and show of will - everything quiet except skirmishing by Light Division until 7 p.m. when 5th Wisconsin and other regiment of Light Division drove in rebel skirmishers and we advanced beyond rifle pits. Whole of 6th Corps crossed over."[21]

Unknown to Lieutenant Latta, or the rest of the members of the Sixth Corps, the advance of the Light Division might, if pushed only a short distance further, have resulted in a cheap and stunning victory. Earlier in the afternoon, Confederate General Early who was in charge of the defenders behind Fredericksburg, had been mistakenly ordered to shift most of his men westward to Chancellorsville. Although those wayward troops would be returned late in the day, at the time of the advance of the Light Division, the Southern defenses were manned by only a skeleton force. It is entirely possible that if this fact had been known, and the advance continued, the Light Division would have smashed through the Butternut line, against only token resistance and with minimal casualties.[22]

On the morning of May 3, the 119th was roused at 3:00 a.m., but waited until dawn to move, and then only to get out of range of the Rebel artillery. During this time, the Confederates threw a steady diet of shells in the direction of the Regiment, but without effect.[23] [Some of the following descriptions of the events of May 3 were taken from a letter written on May 5, 1863, by a member of the 119th who identified himself only as " B.A.W., a Bucks Countian." We may assume that the writer was a member of Company B because of references to his captain

---

[21]Latta diary, 5/2/1863.

[22]Sears, *Chancellorsville*, pp. 250-251.

[23]W., *Bucks County Intelligencer*, 5/26/1863.

being Peter W. Rodgers, who was then the captain of that company. There was only one individual in Company B at that time with the appropriate initials, Sergeant Benjamin A. Wildman, who would later be wounded at the Wilderness on May 5, 1864, but would muster out with his company. Other portions of the narrative were taken from a paper presented by G. Norton Galloway, who participated in the battle as a member of the 95th Pennsylvania.] Sometime after dawn on the third, Hooker again demanded, this time with pre-emptory orders, that the Sixth Corps act immediately to storm the city and come to the rescue of the six other corps at Chancellorsville. The orders were of such a tenor as to eliminate any latitude that Sedgwick might otherwise have had for maneuver, and as a good soldier "Uncle John" began to make the necessary dispositions for a direct assault on Marye's Heights behind the city, the scene of the terrible slaughter the previous December. Around 11:00 a.m., as part of those preparations, the 119th and the 95th Pennsylvania were ordered to a new location in a ravine, one-quarter mile from the front, to shield the pending assault from a possible flank attack.[24]

To accomplish that maneuver, it was necessary for the men of the two regiments to cross an open plain, again becoming targets for the Rebel artillery. Fortunately, none of the men were hit, but Lieutenant Cephas M. Hodgson of the 119th would have lost his head to a solid shot had he not ducked just in time.[25] After the change in location was completed, both the Grays and the 95th Pennsylvania were effectively detached from Russell's brigade, and in essence became a separate mini-brigade under the 95th's Colonel Gustavus W. Town. The two regiments were not completely independent, however; instead, they were placed at the disposal of Colonel Henry W. Brown, commander of the First Brigade, First Division, which was known as the Jersey Brigade because of the origin of all its regiments.[26]

It was not long thereafter that the Grays heard volleys of musketry, followed shortly by cheering from the troops of the Light Division, the Fourth Division of the Sixth Corps, which with the 6th

---

[24]W., *Bucks County Intelligencer*, 5/26/1863.
[25]W., *Bucks County Intelligencer* 5/26/1863.
[26]Galloway, p. 16.

Maine and the 5th Wisconsin in the lead, had just carried Marye's Heights by frontal assault.[27] The Philadelphians were only bystanders to this gallant action and probably counted themselves fortunate for it. They would not consider themselves fortunate for long.

[27]Mundy, pp. 114-115.

4

SALEM CHURCH

Immediately after the Heights were carried, Sedgwick ordered his troops forward toward Chancellorsville for the purpose of saving the other six army corps that were by then hunkered down in their trenches. As the march began, the men of the 95th Pennsylvania, and probably the Grays as well, were filled with the recent triumph: "We were happy, shouting and singing, the heights was ours and the celebrated Washington Battery was among the trophies won."[1] By 1:00 p.m. the mini-brigade, consisting of the 119th and 95th Pennsylvania, was on the Orange Plank Road heading west toward Chancellorsville as part of Brooks' leading First Division.[2] Company I of the 119th may have marched along to a cadence provided by its drummer, John B. Cassady, who had returned only days before from Philadelphia after five months of convalescing from an illness.[3]

Almost immediately after marching out of town, Brooks' Federals were confronted by a brigade of Southerners who were intent upon preventing, or at least delaying for as long as possible, the Sixth Corps' rescue effort.[4] Brigadier General Cadmus Wilcox, the Confederate brigade commander, could not have wished for better terrain over which to conduct a delaying action. The stretch of road between Fredericksburg and Chancellorsville passed over a series of low ridges and shallow valleys running perpendicular to the road. Each succeeding ridge became a bastion occupied by a battery of Confederate artillery,

---

[1]Galloway, p. 7.

[2]W., *Bucks County Intelligencer*, 5/26/1863.

[3]National Archives, Military Records of John B. Cassady.

[4]Furgurson, p. 273.

John B. Cassady's I.D. Badge

supported by either Wilcox's infantry or the cavalry under his control; and each was carried only after the Federal artillery was deployed to suppress the Rebel cannon fire and blue-coated troops moved from column into line of battle, to either flank or intimidate the outnumbered Southerners off the ridge.[5] The time consumed in the process was counted in hours rather than minutes.

The Rebel force made a more determined stand in the area of a toll booth about three-quarters of a mile east of the Salem Church, where the men of the 8th, 10th, 11th, and 14th Alabama occupied some rifle pits which had been prepared the previous winter in anticipation of a possible retreat from Fredericksburg.[6] The Alabamians were only driven off when an even larger force of several Yankee regiments were sent to the right to turn their flank, and a Union battery was deployed and began dropping shells into the Confederate position.[7]

It may be inferred from the following, rather vague, description of the struggle toward Chancellorsville provided by Private Galloway of the 95th Pennsylvania that those "several regiments" which cleared the area of the toll gate were the detached Pennsylvanians from Russell's Brigade. "It was 4:00 o'clock when the arrangements were completed.

---

[5]Furgurson, p. 274.
[6]Furgurson, p. 275.
[7]O.R.-1-25-1-566, 568.

In this manner we passed up the plank road under the gallant Brooks, following the enemy closely but meeting no opposition until reaching a point about two miles from Fredericksburg. Here the road describes a slight curve round a small pine grove. As the head of our column was rounding at this point, a section of artillery stationed in the middle of the road about 80 yards distant and near a toll gate, opened upon us with shells. The first felling one of our artillery sergeants. For a few moments defense rails and small pines were hurled about like chaff as the shock [shot?] poured through the woods."

"Confederate skirmishers were soon encountered in the vicinity of the Taylor house. On the right of the plank road, the country was open offering but few advantages for the Confederates to find cover. Occasionally they would take a position behind a rail fence and show a disposition to dispute the ground with us. When our two regiments would trail arms and take up the double quick with a cheer upon which the enemy would promptly come to right about and move off ... We kept the 'Johnnys' moving at a pretty rapid gait. Their artillery limbering and moving down the road as we approached. When, at a safe distance, they would go about unlimber and open fire again."[8]

Unknown to Generals Sedgwick or Brooks, or to the blue-coated infantrymen who were sweeping back the Southern resistance, Lee had earlier in the day taken Hooker's measure and correctly concluded that the Yankees at Chancellorsville posed no threat to the Confederate left flank. Lee then dispatched to the east a large portion of his troops who, thanks to the time bought by Wilcox's delaying tactics, were able to march several miles and to occupy a ridge line to the west of the toll booth, where the Butternuts waited for an opportunity to crush the Sixth Corps. The location chosen for their stand, known as "Salem Heights" after the Salem Church which dominated it, provided the best natural defensive position of all, being higher than the ridges to the east, and with the added advantage that its eastern front was covered with a rather thick and tangled second growth woods. Upon arrival, the Southern units, consisting of the brigades of Brigadier Generals William Mahone, Paul J. Semmes, Joseph B. Kershaw, and W. T. Wofford, wasted little time and soon had excavated emplacements on the ridge line for

---

[8]Galloway, pp. 18-19.

themselves and their artillery.[9] The Salem Church was also quickly converted into a small brick fortress, with Rebel snipers stationed in the balconies at the second story windows, from where the Northerners could be picked off at a distance, even while forming for an attack.

Colonel Henry W. Brown and Brigadier General Joseph J. Bartlett, the commanders of the two leading Federal brigades of Brooks' Division, were apparently aware that the Confederates had some forces deployed in the thicket in front of Salem Heights, although they do not seem to have been aware of the full extent of the enemy force dug in on top of the ridge. Perhaps believing that they faced only another delaying action, the officers deployed their two brigades in line of battle perpendicular to the road facing toward the Heights. "It was now nearly sunset and by this time we reached a point four miles beyond Fredericksburg, near Salem Church. Here our guns went into position on a slightly elevated plateau on the right of the plank road near the toll gate from which the ground sloped gently towards a belt of timber four or five hundred yards on our front. The woodland was a continuation of the forest on the left of the road through which the First and Second brigades were advancing. Our line of battle not being over 1000 yards in length."[10]

Salem Church - 1996

At this point in the battle, consistency between the various sources

[9]Furgurson, p. 275.
[10]Galloway, p. 19.

begins to seriously deteriorate. According to Brooks, in his official report, Brown's Jersey Brigade was arrayed on the north side of the road, with the 2nd New Jersey out front on the skirmish line, and with the battle line having the 1st New Jersey closest to the north side of the road, the 3rd New Jersey on the right flank of the 1st, and the 15th New Jersey, which had just returned from the far right flank, to the right of the 3rd. Finally, the two orphaned Pennsylvania regiments were deployed as support in the second line of battle, with the 95th Pennsylvania closest to the road and the 119th on their right flank.[11] Bartlett's Brigade spread out in similar fashion on the south side of the road.

This deployment is consistent with that described by the Grays' Benjamin Wildman in his letter home. "After forming in line we advanced slowly towards a wood about one mile in front. We had not proceeded more than a quarter of the distance before the enemy opened a battery on us; but their shells were too high to molest our ranks. They did not continue this firing long, nor did we lay a great while where we were before we again advanced. Our skirmishers were now engaging those of the enemy, and the first line of battle nearing the woods, which they soon reached, while we were less than a quarter of a mile in the rear, advancing rapidly."[12]

The foregoing descriptions do not totally agree with the disposition outlined in the recent regimental history of the 15th New Jersey, which is based in large part upon the diary of a member of the 15th New Jersey, Edmund Halsey, or seemingly with Galloway's recollection from his perspective within the 95th Pennsylvania. The former source described the alignment from the road north as the 1st New Jersey, the 3rd New Jersey, the 95th Pennsylvania, and the 119th.[13] Both Bilby and Haines, the latter being the author of the original history of the 15th New Jersey, agree that the men of the 15th New Jersey did not arrive until after the battle had already been engaged in the woods for some time, and therefore they could not have been in the original front line.[14] Galloway's description does not indicate the

---

[11]O.R.-1-25-1-568, Brooks.

[12]W., *Bucks County Intelligencer*, 5/26/1863.

[13]Bilby, p. 65.

[14]Haines, p. 58.

Artillery at Salem Church - *Leslie's Illustrated Newspaper*

Pennsylvanians were in a second line either: "On this descending plain, [from the area of the tollhouse] towards the woods on the right, the 95th and 119th Pennsylvania advanced in perfect order. Our skirmishers now entered the woods and were at once hotly engaged by strong force of the enemy."[15] Perhaps the discrepancy merely resulted from a different interpretation of what size force made up a "skirmish line."

In any case, all the sources seem to be in basic agreement as to what happened next: both Pennsylvania regiments, at the order of the 95th's Colonel Town, lay down. As Galloway described it, "A few rods in advance of this woods, Colonel Town halted the small brigade and we layed down behind a low brush fence for a few moments ..."[16] According to Wildman, "When we were within 400 yards of the wood we were ordered to charge and drive the rebels from their position. A moment more and away we went, rushing toward the foe, who met us with a volley of musketry which led me to believe that a considerable number were concealed behind the thick underbrush. Arriving at the edge of the woods, we halted and lay down till the rebels had fired their second round when we advanced into the wood."

This is probably the point in the battle where the heaviest fighting shifted to the left side of the road, roiling up to, in, and around the House of God. The drive of General Bartlett's men up to the church was described in vivid detail by an anonymous soldier in the 16th New York, the regiment closest to Brown's New Jerseyans:

"There is a rattling of steel against steel as the bayonets are put on and locked. 'Forward, march.' Slowly and steadily, elbow to elbow, we move forward. There comes a shell. We see the puff of smoke from the gun. It falls harmless, but that next does not; it leaves a gap in the line ahead. *hum*, that is a rifle ball, almost spent, yet reaching beyond our line. 'Steady.' Shot and shell multiply; the man at my right falls, my tentmate, but I must not stop to help him. Glancing back, I see him limping to the rear. We come to a rail fence and are just about to spring upon it when the order comes, 'Halt and lie down.' We drop behind the fence, my head close to rail. *Thud*, a bullet strikes the rail, I glance at it and see that it was directly in range and has almost passed through.

---

[15] Galloway, p. 19.
[16] Galloway, p. 20.

It is slivered just in front of my head. Saved by a hair's breadth. We lie perhaps two minutes ... 'Fall in' and we spring up. 'Right face, march,' and we cross the road, raked by the enemy's artillery. 'By the left flank' and we enter the thicket, from which a regiment has just been driven. We press into it, and catch sight of the hedge beyond, and the Church ..." [17]

The 16th New York and 23rd New Jersey made the farthest penetration. As the Union soldiers neared the top of the ridge, their line was pelted by increasingly accurate sniper fire from the second story of the Salem Church, instigating a ferocious firefight between the Rebel snipers in the church and the Federals pressing to surround the building.[18] Within a matter of minutes, an entire company from the 9th Alabama was forced to surrender when the church was surrounded and captured.[19]

The victory at the church was to prove to be shortlived, however. Just moments after the church was captured, the Confederates launched a concerted counterattack all along the front. Given the Southerners' overwhelming superiority of numbers, the advantage of a downhill charge, and that the Union lines were already disordered from passing through the thicket and reduced from casualties, the result was inevitable. Both the 16th New York on the left, and the 1st New Jersey on the right, broke and began running back down the road.[20]

The 95th Pennsylvania seems to have been in a cleared area that allowed them a view of the church as "... the gallant Jersey skirmishers in front peppered the now seemingly broken and confused mass of Confederates who swarmed about the little chapel in front."[21] Galloway and his comrades watched as the Union forces captured the Confederates "In their strong position at the schoolhouse, seizing the stronghold with its miniature garrison whom they made temporary prisoners and were in turn driven off losing heavily." What they saw next, blue-coated soldiers streaming back down the hill, propelled the

---

[17]Unknown soldier as cited in Furgurson, p. 276.

[18]Even after repairs 168 bullet dents still remain on the church, 81 on the east side and 53 on the north. Furgurson, p. 277.

[19]O.R.-1-25-1-858, Wilcox.

[20]Furgurson, p. 279; Bilby, p. 67.

[21]Galloway, p. 20.

Pennsylvanians into action. "Quickly our line of battle sprang to its feet to confront the swarms of rebels now pouring out of the woods, line upon line, firing and yelling with demoniacal fury as they advanced. Bravely our two little regiments under Col. Town strove to resist the overwhelming taint which now overlapped our right and threatened total annihilation."[22] Both Pennsylvania regiments stood and blasted away at the descending Southerners, and then paid for their belligerence by receiving a withering fusillade in return.[23]

It would seem, however, that although the men of the 95th Pennsylvania could see the oncoming foe, the Grays could not, and as a consequence were ordered to position themselves so as to be able to fire blindly in the direction from where the greatest threat seemed to be emanating. "I [Sgt. Wildman] was on the right of the company, which made a one half wheel to the left along a fence. Just as I was about to fire some one called out that we were firing on our own men. Consequently I fired higher than I intended to, thinking that what I took to be rebels was our own front line, which was in the wood. The balls were flying as thick as hail, yet still the cry came that we were firing on our own men."[24]

It is not clear whether the Grays shared the same targets as the men of the 95th Pennsylvania. Although the Union collapse at the church occurred more quickly due to the more open terrain, the Confederate counteroffensive was general along the whole line, and as a result some or all of the Philadelphians may have been exchanging rifle fire with Confederates descending on their front, or even toward their right flank. The effect of the attack on the Pennsylvanians was the same, regardless of the direction toward which they were shooting. "Shortly some one called out for us to fall back, which call went down the line. The men near me were leaving quite fast. I began to fear that our regiment [the 119th] had broken, it never having been in a close fight before, and this I knew to be a hard one. In a very short time I heard the Rebels give a yell. Up I jumped and as I arose some one by my side

---

[22]Galloway, p. 20.

[23]Bilby, p. 67. It is possible that it was at this point in the action that Colonel Town was killed.

[24]W., *Bucks County Intelligencer*, 5/26/1863.

was shot. I turned and ran out of the wood. Then I found that not only our own regiment was in full retreat, but the whole line as far as I could see. The enemy thinking it his turn to drive us, pushed boldly forward. Men were falling in every direction. The balls were flying around us like hail stones. Many of them tore up the dirt at my feet ... My own escape was a miracle. The enemy were almost at my heels when I came out of the wood, loudly yelling, yet their balls touched me not."[25]

Fortunately for the fleeing Bluecoats, the Federal artillery had taken up a strong position on the ridge immediately to the east of Salem Heights, around the Morrison House, which was approximately eight-tenths of a mile from the Church. The terrain gave the Union gunners a critical and unusual advantage. Civil War artillery was primarily used in a direct line of fire method. The exploding shells were often unreliable, and there was no way to adequately direct fire, so shells were very rarely lobbed over the heads of advancing or retreating troops. Here, however, the retreating Union soldiers were in a valley with the artillery placed above them, so the cannoneers were able to fire exploding shells and case shot[26] over their compatriots' heads into the Rebel line during most of the retreat.

The Grays and their comrades did not entirely abandon the field, despite the drubbing administered in the woods. "Some of our officers displayed great bravery using every effort to rally the men [of the 119th] beyond the wood, where they were making an endeavor to form a new line forming some distance back. Our Colonel, who I have spoken of before as a brave man, led us forward to the charge with great gallantry as did the officers generally. Lt. Hodgson during the retreat did his utmost to rally the men around him, but it was of no avail. I thought it best to turn my steps thither. Our regiment I could not find. Some said it was advancing, others that it had fallen further back -- Thinking the former statement correct, I advanced some distance with a Massachusetts

---

[25]W., *Bucks County Intelligencer*, 5/26/1863.

[26]The former consisted of hollow steel shells filled with powder, and the latter contained added steel balls, each designed to explode and throw shrapnel.

Salem Church - May 3, 1863

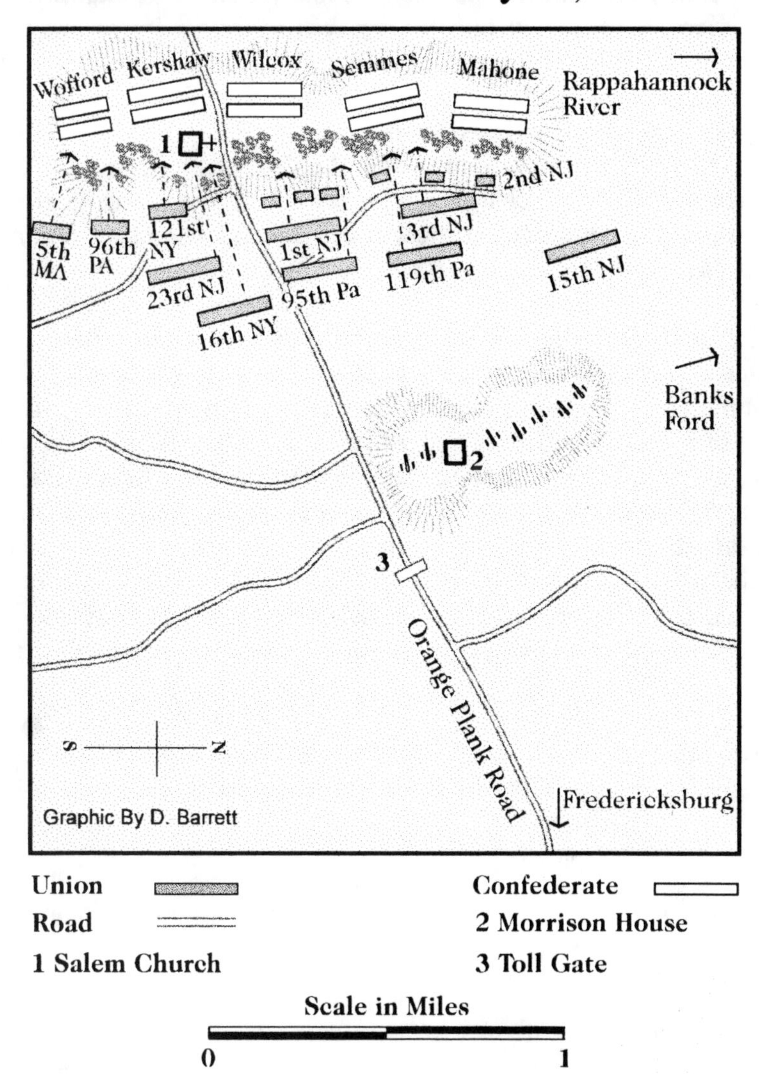

regiment, and then went to the right hoping to find my regiment but without success."[27]

The Union troops fleeing from the ridge found their artillery to be a sanctuary behind which to rally. "Finally after a desperate struggle which scarcely lasted ten minutes, we were forced to give away and together with the troops on the left, seek shelter behind our guns on the elevation just in rear."[28] Joined by reinforcements filing off the Plank Road, the Federal line quickly stabilized.

Now the tables were turned on the Confederates, as they found themselves in the open, charging uphill with their thinned and disrupted lines exposed to murderous artillery fire. The Union gunners continued to fire shells and case shot as fast as their pieces could be swabbed and loaded, filling the air with the "spang" of the brass napoleons and the duller "thud" from the iron parrotts and ordnance rifles; with the near continuous concussions blending together into one gut-shaking din.[29] When the Federal infantry finally cleared from in front of the guns, the cannoneers switched to the far deadlier double-shotted canister, which apparently wreaked the most havoc along the road where the land was clear and relatively flat.[30] "... A storm of shell and canister was rained upon the advancing foe who were quickly driven back to the shelter of the woods leaving prisoners in our hands, who had followed us up so closely they were forced to surrender.[31] Half an hour after we were driven back we again held nearly the same ground as when the line gave way."[32]

The most significant portion of the battle was over, although some fighting continued to the right of the Union artillery as the 2nd Rhode Island and the 37th Massachusetts relieved the 3rd and 15th New

---

[27]W., *Bucks County Intelligencer*, 5/26/1863. At that time there were only three Massachusetts regiments in the Sixth Corps, the 7th, 10th, and 37th, all in the Third Division, Second Brigade. Sears, *Chancellorsville*, p. 462.

[28]Galloway, p. 20.

[29]DeForest, p. 90.

[30]Canister consisted of thin metal cans filled with from 15 to 20 iron balls approximately one inch in diameter which, upon firing, burst out of the end of the cannon barrel with a shotgun-like effect. It was normal to use one canister shell, but for close or desperate work two were employed.

[31]Galloway, p. 20.

[32]W., *Bucks County Intelligencer*, 5/26/1863.

Jersey and pushed the remaining Confederates back up the ridge.[33] According to Elisha Hunt Rhodes, the diarist with the 2nd Rhode Island, his regiment was instrumental in stabilizing the Union line. "After the attack was made by the front line, we could see the [Union] troops waver, and soon men began to retreat down the road. The next we knew the Rebels came in sight, and Col. Rogers was ordered to the front with the 2nd R.I. We advanced across a field to the brow of a hill and opened fire. Here our men began to fall, and the Rebels still advanced. Forward is the word again, and with a yell we rushed on to the Rebel lines which broke and fled for the woods. Men were falling here and there, but 'Close up and forward' was the command and we kept on, cheered by the thought that we were doing good service while our Corps could reform in our rear. We entered the woods, but were stopped by the severe fire. Here we fought for an hour ... The Rebels had as prisoners a regiment of New Jersey troops with their colors. We succeeded in releasing the troops and recapturing the colors ... After the firing ceased we returned to the hill in our rear and reformed our lines."[34]

The chaos, suffering, and dying continued even though the gunfire had all but ceased. "After a long search I found it, [the 119th] about dark. One by one the men joined it ... I learned that our Captain [Peter W. Rodgers] and T. Blakey Walton were wounded, the former dangerously ... I hope I may never witness such a sight as I beheld on that battlefield ... After joining the company and getting a little rest, I went to a house nearby, that was used as a hospital, to see Walton. I found him suffering much pain, having a wound just below the right shoulder. We could learn nothing of our Captain. He was seen to fall, having been shot through the head. When asked what could be done for him he merely replied 'let me lie.'"[35] Both Captain Rodgers and Private Walton succumbed to the wounds each received that day.[36] It may be assumed that during this time the Regiment's surgeon, Philip

---

[33]Bilby, p. 70.

[34]Rhodes, pp. 106-107.

[35]W., *Bucks County Intelligencer*, 5/26/1863.

[36]Bates, *History...*, vol. 4, 119th Pa. Walton's body was subsequently exhumed and returned for proper burial at his family's home in Attleborough (now Langhorne), Middletown Township, Bucks County, Pa. *Bucks County Intelligencer*, 6/2/1863.

Leidy, was pressed to his physical and emotional limits as he tried to minister to the broken, torn, and bleeding casualties of the Grays' first battle, who crowded the floor of his makeshift hospital.

Surgeon Philip Leidy

(Courtesy - The Civil War Library Museum, Phila., Pa.)

Along with the many other Grays wounded that day, James B. Millard of Company I lay in the field hospital groaning in agony from a gunshot wound which shattered a bone. With his wound, James became the first Millard in three generations to shed blood for his country; and although he would not be the first of his family to offer "the last full measure of devotion" he would, several years after the war, succumb to complications from the wound, which continued to discharge fragments of shattered bone until the time of his death.[37]

Although not physically wounded in the action, the Grays' commander, Colonel Ellmaker, seems to have been somewhat psychologically bruised from, or distraught over, the outcome of the fight. As the 49th Pennsylvania from the Grays' brigade marched onto the field at the end of the day, one of its soldiers recognized Ellmaker and asked him what had become of the 119th. As recollected by Private Westbrook, the historian for the 49th, "... His answer was 'all gobbled up ...'" delivered in a "... voice [which] was coarse and sounded very funny ..." Afterwards the phrase "all gobbled up" was used as a running joke amongst the members of the 49th Pennsylvania.[38]

During the evening, the rest of the Sixth Corps came forward, and at about dusk the 119th was reunited with its brigade commander,

---

[37]*Philadelphia Sunday Press*, 12/28/1890.

[38]Westbrook, p. 145.

General Russell, who was then placed in charge of the right wing of the Union forces on the scene. Several factors prevented Sedgwick from using his reinforcements to launch a counterattack against Salem Heights. Night was approaching, and the armies in the Civil War almost never fought in the dark. Further, Sedgwick knew that the Confederates who had been routed earlier that day at Fredericksburg had regrouped in the rear of the Sixth Corps, and were pursuing it down the same road that the Greek Crosses had recently traveled. Finally, "Uncle John" had received reports that there were also Southern units forming to his south. For the prudent Sedgwick, the possible gains of a counterattack were far outweighed by the consequences of losing additional men, when the virtually surrounded Sixth Corps might soon need every possible rifleman to fend off total annihilation.

In preparation for the inevitable coming attack, the blue-coated troops were deployed in a cup-shaped formation, with the 119th and the rest of the Third Brigade facing west toward the heights. To their left, at a right angle facing south, were the brigades of Bartlett and Brigadier General Alfred T. D. Torbert, with the balance of the Corps filling out the southern and eastern perimeter.[39] All the Federals, motivated by the reasonable expectation that their lives would soon depend on their effort, spent the next several hours furiously digging trenches. When the men settled down late in the evening and stillness passed over the field, the men of the Grays' brigade could "... hear the wounded moaning in every direction, but we don't know whether they are rebels or our men ..."[40] The blue and butternut wounded, who had been antagonists in the afternoon, were united in misery throughout the night.

With the advent of daylight on the fourth of May, Lee launched several unsuccessful attacks against various portions of the Union defenses, mostly against Brigadier General Albion Howe's Division, which formed the eastern portion of the Union line, and suffered significant casualties for his efforts. The 119th experienced intermittent skirmishing along its portion of the western front. "Next morning [May 4] around sunrise we were again ordered to the front. We remained most of the day in the same position, advancing about 6 o'clock a short

---

[39]O.R.-1-25-1-568.

[40]Westbrook, p. 145.

distance to the front. We had not been long in our new position before our artillery open on the enemy who were advancing from the road. They were driven back, not relishing the manner in which our grape and canister were thinning their ranks."[41]

Sometime during the day, the men of the Third Brigade were granted a diversion from the grimness of their situation. According to Private Westbrook, "... a herd of cattle is between our skirmish line and the rebels, and it is very amusing to see them run and bellow, first to the right, then to the left, with tails straight out ..."[42] Perhaps some of the Grays, with a sense for the ironic, realized as they watched the spectacle that the Sixth Corps shared a predicament similar to those unfortunate cattle.

Sedgwick held his position throughout the day, because he knew that by so doing he kept Lee from again shifting the weight of his army back to Chancellorsville, and also because, in truth, he had only one viable option, for which he lacked permission. Surrender was not an option that Sedgwick believed was available to him, and he was prepared to fight to the last man if necessary, as shown by the following (perhaps apocryphal) exchange with one of his young staff officers:

> "General, it looks as if the Sixth Corps was [is] going to close its career today."
>
> "It has somewhat that appearance," Sedgwick replied.
>
> "Then if the Sixth Corps goes out of existence today, I hope it will be with a blaze of glory that will light the history of this war for all time."
>
> Sedgwick responded, "I will tell you a secret; there will be no surrendering."[43]

Not wishing to sacrifice the lives of his men solely for a heroic gesture, however, Sedgwick solicited and received permission to save his corps by retreating across the river at Banks Ford. Another later order

---

[41]W., *Bucks County Intelligencer*, 5/26/1863.
[42]Westbrook, p. 145.
[43]McMahon, *Vermont Address*, as cited in Winslow, p. 81.

from Hooker, who was pathetically much more pugnacious with Sedgwick's troops than his own, rescinded the earlier permission to retreat; but fortunately that order was not received until after the corps was safely across the river.

Commencing on the night of May 4, and continuing into the morning of the fifth, the Union forces quietly withdrew towards the ford under the cover of fog and darkness, where they crossed the river one regiment at a time. During the crossing, the Southerners occasionally lobbed artillery shells at the ford, which one Union soldier described as looking "... like so many graceful curves of rockets ..."[44] Because the Confederate gunners could not see their targets, their shelling did little damage.[45]

Probably because of their location, the men of Russell's Brigade shared in the responsibility of covering the Sixth Corps' withdrawal across the ford. The Grays arrived in the area of the bridge around 9:00 p.m., but did not actually cross the river until between 3:00 and 3:30 a.m., while still under shelling.[46] "It was about dark when we began to retreat along the whole line, going in the direction of Banks Ford, about five miles above Fredericksburg. At about 3:00 o'clock this morning we began to cross the river, the enemy throwing shells among us as we went, but not doing material damage."[47]

The 6th Maine, which was soon to be brigaded with the 119th, claimed the honor of being the last unit to cross the river, but only after a narrow escape. Finding themselves alone on the South bank, the

---

[44]Westbrook, p. 145.

[45]Curiously, although the sources agree that the crossing was made without casualties, the Muster Out Roll for the 119th indicates that Private John Cleavenstein of I Company died on May 29 from a shell fragment wound which he received at Banks Ford on May 5, 1863. Pennsylvania Archives.

[46]O.R.-1-25-1-592; Latta diary.

[47]W., *Bucks County Intelligencer*, 5/26/1863. There seems to be some disagreement concerning which ford the Sixth Corps used to escape from the cul-de-sac. Sergeant Wildman of the 119th referred to Banks Ford as the point of crossing, as did General Sedgwick in all his official messages to Hooker. Confederate observers, as well as Lee's noted cartographer, Jed. Hotchkiss, placed the point of the Union escape at Scott's Ford, which was approximately 1-1/4 miles downstream and almost due north of Banks Ford. Perhaps the discrepancy resulted from a lack of local knowledge on the part of the troops on the scene, or perhaps because elements of the Sixth Corps crossed at each ford.

Maine men were forced into a fifteen-minute firefight with the Confederates, who were rapidly closing in from behind the fleeing Federals. Only by sliding down a steep, sixty-foot-high bank while under the cover of the fog and deep darkness, were the men of the 6th Maine able to perfect their escape.[48]

The Grays did not escape from hardship as easily as from the Confederates. Lieutenant Latta chronicled the trials to which the Regiment was subjected over the next several days:

"May 5 - Assumed command of Co. G. Recrossed Rappahannock at 3:30 a.m. under shelling from enemy. Bivouacked at daylight about a mile & 1/2 from the shore - apprehensive casualties and mishaps in the Sixth Corp are more ... [extensive] than first supposed - loss in our regiment about 160 - troops in bad shape as a severe rain storm came on towards evening and continued all night."

"May 6 - ... on the same ground where we camped yesterday - rain continued all day & through part of night ... [rendering] everything damp and unpleasant ..."

"May 7 - Moved to more suitable ground ..."

"May 8 - Commenced return march. Roads heavy and fatiguing. On road all day and returned to old camp 2:30 p.m. everything undisturbed."

"May 9 - Lost clothing, tents, knapsacks in fight of [May 3rd] and must equip regiment anew ..."

Undoubtedly the physical discomforts experienced by the men of the 119th were compounded by the grief and frustration accompanying the unavoidable conclusion that valued comrades had been lost in another defeat brought about by poor leadership at the top. As if to summarize the futility of the Chancellorsville campaign, Latta also noted in his diary one additional senseless casualty. On May 6 a private was accidentally shot by the unintended discharge of a pistol. Although neither the name of the victim nor the circumstances of the shooting were included in the diary, a comparison of the unit muster-rolls against the date show that although Private Thomas Hunsworth of Company G survived the amphibious assault and the charge up Salem Heights, he did not survive the carelessness of a comrade.

---

[48]Mundy, p. 134.

Private Hunsworth was the last, but as Latta reported, far from the only casualty suffered by the Regiment during the first few days in May. As previously noted, Captain Peter Rodgers was killed in the action. Captain Charles P. Warner and 2nd Lieutenant John M. Cook were both severely wounded, and Captain Andrew T. Goodman was slightly wounded. The regiment had 719 men present for duty at the start of the campaign, but the number remaining at the conclusion is a matter of some disagreement.[49] According to the *Philadelphia Inquirer*, May 19, 1863, the unit suffered 135 casualties as follows: killed - 13; wounded - 77; missing - 39; captured - 6. Bates' *History of Pennsylvania Volunteers* provides different numbers: Killed or died from wounds - 24; wounded - 13; missing - 5; captured - 12; totalling 54. The *Official Record* reported the casualties as "...killed, one officer and 9 enlisted men, wounded 3 officers and 71 enlisted men, and missing in action 38 enlisted men, for a total of 122 casualties." Finally, Latta put the total casualties at 160. By any count, the first real fight for the 119th was costly, claiming anywhere from 22 percent to 7.5 percent of the Regiment.

2nd Lieutenant John M. Cook

(USAMHI)

The battle was especially costly for the Fausts of Montgomery County, Pennsylvania. John E. Faust was one of the wounded. His medical records indicate that the bullet which downed him entered the bottom of his right heel, passed through his ankle and exited out the top

[49]Bates, *History...*, vol. 4, 119th.

of his foot.[50] The nature of the wound suggests that it occurred during the retreat from the Heights where Faust, unlike Sergeant Wildman, was apparently not fortunate enough to avoid the bullets snapping around his feet as he retreated.

John next appeared as a patient in the Douglas Hospital in Washington, where he was admitted on May 8, 1863, five days after he was wounded. The young farmer apparently did fairly well for the first few days in the hospital. However, the doctors seemed very concerned about whether the bullet had "opened" his right ankle joint. On the fourteenth they performed an examination of the wound with a probe "... but without anesthetics ...!" The cure in this case was probably worse than the cause. The next day John developed a "severe chill" and much "irritability of system." In response, on the seventeenth he was "etherized," the wound surgically opened, and because it was then determined that the joint was in fact "opened," his foot was amputated. The doctors noted that he was very slow to awaken from the anesthesia, but they still believed during the next twenty-four hours that his chances for recovery were better than before the surgery. Although he was strong enough to survive a gunshot wound to the foot, he was not strong enough to survive nineteenth-century medicine and: "... the following night he slowly sank and died ..."[51]

Doubling the family grief over the mortal wound John received at Salem Church, his cousin Aaron was apparently killed in the same action, although his military records listed Aaron as missing in action during the battle. Although there is no official evidence that Aaron was killed, he had not returned home by 1877, and it is clear that his family members and several neighbors were convinced that he died in the war. Both of the Faust boys joined the Regiment in part to help support their mothers. As a result of the deaths of their children, each mother received a pension of eight dollars a month for life, completing the Faustian bargain.[52]

---

[50] By coincidence, the wound was at almost the identical spot on the same foot where his great-grandson, Clarence P. Maier, would be wounded 81 years later at the Battle of the Bulge, only in the latter case, the bullet entered through the top of the foot.

[51] National Archives, Military records for John Faust.

[52] National Archives, Pension records for John and Aaron Faust.

John E. Faust

5

BRANDY STATION

After Hooker and Sedgwick completed the rather precipitous withdrawal of the Army of the Potomac from the Chancellorsville battlefield, the two armies resumed their former positions on either side of the Rappahannock. Because the Confederates had more of their own wounded than they could handle, the Northerners who were abandoned on the south side of the river were receiving little, if any, care. On May 10 Sedgwick made arrangements with the Southerners for a truce to retrieve the Sixth Corps wounded, many of whom were languishing across the river in and around the Lacey House, a home converted into a hospital. Union ambulances were permitted to cross the river, and between 1,500 and 1,600 wounded were rescued and distributed among Union field hospitals in the area.[1]

Ellmaker's men were not granted a long respite to refit and to heal from the physical and emotional wounds received at Salem Church. Shortly after the Grays' return, the men had to move camp about a mile from the prior location at White Oak Chapel, to a new spot about five miles from Aquia Creek. The new location had good water and shade, but more importantly it was free of health hazards such as garbage, dead animals and effluent which had accumulated over the winter.[2] Lieutenant Latta didn't find this time to be particularly healing in any case, providing this description of a typical day: "Stayed around camp all day, weather almost intolerable, nothing of interest transpiring, the dull monotony of camp life continues; the occasional distant shouts of troops

[1]Winslow, p. 88.
[2]Winslow, p. 89.

whose terms of enlistment have expired may be heard day after day."[3] Latta would soon have some action to relieve his boredom.

Within two weeks after the battle at Chancellorsville, Hooker began to receive warnings, through his newly revised and improved intelligence system, that the Confederates were on the move on the other side of the river. In fact, Lee had begun preparations for another invasion of the North, having directed his army to begin to concentrate in the area of the Culpeper Court House. Lee's plan was to push his army north through the Shenandoah Valley, leaving Lieutenant General Ambrose P. Hill to occupy Fredericksburg for as long as possible, in hopes of freezing the Union forces in place opposite the town.

Hooker decided that the proper response should be to launch an attack across the river and then a drive for Richmond. He proposed this plan to President Lincoln, who rejected the idea, writing that such a maneuver would leave Hooker "... entangled upon the river, like an ox jumped half over a fence and liable to be torn by dogs front and rear, without a fair chance to gore one way or kick the other."[4] Presumably with Hooker's consent, however, on June 6 General Sedgwick ordered a portion of his Sixth Corps over the pontoon bridges at Deep Run below Fredericksburg for a reconnaissance in force.[5]

Although forced to abandon his plan for a drive on Richmond, Hooker nevertheless held to his belief that some offensive action was necessary, if not with his infantry, then with his cavalry, which could be sent on a raid south without the commitment to a full-fledged offensive. In hopes of destroying, or at least scattering, the horsemen of the flamboyant Major General J. E. B. Stuart who were then gathered around Brandy Station, the Union commander directed Major General Alfred Pleasonton to lead his entire cavalry force, together with 3,000 foot soldiers specially selected for their fighting prowess, across the Rappahannock River for an attack.[6]

By midday on June 7, Pleasonton had completed the planning for his raid. The attackers were to be divided into two wings -- the right

---

[3]Latta diary, 5/24/1863.

[4]As cited in Coddington, p. 53.

[5]Coddington, p. 52.

[6]Coddington, p. 54.

wing under Brigadier General John Buford, and infantry under Brigadier General Adelbert Ames, was to cross the river at Beverly Ford, while the left wing under the command of Brigadier General David Gregg, with infantry support led by General Russell, was to launch its assault from Kelly Ford. Both were to embark at dawn on June 9 and close the pincers at Brandy Station, except for a segment of the troopers in the left wing under the command of Colonel Alfred N. Duffie, who were to proceed south to Stevensburg, in hopes of intercepting a Confederate retreat.[7]

Russell received his marching orders on June 7, 1863: "The inclosed copies of orders indicate to you the command to be given you for a temporary duty. You will report to Brigadier-General Pleasonton, at Kelly's Ford, tomorrow for orders, and in your movements from Hartwood Church be careful that your column is concealed from the enemy; that your own command is ignorant of their destination; that any guerrillas, spies or wanderers through the country which you traverse are picked up, to prevent their communicating any information to the enemy. S. Williams Asst. Adjutant General."[8]

Perhaps to spread the glory, or the risk, Russell selected his force from several of the Corps in his area: 600 men from his own Sixth Corps; 600 men from the First Corps; and 300 men from the Second Corps. To meet the Sixth Corps' allotment, Russell chose warriors from the 6th Maine and the 119th, presumably out of respect for attributes he had observed as their brigade commander, and also because of the history of achievement which followed the 6th Maine.

Early on in the war, the 6th Maine, 5th Wisconsin, and the 49th Pennsylvania were brigaded together under the command of Winfield Scott Hancock. In their first serious action, at the Battle of Williamsburg on May 5, 1862, Hancock's men were led to an isolated position on the Southern flank by a young staff officer named George A. Custer. Although the high command squandered a golden opportunity to exploit that position and collapse the Confederate defensive line, Hancock's fighting withdrawal, and the sharp repulse his men administered to Jubal Early's troops, earned Hancock the nickname "Hancock the Superb."

---

[7]Coddington, p. 55.
[8]O.R.1-27-3-29.

At Second Fredericksburg, the 5th Wisconsin and 6th Maine, as part of the Light Brigade, were at the heart of the successful storming of Marye's Heights. Several weeks after Chancellorsville, the 119th was assigned to a newly reconstituted brigade composed of the above mentioned regiments, and thus became an integral part of a unit of solid troops who were known to perform well under competent leadership.[9]

On June 7, the various component units of Russell's force began to move into position for the assault, which was to commence at dawn two days later. Lieutenant Latta was one of the Grays chosen for the raid, and he recorded the day's activities: "Everything quiet during morning. At 2 p.m. a detachment of 260 men under command of Major Henry P. Truefitt, together with ... [the 6th] Maine ordered to Harwood Church -- object of the movement covered in mystery. [As] Acting adjutant of the battalion [I] reached the church after a fatiguing march at 8:30 where other troops join us and General Russell assumes command."[10]

The Grays and the Maine men spent much of the day of June 8 covering the remaining distance to their designated final position: "[The 119th] Moved again at 6:30 [a.m.], everything still mysterious ... at 10:00 a.m. near Groves Church ... reached Kelly Ford about 5:00 p.m. ... the move appears to be to cover the crossing of ... cavalry at that point. Distance marched since Friday 30 miles."[11]

As planned, Buford's force crossed at dawn on the ninth, initially meeting little resistance. The Rebels were soon able to scrape together a force that, although not strong enough to seriously challenge Buford, was able to slow him down. Gregg, on the other hand, was late in getting started because Duffie got lost trying to find the jump-off point; but when Gregg's men finally splashed across the ford between 6:30 and 8:00 a.m., they faced no initial opposition. There was a Confederate force in the vicinity which could have offered a serious challenge to the Yankees, but the Southern commander, Brigadier General Beverly H. Robertson, perhaps following his orders to the letter, held his position

[9]Mundy, pp. 66-71, 74, 94, 138-140; Jordan, pp. 36-37.
[10]Latta diary.
[11]Latta diary.

covering the northernmost road to Brandy Station and merely watched, while Gregg's men proceeded down another.[12]

After riding south for a short distance Duffie, as planned, split off from the main force and streamed south in the direction of Stevensburg. The rest of Gregg's troopers soon came upon what was considered the key position of the area, Fleetwood Hill, which dominated the surrounding countryside. Stuart had chosen this hill for his command post, but at the time of Gregg's arrival it was manned mostly by staff, who were armed with only one six-pound howitzer. Unfortunately, this fact was unknown to the Union general, and when his men began to receive incoming artillery rounds from the howitzer, he deployed his troopers in formation in anticipation of a full-scale battle.[13]

This delay allowed Southern reinforcements to arrive, and as a result, rather than a swift capture of the hill and a humiliating defeat for the butternut cavaliers, the two cavalry forces spent much of the day engaged in wild charges and countercharges, where pistols and sabers inflicted the majority of the casualties. No decisive victory was obtained by either side, but the Union achieved a moral victory, first for having surprised the vaunted J. E. B. Stuart, and also for holding their own against a force which had routinely embarrassed them in the past.[14]

But what of the men of the 119th? "At 2:30 on the morning of the 9th the night's bivouac broke up and the river was forded at 6:30. Following the cavalry closely, line of battle was formed and advanced to a position beyond the Orange and Alexandria railroad [where the railroad crossed the river at Rappahannock Station] some four miles from the river [crossing at Kelly's Ford]."[15] Unlike the infantry with Ames, who became involved in some serious action, the Grays and a portion of the force which crossed over the ford with them, spent the day slowly advancing westward on a road parallel to the Rappahannock River, while engaged in desultory skirmishing with Robertson's dismounted cavalry. Meanwhile, the rest of Russell's infantry remained in the area of Kelly's Ford. Each force was intent on preventing a surprise attack on the rear

---

[12]Coddington, p. 57.
[13]Coddington, pp. 56-60.
[14]Coddington, pp. 57-60.
[15]Latta, *Pennsylvania at Gettysburg*, vol. 2, p. 641.

or flank of their cavalry, and also upon insuring a secure route for the withdrawal of the troopers when the day's work was completed. Around 4 or 5 p.m. Gregg's exhausted troopers filed back across the ford at Rappahannock Station, followed closely by Russell's infantry, including the detachment from the 119th, which crossed the river intact and without a casualty, at 5:30 p.m.[16]

Perhaps the most stressful experience for any of the Philadelphians during the entire expedition occurred while the Regiment was recrossing the Rappahannock. Two options were available to get back into friendly territory -- fording through waist deep water, or marching over the 600-foot-long Orange and Alexandria Railroad bridge, which at its highest point was estimated by Lieutenant Latta to have been ninety feet above the water. The infantry was directed to cross the bridge and the cavalry was sent through the ford. Since no foot-path had been constructed along the rails, the men had to step from tie to tie, a maneuver which was so frightening to one member of the 119th that he began to cross on all fours, apparently convinced that if he tried to walk across he would fall through. An officer of the Regiment, who obviously didn't empathize with the man's fear of heights, began to berate the poor soldier shouting: "'Stand up, walk upright ... where's your nerve, where's your manhood, never mind the depth below, you can't fall through.'" Deciding that manhood was best established in line of battle, the soldier crawled off the bridge and waded across the river with the horses.[17]

The Grays did not withdraw immediately from the area of the previous day's crossing. "Remained in the front during the day [June 10] and relieved at sundown ... Saw flag of truce from our ... [enemy] across the river. Rebel Cavalry show themselves as casually on the flats on the other side, but no demonstration in force has been made. The night passed off in quiet ... [while the] cavalry marched back."[18]

Probably concerned with the possibility of a counter-attack, the Union infantry made a slow and deliberate withdrawal from the ford. On the eleventh Latta reported: "Moved at 7 a.m. to Bealton Station on

[16]Latta diary; Longacre, pp. 68-74.

[17]Latta, *Pennsylvania at Gettysburg*, vol. 2, p. 641.

[18]Latta diary, 6/10/1863.

O & A Railroad, a distance of 2-1/2 miles, from which place a rest of two hours -- moved another half mile further into camp. Have heard nothing from the rest of the Regiment since leaving on Sunday. Heat intense, almost unbearable."[19]

Although the 119th was not involved in any serious fighting during the attack on Brandy Station, its participation was not without benefit. Presumably Lieutenant Latta and his like-minded companions were relieved from their boredom. More importantly, the miles covered on those hot and dusty roads to and from the ford provided excellent physical conditioning for a coming march that would someday be acknowledged as one of the most grueling in the history of American warfare.

---

[19]Latta diary.

6

GETTYSBURG

For several days after the battle at Brandy Station, the Union camps were thick with rumors about a Rebel invasion of the North. The veterans of the Army of the Potomac knew that spring was for fighting, and that sooner or later they would again have to come to grips with the Rebels if the war was ever to be finished. However, the prospects of attempting to repel another Southern invasion added a whole new level of anxiety to the usual fears of death, dismemberment or dishonor; for a battle lost in Virginia was just another loss, and the army had already survived plenty of those; but a loss in Maryland or Pennsylvania might result in the capture of the capital or a major Northern city, and perhaps the loss of the war as well. The men from Maryland and central Pennsylvania bore an extra burden of concern because they had seen, and perhaps participated in, the wasting of northern Virginia, and could justifiably expect a similar fate if the Confederates should proceed into their own home territory. Then, in justification of that anxiety, orders were received propelling the Army of the Potomac in pursuit of Lee's army. On the eve of their departure, most of the men of the 119th not detached to Brandy Station attended a religious service.

On June 13, the remainder of the Regiment that had been excused from the raid on Brandy Station broke camp, crossed back over the Rappahannock, and headed north. Although the following description was provided by Jesse Bowman Young, a lieutenant in the Third Corps, it is safe to assume that a similar scene occurred in the Grays' camp when it received orders to move out: ".. one day couriers were seen flying in all directions with orders to march in two hours with sparse baggage and plenty of ammunition ... The hurry and commotion, the stir and haste, the excitement and effervescence ... that day may be fitly likened to the fermentation occasioned in a wasp's big nest when stirred up by a long pole." Soon, "... long lines of blue-coated infantry, laden with well-filled haversacks, knapsacks, and cartridge boxes, and girded about with their blankets and carrying their muskets 'at will', sallied forth, taking up the line of march and proceeding in utter uncertainty across the hot and dusty plains."[1]

A moving description of the initial phase of the pursuit was provided by Surgeon George T. Stevens of the 77th New York Volunteers [Second Division, Third Brigade, Sixth Corps], whose regiment would have been separated from Ellmaker's men by a mile or less. "Our own Corps being rear guard, started at ten o'clock at night. The darkness was intense, and a thunder shower prevailed. Our route for a long time lay through a thick woods where the branches of the trees, meeting over our heads, shut out the little light that might have penetrated the thunder clouds, and the column was shut in perfect darkness. The road was terribly muddy, and the batteries which were trying to pass over the same route were frequently stuck in the mire. Our men stumbled over stones and fallen trees, often falling beneath the feet of the horses. Men fell over logs and stones, breaking their legs and arms. Thus we continued the hasty and difficult march, while the rain poured in torrents upon us."

"Later in the night the road became more open and the rain ceased. The darkness was not so black; still it was difficult to see the road. We were passing over corduroy [a method of road paving where logs of various sizes were placed side by side, perpendicular to the route of travel]. Some of the logs were a foot, and others a foot-and-a-half through. They were slippery from the rain, and the men, heavily laden with knapsacks, guns, and cartridges, tumbled head-long, many of them going off at the side and rolling far down the steep embankments. A laugh from the comrades of the luckless ones, while someone would call out, 'Have you a pass to go down there?' was the only notice taken of such accidents; and the dark column hurried on, until at three o'clock in the morning we halted at Potomac Creek, where we slept soundly upon the ground until morning."

---

[1]Young, *The Battle of Gettysburg*, as cited in Wheeler, p. 35.

"The following day was Sunday. Our corps did not march until evening ... [they resumed the march at 9:00 p.m. and continued into the next day.] Morning dawned, the march was becoming tedious. The men were faint and wanted rest and coffee, but there was no halt... At length, as the morning advanced, the heat of the sun was almost intolerable, and the dust suffocating. Not a leaf stirred on the trees. Vegetation drooped under the scorching rays, and the clouds of dust were so dense that one could not see half the length of a regiment. The men at length began to fall from exhaustion. One after another, with faces burning with a glow of crimson, and panting for breath, would turn to the surgeons of their regiments and receive passes to the ambulances and a draught from the surgeon's flask; but at length ... the ambulances were crowded and so many were falling on every side that it became useless to require or attempt to give passes, or even for the surgeons to attempt to relieve the sufferers."

"In every corner of the rail fences and under every tree and bush, groups of men with faces glowing with redness, some with streams of perspiration rolling down their cheeks and others with the red faces dry and feverish, strewed the wayside and lined the hedges. Here the color-bearer of a regiment, his color lying beside him, lay gasping for breath; there a colonel, his horse tied to the fence, strove to fan the air into a little life with his broad-brimmed hat ... The spectacle along the roadside became appalling. Regiments became like companies, and companies lost their identity. Men were dying with sun-stroke, and still the march was continued."

"This could not last much longer, for the brave men who still held out were fast losing strength, and soon there would be no troops able to move. At length, at nearly three o'clock, we came in sight of the little old depopulated town of Dumfries. Here, to the joy of all, we saw men filing into the fields for a halt. There was no cheer, no expression of gladness, for the tired men, with feet blistered and raw, worn out by seventeen hours' constant march, almost melted and smothered, cared little for demonstrations. Throwing themselves upon the ground, they rested for half an hour, and then, rousing long enough to cook their coffee, they refreshed themselves with their hardtack, pork, and coffee, and were ready to sleep ..."[2] Elisha Hunt Rhodes, a soldier in the Third Division of the Sixth Corps, succinctly recorded his feelings about the twenty-mile march to Dumfries, Virginia in his diary, "I never suffered more in my life than I did on this march."[3]

Meanwhile, Major Truefitt's 260-man detachment was still struggling to catch up with the rest of the Regiment and the Sixth Corps. On June 14, Truefitt's men left Bealeton Station at 7 a.m., then passed by Bristoe Station, Cedar Run, Catlett's Station, and Warrenton Junction, before being permitted to bivouac at 9 p.m.[4] The next day brought more of the same: "Left bivouac at daybreak, reached Manassas Junction at 8 a.m. ... now surrounded by the rebel fortifications. Moved as far as Union Mills, place reached at 10 a.m."[5] This latter site was an oasis in a world of blistering heat and choking dust, possessing a grist mill with dam and millrace, cool water, lush meadows, and shaded banks, just the sort of place to bathe and recover from the arduous marches of the past several days.[6]

The two halves of the Regiment spent June 16 converging on each other until finally, after Truefitt's men bivouacked for the night at Fairfax Station and Ellmaker's soldiers bedded down on the old Manassas battlefield, the two contingents were only about a mile apart. The Regiment was finally reunited on the seventeenth.[7]

The reunification of the 119th was only a small part of the massing of the Army of the Potomac into a consolidated and manageable fighting force. Although Hooker was able to gather most of his troops in the Centerville, Virginia area by the end of the day on the seventeenth, the striking power of the army was significantly compromised as a result of days of heavy exertion, with minimal rest, in the crushing Virginia heat. Responding to the deteriorated physical condition of his men and the lack of firm intelligence about Lee's objectives, the Union

---

[2]Stevens, *Three Years in the Sixth Corps*, pp. 222-227.
[3]Rhodes, p. 113.
[4]Latta diary, 6/14/1863.
[5]Latta diary.
[6]Latta, *Pennsylvania at Gettysburg*, vol. 2, p. 642.
[7]Latta diary, 6/16,17/1863.

commander paused, allowing his army a week's recuperation in the cool air which blew in behind a cold front on the next day.[8]

On June 18, the Grays shifted their camp about four miles to a position on the Little River Turnpike near Germantown, Virginia, which would prove to be the Regiment's only movement until June 25.[9] Although granted a respite from the ordeals of the previous week's march, the Philadelphians were not able to escape the reality of their situation, witnessing the return of several shot-up cavalry units from a skirmish at Aldie on the eighteenth, and hearing "... heavy and continuous cannonading ... during greater part of the day in direction of Aldie, [and] Middleburg ..." from other cavalry engagements on the twenty-first.[10]

On June 25, it became evident beyond any doubt that not only was Lee in the process of a full-scale invasion of Pennsylvania, but also that he had managed to gain a lead of several days. In response, Hooker began a desperate effort to catch up with the Confederates before they were able to capture a major Northern city such as Baltimore or the key rail center of Harrisburg, Pennsylvania. All through the Union Army, scenes reminiscent of the scramble on June 13 were repeated as hastily issued orders from Headquarters began to arrive at the scattered camps of the various corps.

On the twenty-sixth, the 119th, along with the rest of the Sixth Corps, left its encampment at Centerville and marched to Dranesville.[11] The next day the Regiment was "... Ordered to move at 4 a.m. -- started 6 a.m. and reached Edwards Ferry on the Potomac at 10:30 ... crossed the pontoon at 5:00 p.m. and bivouacked about 1-1/2 miles this side of the river, distance marched eight miles."[12]

On the morning of the twenty-eighth the Grays "Moved at 4:40 a.m., passed through Barnesville and Poolesville and ... [bivouacked] one mile beyond Hyattstown having been on the route about thirteen hours."[13] Those men whose appreciation of the beauty of nature had

---

[8]Coddington, p. 75.

[9]Latta, *Pennsylvania at Gettysburg*, vol. 2, p. 643; Latta diary.

[10]Latta diary, 6/21/1863.

[11]Winslow, p. 95.

[12]Latta diary.

[13]Latta diary.

not been seared away by the horror of combat or the exhaustion of the march, were soon granted a pleasant interlude. "At last we lay down in the bright light of a full moon, and soon were unconscious of pain or weariness in our refreshing slumber. How bright and beautiful the moon shone that night." However, even such a soothing sight could not free the men from the reality of the purpose of their journey. "As I looked upon that pure, silvery orb, I could half imagine how her light would become dimmed with sorrow were she conscious of the cruel desolation being enacted under her light. Perhaps it was so, and for very grief she had hid her face behind a cloud, for before morning it rained quite hard, and when some of the boys awoke they found to their surprise that their blankets were soaking wet."[14]

In addition to being a day of hard marching, the twenty-eighth of June proved to be momentous for the Army of the Potomac, and for the country as well. At the close of the day on the twenty-seventh, the commander of the army was General Hooker, who may not have been beloved by his men, but who was at least a known quantity with whom the army had grown accustomed. When the Bluecoats awoke on the twenty-eighth, they found themselves under the command of Major General George Gordon Meade, who had been elevated by President Lincoln during the night from Fifth Corps commander to the head of the entire army.

The change probably puzzled many of the men both inside and outside of the Fifth Corps, since little was known about Meade other than his reputation for having a foul temper. At least in the opinion of Lieutenant Peck in the Grays' sister regiment, the 118th Pennsylvania, the men in Meade's own corps were less than enthusiastic about the appointment: "The latest news we have is that Gen. Meade of our corps is to take Hooker's place as commander of the Army. The estimation he is held in by the army is very slight indeed. The men of his own corps know him as 'Granny Meade' and the 'Doctor' because he looks so old-womanish. When he is superseded I suppose that some one from a lunatic asylum will take his place."[15] For those men who pondered the implications of the situation, concern rather than curiosity must have

---

[14]Fisk, p. 113.

[15]Peck, Henry T., *Letter*, 6/28/1863.

been the predominant emotion. Moving an army whose size approached 100,000 men was never an easy undertaking. To appoint a new commander to attempt to do so, while facing a seemingly invincible enemy, in the middle of an invasion upon which the course of the war probably depended, must have appeared an incredible blunder, even to men who had come to accept ineptness on the part of their leaders as standard operating procedure.

As loyal soldiers, however, the men strapped on their gear early on the morning of the twenty-ninth and resumed the trek northward, presumably to the refrain of even more grumbling than usual about the leadership of the army; and as with all armies, the usual was quite a lot. Even the officers complained, as illustrated by a captain from Massachusetts who vented his spleen about the quality of the leadership during the march: "There is not more than one in ten officers of high rank that understands the proper mode of moving divisions; and the fatigue that so often results is caused not by merely traveling a large number of miles but by the omission to halt them at regular intervals ... Mounted upon their horses, unencumbered by rations or clothing, and usually carrying a small flask and a light sword, it was a pastime for the subordinate generals and their staffs to ride or race from town to town, and issue stringent orders to court-martial the weary men for what they termed straggling ... Whenever a halt was ordered at the end of a march, a score of servile pioneers pitched his [a general's] capacious tent upon the most pleasant spot of ground, and placed in it a carpet, camp chairs, tables, and an iron bed-stead, so that he was probably more comfortable than he would have been at home."[16] The men's devotion and discipline was such that they endured such indignities; but they surely wondered, as they marched mile after dusty mile, whether their new commander would squander their lives in the same fashion as had McClellan, Pope, Burnside, and Hooker.

After leaving Hyattstown late that same morning, the Grays, probably at the rear of the Sixth Corps' column, marched continuously for a distance of twenty-six miles until finally permitted to stop at New Windsor, Maryland after sunset.[17] "No rest for the weary" was an

[16]Blake, *Three Years in the Army of the Potomac*, as cited in Wheeler, p. 36.

[17]Latta diary.

expression that must have been repeated up and down the ranks of the 119th as the men roused themselves and began another day's march at 7:30 a.m. on June 30, even though, as part of the trailing division, the Grays were able to snatch a few more hours' rest than the balance of their corps, which was on the road at 4:00 a.m.[18] Despite a persistent rain and accumulating fatigue, that day's twenty-three mile march to Manchester was comparatively easy, and would even prove to have a rather pleasant ending.[19] Lieutenant Latta fondly recalled the welcome given to the Regiment when it set up camp about two miles from Manchester: "The next day at Manchester was a novel one; we had no such experiences before or after ... The people in apparent sympathy with the Union cause crowded the camps, mingling freely with the troops. The scene much resembled a county fair ... Men and maidens, matrons and children, afoot and in wheeled vehicles, gathered from far and near for the opportunity to witness the sudden increase of male population."[20] Unfortunately, some of the good spirits shared with the Greek Crosses by the citizenry included the liquid variety, and so many men became drunk that General Sedgwick was forced to issue an order that anyone bringing liquor into the camps was to be immediately arrested. The next day, many Union boys would sorely regret the hangover which resulted from the prior evening's festivities.[21]

The morning of the first of July gave no hint of what was in store for the Philadelphians that day. The men enjoyed the luxury of lounging around camp until about 11:00 a.m., when the morning's tranquility was abruptly interrupted by orders to draw three days' rations and sixty rounds of ammunition.[22] To those veterans, the receipt of such an order was tantamount to being told that a battle was imminent; and most must have experienced the natural psychological, and perhaps physiological, reactions. However, the morning's tranquility soon returned to the camp and for the next eight hours nothing significant occurred, a development which probably puzzled the men.

---

[18]Mundy, p. 145, Latta diary.

[19]Mundy, p. 145.

[20]Latta, *Pennsylvania at Gettysburg*, vol. 2, p. 645.

[21]Winslow, p. 98.

[22]Mundy, p. 145.

Late that afternoon, shortly after the Dutchmen of Major General Oliver O. Howard's Eleventh Corps had been driven through the streets of Gettysburg, but before the Union forces were securely emplaced on Cemetery Ridge, General Meade sent an order summoning the Sixth Corps forward to Taneytown, Maryland with all possible haste, probably to provide support in the event that the Union army was compelled to retreat.[23] At about 8:00 p.m. General Sedgwick received that order, the first of three he would receive during the night; and with its arrival the men of the Sixth Corps were propelled on one of the major feats of endurance of the Civil War. "In a moment more all was hurry and confusion, the bugles sounded the assembly, and orderlies and staff officers were rushing in all directions to the headquarters of the several brigades, whose bugles again sounded the call, and officers rushed out shouting to the men 'pack up, pack up and fall in.'"[24] "Uncle John" Sedgwick's charges promptly answered the call, and the first of the troops were on the road within one hour, soon joined by the Grays at 9:30 p.m.[25]

Apparently in the haste to get the Corps on the move, someone sent at least the Red-Crosses of the First Division in the wrong direction. "Our first division soon took up the line of march and plodded on for about half an hour when the word came from the rear, 'Halt.' Somebody had blundered and we had taken the wrong road and gone two or three miles out of the way. We cursed the luck that had tacked on four or five extra miles to the thirty-two or thirty-five miles we were expected to travel before we reached the battle field."[26] For a time confusion reigned as the officers, "... perplexed and misled, found the column jammed and floundering in a copse of timber ..."[27] Finally the order was given, "'Countermarch by file left,' and back we went over the fields and finally we filed on to the pike as we supposed, began swinging along toward Gettysburg to help our comrades."[28]

---

[23]Hassler, p. 132; Coddington, p. 326.

[24]Anderson, 1903, p. 12.

[25]Winslow, p. 98; Latta diary, 7/1/1863.

[26]Anderson, 1903, P. 12; Latta diary. John C. Anderson was at that time a private in the 5th Wisconsin, one of the regiments in the same brigade as the 119th.

[27]Latta, *Pennsylvania at Gettysburg*, vol. 2, p. 645.

[28]Anderson, 1903, p. 12.

By early evening General Meade, who had become more confident that his Federals would stand and fight on the high ground at Gettysburg, and who needed the Sixth Corps for that fight rather than to support a retreat, sent a second order to Sedgwick: "The Major General Commanding directs me to say that a general battle seems to be impending tomorrow at Gettysburg; that it is of utmost importance that your command should be up. He directs that you stop all trains that impede your progress, or turn them out of the road. Your march will have to be a forced one to reach the scene of action ..."[29] Rather than hedge his bet, Sedgwick told the aide who delivered the order that General Meade could rely upon the arrival of the Sixth Corps on the field of battle by 4:00 p.m. on the afternoon of the second.[30]

At the time this second order was received, the Sixth Corps' column stretched for about two miles, with the 119th probably somewhere toward the rear. By 11:00 p.m., after having marched about seven miles on the route to Gettysburg through Taneytown, Sedgwick received yet a third order, directing a change of route from the Taneytown Road to the Baltimore Pike.[31] General Meade reasoned that such a change would speed the arrival of the Sixth Corps because the new route, although longer, would involve marching on the much better and faster limestone surface of the Pike.[32] Concurring with this decision, Sedgwick countermarched his men back to the Pike which they had passed earlier in the evening, and by 3:30 a.m. the Philadelphians were finally on the Turnpike headed toward Gettysburg.[33]

The change in route to the Baltimore Pike added another burden, limestone dust, to the additional mileage the troops were forced to march. Wagon and artillery traffic had ground the limestone to a fine powder, and the shuffling of thousands of feet created billows of fine white powder-dust which made throats dry, eyes water, and the men even dirtier and more uncomfortable than before.[34] "That hot, dry, dusty, moonlit night of July 1 presented a scene of weird, almost spectral

[29]O.R.1-27-3-467.
[30]Winslow, p. 99.
[31]Coddington, p. 326.
[32]Coddington, p. 326.
[33]Mundy, p. 148; Latta diary, 7/2/1863.
[34]Mundy, p. 148.

impressiveness. The roads to the south and southeast of the town flowed with unceasing, unbroken rivers of armed men, marching swiftly, stolidly, silently. Their garments were covered with dust, and their gun barrels gleamed with a fierce brilliance in the bright moonlight. The striking silence of the march, the dust-gray figures, the witchery of the moonbeams, made it seem spectral and awesome. No drum beat, no trumpet blared, no harsh command broke the monotonous stillness of the steady surge forward."[35]

Not all the men were silent, however, as one of the Grays identified by Latta as "Henry -----" of Company D, attempted to raise everyone's spirits with some wry humor by repeatedly shouting, "Boys, it's rough, but I tell you it's regular."[36] We may never know whether or not Henry's comments had the desired effect, but soon other sounds began drifting along the lines of the Philadelphians in the pre-dawn darkness, which certainly must have helped ease the burden. "Suddenly from away towards the head of the column was heard the strains of a band, breaking through the stillness of the night. The men caught the cadence of the music and fell into the marching step. The band was playing the 'Old John Brown' Battle Hymn and as they reached the chorus, first a score of voices, joined the words to the music, then a hundred, then a thousand and soon ten thousand voices rolled out the battle song, 'Glory, Glory Hallelujah' ... Whoever was responsible for it, it was certainly a happy inspiration and helped the men wonderfully."[37]

Finally, as the early morning sun began to brighten the eastern sky, the column was given the opportunity to rest, eat, and most importantly, boil and gulp down some coffee. This pause did not last long, and did not indicate that any of the sense of urgency had been lost. When several members of the 93rd Pennsylvania lingered too long around their coffee tins, angry officers kicked over the pots and ordered

---

[35]Mark, *Red, White and Blue*, as cited in Pfanz, *Gettysburg, The Second Day*, p. 80.

[36]Latta, *Pennsylvania at Gettysburg*, vol. 2, p. 646. According to Bates, there were only two Henrys in Company D, Henry Bulmer and Henry Thomas. The former would be listed as missing in action at Spotsylvania one year later, and the latter would be discharged at an unknown date by a general order.

[37]Anderson, 1903, p. 13.

the men into line.[38] A short time later, an ambulance driver found a pistol pressed against his forehead by an officer who became infuriated with the driver's failure to move his ambulance from the road with satisfactory speed. The way was then quickly cleared.[39]

At 9:00 a.m. the men began to hear the faint sounds of artillery fire in the distance, an inhospitable welcome for the many Grays who were just then returning to their home state for the first time in a little less than a year.[40] As the sun continued to rise, yet another burden, heat, was added to straps grinding into shoulders, thirst, dust, blisters, and fatigue. "The early morning was fresh, but not bracing, it indicated a withering noon-day heat to be unappeased by no refreshing breezes. A great red sun gave further promise of a fulfillment of these indications ... The sky was cloudless, the air unruffled by the flutter of a single leaf ... It was hot to equatorial figures."[41] "The sun, warm at the beginning, grew hotter and more piercing every hour and his rays gathered fresh force as they were reflected from the hard road. Toward noon the radiating heat could be observed in waves, like colorless clouds, floating from the earth and mingling with the fine dust created by the moving column."[42]

The combined effects of exhaustion and heat had a devastating effect. "Men reeled and staggered along as if they were drunken. Ever and anon a rifle or musket would fall clattering on the stony pike, as the man who carried it collapsed and sank in a quivering heap in the midst of the roadway. He would be seized and dragged to the roadside, his musket laid beside him, and his comrades would resume their places in the ranks and struggle on."[43]

Perhaps almost as hard on the men as the weather, was the fact that they began to encounter wounded and stragglers from the previous day's engagement. One of the wounded, perhaps having been part of the rout of the Eleventh Corps through the streets of Gettysburg, told all the

---

[38]Lame, *Pennsylvania at Gettysburg*, vol. 1, p. 502.
[39]Mundy, p. 150.
[40]Winslow, p. 100; Latta diary, 7/2/1863.
[41]Latta, *Pennsylvania at Gettysburg*, vol. 2, p. 646.
[42]Brewer, *Pennsylvania at Gettysburg*, vol. 1, p. 340.
[43]Anderson, 1903, p. 13.

marchers that would listen, "You fellows will catch it, the whole army was smashed to pieces."[44]

Fortunately, two later incidents involving local citizens surely helped the men of the 119th overcome the demoralizing effects of such comments and energized the Philadelphians for the last several miles of their ordeal. The men's thirst grew in proportion to the miles they traveled, and all were constantly on the lookout for places to fill empty canteens. As each farm along the route was passed, a group of men could be observed crowded around the well trying to slake their tormenting thirst, fill canteens, and perhaps splash some cool water over hot and dusty foreheads before their regiment passed too far down the road. At one farm, however, a woman and her two daughters were found ladling cool water out to any of the parched soldiers who asked for it. When questioned by one of the Red Crosses as to the reason for their efforts, the woman answered, "'... God bless you, ... I have two boys somewhere among you and I would not want them or their friends to pass their mother's house without at least a cup of cold water.'"[45]

Later, as the Philadelphians came on to the scene of the battle, they encountered a family fleeing with what portable possessions could be quickly packed on a farm wagon. The obvious fear on the face of the master of the household generated a certain amount of scorn among the troops, many of whom had left families of their own behind. Perhaps responding to a sarcastic remark, one of the daughters, probably in her early teens, told one of the officers in the Regiment, "I wish I were a man, I should promptly return and lend my feeble support to the cause of my country ...," which caused an officer of the Regiment to tell his men,"... if time were afforded and she would consent ... [I would] then and there unite with her in holy matrimony."[46] We may safely assume that on hearing the exchange, backs snapped straight under suddenly lighter gear.

The time was between 2:00 and 4:00 p.m. when the Sixth Corps, as promised, began to pass to the rear of the Round Tops and Cemetery Ridge toward their immediate destination, an area around the Rock Creek

---

[44]Tyler, *Recollections of the Civil War...*, as cited in Winslow, p. 101.
[45]Anderson, 1903, p. 13.
[46]Latta, *Pennsylvania at Gettysburg*, vol. 2, p. 647.

where the Fifth Corps had recently been stationed as the reserve force for the army.[47] As the head of the Sixth Corps' column began to shuffle onto the battlefield, General Meade was inspecting his left flank, and what he found made him extremely unhappy.[48] Contrary to orders, Major General Daniel E. Sickles, the Third Corps' politically appointed commander, had moved his men forward from the intended line on Cemetery Ridge, to somewhat higher ground out front into the Peach Orchard and the Devil's Den. It was also discovered about this same time that Little Round Top, the anchor at the end of the left flank of the Union army, was unoccupied by infantry. Meade was about to order Sickles to re-deploy his Corps back to the intended location, when at that very moment, the Confederates launched their assault. Sickles belatedly offered to realign his Corps, drawing an exasperated response from Meade, "I wish to God you could, but the enemy won't let you."[49]

The Sixth Corps' arrival shortly before the commencement of the Confederate attack came at a critical time. Because the newly arrived Greek Crosses were available to serve as the new tactical reserve, Meade was able to order the relatively fresh Fifth Corps forward to extend the Union left beyond the Third Corps' position. The stage was set for one of the most dramatic incidents in American history to unfold on the left of the Union line.

After it was discovered that Little Round Top was defenseless against the approaching Southerners, a desperate search began for troops to fill the void. A Fifth Corps brigade under the command of Colonel Strong Vincent was then in the vicinity, having been dispatched southward upon the arrival of the Sixth Corps. Realizing the desperation of the moment, Colonel Vincent ignored an earlier order, and on his own authority sent his men racing up the hill to their destination with history. Led by the 20th Maine, Vincent's Brigade formed on the hill just ahead of the onrushing Confederates, and despite repeated ferocious assaults, held the key position of the battlefield for the Union.

It is certainly legitimate to ponder whether Vincent's Brigade would have been able to arrive on the hill ahead of the Confederates,

---

[47]Rhodes, p. 115; Mundy, p. 151; Latta diary.

[48]Pfanz, *Gettysburg, the Second Day*, p. 81.

[49]Pennypacker, *Military Historians and History*, as cited in Coddington, P. 346.

who were already massed and beginning their attack when Vincent's men dashed for the hill, if the soldiers of the Sixth Corps had arrived any later on the field. The men who fought and died on the line certainly deserve the lion's share of the credit, but the contribution of the Sixth Corps cannot be overlooked. By accomplishing a forced march of about thirty-seven miles [forty to forty-two for the Grays and the rest of the First Division] in eighteen hours, the Greek Crosses provided General Meade with the confidence that he could make an aggressive disposition of the Fifth Corps and still retain the essential tactical reserve.[50] Minutes were critical to the outcome of the battle, and because Vincent's Brigade had a "running start," precious time was saved. The history of this country might well be entirely different had the men from Alabama been a few minutes ahead of the 20th Maine to the top of Little Round Top, rather than a few minutes behind it.

The sudden roar of battle as Alabama met Maine put a quick end to the Sixth Corps' brief respite at Rock Creek; and those soldiers who were fortunate enough to have gotten to the creek in time to soak their aching feet in the cool water, scrambled for shoes and discarded equipment and rushed back into line.[51] Within minutes the 119th, which was probably near the back of the original column of march and may never have had the opportunity to stop and rest, was again on the move, this time in the direction of the fighting on the left of the line. The Grays' brigade was placed to the east of the Round Tops (the side opposite the fighting), approximately in the gap between the two hills, because General Meade was justifiably concerned that the Confederates might attempt to turn his left flank by going around the hills, if unsuccessful in the attempt to take them.[52]

The Confederate commander responsible for the assault on the far left of the Union line was Major General John Bell Hood, who would become more noted for his aggressiveness than his wisdom. According to his after-battle report: "Before reaching this road [Emmitsburg Road], however, I had sent forward some of my picked Texas scouts to ascertain the position of the enemy's extreme left flank. They soon reported to me

---

[50]Latta, *Pennsylvania at Gettysburg*, vol. 2, p. 654.
[51]Pfanz, *Gettysburg, the Second Day*, p. 81.
[52]Latta, *Pennsylvania at Gettysburg*, vol. 2, p. 647.

that it rested upon Round Top Mountain [meaning Little Round Top]; that the country was open, and that I could march through an open woodland pasture around Round Top, and assault the enemy in flank and rear; that their wagon trains were parked in rear of their lines and were badly exposed to our attack in that direction ... I dispatched a staff officer, bearing to you [Lieutenant General James Longstreet] my request to be allowed to make the proposed movement on account of the above-stated reasons. Your reply was quickly received: 'General Lee's orders are to attack up the Emmitsburg Road.'"[53]

From that time to the present, there has been an ongoing debate, first among participants, and later among historians, whether General Longstreet refused to modify Lee's orders out of a fit of pique generated by Lee's refusal to adopt Longstreet's suggested defensive strategy, or a sense of duty and respect for his commander. In any case, Longstreet would not permit, despite a second request, the Confederate army to swing around rather than attack up the hill, and thus occurred the heroic struggle on Little Round Top. Perhaps, if the order had been amended, the First Division of the Sixth Corps rather than Vincent's Brigade would have borne the brunt of the Rebel attack.

In reality, however, the Grays remained in position behind the Round Tops overnight and during the morning of the third, and were not directly involved in combat during that time. Suddenly, at 1:07 p.m. that afternoon, Ellmaker's men froze, and for a time focused their undivided attention on the roar of a huge cannonade coming from the center of the Union lines, the precursor to "Pickett's Charge."[54] It is not clear whether or not any artillery shells from the Confederate barrage overshot Cemetery Ridge to such a degree as to land amongst the First Division, a question not clarified by Latta's diary: "The terrific artillery firing on our lines kept up for about ___ hours -- under shelling but not engaged.", leaving open the question of exactly who was under shelling. In any case, the implications of the barrage were clear enough, and in confirmation the Regiment was soon shifted toward the center of the line as support for the Second Corps, in case Pickett's men managed a

[53]Hood, as cited in LaFantasie, pp. 81-82.
[54]Stewart, p. 127.

breakthrough.[55] By the time the Grays arrived, however, the Confederates were in retreat, and many of the men of the 119th probably offered a prayer of thanksgiving for again having been spared from combat.

By the morning of July 4, the men of the Fifth Corps were in desperate need of relief from their duty on the Round Tops. Russell's Brigade was redeployed to provide that relief, and the Grays "... changed position and formed line behind a stone wall on top of a high mountain ...[probably Big Round Top]."[56] By coincidence the Grays relieved their sister regiment from Philadelphia, the Corn Exchange Regiment [118th Pennsylvania, Fifth Corps, First Division, First Brigade] from the latter's place on the line.[57] Ellmaker's men spent the balance of Independence Day anxiously listening not to firecrackers but to the sounds of "... Picket firing going on all day ...," but without the knowledge that we have, that the battle of Gettysburg had ended with Pickett's Charge.[58] Each spattering of musket fire from the picket line undoubtedly sent hearts racing, in expectation of a line of Rebels bursting out of the woods.[59]

Monument to 119th at Gettysburg

The respite on Big Round Top would prove to be only short-lived. At around 12:30 p.m. on July 5, General Sedgwick was ordered by his commander to: "... push forward your columns in a westerly direction ... time is of great importance as I cannot give orders for a movement without explicit

[55]O.R.-1-27-1-673.

[56]Latta diary.

[57]Peck, Henry L., *Letter*, 7/7/1863

[58]Latta diary.

[59]Latta diary.

information from you."[60] Probably because of their reputation as fighters, and because they had not been engaged during the previous days' fighting, Russell's Brigade was chosen to lead the pursuit of the retreating Confederates.[61]

As ordered, Russell pushed out his skirmishers and the pursuit began. At first, no Southern opposition was encountered, only the broken and torn victims from the battle. The chaplain of the 15th New Jersey, another Sixth Corps, First Division regiment, graphically described some of the carnage witnessed by the pursuing Federals: "We were passing over the battle-fields of the second and third days, and saw many hundreds of the unburied dead. The bodies were often fearfully torn, and generally bloated and blackened past recognition. Dead horses were swelled to elephantine proportions, and dreadful effluvia tainted the air ... At one place a caisson-wagon had exploded, and around it were the dead horses which had drawn it, and sixteen bodies of the cannoneers. Some of the dead were lying across each other. One man in gray had a bullet in his forehead, and had lain there since the afternoon of the 3rd. He was past consciousness, but that life was not extinct was shown by the convulsive kicking of his legs. A large barn had been burned, and we were told that it had been full of wounded men. We could distinguish the charred remains of several, but could not tell whether these had died in the barn, before the fire, or had perished in the flames. Some bodies, with clothing partially burned, were those of Union soldiers, probably wounded prisoners from the Eleventh Corps."[62]

Graphic descriptions by the participants of the horrors of battle, especially in letters sent home, were the exception rather than the rule, and when they occurred were probably indications of the extreme nature of the situation, or its impact on the writer. Wilbur Fisk, a Greek Cross in the Second Division, detailed such graphic observations of the leavings of the battle in a letter to his home newspaper. "Here the troops halted for a short time, and those that wished to had an opportunity of looking over the field. I saw but a small portion of it, but I saw all I wished to. The rebel dead and ours lay thickly together, their thirst for blood

---

[60]Winslow, p. 108.
[61]Mundy, p. 153.
[62]Haines, p. 96.

forever quenched. Their bodies were swollen, black, and hideously unnatural. Their eyes glared from their sockets, their tongues protruded from their mouths, and in almost every case, clots of blood and mangled flesh showed how they had died, and rendered a sight ghastly beyond description. My God, could it be possible that such were lively and active like other people so shortly previous, with friends, parents, brothers and sisters to lament their loss. It certainly was so, but it was hard to realize it. I turned away from the heartsickening sight, willing to forego gratifying my curiosity rather than dwell upon the horrors of that battle-field. I thought I had become hardened to almost anything, but I cannot say I ever wish to see another sight like that I saw on the battle-field of Gettysburg."[63]

Displaying their usual courage, or their amazing ability to quickly detach themselves from gut-wrenching surroundings, Russell's men soon resumed the pursuit of the enemy. Around 5:00 p.m., after marching five miles over rain-soaked roads, the Rebels' rear guard was spotted through the fog, but Russell delayed launching an attack until his artillery could be rushed to the front. Once the Federal cannoneers had swung their pieces into battery, serious skirmishing commenced, with the Grays dueling in the fog with their counterparts from South Carolina.[64] When the fighting for the day was finished, the Union forces had inflicted eight casualties on the Confederates and taken 250 prisoners, while the Bluecoats suffered only one man killed and two wounded.[65]

Given the opportunity for a brief rest, the 119th and the rest of Russell's Brigade "remained in same line of battle that was first formed yesterday. Near Fairfield [two miles to the east] all night and during the day until 5:00 p.m. when we moved, reached a turnpike leading towards Emmitsburg about 12 midnight. Stragglers from rebel army coming in continuously, swelling the number of prisoners considerably."[66] While the Grays rested, the balance of the Sixth Corps resumed the pursuit around noon on the sixth.[67]

---

[63]Fisk, p. 116.

[64]Latta, *Pennsylvania at Gettysburg*, vol. 2, p. 647.

[65]O.R.-1-27-1-666, Wright.

[66]Latta diary, 7/6/1863.

[67]O.R.-1-27-1-671, Bartlett.

Fatigue was probably not the primary reason for the Sixth Corps' leisurely departure time, because during a personal reconnaissance the preceding night, General Sedgwick had observed a great number of Rebel camp fires dotting the hillside to the west. As a veteran soldier, "Uncle John" was justifiably reluctant to attack, since he could well imagine the bloody reception his boys could expect if they tried to force their way through the Fairfield Pass against what was sure to be determined resistance from presumably well-entrenched troops.[68]

Sedgwick had Meade's full confidence, and as a result was granted leave to pursue the enemy according to his best assessment of the situation. Rather than attempt to force the pass, Brigadier General Thomas H. Neill's Brigade was left at its mouth to harass the Southerners, while the balance of the Sixth Corps was sent south in hopes of reaching the passes through South Mountain at Turner's and Crampton's gaps before Lee could erect fortifications similar to those at Fairfield. Instead of another bloody assault, the Grays and their comrades resumed the same type of forced marches which had characterized the trip north, and the Regiment ended the sixth marching through Emmitsburg in the dark.[69]

It is fair to say that George Meade brought to the command of the Army of the Potomac a different martial philosophy than that possessed by most of his predecessors. Previously, a standard tactic was the "heroic" charge into the face of the enemy, with little consideration given to the prospects for success or the probable cost in death and misery. Those "forlorn hope" assaults often seemed to be motivated more by the desire to display appropriate aggressiveness to members of the Administration and Congress, rather than by any real hope of victory.

With Meade, the philosophy seems to have changed to a genuine desire to accomplish valid military goals without the profligate waste of life. Previous commanders would almost certainly have launched a counterattack against the Confederates on Seminary Ridge at Gettysburg, and thus suffered a Union "Pickett's Charge." Burnside would likely have launched a few assaults against Fairfield Pass, and sent home many

---

[68]Winslow, p. 108.

[69]Latta, *Pennsylvania at Gettysburg*, vol. 2, p. 647.

more names for the casualty rolls, before concluding the task was hopeless. Although Meade's tactics lost for him the respect of his President, his efforts to accomplish victory by maneuver rather than brutal assault certainly spared many men meaningless death or injury. Perhaps, in the long run, the final Union victory was in part the result of Meade's unwillingness to squander the manpower and morale of the army.

July 7 was one of the more unpleasant days in the life of the men of the 119th. The day began on the march, as the troops passed through Emmitsburg at 3:00 a.m.[70] After a few hours' rest, the day's work resumed at 10:00 a.m. with a "vigorous tramp" of about fifteen miles south on the turnpike leading to Frederick, Maryland.[71]

At Franklin Mills, the Regiment turned westward and began to scale the Catoctin Mountain.[72] Crossing over a mountain pass was always an ordeal for the infantry, burdened as they were with thirty or forty pounds of equipment; but this trek forced the men to new depths of misery. One man in the 6th Maine described the road as "... the most horrible road that man was ever suffered to walk on ..." inspiring the men of the Grays' brigade to dub the mountain "Mount Misery."[73] As if the grade was not sufficiently onerous, the crossing was made in a "... terrible rainstorm ..." over a boulder-strewn path that was only wide enough for two men to walk shoulder to shoulder. Ellmaker's men were at times forced to crawl over the rocks, and at other places to drag themselves up, hand over hand, where the mud had become slick as ice from the day's continuous downpour and the passage of hundreds of feet. Lieutenant Latta described the ordeal in what was for him unusually vivid terms: "The ascent deflected only enough from the perpendicular to permit the climb, the path, if path it was, was scarcely wide enough for two, the rocks pointed and jagged, and great boulders stood breast high; the darkness was intense, relieved only by occasional flashes of lightning, and the torrent still continued with unceasing pour. The column lost its identity, men crawled and felt and dragged their way

---

[70]Latta diary.

[71]Latta, *Pennsylvania at Gettysburg*, vol. 2, p. 647; O.R.-1-27-1-666, Wright; Latta diary.

[72]Latta diary.

[73]Leighton, as cited in Mundy, p. 154; Winslow, p. 109.

along, and about midnight, wet and hungry, stopped instinctively, because they were out of the woods and into the clearing."[74] As Private Fisk, a White Cross in the 2nd Vermont described it, the waiting to climb was almost as bad as the climbing. "... [T]he road was continually blocked up by some obstructions ahead, so that we had to halt three minutes where we could travel one. It was vexing beyond all control to stand there and hold our aching knapsacks, with that gigantic, never-ending hill looming up in front of us, and the long, hard journey in prospect. We rarely halted long enough to sit down, but if we did the column would invariably start just as we were fairly seated."[75] It is unfortunate that none of the later historians, who were so critical of the effort to intercept Lee, had the opportunity to offer a face-to-face opinion to those exhausted, mud-soaked soldiers that their pursuit was not nearly aggressive enough.

The men seem to have fared better than the animals, however. The horses and mules pulling the Corps equipment and artillery were so broken down from the previous night's struggle up the mountain that on the next day the Corps was compelled to proceed on without them.[76]

At 5:00 a.m. on the eighth, the wet and exhausted men of the 119th were roused by their sergeants in preparation for another day's march. The men soon discovered that they had stopped near a small stream, whereupon most of them jumped in, clothes and all, and washed off the coating of mud which they had acquired the night before during their crawl up Catoctin Mountain. According to Lieutenant Latta, it was only after this bath that the men were actually able to recognize one another.[77]

The pursuit continued on July 9. "Marched as far as Boonesboro, formed line of battle at the South Mountain for the purpose it is supposed of holding the gap. Remained in this position during the day and night."[78] The next day the Grays, "... left base of the South Mountain near Boonesboro at 6:00 a.m., moved out the turnpike toward Funkstown near which place formed line of battle. Our company rear

---

[74]Latta, *Pennsylvania at Gettysburg*, vol. 2, p. 648; Latta diary.
[75]Fisk, p. 118.
[76]Coddington, p. 556.
[77]Latta, *Pennsylvania at Gettysburg*, vol. 2, p. 648.
[78]Latta diary.

guard. After we arrived on the ground sent out on picket along the banks of the Antietam where we remained during the day. Heavy engagement on our right flank."[79]

Sedgwick's men finally re-established contact with the rear guard of the fleeing Southerners on the outskirts of Boonsboro. The Vermont Brigade was sent forward across the Beaver Creek, where it engaged the enemy in skirmishing heavy enough to cost the Union forces nine killed and fifty-nine wounded, while the Confederates lost thirty men killed and 100 wounded. The rest of the Corps was forced to remain helpless spectators on the far side of the stream, as the Vermonters bore the brunt of the engagement, because General Sedgwick was reluctant to instigate a full-scale battle without the rest of the army in position to join in the fray.[80]

On the eleventh, "[The Grays] remained on picket ... on banks of the Antietam all day. No movement appear as yet taken place, not a single gun heard today in any direction. Probably preparing for a coming storm ..."[81] Before the storm could break over the Confederates, however, it was necessary for the rest of the Union army to come up, for the Federal command to thoroughly scout the newly constructed Confederate defenses, and to select the most advantageous point of attack. Finding an exploitable weak point would be a difficult task because the Rebel defenses were both formidable and well situated, General Lee having erected his line of emplacements along a ridge of high ground, with his right flank anchored on the river at Downsville, and his left about one and one-half miles southwest of Hagerstown, a point also protected by a small river.[82]

At 5:00 a.m. on July 12, the 119th left its camp site two miles outside Funkstown, and with the rest of Russell's Brigade commenced what amounted to a reconnaissance in force until, after having marched about a half mile, the movement escalated into the "Skirmish at Ringold Farm."[83] As soon as Rebel pickets were encountered, Russell deployed his brigade on either side of the road in preparation for an assault. On

---

[79]Latta diary.

[80]Winslow, p. 110.

[81]Latta diary, 7/11/1863.

[82]Coddington, p. 565.

[83]Latta diary; Latta, *Pennsylvania at Gettysburg*, vol. 2, p. 648.

the left, the 6th Maine was deployed with its right on the road, and the 5th Wisconsin was placed in support to the rear. On the right, the 119th drew the front line assignment, with its left connected to the 6th Maine, while the 49th Pennsylvania was directed off to the right for support and to prevent a flank attack.[84]

As a result of Russell's decision not to charge, the engagement devolved into a rather protracted firefight between the skirmishers of both sides, and continued in that mode for some time, until the Union commander lost patience with the harassing fire his men were taking from a farmhouse full of Confederate snipers across from the 6th Maine's position. To terminate the annoyance, Russell dispatched the men of Company D of the 6th Maine, who quickly surrounded the house, and captured a captain, a lieutenant, and thirty-three enlisted men. The Brigade suffered no casualties during the entire engagement.[85]

At approximately 5:00 p.m. the Grays' brigade shifted to the left a distance of approximately one mile, to a position in front of a slight rise which sheltered enemy entrenchments and rifle pits. About sunset, after the re-alignment was completed and the First Brigade had connected with the right of the 119th, the entire command surged forward and carried the emplacements, which proved to be only lightly defended by Rebel pickets rather than the massed muskets which the men surely expected.[86]

Because the Confederate army could not be compressed further without a battle, General Meade summoned his Corps commanders for a council of war, which convened around 8:00 p.m. that night. The generals discussed the situation and various alternatives, and in so doing rejected Sedgwick's proposal that he take his and the Eleventh Corps to the right, in order to launch a flank attack in the Hagerstown area, which would hopefully have denied Lee access to the river crossing. Finally, after much discussion, the question was brought to a vote, with the Corps commanders voting five to two against an attack of any sort the next day. General Sedgwick justified his vote against a direct assault by

[84]O.R.-1-27-1-674, Russell.

[85]O.R.-1-27-1-674, Russell; Mundy, p. 154.

[86]O.R.-1-27-1-674, Russell.

stating: "I am tired of risking my Corps in such unequal contests ...," again valuing blood above reputation.[87]

As a result of the vote the preceding night, the thirteenth of July passed rather uneventfully for Ellmaker's men. There was some light skirmishing all along the line throughout the day, but the event of real significance, the withdrawal of the Confederate army across the river, would not occur until after dark. Despite the lack of fighting, tension certainly gripped the men in anticipation of a bloody battle all believed to be imminent. Elisha Rhodes, perhaps speaking for most of the men, said: "I have not changed my clothes for five weeks, but I am still happy, and we are doing good work ... We are expecting a fight here as Lee's army is not far off. I do not understand our movements but suppose them to be all right."[88]

That evening, orders came down from headquarters that the troops were to initiate a reconnaissance in force on the morning of July 14, and presumably the men drew their sixty rounds of ammunition in preparation for a fight. The next morning at 8:00 a.m., Brigadier General Horatio G. Wright ordered skirmishers from his First Division forward. As the Grays and their comrades formed in line of battle and began to press towards the Rebel fortifications, each man braced himself for the anticipated blast of musketry and canister; but to their great relief, instead of fire and death, the Federals encountered only empty trenches abandoned during the night by the

Brigadier General Horatio G. Wright

(USAMHI - MOLLUS)

[87]Winslow, p. 112.
[88]Rhodes, p. 118.

Confederates. Hoping that he might yet intercept the Rebels in transit, Wright pressed his division down the road and into the town of Williamsport. By 11:30 that morning, however, it became evident that the Confederates had made good their escape and were safely back across the Potomac River.[89]

Two men were disappointed that Meade had not launched a full-scale attack on the Southern defenses prior to the Rebel withdrawal -- Abraham Lincoln and Robert E. Lee. The former was convinced that the Union army had squandered a golden opportunity to crush the rebellion once and for all, and would scornfully compare the Union pursuit to "... an old woman trying to shoo her geese across a creek."[90] Lee was disappointed because he hoped and expected that such an assault would have results comparable to the first battle of Fredericksburg -- thousands of United States soldiers left dead on the field, and another blow to Northern morale.

Hindsight indicates that Lee's expectations of the results of an assault on his defenses at Williamsport were probably closer to what would have occurred than were Lincoln's. Union Colonel Charles Wainright, on inspecting the Confederate works around Williamsport, declared them to be "... by far the strongest I have yet seen ..."[91] Clearly the Grays, among the first troops to approach the Rebel trenches, were spared the horrendous casualties which had become an unavoidable component of assaults upon prepared defensive positions. When the Philadelphians had the opportunity to inspect the abandoned enemy works, they surely were grateful that General Meade had learned the lessons of Fredericksburg.

---

[89]Coddington, p. 570.
[90]Foote, vol 2, p. 799.
[91]Winslow, p. 112.

7

VIRGINIA REEL

The Confederates' flight into Virginia did not signal the end of the campaigning season for the Federal army. The day after discovering the empty trenches of the enemy, Ellmaker's men were back on the road, evoking for Lieutenant Latta memories of the first time that he and his comrades had marched on that particular road on their way to join the Army of the Potomac in the fall of 1862. During the day's march, Latta was able to do some calculating and noted in his diary, "... [distance] marched by this command since the 6th of June is 287 miles."[1] Although covering significant distances, the pace of the pursuit was more leisurely than while the enemy remained in Union territory. It took the army from 6:30 a.m. until 2:00 p.m. to travel the ten miles from Williamsport to Boonsboro on the first day's march, which must have seemed, but for the heat, relatively more like a stroll.[2] The men were even allowed sufficient time to bathe and cool down in a clear stream.[3]

For no apparent reason, it took the Sixth Corps three days, from July 16 until early on July 19, to get into position and to actually cross into Virginia.[4] On July 20, the Grays, with the rest of their Corps, marched about ten miles to New Beaver Dam, where at the end of the day a detail was dispatched from the Regiment to return to Philadelphia to bring back some new recruits.[5]

---

[1]Latta diary, 7/15/1863.

[2]Latta diary.

[3]Winslow. p. 115.

[4]Latta diary.

[5]Latta diary.

Although the 119th had not suffered the high level of casualties inflicted upon many of the regiments of the army at Gettysburg, the heavy losses at Salem Church and the deleterious effects of heavy marching and camp life had nevertheless depleted the ranks of the Regiment to an uncomfortable level. The delegation probably had hopes of obtaining volunteers committed to the Union cause; but the mood of the country had changed since the desperate days of August 1862, and the Grays were only able to obtain a few enlistees, and had to be satisfied with mostly draftees, albeit 205 of them.[6]

The conscripts were to prove a mixed blessing. Although their presence helped fill out the thinned ranks of the Regiment, and most would stand in line for at least one battle, many would prove unreliable. A survey of *Bates*' roster of the Regiment revealed nine enlistees and 157 draftees joined the Regiment in late August and early September.[7] Of the 157 draftees, sixty-three would desert the Regiment before the end of the war; seven were AWOL at mustering out; and one would be dishonorably discharged; for a willful failure to complete service rate of a dismal forty-five percent. The shortest service for a draftee, who was probably a bounty jumper, lasted only twelve days. In fairness, however, at least six of the men who would eventually desert did so only after sustaining combat wounds, and another nineteen would stand in line for at least one battle.

It was not only the draftees who deserted. One of the September enlistees lasted only forty-one days before he skedaddled. As a whole, however, the record of the nine enlistees was much better -- only that one deserted, and then only after having been in a battle, while the rest either became casualties or completed their commitment. As a group, the new recruits who stayed suffered terribly in the year and a half left in the war. Of the eighty-eight who stayed, fifty-two became casualties, for a startling fifty-nine percent attrition rate. One must wonder if such a grossly disproportionate rate was the result of a lack of battle

---

[6]Latta diary, 9/8/1863.

[7]The discrepancy between Latta's and Bates' numbers probably results from the fact that for purposes of this discussion the thirty or forty men drafted in mid-July were not included, because it could not be determined when they actually joined the unit. Although Bates' total may be off somewhat, conclusions may still be drawn from the relative proportions between those who served and those who deserted.

knowledge, because the veterans did not share the benefits of their experience with the rookies, or whether there was a deliberate effort to use the newcomers for more dangerous assignments.

While the few fortunate Grays in the delegation enjoyed the comparative luxuries of Philadelphia, the rest of the Regiment continued its amble southward, apparently allowing Lieutenant Latta sufficient time and energy to make more descriptive and legible entries into his diary during the period.

"July 21 -- Remained the entire day on the ground we occupied last night. The men have been plundering around the country to a great extent, but although this is contrary to a discipline, still the inhabitants seem to ... [keep the] provost guards busy."

"July 22 -- Left camp near Snickers Gap (Beaver's Dam) at 1:30 and marched to a point near Rector's Crossroads where we bivouacked for the night. Passed through Union and over the old camping grounds we occupied last fall. Distance marched about eight miles."

"July 23 -- Left at 4:00 a.m. and marched first to Rectorstown and then to White Plains where we went into camp having marched about 12 miles. The march was a hard one, the heat being oppressive."

"July 24 -- Had tents put up expecting to remain for a day or two, but orders came at sundown to move at once, but as usual we did not start until about 10:00 p.m. when our regiment was detailed as guard to corps trains. The companies being split up along the train -- march fatiguing, arduous and at times tiresome and distance made but a few miles ..."

"July 25 -- At daylight found ourselves about six miles on our journey and reached Warrenton at 12 noon. Halted in grove near the town and waited for the brigade to come up, which arrived about 5:30 and we moved about a mile to the right of town and went into camp. Through the town everything looks desolate but the town bears marks of having been a fine one."[8]

Finally, with the arrival at Warrenton, the men were given an opportunity for a more prolonged rest. But the opportunity for recuperation was, at least at the beginning of their stay, to be more limited. Having apparently outrun their supply trains, the men of the

[8]Latta diary.

Sixth Corps faced a serious food shortage, a problem which became so acute that the soldiers were reduced to scavenging for food like animals. "For two days we have had no food except berries. On halting last night we found high blackberries very plenty and everybody ate their fill. They were good, too, for we were nearly starved."[9]

The 119th set up camp first on the Waterloo Road to the northwest of town, and a few days later at a "... pleasant spot in the wood nearer town."[10] A sense of relative normalcy began to overtake the men; on July 27 mail arrived for the first time in days; and on August 2, after church services were completed, the Regimental sutler, R. Pickens, arrived with his wares.[11]

Adding to the illusion of peace, at least the officers of the Regiment were able to attend church services in a real church. "Attended Episcopal church in Warrenton, heard an excellent sermon, quite a number of soldiers present. Everything flavored with sesesh ..."[12] As much as the young lieutenant may have enjoyed the sermon on the ninth, he seems to have enjoyed the next week's service even more, mostly because of the parishioners. "Attended the Episcopalian church in town, heard quite an excellent sermon, and it seems something like civilization and peace to be seated in a house of worship with sprinkling of ladies throughout the audience."[13] Perhaps the lieutenant was so enthralled by the experience of attending civilian church that the heat did not diminish his enjoyment of the services enough to warrant mention, but the weather was certainly having an effect on the army.

In fact, the prolonged stay in Warrenton was due in part to an oppressive heatwave that was gripping northern Virginia. During the early part of August the temperature climbed so high that it was necessary to cancel the regular drilling, and the men spent their days attempting to find some relief under a shady tree or near a quiet stream. It was so hot that privates making only $13 a month were willing to pay their sutlers fifty cents for a cool glass of soda water.[14]

---

[9]Rhodes, p. 120.
[10]Latta diary, 7/26/1863, 8/1/1863.
[11]Latta diary.
[12]Latta diary, 8/9/1863.
[13]Latta diary, 8/16/1863.
[14]Winslow, pp. 116, 118.

Lieutenant Latta made several notations concerning the extreme heat; on August 1 he observed: "... Most terribly hot and mentally feel exhausted in moving the short distance of a mile ..."; the next day similar conditions prevailed: "The heat today has been oppressive in the extreme and at night ... [seems] to be no change ... Marching troops [in such] weather as this would be likely to kill them up rapidly."[15] Although it rained on the evening of August 4, the heat wave was apparently not broken, because on August 11, Latta's diary contained another reference to the heat and that men had possibly died from it: "... Weather still continues warm. Two men of A company have died within a few days of each other."[16]

The Greek Crosses had more than just heat to contend with. "Flies, too, are becoming miraculously abundant, and as annoying as they are abundant. We have the most prolific species of this insect here that I ever saw. I believe they increase fourfold every day, and have done so in regular geometrical progression ever since dog days commenced. They swarm everywhere and torment a fellow from daylight till dark. They hover in his face, fly into his mouth and nose, and with their little tickling feet irritate the flesh wherever the saucy imps can find it. There seems to be a peculiar species of the fly kind that infests our camp. They bite almost as quick as a bee can sting, and their bite is almost as painful ... It would be untrue to say that we are idle; we cannot be in such a nest of flies."[17]

Meanwhile, General Lee, unlike his Union counterpart, was deterred by neither the heat, the flies, nor the high casualties of the Gettysburg campaign, and seeing no necessity to regroup, retained his aggressive instincts. At about the same time that the delegation from the 119th was back in Philadelphia collecting conscripts from the recent draft, Lee announced his intentions: "If General Meade does not move, I wish to attack him," and began planning for a third invasion of the North, or at least for a serious drive into northern Virginia.[18] Lee's plans for another offensive were complicated, however, by the

[15]Latta diary.
[16]Latta diary, 8/11/1863.
[17]Fisk, pp. 132-133.
[18]Foote, vol. 2, p. 786.

politicking of his restive subordinate Lt. General James Longstreet, who occupied himself at this time trying to cajole permission from Richmond to take his corps west to assist in an offensive against Major General William Rosecrans. Permission for the redeployment was finally granted, and on September 9, 1863, Longstreet and his men began the journey west.[19]

Before word of Longstreet's departure propelled the Union army into action, most of the Grays continued to while away the time with routine chores in their pleasant camp near Warrenton. During an idle moment, George C. Booze, the super-patriotic but artistically inclined nurse in the 119th's camp hospital, found time to sketch a Virginia home, and to compose a poem, which he sent to his sister on September 14:

Land of the North imperial land
How proud thy mountains rise
How sweet thy scenes on every hand
How fair thy covering skies
But not for this, oh not for thee
I love thy fields to roam
Thou hast a dearer spell to me
Thou art my Native home.

Thy rivers roll thy liquid wealth
Unequaled to the sea
Thy hills and valleys bloom with health
And green with verdure be
But not for thy proud ocean streams
Not for thy azure dome
Land of the North I cling to thee
Thou art my native home.

[19]Cozzens, pp. 48-49, 60.

Ana, Heaven's best gifts to man is thine
God bless thy rosy girls
Like sylvan flowers they sweetly shine
There [*sic*] hearts are pure as pearls
Ana grace and goodness circle them
Wherever their footsteps roam
How can I then while loving them
Not love my native home?

May rank secession banner ne'er
Wave over thy fertile loam
But should it come then one will die
To save his native home.[20]

Rebel Mansion House near Middletown, Va. - By George C. Booze

(USAMHI)

[20]Booze, USAMHI.

Any plans that General Lee was then harboring to take the "secession banner" northward were put on the shelf, both because of Longstreet's departure and the news received four days later that the Army of the Potomac was coming south. On September 15 at 4:00 p.m. the Grays struck their comfortable camp at Warrenton, and joined the rest of the Sixth Corps in a march toward Culpeper Court House.[21] Reminiscent of the marching done on the way to Gettysburg, the Philadelphians slogged twenty-two miles on the sixteenth, a "... fatiguing and tedious ..." journey that took them over the Rappahannock River and the Hazel Run, and continued until the unit was finally permitted to bivouac a few miles from Culpeper Court House.[22]

The Union "offensive," if it can be dignified by such a term, came to an abrupt halt at that point because the administration, anxious about the Confederate deployment of troops westward, responded in kind and sent two of Meade's Corps in the same direction. With the forces of both sides returned to the same relative balance, General Meade lapsed back into complacency, and the men of the 119th, along with their Sixth Corps comrades, began to set up what they thought would be their winter quarters. In anticipation of a lengthy stay the encampment, which was about four miles from Culpeper Court House, was even given a name, "Camp Sedgwick."[23]

Some of the Sixth Corps troops, probably including some from the Grays' First Division, were pushed out as pickets closer to their adversaries, assuming a defensive position between Cedar Mountain and the Robertson River. Those men probably appreciated the passive attitude of their commander because the Rebel positions observed across the river were judged to be as imposing as those at Fredericksburg.[24]

General Meade may have been content to remain passive, but typically, the Confederate commander was not. Sometime in the two weeks after the Army of the Potomac established its camp, Lee's spies learned that the Federal opposition had become two corps lighter; and,

---

[21]Winslow, p. 118; Latta diary, 9/15/1863.
[22]Latta diary.
[23]Rhodes, p. 125.
[24]Winslow, p. 118.

in response, the always aggressive Rebel leader reactivated his plan for a drive northward.

During the first week of October, elements of the Sixth Corps were shifted around, but whether this was in anticipation of a Southern attack is unclear. Lieutenant Rhodes reported that on October 2, his regiment marched northward to Bealeton in a rainstorm.[25] Two days later, General Sedgwick received orders from Headquarters to shift his men to the Robertson Ford on the Rapidan, to provide relief for the Second Corps.[26] If this order was promptly carried out, the Sixth Corps must have been fairly spread out, because Rhodes placed his regiment the next day at Bristoe Station, a considerable distance to the north of Robertson Ford. The disposition of the 119th in that realignment cannot now be determined.

A Union observation team on October 7 intercepted a message to the effect that the Rebels were on the move again, perhaps producing in the minds of the Federal leaders a sense of deja-vu and a flashback to the perilous days of early June. In response to this bit of intelligence, and the vague reports of activity being received from Sixth Corps pickets, General Meade traveled down to Cedar Run Mountain for a personal look. Based upon what the general observed with his own eyes, and with even more information supplied directly to him by Sixth Corps pickets on the scene, Meade concluded that he was again faced with another Confederate drive against the right flank of the Union army.[27] Determined to avoid a repeat of the June struggle to catch up with the Confederates, who were at that very moment advancing up the south bank of the Rapidan, Meade chose the Sixth Corps as the lead element in a maneuver which he hoped would cut the Rebels off before they could get between the Union army and the capital or Pennsylvania.

For most of the men of the Sixth Corps, the sudden assignment to lead the rush after Lee was at best an inconvenience, but for two Grays the rapid deployment may have been a life saver. On October 6, hard orders were read announcing that two soldiers of the 119th were to

---

[25]Rhodes, p. 125.
[26]O.R.-1-29-2-251.
[27]Winslow, p. 119.

be shot for desertion.[28] No reference has been discovered which indicates that either of the death sentences were actually carried out on the condemned men, but an entry in the history of the 49th Pennsylvania and in the Latta diary for October 28 indicated that two Grays, also unnamed, had their heads shaved and were drummed up and down in front of the Third Brigade.[29] Perhaps by making a good showing during the maneuvers which occurred between the date of sentence and the head shavings, the two condemned men redeemed themselves and earned the right to live.

Those maneuvers commenced on October 10, the day after Lee's men crossed the Rapidan. General Sedgwick quickly received several orders which graphically depict Meade's desire that the Union forces be moved north as rapidly as possible. At 4:30 p.m., an order directed that the Sixth Corps take a position on the south side of Culpeper and to be ready to move north again at 3:00 a.m. the next morning. Three hours later a second order arrived, directing that the disposition of the Corps should be to the north side of Culpeper, where the Corps finally arrived after dark.[30]

It isn't clear whether the men got off at 3:00 a.m. as earlier directed, but at some point during the morning of the eleventh the Greek Crosses resumed the push northward toward the Yew Hills on the south side of the Rappahannock, where they were supposed to connect with pickets of the Fifth Corps.[31] Possibly the entire Sixth Corps, or perhaps just the First Division, received yet another order, because instead of stopping on the south side of the river, the Grays continued across at Rappahannock Station at sunset. By the time the men were permitted to bivouac for the night, the march was twenty-three hours old.[32] When the troops finally dragged themselves off the road, they

---

[28]Westbrook, p. 164; Latta diary. Lt. Latta, who may have participated in the courts martial, referred to a "Fox" and what appears to be a "Murphy" as the two condemned men. Two men, William Fox and John Murphy, both from E Company., appear to have been those sentenced "To be shot to death by musketry..." *General Order No. 93*, 10/24/1863.

[29]Westbrook, p. 167; Latta diary.

[30]O.R.-1-29-2- 285, 286.

[31]O.R.-1-29-2-291.

[32]Latta diary, 10/11/1863.

received an unexpected welcome: "The enemy does not molest us. Only pretty girls with pies for sale invade our camp."[33] As the men cooked rations and enjoyed fresh pie, rumors circulated around the campfires that night that the trailing elements of the Sixth Corps had been involved in a skirmish on the Rapidan.[34]

The orders issued on the twelfth became even more urgent. Sedgwick had suggested to Meade the night before that perhaps what seemed to be a Confederate invasion in the making, was in reality only a sham, which if undetected would reduce Meade's standing with the administration even further. To eliminate such a humiliating possibility, Meade ordered "Uncle John" to lead a reconnaissance in force back toward Culpeper to determine if significant Rebel forces remained to the south.[35] At 7:45 a.m. the infantry was warned to be prepared to move immediately, with only ambulances and ammunition wagons, an order which probably produced groans among the ranks, since it was the same sort of order received before the forced march to Gettysburg on the night of July 1. The actual order to move came at 10:30 a.m., and by 1:00 p.m. the soldiers of the Sixth Corps were trudging back across the river toward Brandy Station, with their counterparts of the Fifth Corps and General John Buford's cavalry.[36] Upon arrival at the site of the cavalry battle in June, the entire force deployed into line of battle, a spectacle described by Isaac Best of the 121st New York, which was posted a short distance from the Grays: "The country was open, and nearly level, the morning was fine and the sun shone brightly. The line of battle, extending about three miles, advanced slowly and steadily, the flags floating in the gentle breeze, the sunlight flashing from their arms, and the batteries in regular formation following close behind the infantry. In front of the advancing line a force of cavalry were in almost constant conflict charging and repelling the charges of a like force of Rebel cavalry, but constantly advancing until Brandy Station was reached."[37] Except for the skirmishing by the troopers, nothing else happened.[38]

---

[33]Rhodes, p. 127.
[34]Rhodes, p. 127.
[35]Henderson, p. 123.
[36]O.R.-1-29-2-295, 296.
[37]Best, p. 97.
[38]Latta diary, 10/12/1863.

Around midnight yet another order was received, directing the abandonment of the hills of Brandy Station and a return to Rappahannock Station.[39] One need not be terribly creative to imagine the sorts of opinions expressed by the Grays about the competence and ancestry of their leadership, as the Regiment recrossed the bridge at Rappahannock Station at 4:00 a.m. in the morning.[40]

The dog-tired infantrymen were permitted to rest until sunrise; but by the time the sun was fully visible, the Grays were traveling northward along the line of the Orange and Alexandria Railroad on a tramp that would prove to be a rival of the one to Gettysburg.[41] First, the Philadelphians and their comrades passed through Bealeton, then Warrenton, and finally, twenty-four hours and twenty-eight grueling miles later, the weary foot soldiers arrived at Centerville. "After marching all night we reached Catlett's Station, having made only five miles by reason of roads being blocked with wagons. The night was bitter cold, and the men suffered severely. After sleeping two hours we moved on and crossed the Manassas Plain Battlefield and the Bull Run and arrived at Centerville more dead than alive."[42]

Although this march lacked the heat and the drama, and ultimately the recognition, of the march to Gettysburg, it accomplished a feat almost unique in the Civil War, the outmaneuvering of Robert E. Lee. When Lee learned that the Federals had won the race and had taken possession of the heights around Centerville, he knew that he could neither attack that position with any realistic hope of success, nor gain the Union right flank. Ever the aggressor, however, Lee took what appeared to be the next best alternative, a strike at the tail of the Union column.

General A. P. Hill was immediately directed to attack the Union Second Corps, then located in the area of Bristoe Station. Unfortunately for the Confederate soldiers, their fiery general sent them, without proper reconnaissance, toward a large contingent of Union troops hidden behind a railroad embankment. When the Southerners were almost

---

[39]O.R.-1-29-2-298.

[40]Latta diary.

[41]Latta diary.

[42]Rhodes, p. 126.

within throwing distance, the Union forces rose and ripped the butternut ranks with a withering fire.[43] The battle was over almost as soon as it had commenced, with Southern losses totaling about 1,900, as compared to 300 Northerners.[44] Meade had again thwarted his opponent, who would soon begin another retreat south.

For the next several days, however, the Confederate commander concealed his intentions, neither attacking nor retreating. "[On October 16] Remained in the same position that was taken up yesterday. The enemy appeared to have left our front or at least do not threaten it. Rained severely at times during the day and night which may have prevented an attack."[45] The next day, "Quite an alarm created about 4:30 p.m. by an advance of a considerable force of dismounted rebel cavalry with two pieces of artillery on the extreme right of our pickets. Skirmishing lasted about one hour."[46] It was not until 7:00 a.m. on the nineteenth, after it was clear that the Southerners were gone, that the Grays finally broke camp. During the day, Ellmaker's men marched through the portion of the Second Manassas battlefield where the "... artillery fire had raged the heaviest ...," and finally, as the sun was setting, bivouacked at Gainesville to the sounds of a cavalry spat in the direction of New Baltimore.[47]

Lee's excursion north was not totally without benefit. As the Confederate army retreated toward its safe haven behind the Rappahannock, it thoroughly destroyed the Orange and Alexandria Railroad, which had previously been the Union army's main supply line. Whether justified or not, Meade would rely upon that disruption of his supply line to resist initiating any further aggressive actions against Lee, at least until the line was rebuilt and operating.

---

[43]Henderson, pp. 179-183.
[44]Foote, vol. 2, p. 793.
[45]Latta diary.
[46]Latta diary, 10/17/1863.
[47]Latta diary.

8

RAPPAHANNOCK STATION

Immediately after the Federal victory at Bristoe Station, the administration began an increasingly more strident campaign intended to pressure Meade into taking the offensive. On October 18, in response to one particularly demeaning telegram from Major General Henry W. Halleck, Meade offered his resignation, which was not accepted primarily due to the feeling that there was no one better qualified to assume the role.[1]

The war of words did not end, however, when the administration blinked over Meade's offer of resignation. The President held a strong desire for aggressive action, but he was justifiably reluctant to give specific tactical instructions, while Halleck was too much the bureaucrat to commit himself to specifics; so both continued to bombard Meade with vague suggestions, encouragements, and platitudes. General Meade would not be prodded, and responded that he would follow direct orders, but as long as he received only suggestions, he would do as he thought best, which at that point was to rebuild the Orange & Alexandria Railroad, and to continue to wait for a target of opportunity. The telegraph lines buzzed with messages from Washington suggesting possible courses of action, but Meade ignored them all and continued a slow and deliberate move south, in concert with the railroad repair crews.

For the 119th, this meant a return to Warrenton, which the men again came to hope and believe would be their winter base until campaigning season arrived the following spring. "Changed camp to a point one-half mile north of Warrenton on New Baltimore road, pitched

[1]Foote, vol. 2, p. 798.

tents regularly and organized everything as if a permanent stay for a few days were anticipated."[2] To put a halt to the suffering of the men as they shivered in their tents each night from the bitter cold that had by then descended upon Northern Virginia, permission was granted to construct winter wooden huts with fireplaces, a concession which only bolstered the belief that the Sixth Corps was finished fighting for the year and would spend the winter in Warrenton.[3]

While the men prepared for the coming winter, events transpired that would dash any hopes for a long and cozy winter encampment. The Confederates did not withdraw their entire army across the Rappahannock in the normal defensive maneuver. Rather, General Lee left a contingent on the north bank of the river at Rappahannock Station -- the point about twenty miles west of Fredericksburg, where the Orange & Alexandria Railroad bridge crossed over the river. His purpose was to create a tactical dilemma for the Federals. With a bridgehead on the Union side of the river, the Southerners were in a position to rapidly deploy forces to attack the flank or rear of any Union offensive, or perhaps to launch a rapid assault of their own. Knowing that Meade would perceive this threat and feel either intimidated by it, or compelled to deal with it, the former Union emplacements at the station were reversed and strengthened to a point that satisfied the Southern commander that the position was virtually impregnable.

Lee's confidence was justified. The fortifications were located at a bend in the river to the west of the railroad bridge with the primary emplacements, consisting of trenches and lunettes, facing almost due north with supporting rifle pits to the east and west. One veteran observed that: "Rappahannock Station is a vile place to approach for attack -- a plain long and wide with a small hill only for a mile or more till you come to the river bank, which is quite high, naturally a strong position made more so by two redoubts ... with rifle pits extending a great distance above & below. These works have been constructed with great care & great labor."[4]

---

[2]Latta diary, 10/22/1863.

[3]Winslow, p. 121.

[4]Whittier, Maj. Charles A., *Holmes Paper*, as cited in Winslow, p. 122.

Not only was the fort well-prepared, it was also well-manned. The "Louisiana Tigers" of Major General Jubal Early's Division, one of the more reliable units in the Army of Northern Virginia, were deployed to man those strong defenses. Later, three North Carolina regiments were sent to augment the defenses of the fortress, and received the assignment of protecting the left flank of the entrenchments, a position that placed them facing west, at a right angle to the works. In all, the Confederate position was manned by eight hard-handed, veteran regiments.[5]

For a time it seemed that Lee had wasted the preparations at Rappahannock Station, because his Northern counterpart had no intentions of launching another offensive that year. In an October 21 message, General Meade expressed an opinion which his superiors in Washington did not wish to hear: "It seems to me therefore, [because of the time necessary to repair the railroad] that the campaign is virtually over for the present season ..."[6] The general was immediately summoned to the capitol, where on October 23 he and the President had a long conversation about what was expected from the army before the year was over -- and the expectation was not for a long winter's rest.[7]

As if to facilitate the administration's desire for more action that year, the cold spell broke at the end of the month, and with the change in weather came perfect conditions for campaigning. Sedgwick received orders on November 6 from the newly motivated Meade that the army was being divided into two wings, and that the next morning Sedgwick was to take one wing, consisting of the Fifth and Sixth Corps, and capture Rappahannock Station. The balance of the plan envisioned that Major General William French would take the remainder of the army and cross the Rappahannock at Kelly Ford, trapping the Rebels in a vise as both wings drove to Brandy Station.

The double wing concept required a shuffling of the chain of command for the attack. Horatio Wright, the Sixth Corps' First Division commander, was bumped up to Sixth Corps commander; Russell advanced from the Third Brigade to Wright's vacated position; Colonel

---

[5]Mundy, pp. 161, 165.
[6]O.R.-1-29-2-361.
[7]Foote, vol. 2, p. 797.

Ellmaker became the new leader of the Grays' Third Brigade; and Lt. Colonel Gideon Clark replaced Ellmaker as head of the 119th. Obviously, there was great confidence in the officers of the First Division.

As usual, Sedgwick justified the confidence placed in him, and had his boys up and on the Fayetteville Road marching toward their objective at sunrise on November 7. As a further testament to their reputation, the Grays and their brigade mates led the line of march toward the battle.[8] By 10:00 a.m. the Philadelphians had passed through Fayetteville, and at 12:30, having arrived in the vicinity of the objective, the men were given a well-earned two hours' rest in some woods.[9]

Almost immediately upon arrival the 49th Pennsylvania was dispatched for skirmish duty, and soon thereafter Lt. Colonel Clark rode out to the line to investigate the desultory exchange of musket fire that broke out as soon as the skirmish line got into position. On Clark's return, Grays' Captain Edwin A. Landell of Company I observed: "When Colonel Clark came riding up after he had been out toward the front having the appearance of an officer very much under the influence of liquor. He addressed some few words to the group [of four officers] ... he swayed to and fro on his horse ... and with apparent difficulty dismounted and lay down and went to sleep."[10]

At about 2:30 p.m., after the Grays and their commander had the opportunity for a nap, the Third Brigade was deployed for action. The 49th Pennsylvania was replaced on the skirmish line by the 6th Maine, with the rest of the Third Brigade arrayed behind them in line of battle -- the 49th Pennsylvania on the left along the railroad, the 5th Wisconsin in the middle, and the 119th on the right.

The order was given and the formation began a deliberate advance which continued until, after crossing a stream, the skirmish line paused about 400 yards from the enemy emplacements and waited in the shelter of a sunken road or swale.[11] About the same time that the 6th Maine was moving into the swale, Union men from Howe's Division

---

[8]O.R.-1-29-1-601, Clark.

[9]O.R.-1-29-1-587, Russell; p. 595, Ellmaker.

[10]National Archives, General Court-martial transcript for Lt. Colonel Gideon Clark.

[11]Mundy, p. 163.

occupied a low hill off to the right of the Third Brigade, which quickly became the site for four twenty-pounder Parrott cannons from a Fifth Corps battery. Those big guns, sighting in from only about a half mile from the Confederate trenches, immediately unleashed a precision bombardment, which compelled prudent Tigers wishing to keep their heads, to remain below the crest of their walls.[12]

The next several hours, until the sun had just about touched the horizon, were employed in softening the enemy position with artillery fire. Toward evening, as the shadows lengthened, the balance of the 6th Maine was ordered forward to join the skirmish line, resulting in a double-strength, one-quarter mile long line with men at approximately six-foot intervals.[13] The historian for the 49th Pennsylvania claimed that this maneuver was a ruse intended to fool the Southerners about the strength of the forces in their immediate front: "He [Russell] brought forward one regiment apparently to relieve the skirmishers who had been in front all day, and another to act as support. The enemy saw the whole operation, but supposing it simply a relief, paid little attention to the matter."[14]

Whether intentional or not, the Southerners do seem to have been deceived about the Bluecoats' intentions. Comfortable in the strength of their position and the belief that even the Yankees would not be foolish enough to attack such a position in the twilight with only one brigade, the defenders continued to hug the ground, more concerned about the shells from the 20-pounders than the skirmish line in their front. The "Tigers" would soon learn a hard lesson about the Third Brigade.

Suddenly the Maine men, under orders to rely solely upon steel, surged forward at full speed, rather than at the more typical slower pace which usually gave the enemy steady targets and plenty of time to hit them. Overcoming a six-foot-deep and fourteen- to sixteen-foot-wide ditch, which was filled with three feet of water and mud, a flat plain covered with tree stumps, and finally a dry moat, the 6th Maine covered the quarter mile to the enemy works in what must have been only a

---

[12] O.R.-1-29-1-588, Russell.
[13] O.R.-1-29-1- 575, Ellmaker.
[14] Westbrook, p. 168.

Rappahannock Station - November 7, 1863

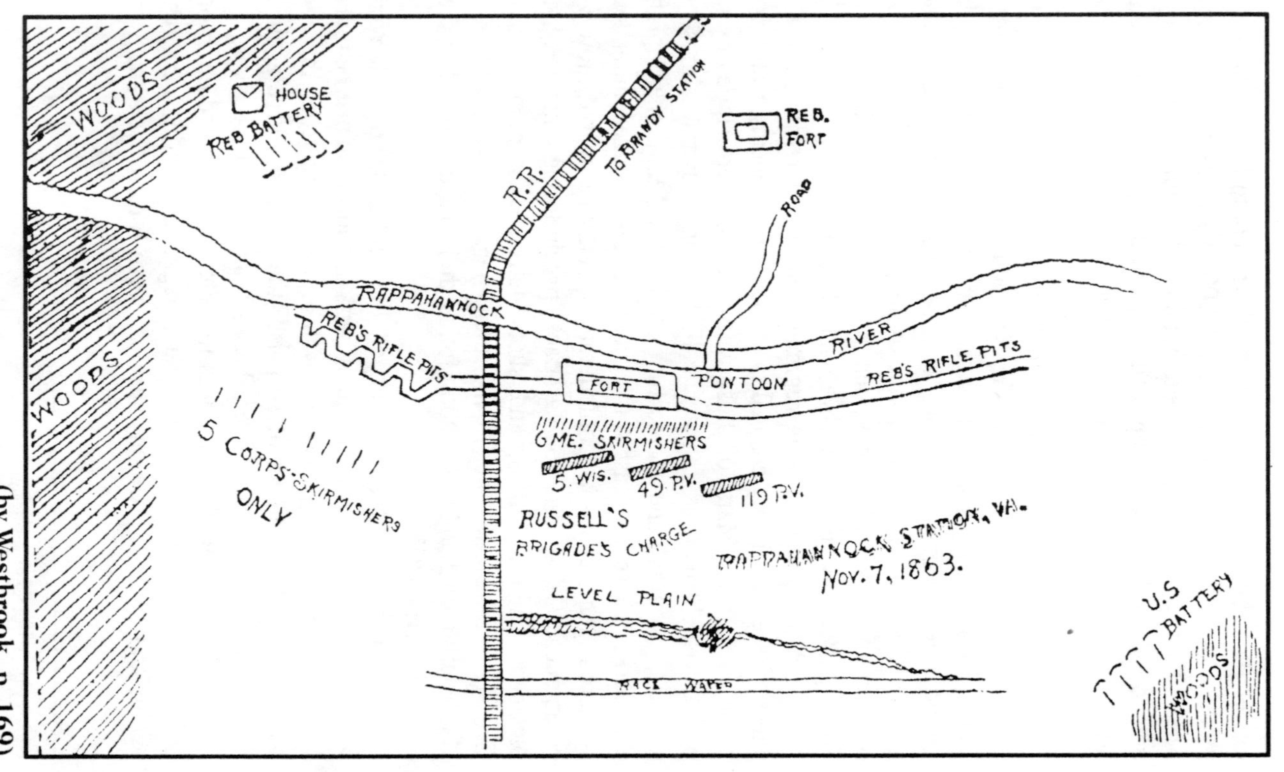

(by Westbrook, p. 169)

matter of a few minutes.[15] The attackers should have been annihilated by the Confederate artillery and the 1,200 to 1,500 Tigers massed in the fort. That they were not is attributable to a number of factors: the defenders' delay in taking up a firing position until it became clear that an attack was under way; the short time of exposure to Rebel fire; the terrain over which the men passed, which took them below the line of fire on several occasions; and in a curious turn-about, Confederate psychological paralysis from a Yankee yell. Usually it was the "Rebel Yell," so dreaded by the Bluecoats, that was blamed for a break in the Union line. Here, however, at least one Rebel credited the noise generated by the men from Maine as a significant factor in the outcome of the battle: "We all allowed that the whole Army of the Potomac were coming, you'uns kept up such a wicked yelling."[16]

Although the Maine regiment avoided extermination from the sheet of fire that finally erupted from behind the enemy walls, it did not avoid casualties. Many of those who were hit were ripped by multiple bullets or clusters of canister balls, leaving several almost shot to pieces.[17] Courage and momentum carried the Maine men up and over the works where, at least for a moment, the shocked defenders were scattered. The tenacious Confederates quickly recovered, however, and commenced a desperate counterattack, precipitating a melee of stabbing bayonets, clubbing rifles, and shots delivered at point blank range. Grossly outmanned, the Maine men began to give ground to the Confederate onslaught, and soon found their backs pressed to the inside of the fortress walls.

At the last possible moment, the soldiers of the 5th Wisconsin, who had been positioned in line of battle a short distance behind the 6th Maine, began pouring over the wall. Benefitting from the additional numbers and the element of surprise, the Federals were again able to drive their foe back away from the wall and toward the river.

The Union advantage was to have only a limited duration. Still holding a significant numerical advantage, the Southerners regrouped again, and again the Union intruders were forced back and were soon

---

[15]O.R.-1-29-1-588, Russell.

[16]As cited in Mundy, p. 168.

[17]Mundy, p. 166.

Battle of Rappahannock Station - *Harper's Weekly*

faced with either death or capture.[18] General Russell, who was directing the action from the field, recognized that the critical moment in the battle had arrived. He raced back to the 119th and 49th Pennsylvania who were waiting in line of battle and ordered them forward. "General Russell gave us orders to charge, and in less than two minutes he gave us orders to not double quick, but to run -- that they were driving the Sixth Maine. We see them and obey his orders."[19] Underscoring how the perception of time is affected by the circumstances, a hard-pressed Badger had an understandably different recollection of the speed with which the Pennsylvanians responded to the crisis; "... There seemed to be an almost interminable delay in their [the Pennsylvanians] coming up, and staff officers were sent in quick succession to hurry up the movements ..." In any case, Anderson acknowledged that "At last they came and with a cheer the 49th and the greater part of the 119th, went up to the assistance of their comrades."[20]

It is difficult to determine what, if anything, happened to the rest of the 119th that Anderson implies did not come up. Perhaps the reason for the seeming disappearance of a portion of the Regiment can be gleaned from Private Westbrook's description of the charge: "In the charge, the 119th Pa. Vol. being on the right and anxious to get to the fort as quick as possible, came in on the left, oblique, lapping over about two companies of the 49th ..."[21] In the confusion Anderson may have mistaken the missing Grays for part of the 49th Pennsylvania.

In any case, it was now the Pennsylvanians' turn, with the 119th on the right and the 49th to their left, to scale the works and leap into the caldron. For the third time, the shock of reinforcements threw the Tigers into retreat. This time, however, a new element was added to the equation. As the men of the 119th drove the Rebels toward the river, they passed behind the three North Carolina regiments who had been stationed on the left of the enemy works. Why the Carolinians held their fire previously is unknown, but they chose this moment to deliver a "disastrous flank fire" into the exposed right wing of the 119th.[22]

---

[18]Mundy, pp. 172-173.
[19]Westbrook, p. 168.
[20]Anderson, 1901, p. 34.
[21]Westbrook, p. 168.
[22]O.R.-1-29-1-601, Clark.

As Anderson described it, "A part of the force on their [the Confederate] left, which had not been engaged, was brought up to assist the disordered ranks of the Louisianians and a hot enfilading musketry fire had already been opened on the over-taxed forces in and around the large redoubt. This fire passing through the thin and shattered ranks of the 5th Wisconsin and the 6th Maine, smote full on the right wing of the 119th Pennsylvania ..."[23] The Grays were momentarily thrown into confusion, and according to Anderson, "Many cast themselves into the dry ditch at the foot of the slope and added to the horror and confusion of the moment by returning the fire of the rebels regardless of the fact that a line of their own comrades was between the two fires. They were in a moment, however, gallantly rallied by their major and led up in line with the rest."[24]

Clearly, however, the 119th, and the battle, were again in jeopardy. In order to relieve the pressure, General Russell next ordered three of the regiments under the command of Colonel Emory Upton to attack the North Carolinians from the front. As Upton's Federals approached from the west, the 119th managed to change fronts and began exchanging nearly face-to-face volleys with the North Carolinians.[25] Almost immediately thereafter, Upton's men struck the Confederates who, being assailed by fire from the flank and rear, and facing oncharging troops in front, broke and surrendered "en masse."[26]

When the North Carolinians crumbled, serious resistance from the Tigers ceased and a rout to the rear commenced, drawing the men from Wisconsin into what could have been considered an atrocity, and what was certainly a tragedy. "A number of them [Confederates], however, were cut off and attempted to escape by passing out of their works at the extreme [Union] left and wading the river near the abutments of the railroad bridge. Here a terrible affair happened. The

---

[23]Anderson, 1901, p. 34.

[24]Anderson, 1901, p. 34. Anderson's statements about the 119th's performance at that point may have been overly critical due to his own bias, having earlier referred to troops from the east as "... renegades and outcasts of society..." when he expressed his displeasure at being brigaded with the 119th and 49th Pennsylvania. Anderson, as cited in Russell, p. 134.

[25]O.R.-1-29-1-601, Clark.

[26]O.R.-1-29-1-589, Russell.

water was up nearly to their armpits and as they were in the stream the Union soldiers, mad with the rage of battle, pushed down to the water's edge and poured a pitiless fire upon them. Many sunk wounded in the water, with a bubbling shriek, losing thus whatever chance of life was left after the bullet had done its work. The horrors of the situation struck even the battle maddened soldiers and suspending their fire they shouted to the confederates to come back and surrender. The greater part of those in the river started back to surrender but when they came near the shore an officer [probably Colonel Goodwin, commander of the Louisiana brigade] stepped from behind a stone abutment and ordered them to return again, enforcing his order by flourishing his sword. The men again wheeled around in the water and began splashing their way to the opposite shore and again the pitiless hail of bullets was showered upon them. At last they gave up the attempt and sheltered themselves behind the ruined abutments of the bridge where they cried for 'quarters' and about seventy-five surrendered."[27]

For all intents and purposes, the battle of Rappahannock Station was over, and the soldiers of the Third Brigade had achieved one of the most stunning victories attained by the Army of the Potomac during the course of the war. Northerners hailed the triumph as the most decisive victory of the war, while a Confederate referred to the defeat as: "... the saddest chapter in the history of this army."[28]

The numbers confirm the lopsided nature of the Union triumph. The Confederates suffered a total of 1,674 casualties, most of them captured, while the attackers, who usually suffered two or three times as many casualties as defenders, suffered only 419. For the Third Brigade, which suffered the majority of the Union losses, there were fifty-eight officers and men killed and 205 officers and men wounded, for a total of 263 casualties. Of those, the 119th lost two officers and sixteen enlisted men either killed, dead from wounds received, or missing in action; sixteen noncommissioned and enlisted men wounded, and four men captured.[29]

---

[27]Anderson, 1901, p. 34. After Anderson related this event, he went on to describe the two Pennsylvania regiments joining the fray, implying that the tragedy at the river occurred during the battle rather than at the end, a circumstance which seems rather unlikely.

[28]Winslow, p. 124.

[29]O.R.-1-29-1-590, 602, Russell & Clark; Bates, *History...*, vol. 4, 119th.

Of the two Grays' officers killed, Company B commander Captain Cephas M. Hodgson died on the field. The other, twenty-four-year-old 2nd Lieutenant Edward E. Coxe, was evacuated to Harewood Hospital in Washington where, on November 22, 1863, he finally succumbed to complications from a "shell contusion of the back." Incredibly, the War Department deducted $10.50 from the young lieutenant's accrued pay for "... board at above named hospital from 8th to 22nd Nov. 1863."[30]

Although the reputation of the Grays' brigade was significantly enhanced by its stunning victory, there was no practical reward or noticeable benefit for the conquerors such as special light duty. After consolidating the position, and perhaps briefly celebrating the victory, Ellmaker's Red Crosses remained in the fortress for the night while tending to the wounded and burying the dead, including the thirty-five men from Maine, who were provided with a final resting place within the walls where they fell.

2nd Lieutenant Edward E. Coxe

(USAMHI)

The next morning orders were received to advance south toward Brandy Station, where it was intended that the Sixth Corps would connect with the left of the Third Corps. Fortunately, the Confederates had abandoned the south side of the river and the Federals were spared the necessity of assaulting the opposite bank. "... Sunday, after lying upon our arms all night, we expected to renew the fight the next day, and to make vigorous

[30]National Archives, Military Records, Coxe.

endeavors to cut in two the army of Lee. We, however, simply crossed the river, on the rebel bridge, in the afternoon ..."[31]

On the November 9 most of the Sixth Corps was ordered to proceed to Wellford's Ford on Hazel Run, the location that would eventually become that Corps' winter encampment. The 119th and the other regiments of the First Division were detailed to remain at Rappahannock Station until further orders were received, perhaps because the surgeons and the burial details had not had sufficient time to complete their grisly duties.[32] Towards evening the Grays relocated their camp a distance of about two miles to the "Booth farm" which, if providing no other benefit, relieved the men from post-battle sights, sounds and smells.[33]

The next several weeks were relatively peaceful and pleasant for the men of the 119th, but were decidedly unpleasant for their commander, George Meade. Meade was convinced that any further offensive action for the year would be ill-advised, first because the lateness of the season would prevent the army from significantly exploiting any victory it was able to gain in the field, and also because the army had again advanced beyond the repaired portion of its rail supply line. As a result of his unwillingness to advance, Meade became the target of serious criticism in the press and in the administration, which prompted President Lincoln to summon his reluctant general for another consultation at the White House on November 14.[34] Whatever was discussed did not, however, have the effect of producing an instant offensive from the Army of the Potomac, and despite the meeting the army continued to lie in wait between the Rappahannock and Rapidan Rivers.

The daily routine fostered by Meade's reticence toward resuming offensive action was interrupted on November 20, when the Sixth Corps was given the opportunity to put on a grand review for some visiting English officers. Although the men undoubtedly complained about the extra effort, they were also probably grateful for a break in the monotony of camp life and the opportunity to bask a bit in the afterglow

---

[31]O.R.-1-29-2-437; Haines, p. 116.
[32]O.R.-1-29-2-440.
[33]Latta diary, 11/9/1863.
[34]Winslow, p. 125.

from Rappahannock Station.[35] The weather, too, provided fodder for complaining, a soldier's favorite pastime. During this lull, the men were subjected to alternating periods of cold and rain, prompting Lieutenant Rhodes to complain to his diary: "Last night it rained, and as the weather is cold we are far from being comfortable ... It is raining, and we all live in mud, sleep in mud, and almost eat in mud."[36]

The lull continued until November 25, when several events occurred which would propel the army back into motion. First, the repairs to the railroad bridge at Rappahannock Station were completed, extending the ability of the army to feed itself if it progressed further south; and second, the weather broke, ending two days of rainstorms. Orders were swiftly drafted and distributed, placing the army on the alert for a movement the next morning.

The Sixth Corps received its orders, and in response the men were roused the following morning at 4:00 a.m. The receipt of the orders, however, did not necessarily generate a sense of confidence in the plan. One Union officer was skeptical: "When we received the order to move, I do not believe there was a single officer at our headquarters but felt apprehensive in regard to the result. It seemed as though we were just going to butt our heads against a very thick stone wall."[37]

Skeptical or not, the Grays "left camp near Brandy Station at daybreak and marched all day and until after midnight, crossing the Rapidan at Jacob's Mill on a pontoon bridge. Bivouacked at 1:00 a.m. and slept soundly."[38] It was not, however, as easy a march as implied by Latta's terse record. The roads were crowded and frequent jam-ups ensued, causing the men to suffer through many irritating pauses which were too short to rest, but long enough to break the rhythm of the march and to allow the cold to seep back into feet and joints. Although the weather did not seem to trouble Lieutenant Latta, who probably enjoyed the benefit of a tent, most of the Regiment spent a short night out in the open, shivering from the cold and wind.[39]

---

[35]Winslow, p. 125.

[36]Rhodes, pp. 132-133.

[37]Halstead, *Letter to Emily Sedgwick*, as cited in Winslow, p. 126.

[38]Latta diary, 11/26/1863.

[39]O.R.-1-29-1-796.

Upton's Brigade, which had spent the night on the north side of the river, joined the rest of the First Division early in the morning, and by 7:00 a.m. on the twenty-seventh, the entire Corps was ready to march. Instead of heading down the road, however, the men in the column stood and waited for hours due to delays caused by the Third Corps, and as a result the column made "No progress" until about 3:00 p.m.

As the Grays and their comrades marked time, perhaps squatting around small fires and coffeepots, the head of the Third Corps, as a result of making a wrong turn in the dense undergrowth of the Wilderness, inadvertently marched into the Confederate division commanded by Major General Edward Johnson. When the surprised skirmishers of both sides began an exchange of sniping, which soon escalated into a serious firefight, the soldiers of the Third Corps left the road to deploy into line of battle, suddenly opening the way for the Sixth Corps behind them. The road cleared at an opportune time, because as his men began to drift back out of the fight, General French found it necessary to call for the immediate support of Sedgwick's soldiers.

Upon receipt of the request, the First and Second Divisions of the Sixth Corps were quickly dispatched to the center of the fighting. At the point of contact, the woods to the right of the road were blanketed in powder smoke and filled with the roar of musket and artillery fire, while wounded and shirkers streamed out of the haze.[40] Expecting the worst, the First Division formed in line of battle, with the 119th and the rest of the Third Brigade on the right of the formation, and Neill's and Upton's brigades to their left.[41]

The exact role of the First Division in this engagement is unclear. There is no question that the men of the Third Brigade were ready for a fight. "The Third Corps was breaking in all directions. Russell's Brigade went in yelling for them 'to get out of the way, and give the Sixth Corps a chance.'"[42] The wording "... went in ..." implies that Russell's men launched an attack, and there were clearly several charges and countercharges at this point by someone. In his

---

[40]Latta diary.

[41]O.R.-1-29-1-796, Wright.

[42]Haines, p. 118.

diary, Latta also stated that the Grays "... went in heaviest musketry for a time ..." However, General Sedgwick, in his official report, stated that his Corps was not engaged.[43] Whether exposed to direct fire, or merely to the stress of anticipation, it is certain that all of the men of the 119th were greatly relieved when darkness finally put an end to the fighting.

With the onset of darkness, the Philadelphians were given a brief opportunity to boil some coffee, eat their hardtack, and perhaps steal a few hours sleep. If any of the men did manage to fall asleep, they certainly weren't blessed with much rest, because at 11:00 p.m. the Corps received marching orders, and by 1:00 a.m., all of the weary infantrymen were back on the road headed toward the Turnpike and a rendezvous with the Fifth Corps.[44]

After marching five or six hours in the rain, the men reached their destination at Robertson's tavern at dawn, taking a position on the extreme right flank of the army where, at 7:40 a.m., the order came down the line to form a battle line to the right of the road in preparation for an attack. The Greek Crosses rushed to form up, surged forward into the thicket, and after a brief time spent struggling through underbrush, vines and tree branches, the entire line broke out into the open on the top of a hill. There, rather than receiving the shot and shell for which nerves had been steeled, the soldiers were presented with an unusual spectacle. On a hill on the opposite side of the Mine Run valley, the enemy could be seen out in the open and arrayed for battle. "Here, we found the enemy in the strongest position that I have ever seen. They were posted on the top of and behind a hill that extended some 5 or 6 miles in a straight line and at each end of the line was rounded as if by the work of engineers. The crest of the hill was about a mile from the hills upon which our line was formed. The rebels had strengthened their position by throwing up earthworks, making an abatis and damming up a creek in the valley, so that it was in many places six feet deep."[45] "We never saw them so conspicuously posted before. On a large, cleared field, especially their gray lines of battle were very

[43]O.R.1-29-1-796.

[44]O.R.-1-29-1-796; Latta diary, 11/28/1863.

[45]Peck, Henry T., *Letter*, 12/4/1863.

Mine Run - *Leslie's Illustrated Newspaper*

showy, with artillery and rifle pits dotting the face of the hill."[46] Those hard-handed veterans had long since abandoned any illusions about the "glory" of battle, but occasionally the grandeur of it could still impress them.

It didn't take very long before the novelty of the spectacle wore off, and the reality of the situation began to sink in. The enormous hazards which faced potential attackers, including the Mine Run itself, which was described by another Yankee as "... waist deep and eleven feet wide ...," were obvious even to the most fatigue-dulled private.[47] Dark recollections of Fredericksburg must have filled the soldiers' minds as they stood contemplating an attack across that stream and up that hill, with cannon loaded with canister, and ranks of Butternuts waiting at the top.

Perhaps as a blessing, "It soon commenced to rain hard, continuing until late in the afternoon."[48] Morbid thoughts were interrupted by more immediate concerns -- the discomfort of being cold, wet, and out in the open on a late November morning. Although there would be no assault that day, anxiety soon returned to the men, who found themselves either involved in a day-long skirmish between pickets, or in the midst of the prolonged artillery duel which soon developed.[49]

The lack of action the next day, the twenty-ninth, probably puzzled the soldiers on the line as much as their commanders were puzzled about what to do next. Meade spent the day pondering the Rebel defenses, which he considered the equivalent of "'... another Gettysburg ...,'" as well as the reconnaissance reports indicating that the Southerners were working furiously to make their defenses even stronger, by slashing timber and digging more elaborate trenches.[50] Finally, after dark, the Union commander convened a council of war where, after considerable discussion, Meade adopted Sedgwick's suggestion that the troops of the Fifth and Sixth Corps attempt to turn the Confederate left flank.[51]

---

[46]Haines, p. 119.
[47]Haines, p. 120.
[48]Haines, p. 119.
[49]Rhodes, p. 134; Latta diary.
[50]As cited in Winslow, p. 128; O.R.1-29-2-928.
[51]Winslow, p. 129.

The full plan, as finally developed, called for a one-hour barrage, followed by an assault along the entire line in support of a turning movement by the Sixth Corps, a portion of whose line already extended beyond the left of the Confederate trenches. Leaving two brigades in position, the balance of the Sixth Corps crept out of its lines at about 2:00 a.m. and began a two-mile movement to the right. Russell's Brigade was most likely one of the two which remained in place, since it was aligned next to the right of the Fifth Corps, with the First Division's First Brigade to its right and Howe's Division at the end of the formation.[52] It is probable that the 119th was not far enough to the right to have been beyond the Rebel trenches, and no one in the Regiment could have had any illusions about the carnage that would follow the order to attack. The men in the 49th Pennsylvania clearly harbored such dark thoughts, because they began to write their names onto scraps of paper and then pinned the makeshift dog-tags onto their coats, to allow for easier body identification.[53]

The artillery started bombarding the Rebel trenches precisely at 8:00 a.m. as planned. The men commenced their pre-battle rituals, probably similar to those the soldiers of the Sixth Corps observed on another battlefield nearly a year later: "Everywhere along the line of battle men might be seen to stoop and retie their shoes; to pull their trousers at the ankle tightly together and then draw up their heavy woollen stockings over them; to rebuckle and tighten their waist-belts; to unbutton the lids of their cartridge-boxes and pull them forward rather more to the front; to rearrange their haversacks and canteens, and to shift their rolls of blankets in order to give freer scope to the expansion of shoulders and an easier play to their arms; to set their forage caps tighter on their heads, pulling the vizor well down over their eyes; and then ... the rattle of ramrods and snapping of gunlocks as each man tested for himself the condition of his rifle."[54] For others the ritual involved the mind rather than the body; perhaps offering a prayer, joking with a friend or relative from home, or recalling a precious moment with a wife, lover, or child. It didn't really matter what diversion was chosen,

---

[52]Haines, p. 120.

[53]Westbrook, p. 174.

[54]Forsyth, George A., *Thrilling Days in Army Life*, as cited in Lewis, p. 263.

because each man knew deep in his heart that nothing would stop the pitiless course of the screeching lead if his time had finally arrived. Rather, the exercise was intended to focus attention on anything other than what was waiting on the other side of the valley.

Just moments prior to the jump-off time, however, an order was passed down the line that the attack was postponed indefinitely. Major General Gouverneur K. Warren had advised his commander that the enemy position in front of the Fifth Corps was impregnable, and that the only outcome of an assault by his troops would be massive casualties. In what was arguably the most courageous decision made by any commander during the entire war, Meade called off the attack.

Concerning Meade's decision, Ellmaker's men probably came to share the sentiments of the members of their sister outfit, as described by Lieutenant Peck of the 118th Pennsylvania, since both groups shared almost identical backgrounds and culture. It was Peck's observation that: "The soldiers think great things of General Meade since this last move [calling off the assault]. They like him now more than, if possible, they did McClellan. A general who can see an impossibility, without having to demonstrate it as Burnside did at Fredericksburg, is appreciated. An article in a Baltimore paper of yesterday, saying that government has lost confidence in Meade and is going to put Hooker in command of this army has excited great indignation among the men."[55]

During the weeks that led up to this day Meade had been compared to an old woman by his president, as a result of his conduct of the pursuit of the Rebels after the victory at Gettysburg, and had been subjected to relentless criticism in the Northern Press, much of which questioned his courage and contrasted the eastern army's lack of accomplishments with Grant's successes in Chattanooga. A moral coward would have ordered the troops forward for an assault or two, and after the bloody sacrifice was deemed adequate, a telegraph message would have been sent extolling the courage of the men and providing excuses for the failure of the assault. Thousands of men were spared death or disability, and lived to fight another day, because George Meade had the guts and the compassion to say no to another "forlorn hope."

---

[55]Peck, Henry T., *Letter*, 12/4/1863.

After the order to cancel the assault was issued, a flurry of correspondence passed back and forth from the field to Headquarters, as Meade attempted to find some way to salvage a benefit from the situation. Unfortunately, the delay only made the tactical situation worse, because the Confederates were given the opportunity to adjust their alignments in response to the intelligence gained from the artillery barrage.[56] In response to one inquiry from his commander, Sedgwick responded: "In answer to your dispatch just received, I respectfully report that I do not believe the enemy's works can be carried in my front by an assault without numerous sacrifices. I regard the chances as three to one against the success of such an attack."[57] Practically speaking, after that statement, the war in the east was over for 1863. Unfortunately, the suffering was not.

The Federals spent the rest of the day lying in their pits huddled against the weather, which was so cold that the water froze in the men's canteens. Although the commanders knew that no attack would be ordered that day, it is doubtful this information was passed down to the privates shivering in the field. Lieutenant Peck of the 118th Pennsylvania, a short distance to the left of the Grays said, "Every minute until late in the afternoon we expected to go forward."[58] It was not necessary for the lieutenant to tell his mother in his letter home, but it was almost certainly true, that many of those minutes were spent in contemplation of the horrors of an attack, an activity which surely did nothing to warm the men. After dark, the Greek Crosses were ordered back to their position of the previous day, a disposition which proved to be too late for several soldiers who, as a result of plummeting temperatures, froze to death while on picket duty.[59]

It was clear to everyone by the morning of December 1 that retreat was the only viable option available to the Army of the Potomac. Supplies and forage were almost exhausted, and the weather could only be expected to deteriorate; and, as a result, even a significant victory could not be exploited in any meaningful way. Orders were issued, and

---

[56]O.R.-1-29-2-930.
[57]O.R.-1-29-2-929.
[58]Peck, Henry T., *Letter*, 12/4/1863.
[59]Winslow, p. 129.

the withdrawal of the Sixth Corps commenced at 9:00 p.m. However, a price would be exacted from the men for their escape from that valley of death. The temperature remained bitterly cold, and "The marching for a time was very tedious, the column halting every few steps, so that we could not get exercise enough to keep warm."[60] When finally able to march, the Federals had to contend with roads lined with wagon ruts made in the mud, but by then frozen solid. The hours of misery did not end until noon on December 2, thirty numbing miles later. The Grays finally reached their earlier campsite at Wellford's Ford on December 3, after marching through Stevensburg and Beaver Station.[61]

The men of the Regiment spent the rest of December finishing off the camp and their huts, and in routine chores and duties. Fortunately, not every day of the month was subject to the same arduous weather conditions which prevailed during the Mine Run campaign. On December 13 Latta noted in his diary, "Cleared off -- warm spring-like day. Miss Payne, pretty Secesh damsel, at headquarters in ... [celebration of the] anniversary of the great battle of Fredericksburg." Four days later, Latta headed home on two weeks' leave, a trip interrupted early on when his train ran into some guerrillas who had just burned a bridge at Pope's Run.[62]

The young lieutenant was able to spend the holiday with his family, while his comrades in Virginia celebrated as best they could under the circumstances. If toasts were offered in the Grays' small huts that Christmas, several were surely made to General Meade, in thanks for the members of the Regiment who were present to celebrate, rather than lying in the cold earth at Mine Run.

---

[60]Haines, p. 120.
[61]Latta diary.
[62]Latta diary.

9

WINTER AT WELLFORD'S FORD

Winter encampment for the enlisted men had a consistent pace and texture entirely different from campaigning -- long periods of boredom interspersed with drill, picket duty, and camp chores, all spiced with uncomfortable weather. If there was a significant difference between the encampment at Wellford's Ford, and that of the previous year at White Oak Church, it was in the men, both those remaining, and those who were lost. By their second winter, the surviving Philadelphians were hard-handed veterans tempered by combat and physical ordeal. All understood that each winter's day would pass no matter how unpleasant, whether spent shivering on the picket line or slogging through a muddy drill for the thousandth time, but with its passing the next and perhaps fatal battle was one day closer. The Grays grumbled, cursed, and complained about the physical privations of winter camp, but each knew that camp was better than what was surely coming, but not much better.

The weather of the winter of '63-'64 tested the stoicism of the troops, alternating between bitter cold, driving snowstorms, wind, thaws, torrential rain, and then more cold and snow. Latta's diary during that winter reads in parts like the chronicle of a picket's nightmare: "... The morning is clear and bracing but the wind is awful (1/1); ... The weather most intensely cold (1/2); ... Snow turned to rain before night (1/4); ... Weather during the morning intensely cold, towards night slight snow accompanied with rain sets in (1/7); ... continues cold, we had no such weather last year (1/9); ... Mild and spring-like ... producing an abundant supply of mud (1/15); ... raining severely (1/18); ... The weather for the past few days has been more like that of May than January. The inhabitants tell us that they have never known it to continue so fine for such a length of time. We should be likely to pay for this in February and March, however. (1/25); ... A severe thunderstorm occurred during the evening, accompanied with lightning and rain (2/2); ... the wind howls tremendously (2/3); ... cold and blustery (2/4); ... Towards evening quite a snowstorm set in (2/15); ... The weather has become intensely cold, the wind howls prodigiously, there is not a tent that is really comfortable (2/17); ... Rain, snow and hail combined have visited us ... for the last few days (3/5); ... Heavy rains have been prevailing for several days and the streams on all sides are swelling to an enormous magnitude (3\9); ... one would hardly know the placid Hazel. It has overflowed its banks and assumed the proportions of a navigable river, and in its sweeping torrents is carrying with it all the temporary bridges hereabouts (3/10); ... A severe snowstorm set in during the afternoon (3/22); ... the ground is everywhere covered with at least eight inches of snow (3/23); ... Rain set in ... and continued with severity until long after we had retired (3/25)..."

It should come as no surprise that when given the opportunity, the men looked to the bottle for an escape from the boredom, the weather, and perhaps the future as well. "The usual scenes of intoxication and debauchery which follow the arrival of the paymaster are things being enacted tonight, although not so extensively as usual. No one of course knows where the whiskey is obtained."[1] Sadly, in this war even alcohol seemed to generate suffering and death. On Christmas Day 1863, Private Stephen Dempsey of K Company was "... burned so badly in a fit of intoxication ..." that he was left barely clinging to life.[2] The poor man lingered for twenty-four more days, probably in continuous agony, until he finally gave up the struggle on January 18. Latta's somewhat callous comment on his passing was that the private's "... tenacity to life [was] remarkable."[3]

Latta recognized that he, and probably most of the men in the Regiment, had become hardened as a result of the things he had done

[1]Latta diary, 3/17.
[2]Latta diary.
[3]Latta diary, 1/18/1864.

and seen the previous year. Several days before Dempsey died, Latta recorded the death of I Company's Private Thomas Sheetz, who was claimed by disease while at the Regimental hospital. The next day, January 17, the band arrived in camp, apparently for a funeral service, prompting Latta to note, "... The slow notes of the fife and the roll of the muffled drum remind that he whose death we noticed yesterday is about to be deposited beneath the [earth]. A scene such as this does not strike us with the same force as when they would first happen."[4]

Not surprisingly, it was much easier for the officers of the Regiment to find diversions from the weather, dreary camp duties, and the occasional death, than it was for the enlisted men. Latta made numerous social calls on his fellow officers, which consisted primarily of friendly conversation around the fire of the host's hut or in the host unit's command post, followed by card-playing and the consumption of "... hot whiskey ..." "Many leisure moments are occupied with cribbage, a game which seems to have taken quite a hold on the officers of this command."[5] For variety, the officers of the Regiment played whist or a game which Latta called "Lou," and on occasion, if the weather was not too foul, the Regiment's band or glee club was dragged out for a serenade.

Certainly few of the men, including the officers, would have chosen winter camp over home, but given human nature, a certain comfort level soon developed in the Army of the Potomac. Unfortunately, in every organization there is always someone who will not let well enough alone, no matter how marginal well enough may be, and the Army of the Potomac was no exception. The previous year it was General Burnside who felt compelled to take the army on the "Mud March." In early 1864, Union Cavalry Brigadier General Judson H. Kilpatrick filled the role. On February 11, he was able to convince the administration that, given the opportunity, he would be able to lead a cavalry raid into the Confederate capital and free the thousands of Union prisoners held captive in Libby Prison. Undoubtedly to their unanimous disgust, the men of the Sixth Corps, along with a cavalry contingent under Brigadier General George Custer, were assigned the duty of

---

[4]Latta diary.

[5]Latta diary, 2/4/1864.

creating a diversion intended to convince Lee that the Union forces were attempting to turn the Confederate left flank, while Kilpatrick went around its right.

On February 27, the Greek Crosses commenced the diversion and marched off in the direction of the Madison Court House. The next day the force reached Robertson's Bridge, rebuilt the bridge, and bivouacked for the night on the southern shore, where Sedgwick was ordered to remain until Custer's troopers, who continued southward, were able to return. The men of the 119th spent two miserable days hunkered down in the mud and a cold rain, expecting the entire Confederate army to come crashing down on them at any moment.

Custer's troopers returned on March 1, having narrowly escaped an encounter with much of Lee's army. Fearing that his men might be trapped on the south side of the Rapidan by the rising water from the previous two days' rain, Sedgwick took his charges back across the river at 6:00 p.m. that same evening. More misery followed. The equipment train with the blankets and tents became separated from the infantrymen, who were forced to spend a sleepless night huddled around their campfires, while no doubt cursing the teamsters, their officers, and probably the war as well. As if that ordeal was not a high enough price to pay for the privilege of returning to their snug winter quarters, the Philadelphians and the rest of the Corps finished off the expedition with another twenty-three-mile march back to camp in the cold, under "... trees loaded with ice ... with every bough and twig ... an icicle, which sparkled like pearly crystals in the glittering sunlight."[6] The beauty of the scenery didn't help the Vermonters in the Second Division, many of whom "... fell out completely exhausted and helpless as infants ...," and presumably it didn't do much for the Grays either.[7]

Like the "Mud March" the year before, Kilpatrick's excursion was also an exercise in futility, resulting in no significant military benefit for the Union. In fact, the only significant military developments for the 119th during the entire winter came by way of a shuffling of the organization of the Regiment, and much of the rest of the army as well. Perhaps most pertinent to the Grays was the loss of a large number of

---

[6]Winslow, pp. 140-141; Fisk, p. 198.

[7]Fisk, p. 198.

the Regiment's experienced officers, starting with the resignation of the founder of the Regiment, Colonel Ellmaker, offered on November 3, 1863, and accepted January 12, 1864.[8]

Ellmaker gave the following as his official reasons for requesting permission to resign his commission: "First, I am and have been ever since I entered the service, and indeed long before, afflicted with the Rheumatism to such an extent as to almost incapacitate me for active duty in the field, notwithstanding which I have always endeavored faithfully to perform my part - Second - A suit is now pending in our Supreme Court, which if decided against me will bring utter ruin upon myself and family - My presence there might avert this contingency - Third - Our only son has recently enlisted in the service and my family is left without any male protector."[9] There was no documentary evidence discovered which challenged the sincerity of the reasons given.[10]

However, if Lieutenant Latta's diary is an accurate reflection of the thoughts of the men of the 119th generally, rather than the venting of strictly personal ill-will, then dissension among Ellmaker's officers and amongst the ranks may also have been a factor in his decision. Although Latta would later give his colonel lavish praise in the book he authored years after the war, several entries contained in the privacy of his diary around the time of the resignation and shortly afterwards tell a different, and perhaps more credible, story. "[A] ... grand howl going on in the tent of the commandante of this battalion ... although he [Ellmaker] may be a soldier [he] certainly lacks the qualities which adorn and grace the gentleman. [He is] 'Noisy in camp and quiet in battle.'"[11] On January 14 Latta penned, "Col. Ellmaker left the command this morning possibly with the regrets of some ..." A month later Latta made another entry concerning his former commander, "The regiment was today inspected by the brigade inspector ... men appeared to be in excellent condition, since the date the Colonel [Ellmaker] left a great and

[8]National Archives, Ellmaker Military Records.

[9]National Archives, Ellmaker Military Records.

[10]A search of Court records did not reveal a lawsuit involving Ellmaker in either the Pennsylvania or United States Supreme Court during the war years, so perhaps his presence did lead to an amicable settlement of the matter.

[11]Latta diary, 1/1/1864.

pleasing change has come over the entire command. No more midnight visits like at brigade headquarters. Things behave with much more harmony and good will than they did before."[12] In a writing notable for its lack of editorializing, these comments stand out as extremely rare, negative comments unlike anything contained in the balance of the diary, including notations concerning the many soldiers in whose courts-martial Latta participated. The diarist's dislike or disrespect for his commander must have been deeply held.

It must be noted, however, that on January 9, 1914, perhaps in anticipation that his diary would soon pass beyond his control, or in recognition that when written the author was unseasoned, Latta appended a note which attempted to take the sting out of his comments made fifty years earlier. In that notation he stated: "He was really a superior officer as a ... [disciplinarian] in exacting a full performance of duty." Perhaps it was only the demeanor of the colonel which generated irritation, because with the sole exception of the "quiet in battle" comment, Latta never criticized Ellmaker's courage or the performance of his duties when the bullets began to fly.

If there had, in fact, been generalized friction between Ellmaker and his officers when he commanded the Regiment, the situation in the Grays' camp markedly deteriorated when Ellmaker moved up to the command of the Third Brigade for the Rappahannock Station expedition in November. Soon after that move in the fall, Lt. Colonel Gideon Clark, an artist at self-promotion, initiated a behind-the-scenes and largely secretive campaign to secure for himself the rank of colonel, in order to solidify his temporary command of the 119th. Either in anticipation of such a maneuver, or after news of the effort leaked back to Wellford's Ford, the field officers of the Regiment split into two factions, the much larger anti-Clark and pro-Major Truefitt (the third-ranking officer in the Regiment) group led by Captain Andrew T. Goodman of Company C, and the smaller and much more timid Clark supporters apparently backed by Ellmaker.

Dissension, which had begun smoldering amongst the line officers following Ellmaker's promotion to command of the Brigade, and perhaps even before that, exploded upon his resignation into a fire storm

---

[12]Latta diary, 2/16/1864.

of bickering, back-biting and intrigue, which for a time threatened to tear the Regiment apart. Captain Goodman, in a February 1864 letter home to the founding committee of the 119th, exposed the depth of many of the officers' animosity towards Clark. "You already know how bitterly we have been disappointed in the abilities, conduct and habits of Lt. Col. Clark. We/I refer to the greater part of the line officers [who] had long ago seen the mistake that had been made in giving him that position and had decided in the event of the Colonels [Ellmaker's] death or resignation to use every means in our power to prevent his promotion to the colonelcy."[13]

Goodman, who may not have been an exemplary officer himself, given that his company had the highest desertion rate in the 119th, with almost forty percent of the soldiers under his command choosing to risk a firing squad rather than remain in the army, went on to present what amounted to a bill of indictment against his acting commander. First, it was noted that Clark had missed, under suspicious circumstances, the campaigning in the spring and summer of 1863, with the suggestion that Clark's disability was more attributable to a cooperative doctor than to a genuine illness. Second, Goodman claimed that Clark refused to return to the Regiment to assist its depleted and overworked staff, despite repeated requests from his beleaguered fellow officers. The third broadside was that "Lt. Col. Clark was too Drunk [at Rappahannock Station] (I do not say intoxicated) to know what he was about. Fortunately we were not engaged until he had time to recover somewhat his senses ...." Finally, Clark was attacked for being negligent, careless and a poor disciplinarian. This assault was bolstered on February 15 with a petition signed by Dykes, Brown, Humes, Goodman, Logo, Gray, Lovett, Saylor, Landell, Henry C. Warner, Ward, and Ford, all officers of the 119th, and all asking that Major Truefitt be promoted to the colonelcy.[14]

Presumably, these letters hit the founding fathers of the Regiment, as well as concerned families and friends back home in Philadelphia, like a bombshell. The Regiment's finance committee fired off a letter to Pennsylvania's Governor Curtin supporting the promotion

---

[13]Goodman, Pennsylvania State Archives.

[14]Goodman, Pennsylvania State Archives.

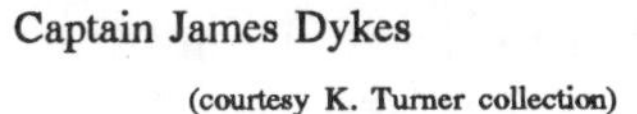

Captain James Dykes

(courtesy K. Turner collection)

Lieutenant Frank Logo

(courtesy K. Turner collection)

of Truefitt, while Ellmaker, still active in the First Regiment from which the 119th was created, responded with his own letter challenging the veracity of the charge of drunkenness. The Regiment's former commander wrote that he had the opportunity to observe Clark's performance during the battle and that Clark was, "... perfectly sober and acted with great gallantry on that memorable day."[15]

Clark was apparently an accomplished bureaucratic warrior as well as a smooth politician, and he immediately initiated a counterattack, first by requesting a copy of the Goodman letter, and then by following its receipt with charges against Goodman for insubordination. Not to be outdone, Goodman responded with charges of his own against his commander.

If Clark had hoped to escape any repercussions from his suspect conduct in the woods prior to the battle of Rappahannock Station, he was certainly very disappointed when Goodman's charges were pressed and

---

[15]Ellmaker, Pennsylvania Archives.

his court-martial convened on April 11, 1864. Goodman was actually able to come up with three charges: drunkenness on duty on November 7, 1863; violation of Article 15, which involved signing an allegedly false muster record in order to secure a promotion to lieutenant for Sergeant Alfred Hannings; and violation of Article 18 for knowingly filing a false report as to the condition of the companies of the 119th on December 12, 1863. Clark chose Captain Latta, who had just received a promotion, partly as a result of Clark's recommendation, as his defense counsel. Latta was probably chosen because he had been a lawyer before the war, had participated as a judge advocate in numerous courts-martial, was not part of the opposition, and perhaps because he seems to have known about, but not been offended by, the conduct which generated the latter two allegations. Rather than indignation, Latta's flippant comment in his diary on the muster roll issue was, "... a small trick has been played by the Lieutenant Colonel commanding..."[16]

Probably because of its seriousness, the charge of drunkenness on the field was the most hotly contested of the three, with each side calling several witnesses. In addition to the testimony from Captain Landell previously referenced, Major Truefitt testified, "I think he was under the influence of liquor ... I think he was very considerably under the influence of liquor [and] ... He was asleep most of the time."[17]

The defense took its turn, and in true lawyerly fashion attacked both the fact of the intoxication and, in the alternative, its significance if, in fact, it had occurred. In regards to the former, 1st Lieutenant Albert Leidy, also of the 119th, testified, "There was nothing in his condition at the time I saw to lead me to believe he was under the influence of alcohol." Leidy was joined in this perception by two members of the 5th Wisconsin, as well as the Grays' Chaplain Benjamin R. Miller. For the alternative defense, Clark relied on another part of Truefitt's testimony to the effect that "... he done his duty when engaged" and that nothing of significance occurred while he was asleep and the rest of the Regiment rested in the woods. Even the chief witness for the prosecution, Captain Landell, was forced to concede during cross-

---

[16]Latta diary, 12/31/1863.

[17]National Archives, Clark Court-Martial papers.

examination that Clark went back out to the skirmish line when the fighting started.[18]

The prosecution presented a much stronger case on the other two points. In essence, both charges alleged that Clark had taken the muster rolls for December 12, 1863, and manipulated the numerical sizes of a number of companies, without actually reassigning the men, in order to increase the paper size of one company to eighty-one, so as to justify an additional lieutenancy for Sergeant Hannings. The only defense offered to the second charge, signing a false muster record, was that Colonel Ellmaker had suggested the ploy before he either was promoted to command of the Brigade or resigned. No factual defense was offered to the third allegation of knowingly submitting inaccurate company strength reports. Instead, Latta relied upon legal technicalities concerning the wording of the charges. Curiously, Clark did not offer testimony that he was not aware of the contents of the report when he signed it, although later, when not under oath, he offered that exact defense in a letter attempting to win a reinstatement.

After deliberations which lasted over a period of two weeks, the court handed down a split decision. Lt. Colonel Clark was acquitted of the charge of drunkenness on duty and filing false muster rolls, but was convicted of knowingly submitting an inaccurate report on company strengths. The commander of the regiment was "Cashiered" for his misdeed. Effective April 25, 1864, on the very eve of the upcoming campaigning season, Major Henry P. Truefitt, Jr. became the new Regimental commander. At about the same time, Captain Goodman was also dismissed from the service by another court for insubordination.

The Grays, for various reasons, some regrettable and some not, lost numerous other officers during the winter. Certainly the most unfortunate was the loss of William C. Moss, captain of Company D, who became desperately ill shortly after the first of the year. The young captain's rank did not protect him from disease, but it did entitle him to nursing care from his sister and widowed mother, who arrived in camp on January 23.[19] Although he had been sick with typhoid fever for some time, Moss remained in the Regimental hospital until February 2,

---

[18]National Archives, Clark Court-Martial papers.

[19]Latta diary, 1/23/1864.

Captain William C. Moss

(USAMHI)

when he and probably his mother and sister "... left with the other sick of the brigade for a general hospital." Despite loving attention from his family, Latta knew when Moss left that his condition was grave, noting "... Moss really looks bad, he seems not to improve any, and has been reduced to a perfect shadow."[20] Captain Moss struggled with his illness for another nine days, but was finally claimed on February 11, 1864.

Perhaps Lieutenant Latta, of all the Grays, was most affected by the loss: "Poor Moss has gone. Gray returned this evening and brought the ill-fated news of his death. He died at the Kirkwood house at daylight. Although I never expected to see him in the service again, I certainly did not look so soon for his dissolution. An intimate friend and companion of former years and with whom we entered the service, has at last fallen by the ... hand of a disease contracted in camp."[21] Latta's sorrow was certainly surpassed by the grief felt by Moss's mother when she learned of, or witnessed, the passing of her remaining son (her other son had disappeared in 1861), and with him the primary source of her support. If there was any consolation for her, it was perhaps that she was with her son when he died, and that unlike so many mothers, her son's remains would not lie in some unidentified pit, on a far-away battlefield.

Although Company G's loss of 1st Lieutenant Francis R. Faust in January did not result from his own death, it was nonetheless a product of a tragedy similar to that which had befallen the Moss family.

---

[20]Latta diary, 2/2/1864.

[21]Latta diary, 2/12/1864.

Faust [no known relation to John or Aaron Faust, or the author] was one of the original members of the 119th, mustering into the Regiment on August 4, 1862, as a 2nd lieutenant. He was at least adequate in his performance, receiving a promotion to 1st lieutenant on July 17, 1863, and presumably, if family tragedies had not interfered, he would have completed so much of his term of service as fate permitted.

Francis was not the only member of the immediate Faust family to enlist, or even the first, because his younger brother, Horace B. Faust, had enlisted in the 91st Pennsylvania ten months earlier on October 7, 1861. Presumably from a substantial Philadelphia family (the Faust brothers' father was on the 119th's Finance Committee), Horace commenced his military career as a 2nd lieutenant at the age of nineteen. Although blessed with a good family, the younger Faust was not equally blessed with a strong constitution; and as a result, during his time in the military the young man was plagued by poor health, suffering from rheumatism, a bout of typhoid fever, and commencing in December of 1863 from protracted diarrhea and pneumonia.

In the belief that only home care could save him, Horace's father arrived at the camp of the 91st to take his desperately ill son home the moment that a resignation could be pushed through channels. A day before the approval arrived, however, the elder Faust was forced to look on helplessly as his son passed away. The next day the grieving father wrote to headquarters, pleading that the resignation be rescinded so that his son would have the honor of having died while in the service of his country, a request that was much more promptly granted.

Meanwhile, Francis had taken an emergency leave from the 119th so as to return to Philadelphia to be with his mother, and hopefully to assist in his brother's recovery. Obviously, not every soldier with a sick sibling was granted permission to return home to lend support to a worried mother, but this was an unusual situation because ten years earlier the Fausts' mother "... was entirely insane for the space of six months, caused mainly by the death of a favorite child ...."[22] By his presence, Francis was apparently able to forestall a recurrence of the mother's emotional breakdown, despite the news of the death of his

---

[22]National Archives, Francis R. Faust Military Record.

younger brother; but the family dreaded the mother's reaction should Francis return to the war, or worse, be killed in it.

The family's physician justified the necessity for Francis' resignation in his affidavit of January 23, 1864: "... the recent sudden and untimely death of another son in the service, Capt. Horace B. Faust, of the 91st Regt. P.V., has very much affected her mind; and in as much as she so particularly presses the return of her son Francis R., I am of the opinion that the acceptance of his resignation and his return home, is the only condition on which, in her peculiar state of mind, a return of her old complaint may be averted."[23] The request was granted, but unfortunately, it is now impossible to determine whether Mrs. Faust's sanity was preserved.

The depletion of the ranks of the Regiment's officers continued throughout the winter. Two, Quartermaster John J. Hess and Captain James Dykes of Company A, were discharged, and another, 2nd Lieutenant Joseph A. Seffarlan of Company E, was dismissed. Two other officers resigned -- 2nd Lieutenant Samuel L. Ward and Captain Stacy B. Campion, both from H Company. As a result of the winter's hemorrhage of line officers, when Major Truefitt assumed command of the Regiment in late April he was faced with the daunting task of making final preparations for the imminent campaign with a severely reduced staff. In response to that crisis, Truefitt petitioned the governor of Pennsylvania almost immediately after taking command for over a dozen promotions to fill most of the vacancies.[24]

The shake-up in the command structure moved down toward the 119th as well as up from it. The entire organizational structure of the Army of the Potomac was changed in March, in part as a result of attrition in the ranks from the previous year, and also for the purpose of the tightening the chain of command. The several corps of the Army of the Potomac were consolidated with only four surviving: the Second Corps under the command of Major General Winfield Scott Hancock; the Fifth Corps under Major General Gouverneur K. Warren; and the Sixth Corps which remained under the command of "Uncle John" Sedgwick. In addition, the Ninth Corps, under the command of the somewhat

---

[23]National Archives, Francis R. Faust Military Records.

[24]Truefitt, Pennsylvania Archives.

suspect General Burnside, was also retained; but in order to allow Meade to remain in command, despite having lower seniority than Burnside, the latter Corps was not technically incorporated into the Army of the Potomac.

The Sixth Corps itself was also rearranged. The former three divisions were consolidated into the First and Second Divisions, and new troops were grafted onto the Corps as the Third Division. The Grays' First Division received an additional brigade under the command of Brigadier General Alexander Shaler.[25] It is doubtful that many of the men of the Greek Cross were enthusiastic about sharing their emblem with the newcomers. Although Shaler's men were old hands transferred from the First Brigade of the former Third Division, the soldiers who formed a substantial portion of the new Third Division came to the Corps with decidedly negative credentials. The 110th and 122nd Ohio regiments, assigned to the Second Brigade of that division, under Brigadier General Truman Seymour, and the 87th Pennsylvania which had been assigned to the division's First Brigade, were known in the army as "Milroy's Weary Boys." That nickname referred to the poor showing made by those soldiers and their comrades in the Shenandoah Valley in general, and in particular, to their embarrassing performance during the early stages of the Gettysburg campaign. Much of Milroy's command had been truly "gobbled up" by Lee as he marched north, and the rest straggled into Harper's Ferry in dribs and drabs after a humiliating rout and retreat.[26] Like the poor Dutchman of the 153rd Pennsylvania one year earlier, a black cat would seemingly follow these troops during the coming campaign.

One final modification was made during the winter that at the time was probably not fully appreciated by the Philadelphians as having any particular personal significance, but which for many of them would soon mean the difference between life and death. Knowing that 1864, with the coming presidential election and growing peace movement, would be the critical year of the war, and convinced that a more aggressive course was essential, President Lincoln reactivated the rank of lieutenant general, and promptly filled the position with Ulysses S.

---

[25]Humphreys, vol. 6, p. 18.
[26]Prowell, p. 69.

Grant. The hero from the west was placed in overall command of the entire army, but it soon became apparent that he intended to stay with the Army of the Potomac, and as such would eventually assume direct control over its day-to-day tactical operations.

Grant brought a somewhat different military philosophy with him to the Eastern Front. From the time of his promotion, the extent of Federal casualties became only a secondary consideration, and in the war of attrition which Grant would wage, the only wasted life would be one not accompanied by a corresponding Confederate death. Grant had heard and understood Lincoln's desire for the application of the "awful arithmetic" and was determined, either from personal agreement or for political expediency, to apply it to the Rebels. No longer would the capture of Richmond be the primary objective of the army. Rather, President Lincoln had finally found a general who seemingly shared the belief that the destruction of the Army of Northern Virginia, whether by defeat or attrition, should be the real objective, and that a drive toward Richmond should be only a means to bring Lee's army out from behind its defenses so that it could either be crushed or bled to death.

The men of the 119th were finally granted the opportunity to observe the newcomer from the west at a grand review of the entire Sixth Corps held on April 18, 1864. Blessed with good weather for a change, the soldiers paraded past their new leader in white gloves, with all the spit and polish precision that they could muster. Colonel Theodore Lyman, an officer on Meade's staff, was duly impressed by the spectacle: "We took our station on a swell of ground, when we could see a large part of the Corps in line; but there was so much of it, that, though drawn up by battalions (that is, ten men deep), there could be found, in the neighborhood, no ground sufficiently extensive, without hollows. At once they began to march past -- there seemed no end of them. In each direction there was nothing but a wide, moving hedge of bright muskets; a very fine sight ... General Grant is much pleased and says there is nothing of the sort out West ..."[27]

Apparently Russell's Third Brigade did not impress all of the staff officers, prompting Oliver Wendell Holmes, Jr. to record a somewhat snide evaluation: "There are some fine fighting regiments in

---

[27]Lyman, p. 84.

this brigade, e.g. the 6th Maine -- But none of them are first rate -- hardly second rate in soldierly appearance and setting up -- or I suspect in discipline."[28] Considering that General Sedgwick repeatedly employed the 119th's brigade as his spearhead, it may be assumed that he did not share the opinion of the staff officer, at least in regards to the issue of prowess in combat.

It is doubtful that Grant formed any particular impression of the 119th as column after column of blue-uniformed soldiers passed by him in a process that must have taken hours. There can be no doubt that every member of the Grays who could see him formed some sort of opinion about the rather plain-looking officer for whose benefit this spectacle was staged. One may wonder if any of the Philadelphians had a premonition, as they paraded by on that lovely early spring day, that this unimposing man would soon lead them on a guided tour through hell.

---

[28]Holmes, *Touched by Fire*, as cited in Mundy, p. 184.

10

THE WILDERNESS

For the first time, sole responsibility and authority for the strategic and tactical conduct of the war to reunite the Union rested in one man, Ulysses S. Grant. Knowing that he had the power to insure cooperation among the various commands throughout the country, Grant decided that for once the Federals would launch a concerted offensive against the Confederacy at several key points simultaneously. The expectation was that by so doing, the Southerners would be denied the ability to minimize the manpower advantage of the Federal government, by transferring reinforcements as needed along interior lines.

The centerpiece of the master plan was to be a drive into Virginia toward the capital of the Confederacy, not primarily for the purpose of capturing it, but rather to draw Lee's army out from behind its defenses and to smash it. The dilemma facing the Union command was exactly where to strike. Each possible route south had its own advantages and disadvantages -- a direct attack meant hammering across heavily defended fords in Lee's front; a swing to the Union right would avoid the enemy's fortifications, but leave Washington vulnerable and severely extend supply lines; while a drive to the left avoided the former problems, but would lead the army into the Wilderness, the scene of the humiliating defeat the prior May at Chancellorsville, and the stalemate at Mine Run only a few months past.

The Wilderness was a particularly nasty place to have to fight. Aptly named, the area, roughly fifteen miles east to west and ten miles north to south, consisted of a second growth jungle of vines, thorns, and scrub trees interspersed with swamps, streams and steep-banked gullies. The main roads through the area, the Orange Turnpike, the Orange Plank Road, and the Brock Road, were marginal at best, and in places were like tunnels, with dense foliage pressing in on the sides and often canopied with a dark green ceiling. In short, the Wilderness was a nightmare landscape for officers who knew that survival often depended upon maintaining unit alignment and cohesion, and thus ensuring an organized regiment on either flank.

Despite all of the drawbacks, the decision was made to push south through the Wilderness, .but only because Grant and Meade were confident that the army could clear the area before Lee would be able to organize an assault on the Union line of march. To insure the necessary speed, the final plan called for the army to be divided into two wings. The right wing, consisting of Brigadier General James H. Wilson's cavalry division and the Fifth, Sixth and Ninth Corps, in that order, was directed to cross the Rapidan River on the westernmost flank at Germanna Ford, closest to the Southern army. The Second Corps, comprising the left wing, was detailed to cross several miles to the east at Ely's Ford.

Orders for the movement south were cut on May 2, and delivered to the 119th on the third. Instantly, the camp was propelled into a frenzy of activity: "Camp in confusion, packing up, etc ..."[1] The Regiment's sutler, R. Pickens, and the other camp hangers-on, had been sent away two weeks earlier; but the company gear remained to be packed, and each man had to face the agonizing process of deciding which possessions were dispensable and which were important or cherished enough to lug around on the long, hot marches that were sure to come. After the excess items were jettisoned, each soldier had his personal burden increased by the issuance of six days' rations and fifty rounds of ammunition, a harbinger of an especially long and bloody initial movement.[2]

On the morning of May 4, the approximately five hundred men that then constituted the 119th, along with the rest of the Sixth Corps, were up by 2:30 a.m. and on the road by 4:00 a.m., filling the road behind the Fifth Corps, which drew the assignment to lead the wing.[3] Among the Greek Crosses, Brigadier General George W. Getty's

---

[1]Latta diary.
[2]Winslow, p. 150.
[3]Latta diary.

division led the way, followed by Wright's First Division, while Brigadier General James B. Rickett's men brought up the rear. At 7:00 a.m. the men were allowed to stop for a short while to eat breakfast, but were quickly back on the road after wolfing down a cracker or two, washed down with some quickly boiled coffee.[4]

The day grew progressively warmer, and the men correspondingly more weary, as the column pounded its way south through Brandy Station, then Stevensburg, and on to the ford. Six months earlier, when the men were in marching trim with strong legs and tight back muscles, this march would have been handled like a stroll in the park. Now, however, the Yankees were winter soft, and, perhaps worse, were burdened with pounds of newly issued equipment. There was no instant way to bring back the physical conditioning lost over the winter, but there was an instant remedy for the weight: "Blankets, overcoats and dress coats were thrown away by the thousands ..."[5]

John D. Billings, in an artillery unit following the Second Corps, described that carnival of waste in detail: "It is growing warmer ... The road is evidently clear of all obstructions, but the heat and speed begin to tell on the men. Look at the ground which that brigade has just vacated after its brief halt for rest. It is strewn with blankets, overcoats, dress-coats, pantaloons, shirts -- in fact, a little of everything from the outfit of the common soldier ... I saw an area of an acre or more almost literally covered with the articles above named, many of them probably extras, but some of them the sole garment of their kind, left by the owners, who felt compelled, from the increasing weight of their load, to lighten it to the extent of parting with the blankets which they would need that very night for shelter. This lightening of the load began before the columns had been on the road an hour. A soldier who had been through the mill would not wait for a general halt to occur before parting with a portion of his load, if it oppressed him; but a recruit would hang to his until he bent over at an angle of 45° from a vertical, with his eyes staring, his lower jaw hanging, and his face dripping with moisture ... It did not take an army long to get into light marching order after it was once fairly on the road ... if a man clung to his effect till noon, he was

---

[4]Rhea, p. 64.
[5]Haines, p. 141.

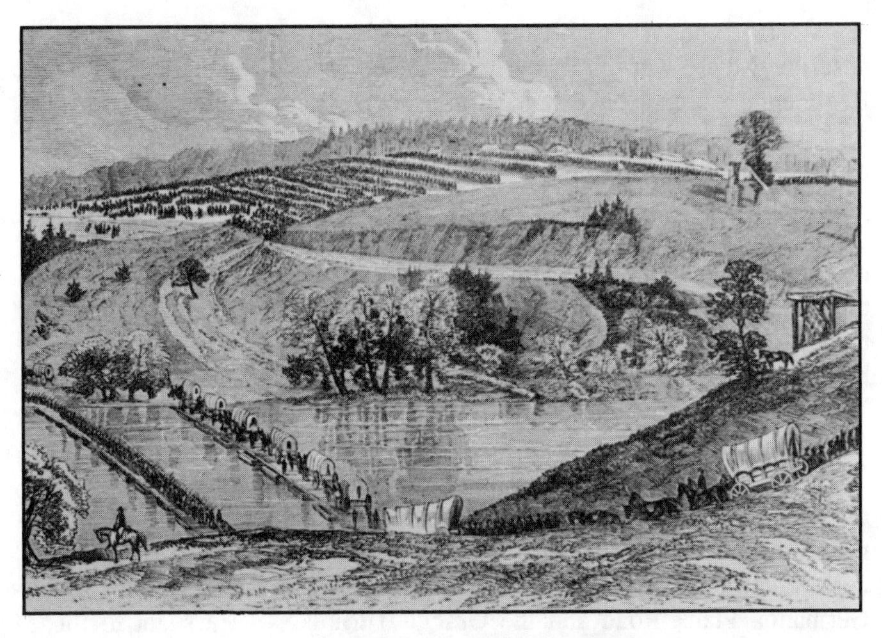

Crossing the Rapidan Toward the Wilderness

Leslie's Illustrated Newspaper

likely to do so for the day, as after noon the thought of shelter for the night nerved him to hold on."[6] There is no reason to suppose the scene along the route of the Sixth Corps was any different.

Not only muscles lost marching condition over the winter, but so did feet; and many of the marchers suffered from another plague -- blisters. "... Men would drop out in the afternoon of the first day for another reason. They blistered or chafed their feet and sat down at the first stream to bathe them, after which, if the weather admitted, they could be seen plodding along barefoot, their pantaloons rolled up a few inches, and their shoes dangling at the end of their musket-barrel."[7] Presumably, similar sufferers in the 119th took the opportunity to cool their hot and aching feet when the Regiment finally crossed the ford near the end of the day.

---

[6]Billings, pp. 342-343.
[7]Billings, pp. 343-344.

If some of the blistered Philadelphians appeared as Billings described, there were probably more than a few extremely embarrassed Regimental officers on that May afternoon, because after crossing the ford, the Regiment passed by an old farm house where General Grant sat on the front porch, smoking a cigar and watching the procession.[8] After passing their commander, the infantrymen from Philadelphia finished the day's "hot and dusty" thirteen-hour, sixteen-mile march with a short hike of a mile and a half to a grove of pine trees, where at around 5:00 p.m. the unit bivouacked for the night.[9] Although the night of the fourth was to prove to be "...quiet and peaceful, as if there was not a reb within a hundred miles, or ever had been ...," Captain Latta wrote in his diary, "We are on the eve of a great battle ...," a perception undoubtedly shared by most of the men in the Regiment.[10]

At about 6:00 p.m., the next day's marching orders were received. The Sixth Corps was directed to take up a position on the right flank of the Fifth Corps, approximately in the area of the Wilderness Tavern, a country inn on a slight rise at the intersection of the Germanna Plank Road and the Orange Turnpike.[11] Pursuant to those orders, the Grays, along with the rest of their Corps, were roused at 3:00 a.m. on the morning of May 5, and resumed the march by around 6:00 a.m.[12] Wright's First Division was only able to progress about two miles until it was countermarched a short distance; and then the Red Crosses were made to stand aside and choke on dust for a time, while artillery passed by on the road.[13] In the intervals between the passing of each clattering gun team, the ominous sounds of musketry began to drift to the idled foot soldiers, from the area to the south occupied by the Fifth Corps.[14]

In mid-morning the Union command made the decision, for reasons still not entirely clear to historians, to change the fundamental strategy from a race to exit the Wilderness as fast as possible, to an

---

[8]Winslow, p. 151.

[9]Latta diary; O.R.-1-36-1-672; Humphreys, vol. 6, p. 19; Winslow, p. 151.

[10]Shaler, Alexander, *Diary*, as cited in Rhea, p. 76; Latta diary.

[11]Trudeau, *Bloody Roads South*, p. 39.

[12]Latta diary.

[13]Haines, p. 141.

[14]Latta diary.

attempt to defeat the Confederates in detail as Butternut divisions were fed into the jungle. As the lead Federal force on the flank nearest to the Southerners, the Fifth Corps began to experience hostile contact from the west early in the morning. Meade, in conformance with the new strategy, began a deployment of Warren's Corps from marching column into line of battle; but instead of waiting for a completed formation with the Sixth Corps on the right flank and the Second Corps on the left, Warren's men were fed into the forest as fast as individual brigades were fronted to the west. Those battle sounds heard by the Red Crosses as they stood aside for the artillery were generated by the collision of the advancing Fifth Corps troops, and the Confederates who had just established initial lines of defense.

With the first sounds of serious combat, the pace of events began to accelerate. First, the striking power of the Sixth Corps was significantly diminished when orders were received for Getty's lead division to press southward on the Germanna Plank Road to the Wilderness Tavern, so as to be in position to support the Fifth Corps' offensive, and for Rickett's trailing division to remain midway between the Spotswood House and the Old Wilderness Tavern to serve as a manpower reserve for both the Fifth and Sixth Corps.[15] Next, Getty notified his Corps commander, General Sedgwick, that he was receiving reports of enemy skirmishers as his division proceeded south. Finally, in response to the increasing volume of fire from the area occupied by the Fifth Corps, Wright's division, all that remained of the Sixth Corps for the moment, was ordered to hasten to the south to connect with, and protect the right flank of, Warren's embattled infantry.

Spared the role of acting as the point of the advance, Russell's men followed Upton's Second and Brown's First Brigades "... along the Fredericksburg and Gordonsville Plank Road, till we struck 'Old Verdersville Road' where we turned right and commence[d] advancing carefully ..." down a country lane known as the Spotswood Road, which was in reality little more than a dirt path.[16] Upton's lead Second Brigade pushed skirmishers out to the front, while the rest of the division was deployed so as to march south, but in readiness to face an attack

---

[15]O.R.-1-36-2-421; Priest, p. 47.
[16]Anderson, 1900, p. 2.

from the west. At about 10:00 a.m. the Confederates began an attempt to block, or at least seriously delay, Wright's connection with the Fifth Corps; and within a short time the staccato popping of skirmish fire broke out at the head and along the western flank of the advancing column.[17]

Knowing that his division was in the presence of the enemy, General Wright would have much preferred to advance down the path in line of battle, but as Colonel Upton observed: "It was impossible to march in line of battle on account of the dense pine and nearly impenetrable thickets [which] met us on every hand."[18] Private Keiser, of the 95th Pennsylvania of Upton's Brigade, described the terrain through which he passed as "... the awfullest brush, briars, grapevines, etc. I ever was in."[19] The Federals pressed through the jungle, desperately trying to make progress while attempting to remain vigilant for, and defend themselves against, bushwhacking by the Southerners. Fear and frustration were as thick as the undergrowth as the men peered ahead searching for signs of the enemy, only to be struck by a burst of musket fire against which they could neither prepare nor retaliate: "Our line would suddenly encounter a line of Rebels lying on the ground and hidden by brush and leaves. Then they would spring to their feet, fire a deadly volley and pull back."[20]

After struggling ahead in that fashion for about a mile, "... we found the enemy in heavy force, when we [Russell's Brigade] formed in line of battle ..." by columns of regiments on the north side of the path, with the order from front to rear being the 49th Pennsylvania, 119th, 6th Maine, and the 5th Wisconsin. Simultaneously, Brown's Jersey Brigade formed in a similar fashion in the center of the formation, and Upton's brigade took the left flank on the opposite side of the trail.[21] The alignment by columns of regiments, when combined with the extremely diminished visibility, soon caused some unanticipated and unwelcome problems for the leading soldiers of the 49th Pennsylvania: "Now the 119th Pennsylvania Volunteers are coming up, and they fire into us. We

---

[17]Priest, p. 47.
[18]Michie, *Life and Letters of Emory Upton*, as cited in Winslow, p. 154.
[19]Keiser, 5/5/1864.
[20]As cited in Mundy, p. 188.
[21]Anderson, 1900, p. 2; Steere, p. 243.

drop to the ground and are very angry. We say some bad words and fire a few shots at them and hollow [*sic*] that they are firing into the Forty-ninth Pennsylvania Volunteers."[22]

Fortunately, it does not appear that any of Westbrook's comrades were hit by the errant gunfire. When finally properly organized and formed, "We [Russell's Brigade] charged on their skirmishers with a yell and drove them out from behind their logs and trees in a hurry, but not until they had killed and wounded quite a number of our men."[23] The three parallel columns again pressed forward, but the total advance of about one and a half miles, which should have been completed in an hour at most, took three; and it was not until around three o'clock that the connection was finally made with Brigadier General Charles Griffin's division on the right flank of the Fifth Corps.[24]

Upon arrival in the vicinity of Warren's flank, the Grays were greeted by suffering wounded pleading for assistance, and the gruesome, brushfire-charred corpses of Bluecoats killed in earlier action. Despite the nerve-wracking gauntlet through which they had just passed, and the horror of their new surroundings, none of the Red Crosses wavered; but it is probably fortunate that the men were spared a prolonged opportunity to contemplate the implications of their situation. Not a moment was spared as the officers hustled the Grays' brigade into a proper line of battle. Within a relatively short period of time, Truefitt's men were poised to launch a westward assault from their position on the crest of a low ridge, with a New Jersey regiment on their left, and their right guarded by a portion of the 5th Wisconsin.[25]

By about four o'clock, before the Federals had the chance to launch their own attack, Russell's men began to hear the unmistakable sounds of a large force of infantry clawing its way toward them through the smoke-filled underbrush. "Failing to see the enemy [the men] soon began to fire by *ear-sight*."[26] After several devastating volleys the Rebels were thrown back in disorder, losing a brigade commander, Brigadier General Leroy A. Stafford, to a shot through the spine. The

---

[22]Westbrook, p. 187.
[23]Anderson, 1900, p. 2.
[24]Humphreys, vol. 6, p. 28.
[25]Priest, p. 98.
[26]As cited in Trudeau, *Bloody Roads South*, p. 65.

Confederates also lost almost an entire regiment to the 5th Wisconsin when, as a result of faulty alignment and the fortuitous deployment of several companies from the 5th, the attacking Butternuts came in with a detachment of the Badgers beyond their left flank. As the Southern line broke and began to retreat, the detached Wisconsin men swooped down on the exposed flank and captured virtually the entire 25th Virginia regiment.[27]

For the next several hours the Red Crosses and their opponents blasted away at each other through the forest, as volley after volley rolled up and down the lines of the Union right flank. Between volleys, the Red Crosses heard ominous sounds which they recognized would soon add to the growing list of casualties: "The Confederates now commenced to strengthen the position on their side of the ravine, felling timber and covering it with earth. The woods resounded with the strokes of their axes as the busy workmen plied their labor within three hundred yards, and in some places less than one hundred yards of our line, yet so dense was the thicket that they were entirely concealed from our view."[28]

William Busby

(courtesy K. Turner collection)

During this period, Grant and Meade resolved to attempt a grand offensive involving all the Union forces then strung out along the entire line. Pursuant to this plan, as dusk approached around 7:00 p.m., the Philadelphians, along with the rest of their division, formed up for battle as best they could and then

[27]Steere, p. 249.
[28]Stevens, p. 306.

Wilderness - May 5, 1864

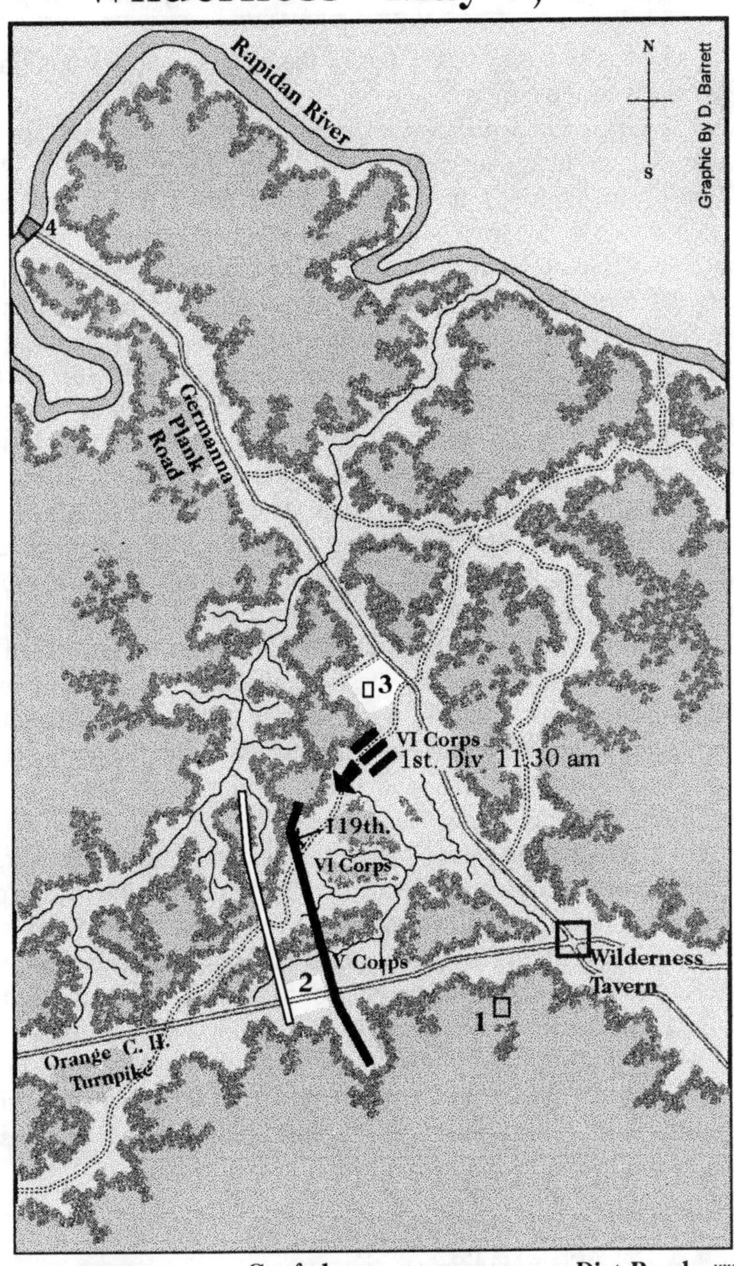

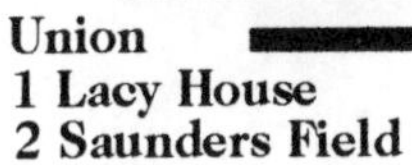

Union
1 Lacy House
2 Saunders Field

Confederate
3 Spotswood House

Dirt Road
Road
4 Germanna Ford

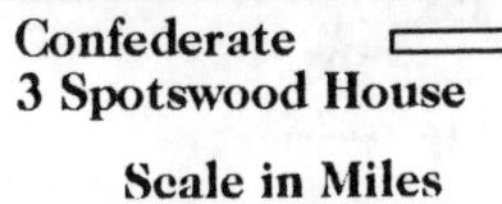

Scale in Miles
0 1

began to advance into the thicket toward the enemy, who were not more than 300 yards to their front.[29]

The Grays soon realized, to their dismay, that the terrain was even worse than that experienced earlier in the afternoon. After struggling down the slope through vines and brush which constantly became entangled with cartridge boxes and bayoneted rifles, while trying to ignore the Confederate dead and wounded strewn along the way, the attackers discovered that the enemy was positioned behind a swamp on a corresponding ridge on the other side of the valley.[30] The battle line pressed onward, and like the battle on Salem Heights one year earlier, the Grays received the withering fire which every veteran in line knew was coming. The attack was repulsed, and the Federals withdrew to their own ridge, firing from tree to tree as they went.[31]

At this point, the battle again devolved into a heavy and generalized firefight all along the line. Near the 119th, a member of Brown's Jersey Brigade described the action: "It was impossible to see the enemy; and though we peered into the thick woods, we were fighting invisible foemen. We soon began entrenching. Our men scraped the stones and earth before them as best they could, until spades were brought. All the time the enemy were sending a shower of bullets over and past us ... One volley, just at dark, commenced far away on the right, possibly two miles off, and came rolling down the line, like thunder, until opposite us, when it stopped."[32]

No significant advantage had been gained by either side from the day's bloody contest. Each sègment of the Union force, the Fifth Corps in the morning, then the Sixth Corps on the right, and finally the Second Corps on the left, had thrown itself against the Butternut defenders, who managed each time to shift just enough troops to the scene of the fighting to stall the Federal attack. Unlike most battles, however, the conflict did not end with the setting of the sun: "All night we lay with arms in our hands, drawing a volley every few moments from the rebel skirmishers a few yards off. This made us lie low and kept us in constant

---

[29]Priest, p. 126; Winslow, p. 155.
[30]Wheeler, *On Fields of Fury...*, p. 106.
[31]Winslow, p. 155; Priest, pp. 128-129.
[32]Haines, pp. 145-146.

wakefulness. The dead were lying thick about us and some wounded in a field to our left, between the lines, crying out for water, and to be carried off."[33] In front of Upton's portion of the line, a few hundred yards south of the 119th, Colonel Beckwith described a similar heart-rending scene: "We lay in line of battle upon our arms and shortly after dark when the firing slackened, the cries of the wounded between the lines ... was something terrible to hear. Some prayed, some cursed, some cried and some asked to be put out of their misery."[34] Along with the soul-wrenching pleas from the injured as they suffered and died in the no-man's land between the lines, came the incongruous calling of the whippoorwills, which only added to the horror of the situation, prompting one Southern captain to record: "The loneliness is of itself sufficient, and these birds seemed to mock our grief, and laugh at the groans of the dying ..." with "... the most hideous of all noises that I ever heard on a battle field."[35]

No one, regardless of how compassionate or well-intentioned, was able to satisfy the pleading wounded, because each potential good Samaritan recognized that the most likely outcome of any rescue attempt would only be to add one more corpse or sufferer to the already ample supply. Neither was anyone able to rest because "... we remained under fire until long after dark ... with no prospect of being relieved."[36]

While the infantrymen on the front line were giving their full attention to avoiding being hit by musket fire or trying to shut out the moans from the wounded, the Union command was hatching plans to renew the offensive on the sixth. The primary assault was to be the responsibility of Hancock's Second Corps, located at the southern end of the battlefield. For their parts, both the Fifth and Sixth Corps were ordered that evening to join in the offensive at 4:30 a.m. the next morning, intended mainly to freeze the Confederates in place and prevent reinforcements from being shifted to the south.[37]

Having slept on their arms all night, the Grays had little to do in the predawn hours of May 6 to prepare for the upcoming fight, other

---

[33]Haines, p. 146.
[34]Best, p. 121.
[35]*Samuel Buck Papers*, as cited in Priest, p. 208.
[36]Latta diary, 5/5/1864.
[37]Winslow, p. 150.

than cautiously stretch out kinked muscles, prepare coffee in hopes of energizing their groggy minds and fatigued bodies, and perhaps clean a fouled rifle. As the Yankees were beginning the process of forming up for the attack, which had been postponed until 5:00 a.m., they were undoubtedly startled when fifteen minutes prior to the planned jump-off time, the unmistakable sounds of a Confederate assault wafted up from the valley below, followed almost immediately thereafter by retreating Union pickets crashing through the brush and back into the main line. Within minutes, a ferocious firefight erupted all along the entire Federal line.[38]

Unfortunately for the Southerners, they had devised no new tactic to allow them to overcome the obstacles of the Wilderness or the Union defenses, and their advance was quickly repulsed. As if attached to their retreating foe by some invisible cord, the Union forces followed the recently vanquished Confederates down into the swamp, where the Union counterattack quickly deteriorated into a bloody exchange of musket fire, which finally ended in a storm of Rebel canister and an inevitable retreat.[39] By 10:30 in the morning, the Red Crosses had mustered sufficient courage and energy for three more assaults on the Rebel defenses, two reaching the top of the western ridge, but all ending in failure and heavy casualties.[40]

George T. Stevens, a Sixth Corps surgeon, witnessed the morning's fighting: "The volleys of musketry echoed and re-echoed through the forest like peals of thunder, and the battle surged to and fro, now one party charging, and now the other, the interval between the two armies being fought over in many places as many as five times, leaving the ground covered with dead and wounded ... Those of the wounded able to crawl reached one or the other line, but the groans of others, who could not move, lent an additional horror to the terrible scene whenever there was a lull in the battle."[41]

On the southern end of the battlefield, the pendulum swung even more wildly. At first, it appeared that Hancock's men would smash

---

[38]Rhea, p. 318.
[39]Anderson, 1900, p. 2.
[40]Winslow, p. 158.
[41]Stevens, p. 309.

Hill's Corps while in the process of driving deep into the rear of the Southern lines. Just at the moment when the rout was to be completed, Confederate General Longstreet appeared with the relatively fresh troops of his First Corps, who stopped the Union drive and slowly began to regain some of the lost territory. Soon thereafter, Longstreet dispatched a small contingent of his troops through a partially completed railroad cut around the left flank of that portion of Hancock's Corps which had just been within an eyelash of a stunning victory. Repeating the performance of a year earlier, the Confederates fell upon the exposed Federal flank and rolled it up, failing to achieve a total victory only because of a few well-placed Union cannons and a heroic stand at some abandoned Southern emplacements.

Recognizing the potential for a real disaster, Meade sent a circular to his right wing around 11:00 a.m., ordering the Fifth and Sixth Corps to cease aggressive actions and to dig in so that reinforcements could be safely drawn from the right and sent to the left. General Sedgwick responded about a half hour later that it would be very difficult for his men to carry out that order, because the construction of trenches would draw the fire of four Rebel batteries across from his position and would generate severe casualties.[42]

At the same time that the order went out for the right wing to hunker down, Meade also solicited information concerning the availability of units that could be released for re-deployment to the left, to which Sedgwick responded that he could only offer Russell's Brigade, "... which has suffered the least."[43] Fortunately for the Grays, the order dispatching them into the inferno to the south never arrived, and the entire division continued to slowly and cautiously entrench. By mid-afternoon the defenses were completed, despite the enemy artillery fire, at which point Sedgwick felt confident enough to offer Upton's and Morris' Brigades as reinforcements. The offer was declined because by that time the situation in the south had stabilized. For the balance of the day the 119th "... laid under a severe fire from the enemy's sharp-shooters ...," and later in the afternoon sought refuge in their pits from

---

[42]O.R.-1-36-2-459,460.
[43]O.R.-1-36-2-460.

heavy doses of "... shot, shell and canister ..."[44]

There is a finite limit to the length of time that the human body can continue to pump adrenaline, and as a result the Philadelphians were probably in an exhaustion-induced semi-stupor by the time sunset arrived. Any hopes for serious rest that night were shortly to be dashed, by events about to occur on the far right flank.

John B. Blackburn

(courtesy of K. Turner collection)

That flank was manned at the end of the day by "Milroy's Weary Boys" under the command of Brigadier General Truman Seymour, with support to their right and rear provided by Shaler's small brigade, which had been dispatched to that position despite having suffered heavy casualties during the morning's assault. Shaler, who was justifiably apprehensive about the situation wrote: "... the most extraordinary fact was seen that an army of 100,000 men had its right flank in the air with a single line of battle without entrenchments. I lost no time in informing Genl. Seymour that I would not be held responsible for any disaster that might befall the troops at this point, calling on him for at least 4,000 or 5,000 more men to properly defend that point."[45]

Despite Shaler's identification of the peril, and his alleged notification to Seymour, the former commander seems to have taken no extraordinary defensive precautions, such as preparing elaborate emplacements, refusing a portion of his line, or even posting extra pickets, while the latter did not send the requested reinforcements. With an eerie similarity to the behavior of the Eleventh Corps one year earlier

---

[44]As cited in Rhea, p. 319; Latta diary, 5/6/1864.

[45]Shaler, *Diary*, as cited in Steere, p. 438.

at Chancellorsville, the most suspect units in the Sixth Corps sat, perhaps with fingers crossed, like lambs waiting for the slaughter. They would not have long to wait.

At sunset, Brigadier General John B. Gordon's and Brigadier General Robert D. Johnston's brigades of Ewell's Corps came crashing into the camps of the unprepared Union soldiers, routing Shaler's Fourth Brigade first, then Seymour's troops almost immediately thereafter. In concert with the assault on the end of the Union line, the Confederates threw another wave against the length of the entrenched Sixth Corps front, but "Our [Russell's] brigade front ...," which was posted about a quarter of a mile south of the disaster, "... repulsed them handsomely."[46] Although the Rebel assault from the front was easily broken, the Grays certainly experienced some serious anxiety while lying in their trenches listening to the roar of a battle to their rear.

Most of the men from the broken brigades ran wildly to the rear, except for a few small groups which were induced to stand and fight until they were again overwhelmed by the onrushing Confederates. Neill's brigade, which had been positioned to the left of Seymour and the right of Russell, refused its line and took on the Southerners front to front. A portion of the two attacking Rebel brigades were halted in front of the refused Union line; but the other portion, rather than turning on Neill's exposed flank, continued on to the south and east.

At about the same time that Neill was shifting his brigade, portions of Upton's Second and Brown's First Brigades swung out of the line facing west, and moved to the north to meet the Rebel incursion. By the time the detached men of the First Division were able to get into position to meet the enemy, the Confederate units were already thoroughly disorganized from the darkness, the forest, and the resistance of Neill's Brigade. The combination of those factors and the ensuing confrontation with the detachments from Wright's Division brought the Southern offensive to a halt. Recognizing that they were now at serious risk from a Union counterattack, the Rebels began a slow withdrawal; and within a matter of hours, the Southerners were back to their original lines.[47]

---

[46]Anderson, 1900, p. 2.
[47]Steere, pp. 442-446.

The Grays did not entirely escape the effects from that near disaster, however, because orders were received later that night for several of Sedgwick's brigades, Russell's included, to pull back and retrench in a better defensive position. The Wilderness was even harder to traverse in the dark than during the day, and as a result it took the men several hours of struggling through the undergrowth to reach the new position, about a mile northeast of the old lines. The new line across the "... Fredericksburg and Gordonsville Plank Road ... [Germanna Plank Road]" was admittedly better, being on higher ground and having a stream, Caton's Run, in front providing extra protection.[48] One must wonder, however, how much the men appreciated the new position, given that marching and digging new trenches cost them another entire night's rest.

General Horace Porter, from Grant's staff, summarized the fighting on the fifth and sixth of May: "There are some features of the battle which have never been matched in the annals of warfare. For two days nearly 200,000 veteran troops had struggled in a death-grapple, confronted at each step with almost every obstacle by which nature could bar their path, and groping their way through a tangled forest the impenetrable gloom of which could be likened only to the shadow of death. The undergrowth stayed their progress, the upper growth shut out the light of heaven. Officers could rarely see their troops for any considerable distance, for smoke clouded the vision, and a heavy sky obscured the sun. Directions were ascertained and lines established by means of the pocket-compass, and a change of position often presented an operation more like a problem of ocean navigation than a question of military maneuvers. It was the sense of sound and of touch, rather than the sense of sight which guided the movements. It was a battle fought with the ear and not with the eye. All circumstances seemed to combine to make the scene one of unutterable horror. At times the wind howled through the treetops, mingled its moans with the groans of the dying, and heavy branches were cut off by the fire of the artillery, and fell crashing upon the heads of the men, adding a new terror to battle. Forest fires raged, and ammunition trains exploded; the dead were roasted in the conflagration; the wounded, roused by its hot breath, dragged themselves

---

[48]Matter, pp. 10-12; Anderson, 1900, p. 2.

along, and with their torn and mangled limbs, in the mad energy of despair, to escape the ravages of the flames; and every bush seemed hung with shreds of blood-stained clothing. It was as though Christian men had turned to fiends, and hell itself had usurped the earth."[49]

Accepting the fact that the contestants had fought themselves to a stalemate, and fearing that the men had reached the end of their physical and psychological endurance, neither side launched an attack against the other on May 7. Light skirmishing broke out sporadically throughout the day, but the Grays spent most of the time resting, regrouping, and generally benefitting from a respite from the carnage. The Philadelphians had been either fighting, under fire, marching, or entrenching almost continuously for four days, and had they not been permitted such a break, the entire Regiment might have been of as little use to the army as if it had been wiped out.

Although not wiped out, the Regiment's losses were substantial: twelve enlisted men were killed, and one officer and seventy-three enlisted men were wounded, for a total casualty rate, assuming the Regimental strength to have been approximately five hundred, of seventeen percent.[50] In Russell's Brigade, only one other regiment, the 5th Wisconsin, had a higher casualty rate for the two days of the battle than did the 119th.

Late that same day, orders were received from headquarters to move out at 8:30 p.m. that evening toward Spotsylvania Court House; first eastward by way of the Pike to Chancellorsville, then southeastward by country roads past Aldrich's and Piney Branch Church. As word of the movement, but not the route or destination, spread through the ranks, the men certainly had mixed feelings and interpretations. Of primary importance, the order meant another sleepless night on the road. On a deeper level, the men probably harbored suspicions that another retreat was in progress, meaning that another pointless slaughter of comrades

---

[49]Porter, pp. 72-73.

[50]O.R.-1-36-1-126. Bates, as usual, provided slightly different figures; killed, 11; died of wounds, 5; wounded, 31; Missing in action, 1, for a total of 48 casualties or approximately 10% of the unit. One officer, Lieutenant George G. Lovett, eventually succumbed to the wounds he received at the Wilderness. His loving family retrieved his remains and brought them home to a final resting place in Tullytown, Bucks County, Pennsylvania. *Bucks County Intelligencer*, June 7, 1864.

and relatives had occurred. Seemingly, the only consolation available was that no matter what awaited them at the end of the night's march, it couldn't be any worse than the battle in the Wilderness. As it would turn out, only one of those conclusions would prove to be correct, that there would be no sleep that night.

11

SPOTSYLVANIA: UPTON'S CHARGE

By 8:30 p.m., shortly after darkness covered the Wilderness on the night of May 7, the soldiers of Wright's First Division were ready to take to the road toward an unknown destination. Due to a postponement ordered from headquarters, the men of the 119th and their comrades did not begin the march until 9:30, with Wright's Division in the lead; Upton's Brigade out front, followed by Russell's Brigade; the Fourth Brigade next; and the Jersey Brigade in the rear.[1] As soon as the men had marched a sufficient distance eastward on the Pike towards Chancellorsville and Fredericksburg so as to be beyond the hearing of their enemy, they began to grumble and complain about what appeared to them to be another retreat. Given the direction of the march, the history of the Army of the Potomac, and ignorance of the personality of Ulysses S. Grant, such an interpretation was entirely reasonable, but was nevertheless completely wrong.

At 4:00 a.m. on May 8, after having trudged only five and one half miles in six and one half hours, the column passed Chancellorsville; but it would be several hours later, not until 8:00 a.m., when "Uncle John" Sedgwick would allow his weary charges to break the march for a brief rest and breakfast.[2] The cumulative effects of this march and the previous four days' action were severely taxing the stamina of the men as well as their officers, including staff officer Major Thomas Hyde who

---

[1]O.R.-1-36-2-510.

[2]Keiser diary, 5/8/1864.

described himself as "... positively light-headed as well as ragged and dirty, hungry and thirsty."[3] James Bowen of the 37th Massachusetts of the Sixth Corps' Second Division, described the march on the tinder dry road as slow torture, "... the dust rose in stifling clouds which hung with tortuous persistency close to the earth, choking the lungs, the throat, the eyes, and settling in disgusting quantity upon the sweaty flesh wherever it could penetrate."[4] Latta's sardonic comment on the march was "The order of the day seems to be fight all day and march all night."[5]

Despite exhaustion, the column of the Sixth Corps pressed on, passing a wagon train loaded with groaning wounded, before turning off the Plank Road and onto the Catharpin Road toward the Piney Branch Church, which was about one and one half miles to the southwest. When the realization spread along the line that, rather than another retreat, the army was driving for the flank of its opponent, spontaneous cheers and singing erupted, demonstrating that despite all of the horrors of the Wilderness, the average Union soldier still preferred the opportunity to defeat the enemy over personal safety.[6]

Patriotism, however, was not a cure for suffering, only an incentive to persevere in spite of it: "We suffered much from weariness, but our men could not rest, and we were obliged to keep closed up, through all hours of that tedious night."[7] As the ordeal continued, the condition of the men deteriorated even further: "We were so overcome by weariness and lack of sleep that we in the ranks neither knew, nor cared much where we were."[8]

Grant had a reason for driving his men. Civil War armies were particularly road-bound, and the best roads to Richmond in the vicinity led through Spotsylvania Court House, a sleepy little county seat which consisted of barely more than the courthouse itself and an intersection of several roads. It was clear to the Union commander that if he were able to control the crossroads at Spotsylvania Court House, he would not only

---

[3]Hyde, p. 325.

[4]Bowen, *History of the Thirty Seventh Regiment Massachusetts Volunteers*, as cited in Trudeau, *Bloody Roads South*, p. 128.

[5]Latta diary.

[6]Matter, p. 71; Wheeler, *On Fields of Fury...*, pp. 153-154.

[7]Haines, p. 153.

[8]Winslow, p. 167.

secure the best roads south for his army, but would also deny the route to the Confederates, and thus gain his opponent's right flank. The first portion of the battle now known as Spotsylvania revolved around the contest for control of the roads to and around the Court House.

Before the critical intersection could be controlled, it had to be reached by troops capable of fighting; but by 10:00 a.m. the men of the Sixth Corps had just about reached the limits of their endurance. As the men shuffled up to the area of the Piney Branch Church, they were permitted to file off the road into a grove of trees for another break to rest and eat. While the men spread out looking for some shade, they could hear the distant sounds of battle as elements of the Fifth Corps, which had been dispatched to the same destination but by a more direct southerly route, began the contest for control of the roads to Spotsylvania Court House. Before having a chance to get settled, the soldiers were sent back onto the road; an order the men were probably too weary to even curse.[9]

After having traveled only about another mile, Wright was presented with an urgent request for assistance from Fifth Corps commander Warren, who desperately needed support for his left flank. Without waiting for formal orders, which were apparently not issued until 1:00 p.m., Wright led the First Division to lend the necessary support.[10]

Upon arrival at the Alsop farm, the infantrymen had to break off the road and struggle through a thick tangle to find the left end of the Union line. As the Grays marched onto the field they found "... the woods afire and bodies of Rebs and our men just killed and scorching."[11] Russell's men were immediately propelled into action. "... On emerging into an open field, [we] saw the 5th Corps boys driving the rebels before them up a hill. The enemy however were flanking them on the right and our brigade was thrown into position on the run and skirmishers advanced which checked the rebels in their onward career. They then opened with shell which did not hurt any one much."[12]

---

[9]Matter, pp. 73-74.

[10]Humphreys, vol. 6, p. 65.

[11]Howe, *Justice Oliver Wendell Holmes...*, as cited in Winslow, p. 169.

[12]Anderson, 1900, p. 4.

For the next several hours both sides paused to gather themselves for more fighting, while the Grays "... dug our usual entrenchments."[13] As previously noted, at 1:00 p.m. General Sedgwick received the following order: "You will proceed with your whole Corps to Spotsylvania Court House and join General Warren in a prompt attack on the enemy now concentrating there. Use every exertion to move with utmost dispatch." Sedgwick responded: "... a division and Brigade of Sixth Corps will commence on the left, to be followed up if any impression is made. There is a very thick tangle to get through before reaching them."[14] Grant was not entirely satisfied with the actual performance of the Sixth Corps commander, as opposed to his promise: "Sedgwick was slow in getting up for some reason -- probably unavoidable, because he was never at fault when serious work was to be done -- so that it was near night before the combined forces were ready to attack."[15]

At some uncertain point after arrival on the field, all of the other brigades from the First Division, excepting the Jersey Brigade, were sent to the right flank of the Fifth Corps to support the famous "Iron Brigade" in the general assault -- with Upton's men on the right, the Grays' brigade in the middle, and Colonel Nelson Cross' [Shaler was captured during the rout of his brigade on the evening of May 6] Fourth Brigade on the end. The attack, originally planned for earlier, was postponed until 6:30 due to the exhausted condition of the men.

When the designated hour arrived, the promised assault was commenced by the Jersey Brigade. The Jerseymen's attack was quickly repulsed after a brief advance, which seems to have ended serious aggressive action for the night.[16] The Philadelphians and their comrades never really got started, "We [Russell's Brigade] were, however, stopped by the rebels, who made demonstrations as if about to charge upon us, which would have been all we could have desired, as at that point our troops were massed column after column. They did not charge, however, although they drove our skirmishers inside of the

---

[13]Latta diary, 5/8/1864.
[14]O.R.-1-36-2-545.
[15]Grant, vol. 2, p. 214.
[16]Haines, pp. 156-159.

breastwork we built. This of course stopped our movement and thus ended the day of the 8th."[17]

At a different point on the line, and somewhat earlier in the day, a small drama was played out that would soon have significant consequences for the Grays and their fellow brigade members. The Second Division of the Sixth Corps was attempting to form its battle line when General Sedgwick observed that one brigade, under the command of Brigadier General Henry L. Eustis, was having a great deal of difficulty getting organized. "Uncle John" was so embarrassed by this performance, in plain view of both Grant and Meade, that he replaced Eustis with a staff officer. It was later reported that Eustis could not control his men because he was drunk.[18]

The Grays spent another dreadful night, subject to conditions seemingly designed to insure that none of the men obtained the rest that they desperately needed. "The sun was just set as [volley] after volley is discharged on our left ... incessantly after dark ... got a partial night's rest."[19] Even the staff officers of the Corps suffered, as Major Hyde vividly described: "The dismal night in the tangled forest, the hooting of owls, the embrace of the wood-tick, bang-bang from the picket line, then a dozen more, then the dreamless rejoice of utter fatigue."[20] It is safe to assume that the men on the line suffered much more from the problems described, and enjoyed much less of the "dreamless" sleep than did staff officer Hyde.

General Sedgwick was also denied a full night's sleep. At 3:00 a.m. on the morning of the ninth he was issued an order to attack the Rebel position in the morning, and at 6:30 a.m. he received another order to extend his pickets to the left.[21] At 8:00 a.m. the First Division, pursuant to the latter order, was back on the road, marching to the far left of the Union line, where it was reunited with the balance of the Sixth Corps at the scene of the previous day's fighting.[22]

---

[17]Anderson, 1900, p. 4.
[18]Matter, p. 90.
[19]Latta diary.
[20]Hyde, pp. 191-192.
[21]Matter, p. 90; O.R.-1-36-2-576.
[22]Latta diary, 5/9/1864.

About the time that the Grays were arriving on the left flank, Sedgwick went to the front line to supervise the positioning of his men and the construction of trenches and earthworks to protect them. While he was patrolling the area occupied by the 14th New Jersey and the 87th Pennsylvania [Sixth Corps, Third Division, First Brigade], a Southern sniper began firing into his vicinity. The general mocked a private who dodged at each crack of the sniper's rifle, assuring the man that, "They couldn't hit an elephant at this distance." Perhaps the private, unlike his commander, was aware that this sniper had already claimed nearly twenty Union casualties that morning, including Brigadier General William H. Morris, who until shot in the leg about a half hour earlier at nearly the same location, had been the commander of the Blue Crosses' First Brigade. In the next instant, the men around Sedgwick heard another crack of a rifle, and then the all-too-familiar sickening thud from a bullet hitting flesh, and saw their leader sink to the ground with blood spurting from a wound under his left eye. In moments, "Uncle John" Sedgwick was dead.[23]

The carnage-hardened veterans of the Sixth Corps were truly saddened by the death of their leader. The writings of his soldiers were replete with expressions of remorse for the man who was known to care for the lives and welfare of his troops. These comments, the first by the historian for the 5th Wisconsin, and the second by Joseph Downing of the 49th Pennsylvania, are fairly representative of the emotions expressed: "We could not believe for a long time that our kind old leader had fallen but soon it was confirmed that he was indeed gone." "This calamity threw a gloom over everyone. All felt that while the army and country had lost a valuable and able commander, every member of his gallant corps had lost a personal friend." [24]

War does not pause for the death of one man, regardless of how valued or esteemed; and within hours the chain of command had been reorganized, seemingly as if John Sedgwick had never existed. Horatio Wright succeeded to command of the Sixth Corps; Russell, who had been temporarily with the Second Division, replaced Wright as

---

[23]Haines, pp. 160-161; Winslow, pp. 174-175; Prowell, p. 134.

[24]Moore, *The Anderson Papers*, as cited in Slade, p. 165; Downing, *Pennsylvania at Gettysburg*, vol. 1, p. 295.

Brigadier General David A. Russell (at left)

(USAMHI-MOLLUS)

commander of the First Division; Henry L. Eustis, who had just been relieved for suspected drunkenness, was appointed commander of the Grays' Third Brigade; while Major Truefitt remained in command of the 119th, the role he had assumed after Lt. Colonel Clark was "Cashiered." Given the grind of the past week, the loss of the beloved General Sedgwick, and the arrival of a new brigade commander who even on his best day could not equal his predecessor David Russell, morale in the 119th on May 9 must have been abysmal, even if the men had not heard the allegation that Eustis was drunk while on duty the previous day.

To the men on the line, the new brigade commander may have created a nagging concern, but the issue of survival remained, as always, a pressing demand. As a matter of survival, both armies had by this point in the war evolved a routine of either moving, attacking, or digging in; and since neither of the former activities were in progress, the army spent most of that day earnestly doing the latter.

The only fighting for the Sixth Corps during the day resulted from contact between Union skirmishers pushed out to find the enemy, and the Confederate pickets which they located. Early in the afternoon,

Wright reported to headquarters that his pickets had advanced about a mile without making contact with the enemy, and he proposed to stop without pressing further ahead.[25] Later in the day, either as the result of prodding from above or as a result of better judgment on Wright's part, elements of the Sixth Corps renewed the effort to locate the enemy. Skirmishers from Rickett's Division advanced through a swamp, were hit by a severe crossfire, and fell back having learned by way of twenty casualties where the Southerners were located. Neill advanced his division's skirmishers about a quarter mile forward, and stopped after encountering feeble resistance. Russell, on the left of the Corps, detailed a reconnaissance in force under the command of a Captain Paine, who led his men to within sight of the road and a small force of Southerners, and then stopped without engaging the enemy.[26] Latta summarized his feelings about the ninth when he wrote: "The day insufferably warm, the fighting has continued so long that it has begun to be a regular business."[27]

It was the wounded, as opposed to the men on the line, who did most of the suffering that day. After an excruciating fifteen-mile ride, the Sixth Corps' casualties from the previous days' fighting, borne in hot and overcrowded ambulances, began to bounce and clatter into the town of Fredericksburg. Dr. Stevens, a Sixth Corps surgeon described the scene: "The process of unloading the wounded at once commenced. All the churches and other public buildings were first seized and filled.... The churches were filled first, then warehouses and stores, and then private houses, until the town was literally one immense hospital.... The surgeons were too much engaged in transferring the men from the wagons to the houses to find time that day to dress many wounds, and many an unfortunate soldier whose stump of an arm or leg had not been dressed since the first day of fighting became the victim of gangrene, which set in as the result of this unavoidable want of care.... No men, except Negroes and white men unfit for military duty, were left in town, but the women were bitter rebels. Some of them made fierce opposition

---

[25]O.R.-1-36-2-577.
[26]O.R-1-36-2-577, 578, 579.
[27]Latta Diary, 5/9/1864.

to the use of their houses as hospitals, but they were occupied notwithstanding their remonstrances."[28]

While the wounded continued to suffer, and the men at the front were again being denied a full night's rest, due to heavy cannonading and the repeated eruptions of musket volleys throughout the night, plans were being formulated at Headquarters for the next day's fighting. At 3:45 a.m. on the tenth, General Wright received orders indicating that aggressive action was expected from him that day, although no particular plan was included.[29] Between 6:30 and 7:30 a.m. the new Sixth Corps commander sent two notes to Headquarters, the first advising that pickets had pressed out and discovered the enemy across Alsop Road, and the latter confirming that two regiments, presumably from Eustis' Third Brigade, had spread to the left and connected with the line of Mott's Second Corps Division.[30] While the brass exchanged messages, the skirmishers of the 15th New Jersey drove forward and made the first direct contact with that portion of the Rebel position which would soon come to be known as the "Bloody Angle."[31]

The fact that there was such a formation to become known as the "Bloody Angle" was an unusual coincidence. It was an accepted principle during this war that defensive lines should be straight, or at worst, slightly bowed toward the enemy. Often, desirable topography was sacrificed to insure a uniform front, a notable exception being Union General Sickles' ill-fated decision to push his Third Corps out of line to higher ground at the Peach Orchard at Gettysburg. The point of this doctrine was to insure the defensive army maximum exposure of its guns to the attacking enemy, and to eliminate the disastrous effects that a breakthrough on one side of a salient could have on the rear of the opposite side.

The Confederates seemed to forget this concept as their forces spread, amoeba-like, toward the east. As Major General Edward Johnson's men of the Southern Second Corps moved into the area of the Harrison and McCoull farms in the dark, they discovered higher ground

---

[28]Stevens, p. 340.

[29]Humphreys, vol. 6, p. 81.

[30]Andrew A. Humphreys was a staff officer at Headquarters. O.R.-1-36-2-607, 608.

[31]Haines, p. 165.

located to the North. A decision was made to occupy the better ground in front, rather than maintain a straight line with the other Southern units, and so was born the salient which became known in general as the "Mule Shoe." Somewhat later, and for very good reasons, the northwest section of that salient would be branded with the name "Bloody Angle."

For the balance of the morning and into the early afternoon, everyone in the Sixth Corps had a problem, although of different types. For most of the blue-coated soldiers on the front line, the primary concern remained how to avoid death or dismemberment from the continuous barrage of minie balls, case shot, shells, and canister thrown at them from the Confederate lines.[32] For the Grays in particular, Abraham Lincoln made a decision that day that would soon create a problem of sorts for the entire Regiment. Ever since his dismissal from the service in April, Gideon Clark had been writing letters, meeting with people, and generally pulling any string available to him to overturn the court's decision which cashiered him. Apparently Clark was able to obtain an opinion from the judge advocate, allegedly endorsed by General Russell, that he ought to be reinstated. On May 10, Clark found himself in the White House awaiting a formal introduction to the President, which was to be supplied by a Judge Kelly. For three hours the nervous former officer paced the hall waiting for the tardy judge until, when he could stand the tension no longer, Clark went to the President's office and knocked on the door.

President Lincoln invited Clark into his office, and upon learning of the purpose of the visit dispatched his secretary to retrieve Clark's file. According to Clark, when the file arrived, the President read the report of the judge advocate in a "loud voice," went immediately to his desk, and signed an order removing the bar to Clark's renewed service in the Union army. Clark quickly took the order and mailed it to the office of Pennsylvania's Governor Curtin; and two days later Clark's commission was reinstated, with orders sending him south to resume command of the 119th.[33] It would take a few days after the executive orders were issued for Clark to be able to rejoin the Regiment. When he did, the Grays found themselves in the uncomfortable position of

---

[32]O.R.-1-36-1-673.

[33]National Archives, Gideon Clark Military Records; Clark, Pennsylvania Archives.

having a commander whose leadership was actively opposed by a large majority of the other officers of the Regiment, and with both a regimental and brigade commander who had faced allegations of intoxication in the face of the enemy.

General Wright also had a problem that morning. He had just received another order from Headquarters directing him to attack the enemy at 5:00 p.m., in conjunction with Mott's Second Corps division to his left; but again, the details of how to crack the formidable Rebel emplacements in his front were omitted, leaving the matter to Wright's discretion.[34] Perhaps hoping to recapture the lightning unleashed at Rappahannock Station, Wright delegated the task of working out the specifics to General Russell and the officers of his First Division.

It is not clear whether engineering officer Lieutenant Ranald S. McKenzie was directed by Russell to scout the Southern lines, or whether he performed the reconnaissance on his own initiative. In any case, he brought back information which, in the hands of a true warrior such as Russell, supplied the seed from which would grow one of the most innovative battle plans of the entire war. First, McKenzie described to Russell the "Entrenchment held by Dole in open ground, two hundred yards from pine woods with abatis in front and traverses at intervals ..."[35] More intriguing, he described a trail that led through the pine woods to a point in front of those lines, and suggested that it would be possible to spirit a large body of infantry close to the Rebel lines without detection.

After considering the possibilities implicit in launching an assault where the attackers would only be exposed to slaughter while covering a mere two hundred yards after discovery, Russell had his plan, and soon he would have his leader. Since Colonel Ellmaker had resigned in the winter, there were only two ranking officers who had participated to a significant degree in the victory at Rappahannock Station -- General Russell himself, and his Second Brigade commander Emory Upton. Given that Upton was already considered an aggressive leader whose star was on the rise, the decision to place him in direct command of the offensive was probably an easy one for Russell.

---

[34]O.R.-1-36-2-609.

[35]Humphreys, vol. 6, p. 83.

Together, the two men formulated an inspired tactical plan of attack. The frequently fatal weakness in the normal method of attack was that there was a tendency on the part of the men in the first line of battle to stop advancing and to begin a gun fight as soon as they began taking hits, a generally unsuccessful maneuver given that the defenders were often behind earthen emplacements while the attackers were out in the open. Further, the thin lines separated by yards did not seem to have much momentum because the rear lines usually stopped as soon as the forward line began the gun fight. So, rather than send the infantry against the position in long thin lines, the two men decided that the Union forces would be deployed in a formation even more densely compacted than at Rappahannock Station. Under normal conditions such a plan would have been suicidal, with canister from the defenders' artillery ripping huge holes in such a formation, each solid shot claiming dozens rather than one or two victims, and even the poorest riflemen being able to hit a victim. Here, however, Russell and Upton were confident that with the element of surprise, their men could cross the short open space between the woods and the emplacements before too much of such carnage could be inflicted.

After personally viewing the planned point of attack, which he described as "... at an angle of the enemy's works near the Scott House, about a half mile to the left of the Spotsylvania Road. His entrenchments were of a formidable character with abatis in front and surrounded by heavy logs, underneath which were loop-holes for musketry ...", Upton probably realized that the mission was not for the fainthearted. Such a reaction would have been reinforced by the orders delivered to him by a staff officer, which purportedly included the following warning: "'Upton you are to lead those men upon the enemy's works this afternoon, and if you do not carry them you are not expected to come back, but if you carry them ... you will get your stars.'"[36] Undoubtedly to his relief, the young commander of the Second Brigade was also presented with a list of the twelve most resolute regiments in the First and Second Divisions of the Sixth Corps which were to participate in the assault, including the Grays and the rest of Russell's (now Eustis') former brigade. Supposedly Upton's response after he had a chance to

---

[36]O.R.-1-36-1-667; Best, pp. 135-136.

Colonel Peter C. Ellmaker's 1st Regiment Hardee hat

(1st Regiment / 103rd Engineer Museum)

Colonel Ellmaker's Dress Epaulettes

(1st Regiment / 103rd Engineer Museum)

1st Regiment Gray Reserve Drum

(1st Regiment / 103rd Engineer Museum)

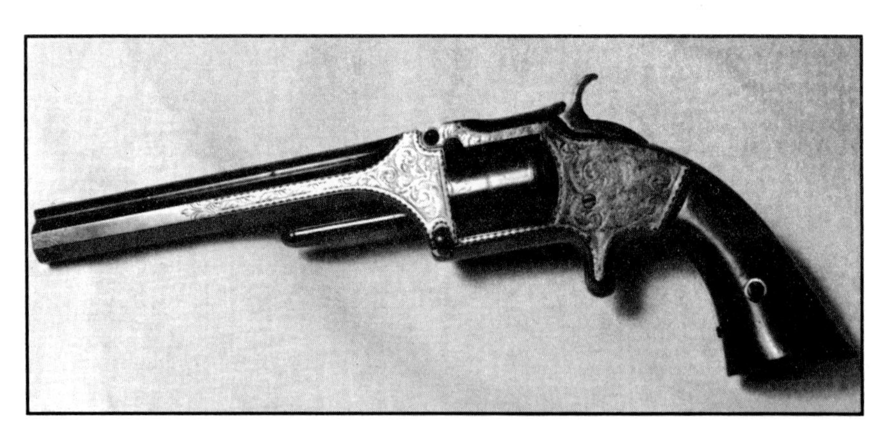

Smith & Wesson Model #2 - presented to
1st Lieutenant Thomas Morris - Feb. 10, 1865

Kepi - Private J. H. Wiedersheim, 119th P.V.

(Courtesy - Don Troiani Collection)

Kepi - Surgeon Philip Leidy, 119th P.V.

(Courtesy - The Civil War Library Museum, Philadelphia, Pa.)

Spotsylvania Court House - May 10, 1864

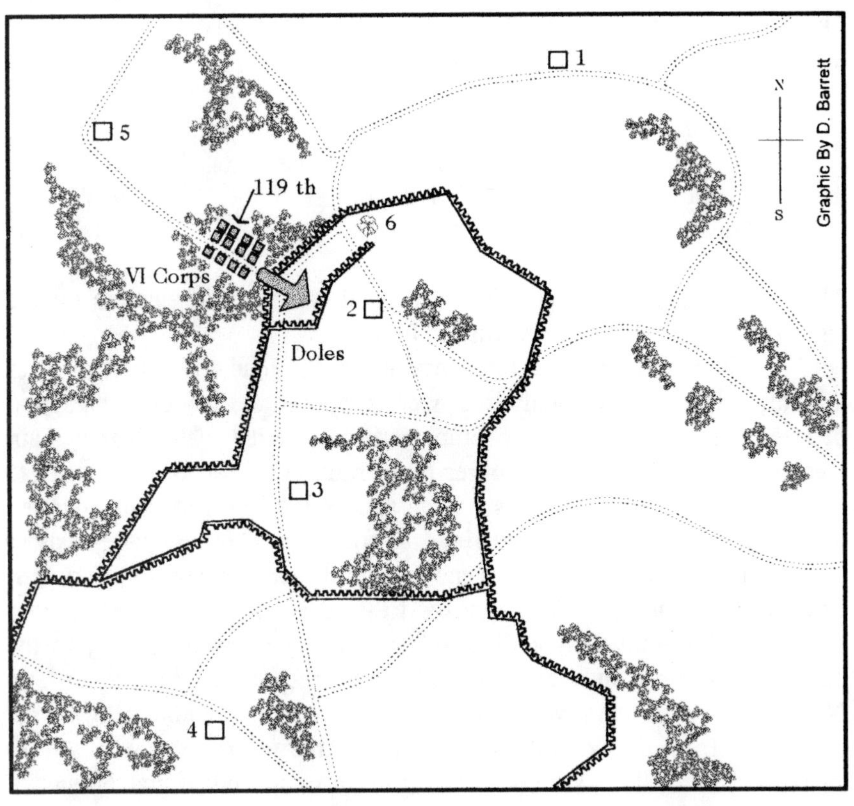

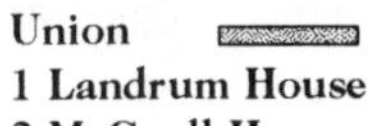

review the list of regiments was, "'... I'll carry those works. They cannot repulse those regiments.'"[37]

The instructions given to the regimental commanders were extremely precise. First, the peculiar formation for the regiments was outlined, requiring each line to be at an interval of only ten feet from the line in front. The planned alignment is illustrated here, with the top of the page corresponding to the Confederate position:

5th Maine	96th Pa.	121st N.Y.
5th Wis.	6th Maine	49th Pa.
119th Pa.	77th N.Y.	43rd N.Y.
6th Vt.	5th Vt.	2nd Vt.

The twelve regiments were to be grouped with four regiments on the right of the path and the rest on the left.[38]

The men in the first line were ordered to load and cap their rifles and, after piercing the enemy line, were supposed to turn to the right and proceed against an artillery emplacement located behind the main trenches. The troops in the other three ranks were all ordered only to load, but not cap, their pieces. Each successive line was also assigned a particular role. The second line, all from the Third Brigade, was to stop after clearing the enemy trenches and direct a steady fire forward. The 119th and its line was supposed to lie down at the enemy trenches and await developments, while the last line was to advance only to the edge of the trees and remain prepared to respond to further orders. Next, "All the officers were instructed to repeat the command 'forward' constantly from the commencement of the charge until the works were carried."[39] Finally, perhaps in recognition of the beneficial effects of the twenty-pounders at Rappahannock Station, the battle plan also included arrangements for a heavy battery to be positioned so as to enfilade the Confederate line and, at exactly 5:00 p.m., to unleash a

---

[37]Best, p. 136.
[38]O.R.-1-36-1-667.
[39]O.R.-1-36-1-667; Matter, pp. 137, 156-158.

ten-minute barrage. The last blast from the artillery was to be the signal to launch the onslaught from the woods.[40]

Late in the afternoon, the participating troops were led down the path in column of fours, while each man concentrated on avoiding a misstep that might alert the enemy to the presence of the Union forces and thereby elicit a storm of death. Anxiety must have been especially high, since it is almost certain that few, if any, of the men in the ranks had seen the position that was their destination, and they had probably heard precious few of the details of the battle plan other than those specific to their own regiment.

A contingent of Truefitt's men had previously been subjected to a rather uncomfortable exploration of the woods through which the entire Regiment was then passing to reach the jump-off point. "About 3 a.m., of May 10, companies D and G [of the 49th Pennsylvania] ... with two companies from the One hundred and nineteenth Pennsylvania Volunteers, all under command of Captain Landell [commander of company I, 119th Pa.], were sent forward as skirmishers into the dense woods. Advanced about three hundred yards and found a strong line of skirmishers of the enemy. We advanced and drove them back on their supports and then back on their line of battle in entrenchments. In this advance we reached a cart road [the same cart road to be used to reach the jump-off point] at which we stopped, still under cover of about seventy-five yards of timber with piles of fence rails for barricades. At this point the officer commanding the right of

Captain Edwin A. Landell

(USAMHI-MOLLUS)

[40]Humphreys, vol. 6, p. 84.

the line, ordered the men to hold this road and to protect themselves behind trees, rail piles, etc. At this moment a field officer, a lieutenant-colonel, rode along and directed the line to advance to the edge of the woods. The lieutenant with his men knowing the attempt would result in certain defeat obeyed the order and moved forward about forty yards and received a galling fire from a line of battle entrenched. The enemy then poured out against us and we were driven back two hundred and fifty or three hundred yards into the woods fighting as we went. We then halted, faced about, and again moved forward under a terrible fire, losing men from our weak line at every step. We fought our way back to the cart road and rail piles at which point we stopped and held that line."[41]

For unknown reasons, the jump-off time was postponed to 6:00 p.m.; but this change was not initially made known to the officers commanding the batteries, and as a result, the barrage commenced promptly at 5:00, but continued significantly longer than originally planned. The exact time that the Federals reached the edge of the pine forest and began to mass in formation is unclear, but it is reasonable to assume that the jump-off time was delayed because the necessary preparations required more time than was originally anticipated. The miscommunication between the infantry and the artillery may have provided an unexpected but welcome dividend, helping to drown out the unavoidable sounds of four or five thousand men moving about in the woods.

According to Colonel Beckwith, who was with the 121st New York stationed in the front line, at some point either prior to, or during the organization of the assault phalanx, the 65th New York, acting as skirmishers, drove the Confederate pickets back into the Southern emplacements. As the Federals took their designated positions, their skirmishers maintained a steady musket fire presumably intended both to keep the Butternuts below the works and also to help mask the activity in the woods.[42] Although Private Kaiser of the 96th Pennsylvania did not mention the Federal skirmishers, he did recall the Confederates "...peppering away at us while the balance of the troops were getting

---

[41]Downing, *Pennsylvania at Gettysburg*, vol. 1, p. 295.
[42]Best, p. 128.

into line."[43] The waiting Yankees undoubtedly suffered a few casualties from the desultory Southern fire, but nothing like the carnage that would have been inflicted had the defenders sensed the true nature of the threat lurking in the woods, and unleashed a storm of shells and canister into the vulnerable formation. The deception which was so successful at Rappahannock Station, apparently also fooled a different group of Butternuts.

At about 6:20 p.m., the last regiment hustled into its position in the rear, while, about fifty feet back from the edge of the woods, the front line waited, time hanging as if the clocks had stopped. When the last man finally took his place, the order came to advance; and, undoubtedly in concert with most of the grim-faced Federals, Beckwith "... felt my gorge rise, and my stomach and intestines shrink together in a knot, and a thousand things rushed through my mind."[44] Next, "... the lines rose, moved noiselessly to the edge of the wood, and then, with a wild cheer and faces averted, rushed for the works. Through a terrible front and flank fire the column advanced ..." while "... Nearly half of our [front] line was shot down before we reached the pits."[45]

Private Westbrook of the 49th Pennsylvania, whose regiment suffered the highest number of casualties in the battle, shared the opinion that the fire inflicted upon the Union phalanx during the rush toward the enemy was ferocious. "Quick as lightning a sheet of flame burst from the rebel line, and the leaden hail swept the ground over which the column was advancing, while the canister from the artillery came crashing through our ranks at every step."[46]

The flank fire was particularly damaging on the Grays' left side of the formation. The musket work of the Southerners, perhaps delivered by men from Walker's Virginia Brigade, was sufficiently accurate to cause the entire left side of the formation to drift to the right, causing some crowding toward the center of the formation.[47] True to orders, the veterans neither broke from the drive toward the enemy line nor stopped to return the fire.

---

[43]Keiser diary, 5/10/1864.
[44]Best, p. 129.
[45]O.R.-1-36-1-668; Keiser diary.
[46]Westbrook, p. 191.
[47]Matter, p. 162.

George Ash

(USAMHI)

In probably less than a minute, the front line reached the enemy works. "Here occurred a deadly hand-to-hand conflict. The enemy sitting in their pits with pieces upright, loaded, and with bayonets fixed, ready to impale the first who should leap over, absolutely refused to yield the ground. The first of our men who tried to surmount the works fell pierced through the head by musket-balls. Others, seeing the fate of their comrades, held their pieces at arms length and fired downward, while others, poising their pieces vertically, hurled them down upon their enemy, pinning them to the ground. Lieutenant Johnston, of the One hundred and Twenty First New York, received a bayonet wound through the thigh. Private O'Donnell, Ninety-sixth Pennsylvania Volunteers, was pinned to the parapet, but was rescued by his comrades. A private of the Fifth Maine, having bayoneted a rebel, was fired at by the captain, who, missing his aim, in turn shared the same fate. The brave man fell by a shot from the rebel lieutenant. The struggle lasted but a few seconds. Numbers prevailed, and, like a resistless wave, the column poured over the works, quickly putting hors de combat [out of combat] those who resisted, and sending to the rear those who surrendered. Pressing forward and expanding to the right and left, the second line of entrenchments, its line of battle, and the battery fell into our hands. The column of assault had accomplished its task. The enemy's lines were completely broken ..."[48] The battle, however, had just begun.

The advancing Federals rushed the next line of defense to the right of the column, a thinly manned trench-line, protected primarily by

[48]O.R.-1-36-1-668, Upton.

a battery of guns belonging to the Richmond Howitzers. The guns were taken by the men of the 49th Pennsylvania, but the captors were unable to use the pieces against the fleeing Rebels, because the latter had the forethought to take the gun implements along with them when they fled. In the center, the attackers drove toward the McCoull House directly to the east of the breakthrough, while the rest of the Federals, apparently including the 119th, commenced an enfilading fire toward the trenches to the left, from where they had just received such punishment themselves.[49]

Had the battle continued to progress as planned, at this point Mott's Division would have come crashing into the Southern lines to the left of the breakthrough, the defense would have collapsed, and the defenders would have fled in confusion. Instead, for reasons not entirely clear, the cup slipped, leaving General Grant entirely disgusted and the attackers without support on either flank. "[Brigadier General Gershom] Mott was ordered to his [Upton's] assistance but failed utterly ... Upton had gained an important advantage, but a lack in others of the spirit and dash possessed by him lost it to us."[50] In fairness to Mott, though, he had already given notice that he could only provide about 1,500 men for the effort; and those men did launch an attack, but met the usual fate of a thin line attacking emplacements filled with alert defenders, albeit defenders under fire.

General Lee, perceiving the threat to his entire line, quickly responded to the crisis and organized a counterattack. Soon the roles were reversed and the aggressors became the defenders, inexorably pressed back by the combined effects of Confederate rifles and cannon. "Re-enforcement arriving to the enemy, our front and both flanks were assailed. The impulsion of the charge being lost, nothing remained but to hold the ground. I [soon-to-be General Upton] accordingly directed the officers to form their men outside the works and open fire, and then rode back over the field to bring forward the Vermonters in the fourth line, but they had already mingled in the contest ..."[51]

---

[49]Matter, pp. 160-163; Mundy, pp. 196-197.
[50]Grant, vol. 2, p. 224.
[51]O.R-1-36-1-668.

The Grays found themselves clustered on the front side of the enemy works, involved in a bitter firefight. Any pretense of organization was gone. Each man fought on his own account, frantically pouring powder and ramming bullets down the barrel of his musket while trying to keep below the barricade, then rising and hurriedly searching for a target, or perhaps not, and firing as fast as possible in order to get back down before being found by an enemy ball. The noise was deafening -- a mixture of musket and artillery fire, screams, curses, the whine of projectiles passing overhead, and the constant drumbeat of minie and canister balls thudding into blue-coated warriors or the logs in front of them.

It was possibly during this phase of the battle that the Confederates exacted revenge upon the Grays' Sergeant Laurens for turning his back on his home state of South Carolina and fighting for the Union. The Southerner-turned-Yankee received a wound which would prove mortal before the day was ended.

The gun fight continued hotly for almost an hour, until darkness began to cover the field. At that point, Upton and Russell conferred at the edge of the woods and concluded that, since no support was apparently going to be forthcoming from the left, the best maneuver was to fall back. As soon as it was dark enough to cover the movement, the Federals were withdrawn from the battle line with some of the wounded, but probably without most of their dead.[52]

The historian for Doles' Confederate Brigade related a curious and touching event which occurred after the Union withdrawal was completed: "... a Confederate band moved up to an elevated position on the line and played 'Nearer my God to thee.' The sound of this beautiful piece of music had scarcely died away when a Yankee band over the line gave us the 'Dead March.' This was followed by the Confederate band playing 'Bonnie Blue Flag.' As the last notes were wafted out on the crisp night-air a grand old-style rebel yell went up. The Yankee band then played 'The Star-Spangled Banner,' and ... it seemed by the response yell, that every man in the Army of the Potomac was awake and listening to the music. The Confederate band then rendered 'Home,

[52]O.R.-1-35-1-668.

Sweet Home,' when a united yell went up in concert from the men on both sides."[53]

In a sad postscript to the battle, Westbrook of the 49th Pennsylvania described the fate of some of the Union wounded left behind the re-established Confederate line. "Our wounded were left on the field eleven days without having their wounds attended to ... They lived eleven days on three days rations, and to get water they would scoop a hole in the ground, then spread their gum blankets out and when it rained, water ... was scooped out of the blankets into canteens. On the eleventh day they were put into wagons and started for Richmond."[54]

Those two hours on May 10 were costly for the 119th. Latta put the Grays' casualties at two commissioned officers and eighty-four enlisted men.[55] According to Bates, the unit suffered thirty-two deaths -- twenty-two either outright or as a result of wounds received; eight missing in action and presumably killed; and two men who were captured and died in captivity. Of that grim harvest, eleven were non-commissioned officers, a particularly disproportionate number claimed for no apparent reason. This brief battle took the lives of more men of the Regiment than would be claimed by any other battle during the war; and, contrary to the normal toll where the number of wounded usually far surpassed the dead, the Grays suffered only

Unidentified 119th Sergeant

(courtesy K. Turner collection)

---

[53]As cited in Trudeau, *Bloody Roads South*, pp. 163-164.

[54]Westbrook, p. 192.

[55]Latta diary. Contemporaneous reports of casualties seem to have been uniformly higher than official tallies taken later, perhaps because minor wounds were included at the time but were not severe enough to be recorded on the muster rolls.

twenty wounded and one other man captured, perhaps because many of the wounded were killed by stray bullets as they lay on either side of the contested works. As for the entire Sixth Corps, the casualty total was approximately a thousand, about equal to the losses (including captured) suffered by their opponents. Perhaps even more depressing for the Federals than the number of casualties, was the fact that they had witnessed a rare opportunity to inflict a crushing defeat on General Lee and his army evaporate before their eyes.

12

SPOTSYLVANIA: THE "BLOODY ANGLE"

In retrospect, it would seem that fairness would have required some benefit to accrue to the Greek Crosses for coming within an eyelash of shattering the Confederate line. Unfortunately, the Grays' only reward on May 11 was to be given the opportunity, along with the rest of the Third Brigade, to spend the day marching about from one point to another, to counter either real or imagined moves by the enemy.[1] While portions of the Sixth Corps were on the move, and the balance of its men remained watchful in their emplacements, General Wright spent much of his day scouting the landscape and the enemy defenses in his sector.[2] The only real excitement during the day occurred when a number of Confederate snipers infiltrated behind Sixth Corps' lines, fired on White and Blue Crosses from the rear for a short time, and then escaped.[3]

While the Union army paused, its commanders pondered the next move to try to wrest control of the roads leading to Spotsylvania from the grasp of Robert E. Lee. Although Grant's battlefield tactics often showed the subtlety and ingenuity of a mace, he usually recognized a good idea when he saw one; and the maneuver arranged by Russell and Upton the previous day was clearly good. Not surprisingly, Grant decided to adopt that strategy, but with the modification that the attack, scheduled for dawn the next morning, would be made by the entire

---

[1]O.R.-1-36-1-673.

[2]Humphreys, vol. 6, p. 96.

[3]Matter, p. 171.

Second Corps in a massive condensed attack against the point of the "Mule Shoe," about a quarter of a mile north of the battle which took place on the tenth.

In the evening, the Grays and their comrades in Russell's First Division received mixed signals as to what was in store for them in the morning. Early in the evening, Rickett's Division relieved both Russell's and Neill's men from duty on the front line, so that the latter divisions could retire a short distance to the rear for a better night's rest. Later, however, any optimism generated by the move to the rear was squelched when the Grays' division received additional orders to be prepared to march by numerical order of brigades at 3:30 a.m. on the twelfth, and to draw two days' rations and ammunition, a sure sign of an impending battle.[4] Normally, the issuance of rations and cartridges provoked tightened stomachs and sent pulses racing; but it is likely that those exhausted and battle-numbed men had little if any reaction to the new order, and were probably much more preoccupied by the discomfort of the driving rainstorm that lashed them during most of the night, than with fears about the coming encounter.

Always justifiably concerned about the possibility of a flank attack, General Meade sent the Sixth Corps' First Division marching off before dawn toward the far right flank of the army, leaving behind the unmistakable sounds of battle breaking out in the area which the division had just vacated. While the Grays were moving to the right and assuming a blocking position against a flank attack, the Second Corps' assault initially achieved stunning results and drove deep into the "Mule Shoe," while capturing large numbers of Confederates. After several hours of intense fighting, however, like the attack two days earlier, the initial breakthrough was blunted and Southern counterattacks had regained most of the captured ground, driving the Federals back to the exterior of the Southern works. Probably because the loss of the breakthrough was more probable than a flank attack, at 7:00 a.m. the Grays' First Division was ordered to hustle back to its original position, where it arrived at about 9:30 a.m.[5]

---

[4]O.R.-1-36-2-642; Matter, p. 184.
[5]Matter, pp. 208, 217.

Spotsylvania Court House - May 12, 1864

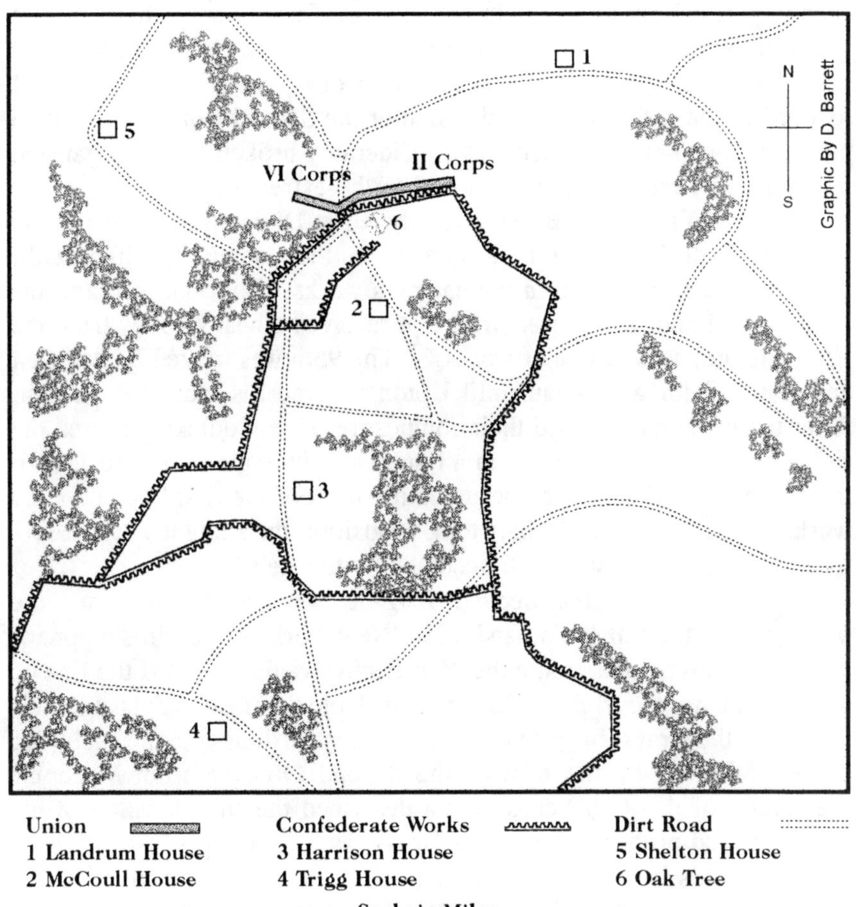

Union
1 Landrum House
2 McCoull House

Confederate Works
3 Harrison House
4 Trigg House

Dirt Road
5 Shelton House
6 Oak Tree

Scale in Miles
0 1

As Truefitt's men and the rest of the First Division marched toward the billows of white gunsmoke which loomed over the horizon, the sounds of a horrendous struggle grew progressively louder until, when almost at the front, the men were engulfed by a deafening roar. Then, "... the Second Corps was found to be hotly engaged with the enemy, particularly on the right and General Russell was ordered to put in his division here as it seemed to be required. The Second and Third Brigades [of the First Division, Sixth Corps] were at once moved forward to the right of Mott's division of the Second Corps, relieving a part of this command, which was considerably broken and disorganized ... while the first Brigade was moved to the extreme right..."[6]

Upton's Second Brigade led the First Division into the inferno with his 95th Pennsylvania Regiment in the vanguard, "[the 95th] reached an elevated point in the enemy's works, about 600 yards to the right of the Landrum House, [where] it received a heavy volley from the [Confederate] second line of works."[7] The 95th was rocked by the blast and wavered for a moment until Upton ordered his men to lie down. After the men had regained their composure, Upton quickly ordered the right-hand companies to form in a line at a right angle to the left half of the regiment, which by then occupied the front of the first line of enemy works. The refused right half took a position on a slight knoll facing trenches to the Southwest still occupied by the Rebels.

The rest of the Second Brigade was rapidly fed into the maelstrom -- the 5th Maine and 121st New York formed in support of the 95th Pennsylvania, while the 96th Pennsylvania extended the line of the brigade to the right. As soon as Upton's men had taken their positions, the Grays' brigade was the next sent rushing into the cauldron, closely followed by the men of the Second Division from Vermont. Westbrook of the 49th Pennsylvania described the final location of his regiment, and probably that of the Grays, as "... laying in a field about 60 or 70 yards in front of the rebel works ... directly in front of where the tree was shot off ..."[8] (The tree referred to was a 24-inch diameter

---

[6]O.R.-1-36-1-661, Daulton.
[7]O.R.-1-36-1-669, Upton.
[8]Westbrook, p. 198.

oak which was gnawed off at its base by musket fire and canister during the battle.)

It has proven to be nearly impossible to determine the exact location of many of the regiments that fought at the "Bloody Angle," due to the confused nature of the battle itself; the fact that many of the officers who fought there died before issuing reports, General Russell and Major Truefitt being the most pertinent examples; and perhaps because the participants were too exhausted or preoccupied to take note of their exact positions. In any case, there are other versions somewhat at odds with the account referenced above, which was taken from Upton's report. One has the order from left to right as the Jersey Brigade, then Upton's men, with the Grays' brigade slightly to the right and rear of Upton's.[9] Another has the initial front line occupied by Edward's [Sixth Corps, Second Div.], Upton's, Lewis A Grant's [Sixth Corps, Second Div.], and McAllister's [Second Corps, Fourth Div.] brigades in front, and with Wheaton's [Sixth Corps, Second Div.], Bidwell's [Sixth Corps, Second Div.], Eustis's [Grays'], and the Excelsior [Second Corps, Fourth Div.] brigades 50 to 100 yards to the rear. Finally, Colonel Beckwith maintained that the 119th was on the front line, almost next to his 121st New York of Upton's Brigade.[10]

Regardless of the original alignment, all of the soldiers of the Sixth Corps, including those in the 119th, were soon drawn into the small corner of hell now known as the "Bloody Angle." What a horrendous scene confronted the Grays from the crest of the small knoll which they occupied, a short distance from the Confederate emplacements. On the left flank the Philadelphians could dimly see, through the rain and gunsmoke, soldiers of the Sixth and Second Corps on the front side of the Rebel works, standing or crouching among, and sometimes upon, the corpses of fallen comrades. Directly to the front were the emplacements of the enemy, wreathed in smoke, and punctuated by death-dispensing muzzle flashes from hundreds of muskets. Between those enemy trenches and the knoll could be seen the ghostly outline of several abandoned Union cannons; the dark, still forms of the dead; and the crawling or writhing wounded, who added a peculiar liquid aspect to

---

[9]Slade, p. 170.
[10]Matter, p. 248; Best, p. 145.

the field.[11] Only short glimpses were permitted to those who hoped to survive, but a glimpse was more than enough. As Private Anderson of the 5th Wisconsin, only yards from the position of the 119th, described the scene: "We who had been inured for nearly three years to the horror of war, saw new horror here ..."[12]

Just as on the tenth, the Grays were again embroiled in a furious gunfight -- this time lying on swampy ground behind empty cartridge boxes filled with mud; struggling to load while lying on their backs with bullets whistling only inches above their noses, then rolling over and firing from the prone position; or rising amidst the hail of deadly missiles and firing at the enemy trenches as quickly as possible.[13] Most of the men would each fire about 200 rounds during the next twelve hours that they would remain under fire.[14] Private Keiser reported that he fired so many rounds that his right arm was rendered "... almost useless tonight from the re-bound of my rifle."[15]

Francis (Pharos) Brown

(USAMHI)

If it is possible to be fortunate under such circumstances, then the Grays were fortunate to be on be on their knoll rather than along the front of the enemy works with their comrades-in-arms. All shared in the fear, the choking thirst, the cries from wounded and dying comrades, the din, the rain, the mud, and the crushing fatigue; but the men fighting up against the Rebel

[11]Westbrook, p. 198; Matter, pp. 218-219, 248.
[12]Moore, *The Anderson Papers*, as cited in Slade, p. 173.
[13]Best, p. 146.
[14]Latta diary.
[15]Keiser diary.

works faced all of that and worse. "It was not only a desperate struggle but it was literally a hand-to-hand fight. Nothing but the piled up logs or breastworks separated the combatants. Our men would reach over the logs and fire into the faces of the enemy [and the enemy would do likewise], would stab over with their bayonets; [some even threw their bayoneted rifles over the top like javelins] many were shot and stabbed through the crevices and holes between the logs; men mounted the works, and with muskets rapidly handed them, kept up a continuous fire until they were shot down, when others would take their place and continue the deadly work ... Several times during the day the rebels would show a white flag about the works and when our fire slackened jump over and surrender, and others were crowded down into their places ... they [the dead at the Bloody Lane at Antietam] were not piled up several deep and their flesh was not so torn and mangled as at the Angle."[16]

As the horror dragged on hour after hour, the last vestiges of civilized behavior were seared away from the combatants, so that eventually not even a white flag of surrender was honored. "Occasionally a lull would occur in the firing for a little time, and many Rebels, taking advantage of it, would raise a white flag and surrender themselves as prisoners. An incident of this kind would be followed by a burst of firing again, usually better directed than the preceding one, and so we stopped the white flag business, the last squad of surrendering Rebels, about thirty of them, getting the fire of both sides, nearly all being shot."[17] It may be assumed that since the Grays were practically alongside Beckwith's 121st New York, that some of them joined in that particular atrocity.

The suffering and the barbarity were shared equally between the blue and the butternut on that terrible day. A Georgia soldier recorded that "This battle was the worst slaughter I ever saw ... Such groans! such cries! and such pitiful calls for water and other assistance; but none could go to them, for the enemy would not let us go and we would not let them go." South Carolina also shared in the misery: "The sight we

---

[16]Humphreys, vol. 6, p. 99, quoting Brig. Gen. Lewis A. Grant of the Vermont Brigade, Sixth Corps, 2nd Division.

[17]Best, p. 146.

encountered was not calculated to encourage us. The trenches dug on the inner side were almost filled with water. Dead men lay on the surface of the ground and in the pools of water. The wounded bled and groaned, stretched and huddled in every attitude of pain. The water was crimsoned with blood. Abandoned knapsacks, guns, and accoutrements, with ammunition boxes, were scattered all around. In the rear, disabled caissons stood, and limbers of guns. The rain poured heavily, and an incessant fire was kept upon us.... "[18]

The antagonists were trapped in the vortex of a battle that was worse than any nightmare: "So fierce was the incessant shower of bullets that the bodies of the dead were riddled ... At every assault and every repulse new bodies fell on the heaps of the slain, and over the filled ditches the living fought on the corpses of the fallen. The wounded were covered by the killed, and expired under piles of their comrades."[19] "The dead, dying and wounded are lying literally in heaps, hideous to look at. The writhing of the wounded and dying who lay beneath the dead bodies, moved the whole mass ..."[20]

Lee launched five counterattacks during the day, each one adding to the mass of human misery, but none adequate to break the stalemate or end the fighting which continued in unabated fury throughout the afternoon and into the evening. To Captain Rhodes, "It seemed the day would never pass away," a sentiment which was undoubtedly shared up and down the line of Philadelphians.[21] The combatants probably also shared in bitter disappointment that this fight, unlike most Civil War battles, did not end with the setting of the sun, but rather continued on in the darkness with intensified suffering on both sides: "To add to the horrors of the day it rained in torrents. All night the battle raged, and we had to lay there. Sleep would over power us when we were not firing ... May God save me from another such scene ..."[22]

Not every soldier in blue shared in the horror and heroism at the Angle, as evidenced by this report concerning a Second Corps hospital,

---

[18]As cited in *Wheeler, On Fields of Fury...*, p. 209.

[19]Haines, pp. 177-178.

[20]Roback, Henry, *The Veteran Volunteers of Herkimer and Otsego Counties*, as cited in Trudeau, *Bloody Roads South*, p. 184.

[21]Rhodes, p. 147.

[22]Rhodes, pp. 148-149.

which sadly was probably similar to the scene at the hospital serving the wounded of the 119th: "A large number of skulkers concealed themselves in the forests or bivouacked near the hospitals, and feigned wounds by binding up their heads and arms in bloodstained bandages, or limped, with the assistance of a crutch, in apparent pain ... The army thieves who lurked in the rear ... grasped with their remorseless hands the valuables, clothing, and rations of the unwary wounded soldiers, [also] the flattened bullets that had been retained as priceless relics by those from whom they were extracted, and the invaluable swords which officers had borne with honor through scenes of carnage. In the tent to which, with twenty others, I was assigned, a member of the regiment was robbed of everything, including an old knife and a diary, while he was unconscious on account of a ball which entered his head; and another person was plundered in a similar style before he had recovered from the effect of the ether which had been administered when his arm was amputated."[23]

It is not clear when, or even if, the Grays were finally relieved and allowed to fall back from the firing line, so as to spare other Philadelphians from delivery into the tender care of the denizens lurking around the division hospital. Upton's Brigade withdrew around 5:30 p.m.[24] and Eustis' Brigade may have followed soon thereafter. Or, the Third Brigade may have remained until around 9:30 or 10:30 p.m., as the reference to twelve hours of continuous fighting in the Latta diary would imply. Curiously, Upton's report contains the following, which seems to contradict that portion of his report previously referenced: "At the point where our line diverged from the works, the opposing line came in contact, but neither would give ground and for eighteen hours raged the most sanguinary conflict of the war."[25] In staff officer Daulton's report on behalf of the First Division, he reported that "The position was held ... til about 3:00 a.m. on the 13th ...," and presumably he meant held by the First Division.[26] Whenever the men of the 119th were permitted to pull back, each probably collapsed into the mud

---

[23]Blake, *Three Years in the Army of the Potomac*, as cited in Wheeler, *On Fields of Fury...*, pp. 211-212.

[24]O.R.-1-36-1-669.

[25]O.R.-1-36-1-669.

[26]O.R.-1-36-1-661.

and slept on whatever spot was occupied when the order to halt was finally given. It is doubtful that any of the Grays were awake to hear the last few shots as the fighting finally dwindled out and died, sometime around 3:00 a.m. on the following morning, when the Confederates withdrew to their new defensive line across the base of the salient.

After sunrise, the men were drawn to the scene of the previous day's horror, in search of wounded or dead comrades, and perhaps in part from morbid curiosity. Many seemed compelled to recount the carnage witnessed at "the Bloody Angle." "We crossed a ditch filled with the rebel dead three feet deep. The coating of mud upon the fallen told how the living had stood upon the bodies of their comrades to continue the fight."[27] "They [the Union dead] were mostly in the open -- many nothing but a lump of meat or clot of gore where countless bullets from both armies had torn them ..."[28] "On the slope in front of the angle lay dead bodies of men and horses so riddled with bullets that they flattened out on the ground. Not a blade of grass, twig or shrub left standing; the face of the gun carriages and caissons toward the enemy was sheeted with lead from striking bullets."[29] "... I visited the place the next morning, and though I had seen horrid scenes since this war commenced, I never saw anything half so bad as that. Our men lay piled one top of another, nearly all shot through the head ... On the rebel side it was worse than on ours. In some places they were piled four and five deep, some of whom were still alive. I turned away from that place, glad to escape from such a terrible sickening sight. I have sometimes hoped, that if I must die while I am a soldier, I should prefer to die on the battle-field, but after looking at such a scene, one cannot help turning away and saying, any death but that."[30]

Staff officers who were spared from the fighting were also drawn to the scene. General Porter recorded his observations of hell's leavings: "My duties carried me again to the spot [Bloody Angle] the next day, and the appalling sight presented was harrowing in the extreme. Our own killed were scattered over a large space near the 'angle,' while in

[27]Haines, p. 182.
[28]Hyde, p. 202.
[29]As cited in Trudeau, *Bloody Roads South*, p. 187.
[30]Fisk, p. 221.

front of the captured breastworks the enemy's dead, vastly more numerous than our own, were piled upon each other in some places four layers deep, exhibiting every ghastly phase of mutilation. Below the mass of fast-decaying corpses, the convulsive twitching of limbs and the writhing of bodies showed that there were wounded men still alive and struggling to extricate themselves from their horrid entombment. Every relief possible was afforded, but in too many cases it came too late."[31]

Charles Dana, Lincoln's representative on the field, and John Rawlins, assigned to monitor Grant's sobriety, also took a tour of the "Bloody Angle" that next morning. "... I dismounted and climbed up the bank over the outer line of rude breastworks. Within we saw a fence over which earth had evidently been banked, but which was now bare and half down. It was here that the fighting had been fiercest. We picked our way to the fence and stopped to look over the scene ... I remember as I stood there I was almost startled to hear a bird twittering in a tree. All around us the underbrush and trees, which were just beginning to be green, had been riddled and burnt. The ground was thick with dead and wounded men, among whom the relief corps was at work. The earth, which was soft from the heavy rains ... had been trampled by the fighting of thousands of men until it was soft, like thin hasty pudding. Over the fence against which we leaned lay a great pool of this mud, its surface as smooth as that of a pond.

As we stood there, looking silently down at it, of a sudden the leg of a man was lifted from the pool and the mud dripped off his boot ... It was so unexpected, so horrible, that for a moment we were stunned. Then we pulled ourselves together and called to some soldiers nearby to rescue the owner of the leg. They pulled him out with but little trouble, and discovered that he was not dead, only wounded. He was taken to the hospital, where he got well, I believe."[32]

---

[31]Porter, p. 111.

[32]Dana, Charles, *Recollections of the Civil War*, as cited in Maney, p. 52. Although it hardly seems possible, a Confederate soldier sent back to the Angle several days later recalled an even more ghastly scene, "Those [Union dead] who were not very badly mutilated were swollen as long as they could swell. Their faces were nearly black, and their mouths, nose, eyes, hair and the mutilated parts were full of maggots!" Nichols, *A Soldiers Story of His Regiment*, as cited in *Wheeler, On Fields of Fury...*, p. 221.

Not surprisingly, it took the men some time to decelerate, and to suppress the blood lust that had managed to slip the bonds of cultural restraint which normally exerted some influence even during combat. Captain Rhodes wrote, "I smoked most all day [May 13th] and so did we all, we were so excited." Curiously, in the next sentence he related seemingly contradictory behavior: "The men did not mind shells any more then [*sic*] snow balls, they were so tired."[33] Perhaps he meant that the men were so tired of fearing death, that they had ceased to fear it any longer.

The battle on May 12 was fundamentally different from any other battle of the Civil War. First, the time actually spent in combat was much longer than normal. Further, more so than in any other battle, the men seem to have surrendered themselves to the urge to kill for the sake of killing, remaining locked in the deadly contest long after a retreat could have been accomplished by either side. After the Union forces were pushed back to the outside of the Rebel works, the Federals made

Officers of 119th - Major Henry P. Truefitt, Jr., seated at left

[33]Rhodes, p. 149.

no further significant attacks, and from that point until late in the night, the battle raged without reason or strategic purpose other than to stand fast and kill.

For the 119th the battle was also unique -- for the first and only time, the Regiment suffered the death in combat of its commanding officer, when Major Henry P. Truefitt, Jr. was killed early in the action under unrecorded circumstances.[34] Joining his commander in death on the field was Captain Charles P. Warner, commander of Company K. Perhaps a small part of Warner's wife of seventeen years died with him, because Emma Warner survived her slain husband by only five more years; and with her passing, five children, three of whom were still minors, were orphaned.[35]

In addition to the two officers killed in action, Sergeants Isaac Freese of H Company and Richard S. Ridgway of I Company died on the field, along with eleven enlisted men. Eight more men, including two other sergeants and two corporals, would later succumb to wounds received in the battle; and two men were listed as missing in action. One of those men who lingered was Nathan R. Marple, whose father, on learning of his son's injury rushed to Washington to try to locate his son and care for his leg wound. Unfortunately, the elder Marple arrived only in time to transport his son's lifeless body back to the Horsham Pennsylvania Meeting House for proper

Captain Charles P. Warner

(courtesy K. Turner collection)

---

[34]O.R.-1-36-1-673.

[35]National Archives, Charles P. Warner Pension Records.

burial.[36] In total, the Regiment suffered thirty-eight additional casualties, leaving approximately 250 men fit for duty out of the 500 who had crossed the Rappahannock eight days earlier.[37]

---

[36]*Bucks County Intelligencer*, May --, 1864.

[37]Bates, *History...*, vol. 4, 119th. Fox maintained that during the period from May 5 to May 12, 1864, the 119th suffered 231 killed and wounded out of a total of 400 effectives.

13

COLD HARBOR

What was the limit of endurance for the surviving soldiers of the Army of the Potomac? It is reasonable to assume that the question of endurance would have been foremost on the minds of Grant and Meade as they considered the next move for the army, although there is no evidence that it was. Perhaps Grant believed that a pause in his offensive would not have been politically acceptable, or perhaps he knew the mettle of his soldiers. In any case, while the soldiers smoked, trenched, slept, or wandered around the battlefield of the previous day, the high command made its plans, seemingly oblivious to the fact that the army had been either fighting or marching almost continuously for nine straight days.

At 8:15 on the evening of the thirteenth, General Wright received orders to have his Corps ready to follow the Fifth Corps to the left flank of the army, and once there to launch an attack along the Massaponax Church Road at dawn on the fourteenth. Word of the movement was passed down the chain of command, and at 8:45 p.m. First Division Headquarters shared the order with the Brigade commanders, setting the order of march as the Second, Third, Fourth, and First Brigades. The pickets, however, were ordered to remain in place until dawn to cover the withdrawal of the Corps.[1]

It was not until 3:00 a.m. on the fourteenth, after waiting in readiness for six hours, that the column of the Fifth Corps passed by, allowing the Grays and their comrades to move onto the road and begin the trudge eastward. Problems beset the moving column almost from the outset of the march. "The mud was deep over a large part of the route;

---

[1]O.R.-1-36-2-728,730.

the darkness intense, so that literally you could not see your hand before your face ... The march was necessarily very slow. The fatigue of floundering along in such a sea of mud but few can apprehend. In spite of the care taken to prevent it [men were posted at intervals and fires were built along the route, burning intermittently until extinguished by the rain], men lost their way and lay down exhausted, until daylight enabled them to go on."[2] To further complicate and slow the march, "... the troops had to cut trees and corduroy the road a part of the way, to get through."[3]

At about the time the Sixth Corps started moving eastward, Wright, recognizing the reality of the situation, notified Headquarters that he could not possibly have his Corps in position to attack the enemy

Building Corduroy Road - *Leslie's Illustrated Newspaper*

---

[2]Humphreys, vol. 6, p. 107.
[3]Grant, vol. 2, pp. 235-236.

in one hour at the designated time.[4] As it turned out, the Sixth Corps was not able to gather itself into an offensive posture until late in the morning.

General Upton's Second Brigade, arriving in advance of the division, occupied the Myers House on a small hill just to the south of the Nye River. The Confederates under General Mahone did not squander the opportunity to strike the isolated Federal brigade, and in short order Upton was driven off the position, while almost losing his entire command in the process.[5] Private Keiser described the action in more personal terms: "... We ran into two full lines of Rebs, and I tell you, we were not slow in getting back, each one for himself ... I got over the stream by crossing on a submerged log, and got wet to the knees. A poor excited soldier jumped into the stream right below me, with his knap-sack still on his back, and all that could be seen after were a few bubbles."[6]

At the same time, the Grays were enjoying a brief respite, until they were "... aroused by a severe shelling and heavy volley on our left ..." from the attack on Upton's men.[7] "We moved towards this position, then fording the Nye more than waist deep [to] the hill formerly held by Upton and after considerable maneuvering got into position. Not a shot fired tonight. We occupied a position to the left of the turnpike."[8] The hill was secured the second time by both the Grays' brigade and the men from New Jersey in the First Brigade.[9] Taking no chances, the regiments of both brigades entrenched their position, and then settled in for another tense night in front of the enemy.

To the men hunkered down in their rifle pits, it must have seemed that they were grist in some huge machine which was dedicated to grinding them into oblivion. Even though spared from fighting for a day, the Grays continued to suffer the debilitating cumulative effects from days of rain. "An ordinary rain, lasting for a day or two, does not embarrass troops; but when the storm continues for a week it becomes

---

[4]O.R.-1-36-2-762.

[5]Matter, pp. 279-285.

[6]Keiser diary, 5/14/1864.

[7]Latta diary, 5/14/1864.

[8]Latta Diary.

[9]Humphreys, vol. 6, p. 108.

one of the most serious obstacles in a campaign. The men can secure no proper shelter and no comfortable rest; their clothing has no chance to dry; and a tramp of a few miles through tenacious mud requires as much exertion as an ordinary day's march. Tents become saturated and weighted with water ... Dry wood cannot be found; cooking becomes difficult; the men's spirits are affected by the gloom, and even the most buoyant natures become disheartened."[10]

By the fifteenth, the psychological and physical toll taken by the preceding ten days' warfare and weather became obvious to everyone. "The terrible losses sustained, and the continual checks we met, combined with the effects of this marching and counter-marching, from right to left, and left to right again, produced a feeling of listlessness and discouragement, which extended throughout the army. The men felt that they were doomed to slaughter. An order caused by this state of feeling was prepared and read to the troops, 'exhorting them, by the memory of their losses and what they had already suffered, not to be discouraged, but to crown their efforts by victory.'"[11] Wright's order referenced above also stated: "[the command] ... has noticed with regret indications of a failure upon the part of some to appreciate the full importance of the struggle in which we are engaged, and the absolute necessity for exertion and vigilance far beyond what is required of each of you ... remember that indifference at this time to anything that may advance the general good is criminal ..."[12]

The generals may have remained gung-ho and pugnacious, but the exhaustion gripping both armies seems to have overcome any ability to compel a resumption of the fighting. The Confederates massed for an attack which didn't come off. On the Northern side: "It is now 4:00 [p.m.] and it has really been a remarkably quiet Sabbath. Both sides seem to have tacitly agreed to suspend hostilities for the day. I have heard thus far but two discharges of artillery, these some distance to the right. At 5:50 p.m. orders came to be ready to move forward and attack the enemy. First and Third divisions to form the attacking column and Second in support. Supposed to be to [attack] the anticipated rear of the

---

[10]Porter, p. 121.
[11]Haines, pp. 183-184.
[12]O.R.-1-36-2-791, 792.

enemy. [The order was rescinded and] ... we have a good night's rest."[13]

The next day General Grant sent a letter to General Halleck purporting to justify the lack of offensive action. "We have had five days almost constant rain without any prospect yet of it clearing up. The roads have become so impassable that ambulances with wounded men can no longer run between here and Fredericksburg. All offensive operations necessarily cease until we can have twenty-four hours of dry weather. The army is in the best of spirits, and feel the greatest confidence of ultimate success."[14] Given that Grant had been ordering attacks within the previous twenty-four hours, and that at least one of his Corps commanders felt compelled to issue a circular which attempted to overcome apparent demoralization, this letter seems a rather disingenuous obfuscation of the fact that his men were simply overworked, overstressed, and fought out.

Although cited by Grant as an extreme illustration of the effects of days of rain upon the condition of the roads in his theater of operations, the inability of the ambulances to travel to Fredericksburg because of the mud may have been a mixed blessing, sparing the wounded soldiers the ordeal of the passage to the rear. "In the ambulances are concentrated probably more acute suffering than may be seen in the same space in all this world besides. The worst cases only have the privilege of transportation and what a privilege! A privilege of being violently tossed from side to side, of having one of the four who occupy the vehicle together thrown bodily, perhaps upon a gaping wound; of being tortured, and racked, and jolted, when each jarring of the ambulance is enough to make the sympathetic brain burst with agony."[15]

The only fighting that occurred on the sixteenth involved a small-scale attack by Major General John Gibbons' Division of the Second Corps toward the right of the Union army. In the action, Gibbons' men were able to recover six or seven hundred of the Sixth Corps' wounded, who had been abandoned when the army shifted to the left.[16] Fearing

---

[13]Latta diary.

[14]Grant, vol. 2, p. 237.

[15]Reed, William H. Ed., *War Papers of Frank B. Fay*, as cited in Trudeau, *Bloody Roads South*, p. 214.

[16]Trudeau, *Bloody Roads South*, p. 192.

that the Confederates were responding with an attack of their own, Headquarters inquired about the sounds coming from in front of the Sixth Corps. Wright put his commanders at ease with a message to Humphreys: "The chopping referred to was in front of Russell's position. He was making slashings to strengthen his front."[17]

In fact, all the Grays had to do that day was rest and strengthen their front: "Another day ... heard not a single shot ... two days now we have not even been disturbed by picket firing and skirmishing ... [I] rode out along the [front, the] entire brigade posted except 130 men from the 5th Wisconsin. The white in [the] camp of the enemy can be seen stretching out in vast numbers in the direction of Spotsylvania Court House and a long line of eighteen guns and positions face us in our immediate front." [18]

Wars are not won, or careers advanced, by resting and building defenses. Late in the day, General Wright successfully lobbied for his plan to have the Sixth and Second Corps march back to the scene of the fighting on the twelfth, in hopes of surprising the enemy's presumably weakened left flank. The staff immediately thereafter began planning and drafting orders for another night march in the mud.[19]

May 17 began much like the previous two days: "Again do we have nothing to do in the way of actual conflict, and am not disturbed by orders of any character whatsoever ... "[20] The tranquility continued "... until about 6:00 when one [an order] comes to be in readiness to move shortly after dark. Our destination is the point, the vicinity which we fought over on the 12th. After a tedious march which occupied the entire night, we finally after daylight [on May 18] reached the Landrum House and remained under a severe shelling for some time ... Just after daylight, we moved from that position and occupied a line of pits immediately in front of where we charged on the 10th and remained there for several hours."[21]

The Grays and their brigade-mates, despite the grueling march and severe shelling, were far more fortunate than their counterparts in

---

[17]O.R.-1-36-2-822.
[18]Latta diary.
[19]Humphreys, vol. 6, p. 110.
[20]Latta diary.
[21]Latta diary.

the Second Corps, because instead of being ordered to join in the 4:00 a.m. assault, the Philadelphians were positioned as support in the rear. The stalwart men of the Second Corps gathered themselves at the base of the "salient" in front of entrenchments, "... of the most formidable character, being concealed on their right by woods and having on that part of their front a heavy slashing, and in their left front, which was in the open ground on the Harrison Farm, lines of abatis." Despite knowing full well what was coming, Hancock's infantry advanced and was "... met with a heavy musketry and artillery fire which completely swept the ground in front, but notwithstanding, they pressed forward to the slashing and abatis, and made several gallant attempts to carry the enemy's lines, but without success."[22] Dismissing any belief that the death of brave men, tangled in abatis like so many insects in a spider's web, was anything but slaughter, one witness starkly described the tragedy: "... the artillery cut our men down in heaps."[23]

After the murder was halted around 10:00 a.m., the Sixth Corps was sent back to its position of the previous day, perhaps with the Regiment again under the command of Lt. Colonel Clark, who was mustered in on the field sometime on the eighteenth. By the end of the day the Grays were undoubtedly extremely tired, hungry, and not a little disgusted. "Our rations were nearly all gone, and most of us had only one cup of coffee and a hard-tack for the whole day -- our supply wagon not coming up to us while we were marching."[24] Instead of rations, the Sixth Corps received a general order to be ready to move at 3:00 a.m. on the morning of the nineteenth.

Pursuant to orders, the Sixth Corps was up at 3:00 a.m., and moved to a position within a third of a mile from the enemy.[25] The Philadelphians moved "... as far as possible without attacking the enemy and entrench[ed]. Moved forward about one mile and a half. Threw up an excellent line of earthworks. Towards evening [heard] heavy and ... persistent musketry firing ... in the direction of the extreme right. Orders came to be in readiness to move to the support of the Corps

---

[22]Humphreys, vol. 6, p. 111.

[23]As cited in Trudeau, *Bloody Roads South*, p. 195.

[24]Haines, p. 186.

[25]Haines, p. 187.

engaged [the Heavy Artillery regiments of the Fourth Division, Second Corps]. Our division with [Brigadier General Frank] Wheaton's Brigade and a battery moved at 10:00 p.m. Marched all night, no sleep as usual, and halted near the line occupied by [Major General David B.] Birney's Division [Second Corps]."[26]

Sunrise on the morning of the twentieth found the Grays marching down the road while surrounded by, if not appreciating, "... the beautiful spring time ... [when] The woods were the brightest, with the young foliage with dog-woods in blossom, and the spring flowers abundant."[27] Any relief that the men might have been enjoying from the stark reality of their situation was abruptly ended when the Regiment reached the scene of the previous day's fighting. There, the "Heavies," raw regiments of garrison troops fresh from the defenses around Washington, had encountered the experienced Confederate warriors under Lieutenant General Richard S. Ewell. The rookies stood their ground but paid a severe price for their courage. "Mostly the heavy artillery [was involved] suffering severely. Large numbers of our dead cover the ground ..."[28]

As if the bloody battlefield was not enough to shatter any reverie created by the beautiful spring day, the Grays also came upon enemy "... works higher than a shelter tent ... [with] two embankments for guns, [and a] clear field for fire ..."[29] Although no orders had been issued to assault the position, the men certainly must have morosely contemplated the implications of that possibility, until it became clear that no attack was planned. Instead of an assault, the Union pickets were pulled back and the Bluecoats withdrew to the Nye River, followed by enemy skirmishers, and an occasional artillery shell thrown in their direction. Later in the afternoon, Hill's Confederates launched a rather feeble attack, which was easily repelled.

Around 6:00 p.m. the situation became more serious when the Union army was ordered to change its base, and the Grays' division was designated as the rear guard. While the Red Crosses labored to

[26]Latta diary, 5/19/1864.
[27]Haines, p. 187.
[28]Latta diary, 5/20/1864.
[29]O.R.-1-36-3-60, Wright to Humphrey, 7:10 a.m.

strengthen their emplacements, a thunderstorm burst over them, changing the assignment from difficult to miserable. Danger was added to the mix when the rain began to slacken, the sky lightened somewhat with the passing of the thunderclouds, and the Confederates launched an attack. "... The enemy made a charge upon our picket line in such force as to drive it in. They came on, apparently unaware of what strength we might have upon the height. As they emerged from the forest our batteries opened upon them. Suddenly, in the gloom of the gathering night, our pieces shot forth great lines of fire; and canister and shell scattered through the woods below. The advancing line halted, then broke, and quickly disappeared.... The scene was most animated, as from the summit of our hill the cannon blazed away into the darkness, the shell sweeping down the ravine, then bursting and throwing a flood of light through the forest."[30]

Having repulsed the enemy, the First Division was able to pull away by 11:00 p.m. and to commence a "March at night ... [which continued] on that road until daylight, having made a distance of but about two miles ...," all the while suffering the usual annoyances of a slow night march.[31] Although Private Fisk of the 2nd Vermont was describing the night portion of the march to Gettysburg, his commentary detailed one annoyance which was certainly applicable to all such efforts, including this one. "Marching by rods is like dying by inches, and it gets an impatient man into a hell of a misery. Scolding and swearing is dispensed at an awful rate when a regiment is compelled to halt and wait every few rods ..."[32] At midnight Wright reported that: "My column has hardly got out of its entrenchments, and is now halted, the road being blocked ahead by Burnside's column." By 4:30 a.m. the road was still congested, but at least the entire Corps was on the road.[33] After dawn, the Grays and their fellow sufferers intermittently trudged and

[30]Haines, pp. 188-189.
[31]Latta diary, 5/21/1864.
[32]Fisk, p. 114.
[33]O.R.-1-36-3-94.

stood in place, until finally reaching Guinea Station at 2:00 p.m. on the twenty-second.[34]

The weary infantrymen were permitted only four short hours of relief before the ordeal commenced again at 6:00 p.m. The wearers of the Greek Cross "... made a miserable and fatiguing march until midnight, accomplishing only about six miles. The roads were filled with artillery and wagon trains, and the infantry were compelled to grope their way in the darkness, through thickets and undergrowth, and water and mud."[35]

The twenty-third of May would offer no significant relief to the now dangerously exhausted soldiers. "Return to march at 5:00 a.m. but did not get started until about 8:00. Marched all day except about two hours when a halt was ordered and rations distributed."[36] Even getting rations was a problem during this grueling march, compelling General Wright at 7:30 a.m. to plead for help from Headquarters to locate and connect his supply train with his troops.[37] At 11:45 a.m. the connection was made, and the men were permitted the two hours referred to by Captain Latta to eat, boil some coffee, or perhaps just to collapse by the side of the road.

Undoubtedly with the assistance of some creative encouragement from their sergeants, the men were up and on the road again at 2:00 p.m.: "We move on again past Harris Store, and immediately thereafter come within hearing distance of an engagement which seems to be raging both in our front and on the flank, but some miles ahead. Marched on until sometime after dark, placed on our extreme support to watch a flank [with] a battery detailed with us. We are about a mile and a half from the North Anna River and near Mount Carmel Church. The Fifth Corps troops were the only ones engaged."[38] Fearing that a general action was in the offing, Wright deployed his divisions in a defensive

---

[34]Latta diary. On May 21, Latta received a promotion to assistant adjutant on the staff of the Third Brigade. All of his subsequent diary entries were made from the perspective of a staff officer rather than an officer of the 119th, although at that point, the entire Brigade was hardly larger than was the 119th when it embarked for the front in 1862.

[35]Haines, p. 193.

[36]Latta diary.

[37]O.R.-1-36-3-135.

[38]Latta diary, 5/23/1864.

posture, one division facing the river, one at a right angle to the first facing west, and one in reserve guarding the trains.

The Sixth Corps remained in that static defensive position until orders were received after dark to resume the march toward the North Anna River, with the Second Division to lead, the Grays' division in the middle, and the Third Division to follow.[39] The troops shuffled and stumbled southward, probably in a trance-like state somewhere between consciousness and unconsciousness; but General Wright, who was apparently aware of the sorry condition of his charges, failed to make a determined plea on their behalf for a pause, perhaps explaining why he never earned the nickname "Uncle."[40] After advising Meade that he expected that the Sixth Corps would cross the river by 2:00 a.m., Wright whined: "The march of today has been so trying to the men that it is represented that full one-third of the fighting men have fallen out ... if not important that move be made tonight the men might have their night's sleep ... I beg that it not be supposed I wish to spare the condition of the men unnecessarily, but only to get them in good fighting condition by a night's rest ..."[41] In fairness to Wright, however, perhaps his own fortitude had been sapped by the same fatigue grinding down his men.

---

[39]O.R.-1-36-3-133.

[40]Although only mentioned in two sources discovered by this author, one Confederate soldier, Sam R. Watkins of the 1st Tennessee regiment, related behavior which, if credible, might explain in part how the combatants survived days of fighting followed by night after night of grueling marches: "I have seen soldiers fast asleep, and no doubt dreaming of home and loved ones there, as they staggered along in their places in the ranks. I know that on many a weary night's march I have slept, and slept soundly, while marching along in my proper place in the ranks of the company, stepping to the same step as the soldier in front of me did.... Step by step, step by step, we continued to plod and nod and stagger and march, tramp, tramp, tramp.... And then the sun would begin to shoot his slender rays athwart the eastern sky, and the boys would wake up and begin laughing and talking as if they had just risen from a good feather bed, and were perfectly refreshed and happy." Watkins, pp. 68-69. Captain DeForest of the 12th Connecticut apparently described the same phenomenon in his account of a particularly grueling forced march through the night, "The men stagger against each other, and [in] slumber marching." DeForest, p. 100. Based upon these two accounts it would seem that the Butternuts were the more accomplished somnambulists.

[41]O.R.-1-36-3-164.

The Philadelphians moved across the pontoons over the North Anna at Jericho Mills sometime shortly after dawn on May 24. By 6:15 a.m. the lead division of the Corps, probably the Second, had moved up in support of the Fifth Corps; while the Grays' brigade had formed in support of the line manning the forward rifle pits.[42] Lacking any evidence to the contrary, it appears that the men spent the rest of the day in comparative ease, and received the benefit of a desperately needed full night of rest.

The grueling marches of the preceding several days, and the prospects of another assault against the Rebel emplacements encountered on the other side of the North Anna River, caused further erosion of the morale that was already recognized as abysmal one week earlier. Probably reflecting the feelings of all the men, a Ninth Corps soldier recorded: "At North Anna I discovered that our infantry were tired of charging earthworks ... Here I first heard savage protests against a continuation of the generalship which consisted in launching good troops against entrenched works that the generals had not inspected. Battle-tried privates came into our battery and sneeringly inquired if the corps and army commanders had been to see the line. Of course we replied 'No.' 'Well,' said one sergeant of the Pennsylvania Reserves, 'I have fought in this army for three years, and in no other campaign have I seen so many generals shirk as I have in this one ...' At North Anna the rank and file of the Potomac army, the men who did the fighting, and who had been under fire for three weeks, began to get discouraged."[43]

Despite sagging morale, which bordered on active dissension, the pace of the campaign continued; and at 8:30 a.m. on the morning of the twenty-fifth, Wright was able to report that his troops had made a successful connection with the right flank of the Fifth Corps, and that none of his pickets became engaged in hostile contact with the Butternuts during the maneuver.[44] When the Federal skirmish line was pushed out even further, to within a few hundred yards of the Little River, it was

---

[42]Latta diary; O.R.-1-36-3-165.

[43]Wilkinson, *Recollections of a Private Soldier in the Army of the Potomac*, as cited in Maney, p. 59.

[44]O.R.-1-36-3-195.

discovered that both Corps were in close proximity to the enemy works, which could be clearly observed across the water.

While the pickets from both sides occupied themselves by exchanging potshots, the balance of the Sixth Corps undertook a new activity -- the wasting of a three- to four-mile portion of the Virginia Central Railroad. "Slender pines were cut and used as levers to raise one side of the track; then the men, as close as they could cluster, lifted it by hand, until they turned it completely over. This was done for a distance of four miles on both sides, from Noel's Station. They begin to pull the ties from the rails. The ties were piled in heaps, set on fire, and the rails laid across them. The rails were weighted by ties piled upon the end, and when the iron became heated they bent and became useless until again heated and rolled."[45]

As Wright's men were busy destroying railroad tracks, disturbing reports began to trickle into Headquarters which, after a time, alerted Grant and Meade to the fact that the Army of the Potomac was in grave peril. Lee had laid a trap for the Union forces by aligning and strongly emplacing his troops in roughly the shape of a wedge, with the point resting on the North Anna. During the previous several days, the Federals had maneuvered themselves into a position along both forward sides of the wedge, so that neither Grant's left nor right flank could support the other against a Confederate attack without marching around the point of the Southern wedge, while crossing the river twice in the process. For all practical purposes, Lee had split the Union army in half, and had only to attack one isolated wing or the other to defeat the Federals in detail.

Consistent with previous strategy, Grant decided that the maneuver most likely to extricate his army from the trap was to shift his right flank to the left, around the wedge. If the Federal troops to be withdrawn from the right flank could penetrate the natural defense provided to the Confederates by the Pamunkey River, not only would the army escape Lee's trap, but it might gain his right flank as well. In order to successfully accomplish the intended maneuver, however, it was critical that the army quickly establish a secure bridgehead across the

---

[45]Haines, pp. 195-196.

Pamunkey, before Lee could shift enough men eastward to either block such a crossing, or make it an extremely bloody affair.

Grant knew he needed speed, endurance and reliability from the units chosen for the task. Major General Philip H. Sheridan was directed to lead the cavalry in the expedition, and for support Grant further ordered that "... Wright's best division or division under his ablest commander ..." be sent along and, "... as soon as it is dark tomorrow night start the division which you withdraw first from Wright's corps to make a forced march to Hanover Town, taking with them no teams to impede their march."[46] At 9:00 a.m. on the morning of May 26, Russell's Red Crosses, the designated division, began its withdrawal back across the North Anna in preparation for another assignment to act as the spearhead for the army.[47]

The Grays and the rest of the First Division marched much of the day in a downpour in order to arrive at the jump-off point by the designated time; finally halting at Chesterfield Station, where they waited for supplies to catch up and the sun to set. The drive toward the river crossing at Hanover Town began at 9:00 p.m., and the men "... marched nearly all night, no troops are on the road except our division, with two batteries of artillery."[48] The column had covered twenty miles by the time the sun began to rise on the morning of the twenty-seventh, but then "The men showing signs of exhaustion after sunrise ... a halt of an hour and a half was given for breakfast ..."[49] At a different point in the line of march, Private Westbrook of the 49th Pennsylvania recalled only a half hour break for coffee, presumably the same break afforded to the Grays.

Whatever the actual length of the break, it was not nearly long enough to refresh the men from the effects of the grueling march, which by then was about twenty-two hours old. After barely enough time to boil and gulp down some coffee, the soldiers were back on the road. The morning dragged on like slow torture. "The heat of the sun was great, and the men wilted down by scores ..."[50] "Before 11 o'clock the

---

[46]Grant, vol. 2, p. 254.
[47]Haines, p. 190.
[48]Westbrook, p. 205.
[49]Haines, p. 196.
[50]Haines, p. 196.

cavalry horses began to drop, and our route was marked by lines of dead animals on both sides of the road, and by a double stream of cavalrymen straggling on with their saddles over their arms. The whole command straggled badly, but kept pouring on as best they could along the sides of the road, determined to keep as near to their comrades as possible. It was not merely the distance covered, though that was considerable, which broke us up, but it was the pace at which we were forced in order to keep within supporting distance of the cavalry."[51]

At 11:00 a.m. the column reached the Pamunkey and "... crossed the river on pontoons made of canvas boats ...;" then, after another hour's march, the beleaguered troops reached their destination.[52] In retrospect, Private Anderson of the 5th Wisconsin maintained that "This march remains in my memory as the hardest we ever made, harder even than the memorable march of the 6th Corps from Westminster to Gettysburg."[53]

Twenty-two hours of actual marching, and over twenty-seven hours without sleep, finally brought the Red Crosses into position for the real purpose of the mission -- establishing a secure bridgehead and perhaps engaging the enemy. "The cavalry pushed out a mile or so further and a few regiments followed to form a skirmish line, but the rest of us threw ourselves on the ground in an open field, under the burning afternoon sun, and slept."[54] Before they were hardly settled, the exhausted Bluecoats were roused and pushed into a defensive perimeter in line of battle by battalions, because Russell was extremely concerned over rumors he had heard that Confederate Major General John C. Breckenridge was lurking in the immediate vicinity with 10,000 Rebel infantry.[55] Sheridan's troopers and Russell's infantry had successfully secured the necessary bridgehead without significant fighting, but not without ample payment in suffering.

The balance of the Sixth Corps arrived at the river at 7:30 a.m. on the morning of the twenty-eighth, but could not cross for another hour

---

[51]Anderson, 1903, p. 20.
[52]Latta diary.
[53]Anderson, 1903, p. 20.
[54]Anderson, 1903, p. 20.
[55]O.R.-1-36-3-254; Latta diary.

until bridge repairs were completed.[56] As the rest of the Corps began to fill in behind, Russell's Division was pushed northwestward along the Hanover Court House Road a distance of about two miles. The day's work was not completed until the Red Crosses had taken a position approximately four miles from the Court House, to the left of the road and the other two Divisions of the Corps.[57]

The situation on the morning of the May 29, "... remained quiet until 12:00 when orders came to make a movement with entire division in the direction of Hanover Court House. Moved out with a strong skirmish line in front. Met the enemy's cavalry about three miles out, one man wounded, McMahon's horse shot, great difficulty in getting on the right road and had considerable marching to do ... all the brigade but one regiment being deployed as skirmishers made the courthouse and destroyed two bridges on the railroad. Held the position described ... all night."[58]

"At daylight [on May 30] moved out on the direct road to Richmond sufficiently far to allow the ______ corps to get in."[59] The rapid movement of the Sixth Corps had created somewhat of a logistics problem, causing the Sixth Corps headquarters to scramble to get rations to the hungry men. It was not until 10:15 a.m. that Wright was able to notify Meade's Headquarters that "I am issuing rations as fast as they can be got up to the troops, who are generally quite out."[60] At noon, presumably with full stomachs, the Grays' division "... marched toward the Mechanicsville and Richmond Road to make a junction with Hancock's Corps ... our division ... joined Ricketts' on the right and he formed a connection with the left."[61]

General Meade, at 5:30 p.m., directed the Sixth Corps to push out skirmishers to drive the Confederate pickets back as far as possible, and ordered an attack if the Rebels were found to be in weak force.[62] Captain Latta reported the results of that order: "Artillery fire quite

---

[56]O.R.-1-36-3-270.
[57]Latta diary.
[58]Latta diary, 5/29/1864.
[59]Latta diary.
[60]O.R.-1-36-3-353.
[61]Latta diary.
[62]O.R.-1-36-3-354.

brisk and skirmishing lively. Our division skirmish line advances gallantly across an open field."[63] To their dismay, on the far side of that field, the Grays encountered a sobering sight: "... [there is] on a high, steep ridge; timber slashed on the slope and abatis immediately in front of entrenchments. In front of Wright's skirmish line [lies] a thickly wooded swamp 300 yards wide, swamp extends to front of ridge. Their entrenchments extend in front of Russell, the continuation lost in the woods."[64] Frustrated once again because the Southerners had beaten the Federals to the point of attack, Grant was left with only two choices -- assault fortifications, or move to the left.

Initially, the pugnacious Grant's plan was to attack, and pursuant to his orders: "... Skirmishing kept up all day [May 31] with occasional [salvoes] of artillery but no general engagement."[65] Perhaps redeeming himself for his timidity on the morning of May 24, at 3:00 p.m. Wright expressed serious reservations about the advisability of an attack against the enemy fortifications: "Russell occupies nearly position of last night on the crest of a swamp with enemy works on opposite side. I can't cross Russell without serious loss ..."[66] Headquarters soon acceded to Wright's evaluation that an attack would be unwise, and the Grays' brigade was withdrawn into some woods, where they were better sheltered from artillery fire, observing eyes, and deadly sharpshooters.

In anticipation of another stalemate, and perhaps in hopes of avoiding a bloodletting similar to that which followed the Union forces' failure to hold Spotsylvania Court House, Grant dispatched Sheridan and his troopers to the strategically vital village of Cold Harbor. Like Spotsylvania, Cold Harbor was another hamlet which happened to be located at the confluence of a number of roads leading toward the Southern capital which, if controlled by the Federals, would provide a direct route to Richmond. Grant hoped that the possibility of such an eventuality might drag Lee into the much desired stand-up fight for its control. It was not long after Lee discovered that the Union cavalry had taken control of Cold Harbor that the Confederate commander dispatched

---

[63]Latta diary.
[64]O.R.-1-36-3-380, Humphreys to Hancock 10:45 a.m.
[65]Latta diary.
[66]O.R.-1-36-3-382, Wright to Hancock.

his infantry to regain the crossroad, and only a short time later that the Federal troopers found themselves embroiled in a desperate struggle to hold out against the more powerful Southern foot soldiers.

At 9:45 p.m. Meade sent Wright an order dispatching the Sixth Corps to Cold Harbor to relieve the embattled cavalry, adding for emphasis: "... it is of the utmost importance you should reach the point as soon after daylight as possible."[67] The order to move worked its way down the chain of command to Third Brigade headquarters by about 11:00 p.m., throwing the Grays' bivouac into turmoil.

Although remaining prepared to march throughout the night, the Grays finally "Got underway at daylight, marched through volumes of dust and intense burning sun all day. Marched [into] Cold Harbor about noon when we found that the cavalry had been fighting the enemy ..."[68] Dr. Stevens, a surgeon with the White Crosses, provided some additional detail omitted by Latta's characteristically terse description, "The march was a hard one. The day was sultry, and the dust, ankle-deep, raised in clouds by the column, was almost suffocating. It filled the air and hung upon the leaves of the trees like snow."[69] The Greek Crosses moved onto another field of battle where the scene, as described by a private in the Vermont Brigade, may have turned more than a few veterans' stomachs; "... Here we saw a sight which made the blood curdle, and at every thought of which the soul sickens and turns away ... Right over the field where the battle had done its fiercest work, the fire had swept, and many a brave fellow, wounded and dying, unable to move from the place where he had fallen had the little remaining life drawn out of him by the flames, and his body burned to a crisp."[70]

It took some time for Wright's men to get themselves organized into proper fighting order, and perhaps to steady their nerves as well, but by 5:00 p.m. the Sixth Corps' line of battle was set, with the Second Division to the left of the Gaines Mill Road, the Grays' First Division straddling it, and the Third Division deployed on the right. The First Division's alignment found the Fourth Brigade to the far left, the First

[67]O.R.-1-36-3-404.

[68]Latta diary, 6/1/1864.

[69]Stevens, p. 347.

[70]Haynes, *History of the Tenth Regiment, Vermont Volunteers*, as cited in Maney, p. 100.

Brigade with its right on the road, the Grays' brigade with its left on the road, and the Second Brigade to the far right.[71] In front of the first line of the Corps' formation "...was an open space two-thirds of a mile in width, beyond which was a strip of pine wood..." which sheltered the Rebel trenches.[72] For unknown reasons, the Third Brigade's commander, Henry Eustis, was not on the field to lead his troops, and as a result Brigade command devolved to Lt. Colonel Gideon Clark of the 119th.[73]

When the last soldier took his position, the entire line surged forward, intent on dispersing the Rebels. "The troops moved forward most gallantly; those on the right of the road through thick wood, those on the left over an open plain for a half mile under a terrible artillery fire and, as they neared the breastworks of the enemy, received a terrific musketry fire, which prevented further advance, excepting the extreme right of the line, which advanced to the enemies [*sic*] works, capturing some prisoners, these were subsequently withdrawn."[74] The Red and Blue Crosses both captured a portion of the Southern emplacements, but Russell's men were eventually dislodged from their conquest after determined resistance.[75]

Next to the 119th, the Jersey Brigade had a terrible time of it. "The ground was, within a brief space of time, strewn with the fallen; but the charging force swept on through the death-dealing artillery fire, and met the still more destructive discharge of musketry as it passed through a little skirt of woods."[76] Each victim of the pitiless missiles reacted differently when struck. "Some would fall forward as if they had caught their feet and tripped and fell. Others would throw up their arms and fall backward. Others would stagger about a few paces before they dropped." For a time it appeared that none of the attackers would survive.[77]

---

[71]O.R.-1-36-1-662.

[72]Stevens, *Three Years in the Sixth Corps*, as cited in Wheeler, *On Fields of Fury...*, p. 249.

[73]Latta diary.

[74]O.R.-1-36-1-662, Daulton.

[75]Wheeler, *On Fields of Fury...*, p. 249.

[76]Haines, p. 202.

[77]Best, pp. 155-156.

To the Grays' right, the Red Crosses of Upton's Second Brigade were also shredded by a blizzard of lead. A Southern officer described the fate of Upton's "Heavies" of the 2nd Connecticut with obvious relish: "... The discharge from my line at once knocked down the front ranks of the column, while the oblique fire along the right and left cut down the men rapidly all along the column towards the rear. In a few moments the whole column ... lay down. Nothing could have been more unfortunate for them. While they thus lay there, the men of my command continued to reload and discharge their pieces into the thick, dark mass. The officers fired their repeaters, while such as had none borrowed muskets from privates and discharged them at particular individuals. As the survivors lay still to avoid attracting attention, it was soon impossible to distinguish the living from the dead. After some fifteen or twenty rounds had been fired into the prostrate mass I directed the firing to cease ... A portion of the column, not more than a tenth, arose and fled to the rear; many of these, however, were shot down as they attempted to escape." The attack left a memorial to the courage of the men who until that day had been mocked by the veterans as band box soldiers: "The second Connecticut Heavy Artillery ... had joined us but a few days before the battle, its uniform was bright and fresh; therefore its dead were easily distinguished where they lay. They marked in a dotted line an obtuse angle, covering a wide front, with its apex toward the enemy, and there upon his face, still in death, with his head to the works, lay the Colonel, the brave and genial Colonel Elisha Kellogg."[78]

Despite being torn by a murderous fire from yet another set of enemy emplacements, the stubborn Federals refused to run. Instead, the attackers dropped down in place and began to furiously burrow beneath the enemy bullets with whatever implements were on hand, including bayonets, knives, and even tin plates. Attempting to make Wright's men pay for their audacity, "... the enemy fired volley after volley as close as possible to our heads, and making the dirt fly over us. We could only escape by clinging close to mother earth."[79] The Confederate effort to stop the digging failed, and despite the fact that some of the pits

---

[78]Clingman, Thomas; by McMahon *Battles and Leaders*, vol. 4, as cited in Maney, pp. 106-107.

[79]Haines, p. 205.

remained unfinished because the occupants were dead or disabled, within a relatively short time the Federals had scratched out a credible defensive position. Seemingly oblivious to the entrenchments in front of them, and to the havoc which they had just inflicted while fighting from behind their own works, the Southerners attempted several counterattacks, all of which were predictably repulsed. After the last Rebel attack, Captain Latta recorded in his diary that he thought the day's action would someday be known as the battle of Cold Harbor, but that notorious title was to be bestowed on a later, even more bloody, day.

At Headquarters, the frustration must have been nearly overwhelming, as word began to filter back from the front that the Confederates had again managed to construct defensive works across the Union advance. In response to the latest check, Grant issued orders at 10:45 p.m. that as soon as the Second Corps, then in transit, reached the left flank of the Sixth Corps, the assault was to be resumed.[80] While Hancock's men moved to the front, the Grays spent the night under the guns of the enemy, trying to block out sleep-robbing thoughts about what was waiting for them in the morning.

Although expected at daybreak, the Second Corps did not arrive until later in the day, thoroughly exhausted from its all-night march, and in no condition to participate in an assault. As a result, at 1:30 p.m. the assault which had been planned for the morning was postponed until 5:00 p.m.[81]

The experience of the Philadelphians and their comrades while awaiting the arrival of Hancock's men during the morning and afternoon of the second of June was almost as harrowing as an assault would have been. "Shooting of the enemy opened early this morning, and [we] are under their fire continuously. This continues during the entire day ... One is not allowed to expose any portion of his body above the surface of the ground ... we are actually living in the trenches."[82] "The day was hot and dusty ... There was a constant fire from the rebel sharpshooters that hit almost every man who exposed himself ... Rations were exhausted, and more could not be brought up ... Still worse was the

[80]O.R.-1-36-3-458.
[81]O.R.-1-36-3-482.
[82]Latta diary, 6/2/1864.

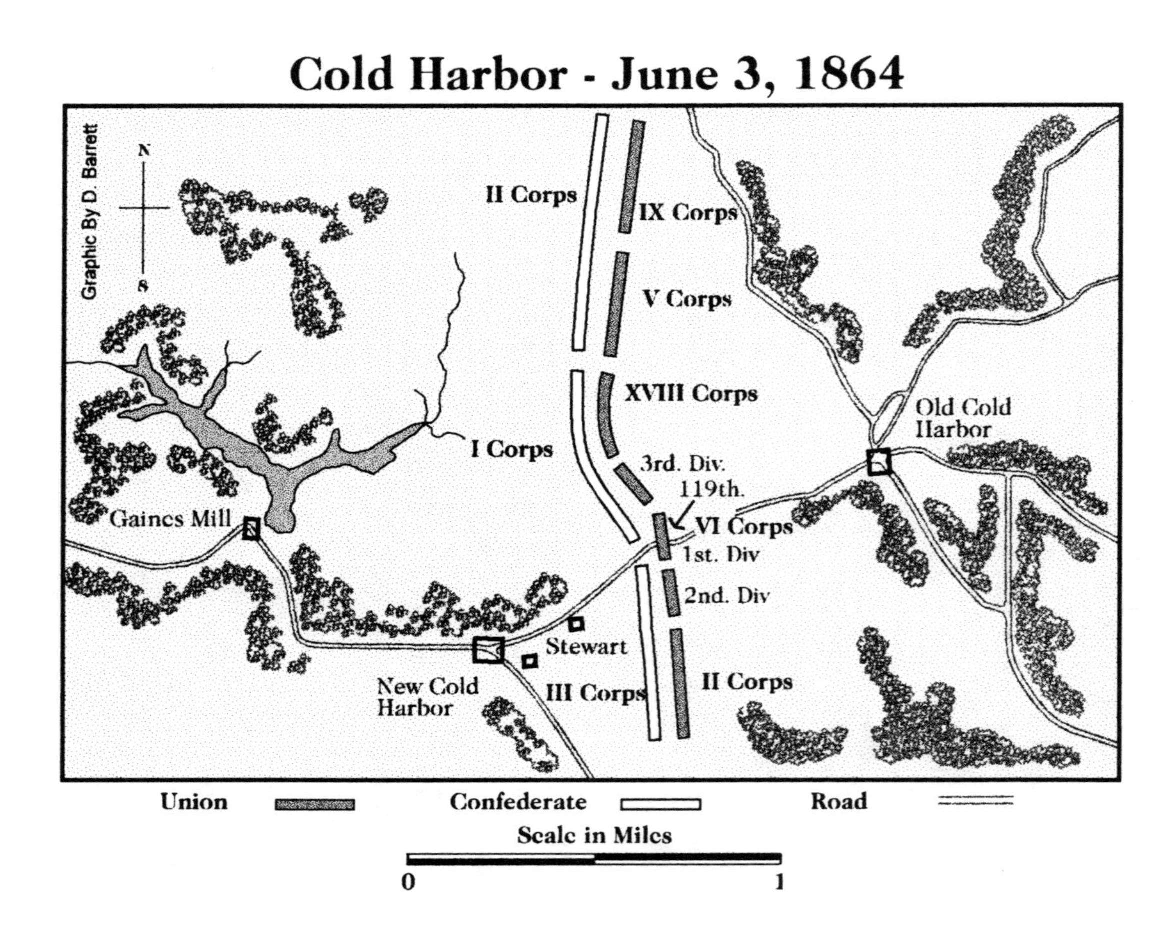
Cold Harbor - June 3, 1864
Graphic By D. Barrett
N
S
II Corps
IX Corps
V Corps
XVIII Corps
I Corps
3rd. Div.
119th.
VI Corps
1st. Div
2nd. Div
II Corps
III Corps
Gaines Mill
New Cold Harbor
Stewart
Old Cold Harbor
Union
Confederate
Road
Scale in Miles
0
1

suffering for want of water ... The dust and smoke were such that the sun could be looked at any time of day without dazzling the naked eye."[83] "... The regiment [49th Pennsylvania] is laying in a rifle pit which it put up last night; the rebel sharpshooters and skirmishers have range of a road on the left flank or our regiment ... we layed [*sic*] in a field in the hot sun all day; our rifle pits keep the balls off, but not the sun ..."[84]

Recognizing that the Second Corps was physically drained, and that the Sixth Corps would be shot to pieces if it attempted to form in proper battle lines in broad daylight, Grant again postponed the assault planned for 5:00 p.m. until 3:00 a.m. on the morning of June 3. Despite the extra day granted to the Confederates to further strengthen emplacements which had already proven to be strong enough to thwart an attack by the Sixth Corps, it appears that Grant never wavered from his myopic determination to launch an assault. In his memoirs, the Union commander made no mention of any effort on his part to personally reconnoiter the front, or to solicit the advice of his field commanders concerning the advisability of an attack, perhaps because Grant had convinced himself that his army had to be at the end of the Confederate line, and that deployment of the Second Corps on the left would necessarily flank his foe. The apparent unwillingness of the Union commander to allow the reality of the situation to intrude upon his plans would soon have fatal consequences.

The ill-fated attack that would make the name Cold Harbor infamous began at 4:30 a.m. on June 3. "Then, at once, rose up sixty thousand men, in a line six miles in extent ..."[85] The Grays' brigade "... advanced our line about 400 yards under a heavy storm of lead from the enemy and halted under the crest of a small hill ... we at once commenced to put up breastworks of fallen timber and brush ... we kept working until we had a complete line of earthworks along our whole front ..."[86] The parallels [trenches closest to the enemy] constructed by the Brigade were "... but 125 yards from the enemy -- and were it not

[83]Haines, pp. 206-207.
[84]Westbrook, p. 205.
[85]Haines, p. 208.
[86]Westbrook, p. 206.

Battle of Cold Harbor - *Leslie's Illustrated Newspaper*

for the protection afforded us by our works, we would suffer terribly from their continuous fire."[87]

A Confederate whose fire contributed to the disintegration of the Sixth Corps attack was not as reluctant as the recipients of that fire to describe the carnage: "Then the musketry began to roll along in a regular wave, coming nearer and nearer as new columns moved to the assault. Now it reaches our front, and the enemy moves steadily upon our works ... As soon as their skirmish line made its appearance, followed by three lines of battle, our pickets in the front of us were relieved, but many fell before regaining our breastworks, and those who were killed [wounded?] had to lie during the day between the most murderous fire in the history of the war, and, sad to say, few survived. When near us the first line came with a rush at charge bayonets, and our officers had great difficulty in restraining the men from opening fire too soon. But when close enough, the word 'fire' was given, and the men

[87]Latta diary, 6/3/1864.

behind the works raised deliberately, resting their guns upon the works, and fired volley after volley into the rushing but disorganized ranks of the enemy. The first line reeled and attempted to fly the field, but were met by the next column, which halted the retreating troops with bayonet, butts of guns, and officers' swords, until a greater number were turned to the second assault. All this while our sharpshooters and men behind our works were pouring a galling fire into the tangled mass of advancing and retreating troops. The double column, like the first, came with a shout, a huzzah, and a charge. But our men had by this time re-loaded their pieces, and were only too eager awaiting the command 'fire.' But when it did come the result was telling -- men falling on top of men, rear rank pushing forward the first rank, only to be swept away like chaff. Our batteries on the hills and rear of those mounted on our infantry line were raking the field, the former with shell and solid shot, the latter with grape and canister. Smoke settling on the ground soon rendered objects in front scarcely visible, but the steady flashing of the enemy's guns and the hail of bullets over our heads and against our works told plainly that the enemy were standing to their work with desperate courage. The third line of assault had now mingled with the first two, and all lying on the ground hidden by the dense smoke..."[88]

As if receiving retribution for the months of ease and security bestowed upon the Heavies while posted well behind the lines, another regiment fresh from Washington, this time from the Second Corps to the Grays' left, was herded to the slaughter across a relatively flat and exposed area. "In this line [Second Corps] was a new heavy artillery regiment of twenty-two hundred men, which advanced in a handsome line, and was cut down like mown grass ... It was the most sickening sight in this arena of horrors; and the appearance of these bodies, strewed over the ground for a quarter of a mile, and in our view for days, can never fade from our recollection ..."[89]

For all intents and purposes the battle of Cold Harbor was over in under an hour, although Grant was not yet aware of the fact. He ordered another assault. What happened next, at another time, under other circumstances, or with more critical observers, might have been

---

[88]Dickert, Augustus, *History of Kershaw's Brigade*, as cited in Maney, pp. 147-148.
[89]Haines, p. 208.

labeled as a mutiny perpetrated by the officers in the field. The corps commanders simply refused to carry out the order to renew the assault, each offering an excuse to justify the decision to stop the murder. Wright was questioned as to why his men were not attacking, and he responded at 7:45 a.m. that he had advanced his center, but could not advance on either his right or left without a supporting advance by the Eighteenth and Second Corps, because if he did so he would be "... taken flank and rear ..." Fearing for his reputation, Wright added: "... My losses will show that there has been no hanging back on the part of the Sixth Corps ..."[90]

Hancock joined in by advising, "Unless success has been gained in other points I do not advise persistence here."[91] Apparently Major General William F. "Baldy" Smith, commander of the Eighteenth Corps, was playing the same game, and also refused to advance for alleged lack of support on his left by the Sixth Corps. When confronted with that allegation, Wright responded at 8:00 a.m.: "As stated, I am a good deal in advance of both the Second and Eighteenth Corps, and the reason why General Smith thinks I am not moving with him is that he is behind me."[92] Was Smith really ignorant of the location of approximately 15,000 Federal troops to his immediate front, all of whom were presumably firing their weapons as fast as possible and generating huge volumes of smoke? Perhaps, given the "fog of war"; but a more likely explanation is that each commander was trying to provide cover for well-intentioned and justifiable insubordination.

General Grant apparently became so frustrated at the lack of further aggressive action, that around midday he personally went to the front to inspect the situation. After his inspection, no further attacks were ordered that day. Grant later provided the best analysis of the battle of Cold Harbor: "This assault cost us heavily and probably without benefit to compensate ... I have always regretted that the last assault at Cold Harbor was ever made ... no advantage whatever was gained to compensate for the heavy loss we sustained."[93]

---

[90]O.R.-1-36-3-544.
[91]Jordan, p. 139.
[92]O.R.-1-36-3-545.
[93]Grant, vol. 2, pp. 271, 276.

Although the Federal infantry would not be called upon again to charge the enemy works, the fighting was not yet over for the day. For hours, the prostrate Union soldiers were subjected to a relentless blizzard of bullets, canister, and shells whistling low over, or punching into the front of, their burrows. Incredibly, despite their own experiences on June 1, and the slaughter just inflicted upon the on-charging Federals, the Southerners attempted two counterattacks -- one at 8:00 p.m. and another at midnight -- but neither achieved any result other than pain, death, and retreat.

On June 4, for the first time since the start of the battle, the nominal commander of the Third Brigade, General Eustis, appeared on the field. Latta did not supply any explanation for the absence, but he expressed his opinion about it: "Russell is indefatigable and Eustis thoroughly inefficient."[94] Eustis' presence might have been of some marginal benefit on the first or third, but there was nothing left for any field commander to do to alter the deadly and exhausting stalemate into which the contest had descended. "Still living under this continued firing and every now and then over goes some one less fortunate than his comrade ... The enemy again attack [and were] repulsed ... fusillades along ... the entire line at times during the night. This is now the fifth day under fire. Just after dark the enemy line opens on both sides with artillery and musketry ..."[95]

Major General Andrew A. Humphreys described the plight of the soldiers in their makeshift trenches under the guns of the enemy: "The labor in making the approaches and strengthening the entrenchments was hard. The men in the advanced part of the lines, which were some miles in length, had to lie close in narrow trenches with no water, except a little to drink, and that of the worst kind, being from surface drainage; they were exposed to great heat during the day; they had but little sleep; their cooking was of the rudest character ... Dead horses and mules and offal were scattered over the country and between the lines were many dead bodies of both parties lying unburied in a burning sun. The country was low and marshy. The exhausting effect of all of this began to show

---

[94]Latta diary, 6/4/1864.
[95]Latta diary, 6/4/1864.

itself, and sickness of malarial character increased largely."[96] A Massachusetts soldier in the Eighteenth Corps to the right of the 119th, who was less reticent about providing graphic detail, recorded the continuous assault on the senses to which the troops were subjected: "Four days of sun and rain, with the severe heat of summer, had passed over our slain, and the air was laden with insufferable putrescence. We breathed it in every breath, tasted it in the food we ate and the water we drank."[97]

Odor was not the only airborne irritant with which the Grays and their comrades had to contend. "To add to the beauties of our situation here we are in an ash heap, as it were. The earth is like a pile of dust, and it dances before every breeze like Vermont snow in midwinter. A man may spread down his rubber blanket for a seat, and one puff of wind will cover it so completely with dust that it will be difficult to distinguish it from the ground around it. Our clothes are filled with dust, and our coffee and everything else we cook is sure to get a clever sprinkling of this fine sand. This dirt goes everywhere. It gets into our haversacks and knapsacks, it fills our hair and mingles with the sweat on our faces. It is universal and there is no getting rid of it."[98]

Late in the afternoon of the fifth, the front line troops did receive relief of sorts from the smells, dust, and some of the danger, when communication trenches were completed to the rear. Those trenches permitted safer passage back and forth so that food, water and replacements could be brought forward, and troops who had been relieved could crawl to the rear. Unfortunately, the trenches were not deep enough to allow for the removal from the front lines of any wounded who could not crawl out under their own power.[99] Not long after completion of the communication trenches, General Russell began rotating brigades amongst three lines -- the front line directly under the enemy guns, an intermediate line, and a "rear" line which was far enough back to avoid sniper fire, but which was just the right distance to be a depository for artillery shells at the end of their trajectory.

---

[96]Humphreys, vol. 6, p. 190.

[97]Derby, William, *Bearing Arms in the Twenty Seventh Massachusetts Regiment*, as cited in Maney, p. 171.

[98]Fisk, pp. 226-227.

[99]Haines, p. 211.

Each day tended to resemble the day before: "The morning [June 6] opens with its usual volley. Mr. Enemy continues firing at intervals throughout the day. We are getting so accustomed to the continuous whiz of the artillery that we do not mind half as much as when it began ... Today [June 7] passes off as its predecessors ... [the enemy is] throwing a few mortar shells which burst in our immediate vicinity ... Our Brigade relieved from the front line [June 8], but placed in a position not much less exposed than that which occupied before ... [a] solid shot ricocheted across the plain. Shells thrown at intervals during the night ... Today [June 11] the artillery of both sides is rather more inclined to fire than yesterday. At noon and before dark they drop ... shrapnel and case .. shells burst within the [area] of the supper table, when we are at it ... The usual shelling and picket firing continues today [June 12]. The shells, however, seem to burst in a closer proximity to headquarters than [before]."[100]

On the evening of June 7, however, an unusual event occurred, which provided a brief respite from the monotony of trench warfare and its pervasive stress. Two days earlier, Grant had written to Lee suggesting a cessation of hostilities to recover the wounded from between the front lines. The message was carefully worded so as not to suggest that the Union commander was requesting a truce, because such a request would have been understood at the time as an acknowledgment of defeat. Lee responded that he would be willing to honor a Union flag of truce. The next day, while Union soldiers continued to needlessly suffer and die, Grant tried again to finesse a truce without actually asking for it, and Lee again declined. Finally, at the end of the day, Grant blinked and asked for a truce, to which Lee agreed, but due to timing problems, the actual truce did not occur until the evening of the seventh.[101]

No records appear as to how many brave men died between the lines during that charade, but there were few survivors to be found after the truce actually began. Colonel Beckwith of the 121st New York, a Red Cross in the Second Brigade a few hundred yards to the right of the 119th, did record some of the suffering endured by the few casualties who survived the ordeal in the no-man's land: "The wounded were in

---

[100]Latta diary.

[101]Grant, vol. 2, pp. 274-275.

a horrible condition ... All the wounded yet alive could have survived but a little time longer. They had exhausted their water supply, and sucked their moist clothing to get the rain and dew from it. They had scooped out holes in the ground to shelter themselves, and put moist clay in their mouths to prolong life. Imagine, if you can, their horrible predicament, lying on a bullet-swept field, without ability to crawl, their wounds infested with maggots, and existing five days or more before being succored, and you can get some idea of the horrors of war."[102] It has been reported that one Union soldier, driven to desperation by the pain of his wounds and the horror of his situation, ended his suffering by slicing his own throat with a pen-knife.

Although of no benefit for most of the unfortunates left out front, the truce was good for the men in the trenches: "A cessation of hostilities from 6 to 8 p.m. to bury dead and bring in the wounded of both sides. This is the first time that we have ever seen a flag of truce in such ... operations. The enemy line their palisades and earthworks [and] shake out their blankets in the front lines, and [it] is the first time they have had an opportunity of raising their heads for several days. A quiet night in our immediate front."[103] Perhaps Latta did not see, or chose to ignore, the gruesome experiences of those unlucky individuals assigned to the mortuary detail: "The burial parties were in most instances unable to handle the dead, corruption had extended so far, and contented themselves with covering as it lay each body with a slight mound of earth."[104]

For those not involved with attempting to bury torn, bloated, and rotting corpses, a certain amount of good will was evident during hundreds of amicable individual encounters between the combatants in the no-man's land -- feelings which seem to have been carried into the next day: "Not a shot fired today in our division front. There seems to have been some arrangement made last night between the men of both sides to stop this incessant popping."[105] Peace of sorts reigned along the lines until early on the ninth, when a Confederate officer apparently

---

[102]Best, pp. 158-159.
[103]Latta diary, 6/7/1864.
[104]Hagood, Johnson, *Memoirs of the War of Secession*, as cited in Maney, p. 183.
[105]Latta diary, 6/8/1864.

decided that such a lack of hostilities was unseemly, and ordered the sniping to resume. A compassionate Butternut yelled to his counterparts in blue across the killing zone, "Hey Yanks! You better git inter yer holes." In a few moments two shots were fired into the air, and then the firing resumed as before.[106]

Not all the communications between the combatants was as friendly or as compassionate as those mentioned above, as this exchange, which occurred in front of the Sixth Corps' Vermont Brigade, and probably within earshot of the 119th, will illustrate. "The other night after it was safely dark, the rebels were as 'bold as sheep.' They jumped upon their breastworks, and invited the 'Yankee sons of b____' to come on. They said it would take a long time for us to *dig* into Richmond. Our boys replied that we should dig them into hell and *walk* into Richmond."[107]

The mutual siege, and the taunting, finally ended on June 12 when orders were received that the Grays' division was to be withdrawn at dark. "We hailed, almost with acclamations, the announcement of our withdrawal from the awful place. No words can adequately describe the horrors of the twelve days we had spent there, and the suffering we endured."[108] For the men in the Grays' brigade there was even more news, which may have been either well or poorly received depending upon which side of the Clark controversy the recipient had been on: "General Eustis relieved from command. We expected this [as] the result of his conduct. Lt. Colonel [Gideon Clark of the 119th] takes command of the brigade."[109] In the evening, "This division [the First] moves back quietly to a new line of pits, the enemy notwithstanding. We are too short a distance from them not to be aware of the movement. They drop a few mortar shells in our immediate neighborhood. The line of march is taken up in the direction of the Chickahominy."[110]

As significant as these events were, unbeknownst to the Philadelphians and their compatriots, movements then taking place behind enemy lines would have an even greater effect upon the future of

---

[106]Haines, p. 214.
[107]Fisk, p. 228.
[108]Haines, p. 215.
[109]Latta diary.
[110]Latta diary.

the Regiment than the end of the stalemate at Cold Harbor. The day before, Confederate Major General Jubal A. Early had received orders to withdraw his troops from the front lines and assemble them, ready for movement, in the area of Gaines Mills. While the Grays were marching south, Early's troops began their march to the Shenandoah Valley.[111]

[111]Humphreys, vol. 6, p. 195.

14

THE SHENANDOAH VALLEY

The infantrymen in the 119th were not aware, as final preparations were made to move away from despised Cold Harbor, how significantly the strategic picture of the war was about to change. The expectation of the average blue-coated soldier on the morning of June 14 was for another of the seemingly innumerable movements to the left flank -- not of the rather dramatic movement that Grant had planned. Instead, as the long blue columns snaked down to the banks of the James River, the realization began to spread through the ranks that something novel was in the works.

At the time the drive toward Richmond was originally planned in the spring, it was only one component of a complex scheme to bring down the Confederacy, with coordinated attacks all across the country. In addition to the part planned for the Army of the Potomac, General Sherman was to march on Atlanta; action was planned in the deep South; Major General Franz Sigel was to control the Shenandoah Valley; and Benjamin "Beast" Butler was to capture, or at least threaten, Richmond by invasion up the peninsula created by the James and Appomattox Rivers.

Initially, Butler's drive toward Richmond showed great promise, but it eventually bogged down in front of the Confederate works across the base of the peninsula at Bermuda Hundred, where Butler's men remained, practically as useless as if they had been stuffed into a corked bottle. Sometime during the siege at Cold Harbor, Grant decided to switch his tactics from a move on Richmond, to an attempt to capture Petersburg, the vital rail hub located to the south of the Confederate capital, by crossing the James River and then launching a concerted attack against that city in conjunction with Butler's idled troops.

Arguably, Grant's new plan had greater strategic depth and political appeal than merely trying to draw Lee's army into the open for a bludgeoning. The huge casualties suffered by the Union forces during the "Forty Days" may have convinced the Union commander that starving the Confederate army by cutting off its supplies would be more humane and politically acceptable than sending home the long lists of dead and maimed that another major battle would necessarily entail. Or, perhaps the loss of so many combat veterans, and their replacement with conscripts and rookies, had shaken the General's confidence in the reliability of his own troops. In any case, the goal became the capture of a town, roads, railroads, and the control of territory, rather than a search solely for another stand-up fight, a philosophical change that would have a profound effect upon the men of the Army of the Potomac. Before this new grand strategy could play itself out, however, the Federal soldiers were confronted with the daunting task of attempting to cross a major river with the Confederate army somewhere in the vicinity. Captain Latta provided a concise account of those movements.

"June 14 -- March at 5:00 [a.m.] as vanguard to train. Reached Charles City Courthouse about 11:00 [a.m.] and after having halted there for about an hour took up the line of march again toward the magnificent James River country and get into position about 1:00 [p.m.], the grounds having far exceeded our expectations..."[1]

---

[1]During 1862 and 1863 Captain Latta's diaries consisted of entries into small 3" x 7" pocket calendars with two dates to a page. Being a Philadelphia lawyer, Latta confined his notes to the space available for each date, resulting in very brief entries, in very tiny script. In 1864 he obtained another such pocket calendar, but fortunately the new booklet had only one date to a page and consequently Latta's content increased proportionately. Unfortunately, much of the content for the "Forty Days" campaign was undecipherable to this author. The translation problem resulted from a number of factors, the tiny script cramming hundreds of words into a 3" x 7" space, poor penmanship undoubtedly the result of Latta's fatigue, the lack of available time to compose his thoughts and write, the physical circumstances under which many of the entries were made, and also to his unfortunate decision to write originally in pencil and then to go over the pencil with pen, making many words a tiny jumble of wavy lines. As may be apparent from the increasingly long and detailed quotes included after Latta was appointed to the Third Brigade staff, the entries became increasingly easier to decipher. Given the benefit of more available content, the

"June 15 -- Remained on the bank of the [James] river all day ... The river is studded with warcraft and shipping of all kinds."

"June 16 -- Again on board the Atlanta. The executive officer and chief engineer accompanied us on shore and dined with us ... Our corps is to remain until all the transportation of the army crosses the pontoon ... before the night is altered we are shipped on the transport steamer *Dictator*, for Bermuda Hundred, the 1st and 3rd Division formed by water and the 2nd Division by land. We are accommodated with a stateroom."

"June 17 -- Reached the landing at Bermuda Hundred at 2:30 a.m. and marched out in the direction of Butler's Works, where we remained behind the entrenchments ... annoyed by heat and swarms of flies until afternoon when we arrive back and go into camp. After dark, heavy cannonading and musketry heard in the direction of Petersburg. We afterwards learned that the Ninth Corps had been engaged on the 15th. Smith with the Eighteenth Corps captured the first line of the enemy's works and a position which commands Petersburg."

"June 18 -- At 12:30 midnight we move out ... the right center sally port [with] the intention of attacking the enemy. A few shots fired and the attack for reasons unknown appears [to] be abandoned and at daylight we return to our position of yesterday. A heavy [firing from the] ... direction of Petersburg in the morning. No news of satisfactory change ... as night closes we are [hopeful] that we may have a comfortable rest."

"June 19 -- Moved at 4:00 a.m. towards Petersburg crossing the Appomattox on pontoons -- arrived at the front within the works captured by the Eighteenth Corps on the 15th instant. Petersburg is in plain sight. We hold the hills commanding the town on this side of the river whilst the environs on the other side are occupied by the enemy. In the afternoon we relieve General ________'s division of troops who are picketing the river. Our headquarters are established in the yard of a house. This is as pleasant a town as we have had for some time. Too fine to last long."

---

history of the Regiment for the Shenandoah Campaign will be provided primarily from the Latta diary with narrative added where fuller detail may be of interest. All of the following un-annotated quotations are from the Latta diary for the date given.

"June 20 -- Remained in the same position all day. Extended our lines. Shelling pretty lively during the morning. Division headquarters shelled out. The enemy's batteries are planted along the river from Fort Cliffton to the city. Fighting going in the left during the afternoon. Have heard as yet nothing from that quarter. Men were at some handsome places in the neighborhood."

"June 21 -- Remained all day in same position. Brigadier General [John H.] Martindale and Major General Smith had advanced quarters. The pickets of our brigade are relieved by colored troops during the afternoon and we are under orders to move shortly after dark. Ben Smith posts a battery of 20 pounders near the wagons which draws a fire in that neighborhood and a piece of shell goes through one of them which causes a sudden decamping of teams. Start just after dark and continue the march all night in what direction or whither bound it is not known."

"June 22 -- Reached a position just after daylight to the left of General Hancock's corps somewhere to the southwest of Petersburg. The intention seems to be to reach the Weldon Railroad. We move forward to attack, our skirmishers meet the enemy and we throw up entrenchments. A tremendous attack is made on the right and the Second Corps are worsted, losing a battery and some prisoners. We fall back to our original position and attack again ordered and at 7:00 p.m. After dark we in obedience to this order move forward through a dense underbrush ... reaching the rifle pits."

The plan called for the Sixth and Second Corps to drive to the south of Petersburg, in hopes of turning the Confederate right flank, and also to occupy a portion of the Weldon Railroad, one of the supply routes for Lee's army and Richmond. In the process of passing through dense woods on the way to their destination, the two corps became separated. The Southerners froze the Sixth Corps in place with one division of A. P. Hill's Corps, and launched two other divisions against the Second Corps, beating them badly and taking numerous prisoners.[2]

At the same time, the cavalry under Union Brigadier Generals James H. Wilson and Augustus V. Kautz drove further to the south of the infantry's incursion, intent on breaking the Weldon, Southside and

---

[2]Foote, vol. 3, pp. 442-445.

Richmond & Danville railroads, and destroying several key railroad bridges that would require months to repair. As the result of a number of mishaps, none of the bridges were destroyed and much smaller portions of the railroads were wasted than was originally intended. Even worse, the swift response from the Confederate cavalry created the possibility that all the Union horse soldiers would be captured. While the Grays maneuvered through the woods for the next several days, the Union troopers to their south struggled to avoid capture, abandoning most of their artillery and supply wagons in the process.

"June 23 -- An attack again ordered at 3:30 a.m. The hour arrives, lines in confusion from a lack of concert of action in division commanders or some other cause. The advance is not made and we lay sweltering in a [hot sun] until about 3:00 p.m. until we are ordered to the left which is seriously threatened. Rifle pits thrown up speedily. Another attack ordered which does not come off. Everything in the way of movements seems to have been in confusion for a day or two just past. We again fall back to our old position where we remain all night."

"June 24 -- Commence the erection of another line of works and continue the same until they are nearly completed when orders come to discontinue in readiness to move forward. Shortly after this another order arrives to resume operations and referring to the probability of the corps remaining in its present position for a day or two. Just after daylight cannonading equal in severity almost to that at Gettysburg ... on the right."

"June 25 -- The heat has been thoroughly oppressive today. Orders came to the effect that a position of the troops of the division would not be changed. We moved headquarters for a more desirable spot. During the night heavy cannonading and musketry heard on the right. Horses saddled and brigade commander and staff [move] to the front. The band reported to the command yesterday. Matters became quiet and we returned to headquarters."

"June 30 -- Remained in the position taken up near Reams Station until about 5:00 p.m. when orders came to move back and resume the old position near Williams House. The command moved through the most blinding volumes of dust that I have ever experienced. The order to take old position countermanded and we halt for the night about 3-1/2 miles from it on the Plank road, being still under the command of Sheridan and ... Wilson ... he refuses to let us up ..."

While the Grays were marching and countermarching, the nearly surrounded troopers were cutting through swamps and fording streams in a desperate effort to avoid capture. Because Sheridan and Wilson were understandably concerned that the horse soldiers might become trapped, the First Division of the Sixth Corps was detailed to maintain a position in the area of Reams Station in hopes of keeping open an avenue of escape for whenever the cavalry might emerge from the back country. Eventually, the troopers escaped the trap at a point some distance from the location of the Grays' division.

"July 1 -- Remained in the position of last night all day today. Headquarters near the road. Weather hot and dust is thick, impenetrable masses envelope us."

"July 2 -- at 5:00 p.m. move back to take up as we again supposed to the ground we occupied before but we are disappointed and the troops are thrown some distance to the left in an open field where the sun and sand render everything almost untenable. Establish headquarters in a pine woods in rear of the open field near Williams House where the troops are encamped."

"July 4 -- The natal day of independence passes off rather quietly. No noise or alarm from any direction except the occasional booming of cannon that we hear continually from the right. In the evening went over to Harris's Battery where the occasion was celebrated with all accompanying convivialities. The heat of the weather still continues with its former intensity. A reviving breeze however during part of the day rendered it in a measure more pleasant than heretofore."

"July 7 -- This morning at 2:00 the third division of the corps left us and proceeded to City Point and from thence by transport it is supposed to Harper's Ferry. The organization of the brigade is effected today, the 37th Massachusetts and the 82nd and 23rd Pennsylvania assigned to it [also assigned to the Third Brigade was Elisha Hunt Rhodes' 2nd Rhode Island regiment].[3] Colonel [Oliver] Edwards of the 37th will assume command ... The command being quiet all day nothing of interest occurring until 9:15 when orders came to be in [readiness] to move at once to City Point. Got ready as speedily as possible. We ...

[3]Rhodes, p. 167.

Sixth Corps loading for Washington - *Leslie's Illustrated Newspaper*

at 11 pulled out on the road. All seemed pleased with the movement, believing it to be precipatory to an embarkation."

At the same time that the Grays were involved with the debacle at the Weldon Railroad, Early's Butternuts were in the process of pushing Major General David Hunter's forces westward from the Shenandoah Valley into what is now West Virginia, leaving an open road to Washington. Pursuant to Lee's plan, Early then began a dash toward the Federal capital, and in response the Third Division of the Sixth Corps was shifted to Washington to assist its defense. That division, along with other odds and ends of Union garrison troops, were defeated on July 9 at a crossing over the Monocacy River to the west of Washington. Although badly mauled, the Union effort bought desperately needed additional time to gather reinforcements to the capital. It was in response to that crisis that the balance of the Sixth Corps was redeployed.

"July 10 -- Remained loafing about the wharf all day awaiting the arrival of transports and the shipment of the 2nd Division. The heat almost unbearable. Got dinner on board the Sanitary Commission boat.

At 9:00 finally got shipped on board the Eliza Hancon ... We had the band on board at 11:00. Shoved off to patriotic airs. A beautiful night and we enjoyed an excellent sleep. The boat is a swift one and we will make Washington ahead of all other steamers."

"July 11 -- Passed Fort Monroe at 2:30 a.m. and awoke at daylight finding ourselves on the waters of the Chesapeake just out of sight of land. Had a pleasant trip up the Bay and Potomac, passing all the transports that had left ahead of ours, reaching Washington at 5:30 p.m. Immediately disembarked. Skirmishing going on in front of Fort Stevens out 7th Street. The citizens in a great state of excitement. Headquarters at the National ... Wrote home."

The most grateful citizens seem to have been former slaves who had escaped from their Southern masters and sought refuge in the nation's capital, and who faced the greatest risk should the city fall to the Confederates. Colonel Beckwith in Upton's Brigade described the reaction of those desperate people to the arrival of the rest of Wright's men. "The negroes were very demonstrative and saluted us with many quaint remarks one of which was, 'God bress massa Lincum for the Six Co.', and another, 'Dey's done got to clear out for dem red cross sojers. Wee's all saved now.'"[4]

"July 12 -- The brigade arrives at 12:00 noon. March up the avenue with a full band and out 7th Street where within 4-1/2 miles of the Capital the skirmishers are engaged with the enemy and Fort Stevens discharges her heavy guns. At 7:00 p.m. two regiments of our brigade go in and ... the President witness[es] ... the demonstration ... by the artillery [and] the handsome advancement of our skirmishers."

"July 13 -- In the morning the enemy are found to have left our front. At 2:00 p.m. we move via the military road along the line of fortifications to Tennallytown, thence via the river road to Crossroads which point is reached shortly after dark. Headquarters established at ____ house. What a glorious change from the dry and sands of Virginia to the fertile well-cultivated land of Maryland."

"July 14 -- Detailed this morning as rear guard to the corps train. The march of the troops commences about 5:00 a.m. but we [do not] get off until 2:00 and then delayed by weapons drawn by ____ mules and

---

[4]Best, p. 170.

Skirmishing at Fort Stevens - *Leslie's Illustrated Newspaper*

awkward teamsters, were made but about ten miles and 12:00 midnight bivouacked at Mills."

"July 15 -- Awaiting the arrival of trains we do not move until 11:00. Reach ... the rest of the division near Poolsville in the afternoon where we went into camp. The enemy have left Maryland it is supposed and thus escaped once more into Virginia. [They] have actually made one of the most daring and successful raids on record."

"July 16 -- Moved at 5:00 a.m. crossing the Potomac at Whites Ford where we are met with some opposition from the enemy's cavalry. Marched on following closely the rebels' rear. Passed through Leesburg and from thence to Clarks Gap where we bivouacked for the night. It is a beautiful sight from the top of the mountain across Loudoun Valley. Stopped for a short time at the house of one Barrett which seems to have been a guerilla headquarters."

"July 18 -- Moved again at 4:30 a.m. via the turnpike to Snickers Gap, crossed the mountain and came up with the enemy at the Shenandoah. Crook's forces [Bvt. Major General George Crook, commander of the Army of West Virginia, a/k/a the Eighth Corps, which formed a portion of the Army of the Shenandoah created to meet the challenge presented by Confederate Gen. Early] ... repulsed, quite a fight which lasted from 5:00 p.m. until 8:00."

"July 19 -- Remained in the same position all day. May have crossed the Shenandoah about 9:00 a.m. Found no enemy to impede our progress ... we move in column ... out the Winchester Turnpike about two miles this side of Berryville. Had a severe thunderstorm today which was quite refreshing. Remaining in position until night when orders came to move at once back to Washington. Commenced the march at 10:00 p.m. Continued all night crossing the Shenandoah at Snickers Ford. Quite a picturesque sight, the column fording the stream under the light of the moon."

"July 20 -- The march continues until 4:00 p.m. passing through Leesburg, Clark's Gap, Hamilton and bivouacked for the night at Goose Creek. The march was hard, fatiguing and exhausting and the ... guerrillas followed closely upon our heels and gathered a great many stragglers."

The Union column was dogged by the men of the infamous Confederate partisan raider John Singleton Mosby who, for example, was able to scoop up 102 weary Yankees who fell behind their comrades on July 18.[5]

"July 22 -- Moved at 7:00 p.m. Marched through Franesville, and after dark halted on the north side of Difficult Creek ... having had a march which lasted all day, bivouacked for the night ..."

"July 23 -- Moved at 4:30 a.m. along with the trains passed through Levinsville, Langley and crossed Chain Bridge about 11:00 a.m. encamping in the rear of Fort Gaines. Immediately went into the city where we remained until 6:00 p.m. dining at the Metropol."

"July 24 -- Went into the city at 4:00 a.m ... Returned to camp at once where we remained the remainder of the day. Rained and blew tremendously during the night. Transports await us in the [harbor] and ... [we] expect to be shipped tomorrow for City Point. In fact the order for the movement had been issued."

---

[5]Wert, *Mosby's Rangers*, p. 182.

"July 25 -- ... Young and self went into Washington in all the rain. It slacked up towards noon and was very pleasant ... Remained in town all day. Moved down to the arsenal in the afternoon ... Left town at 11:00 p.m. Orders came to be ready to move at an early hour in the morning and as such a character to lead us to suppose that we are not for City Point."

"July 26 -- Moved at 12:00 as the rear division of the corps, marched out the Rockville Road, passed through Rockville, took supper at a hotel in that place. March continued until 11:00 p.m. when the command bivouacked four miles beyond Rockville on the Frederick Road."

"July 27 -- Moved again at 4:30 a.m. Marched until 2:00 p.m. Passed through Clarksburg and encamped near Hyattstown."

"July 28 -- Moved early in the morning, passing through Hyattstown, thence via the turnpike ... [to] the Monocacy -- near the railroad bridge when we halted. Bathed in the stream. Pitched camp ... intending to remain for the night, but suddenly orders came to move again. The troops forded the stream, the turnpike bridge having been destroyed. The march continued until midnight when the tired and exhausted command halted at Jefferson."

"July 29 -- Moved at 6:00, passed through Jefferson and from thence through Petersville, Knoxville and Sandy Hook, crossing the Potomac on the pontoons at Harper's Ferry -- through that place and on to Halltown, where at 6:00 p.m. the command took up a position and encamped. The scenery in passing through the gorge of the Blue and Elk Ridge is grand and magnificent. The troops have been marched to such an extent that they are, with the terrible heat of the weather, and accompanying fatigue almost exhausted."

The pause at Halltown allowed Lt. Colonel Clark to indulge in one of his seemingly favorite pastimes, self promotion. From that town he wrote a letter to Pennsylvania's Governor Curtin suggesting that since the initial enlistment term for the soldiers of the 23rd Pennsylvania, which had recently been added to the Third Brigade, was about to expire, that it would be a good idea to merge any veteran re-enlistees, and draftees with time remaining, into the 119th. This, he added, would entitle the newly expanded Regiment to a full colonel, a position which he would most humbly have been willing to fill.[6]

"July 30 -- Remained encamped until 2:00 p.m. when orders came to move at once. We pulled out right in the heat of the day, halted under a burning sun just at the foot of Bolivar Heights, and did not get [back] across the pontoon until 11:00 p.m. The line of march lined with men overcome by sunstroke. It was some mismanagement that the corps was started when it did. Reached Petersville at 3:00 a.m."

"July 31 -- Ordered to move at 11:30, the day fearfully warm. Do not start until 1:30. Halt at the Antietam for 15 minutes and in woods just beyond for an hour. Pass through Jefferson again over the same route we came -- Citizens all dressed in Sunday clothes. Marched to within 1-1/2 miles this side of Frederick City, where we encamped. Distance marched during the month 239 miles."

As always, Captain Latta preferred the use of understatement when describing the burdens under which the troops were required to perform. A soldier from the Vermont brigade was not so restrained when he described the same day's march: "The heat was intense; the day was the very hottest of all the season; the clouds of dust were actually blinding; the pace almost a gallop," while a lieutenant in the 2nd Rhode Island noted that as a result of the march "The men was about as near plaid out as ever saw them ..."[7]

"August 1 -- Remained in same camp all day, visited Frederick City in the afternoon, and we remained in town until 11:00 a.m. News came to hand from Petersburg, not of a very favorable character. Chambersburg [Pa.] reduced to ashes."

"August 2 -- Moved at 9:00 a.m. according to orders. They are subsequently countermanded and go back to our old position. Orders came at night to move at 4:30 a.m. tomorrow."

"August 3 -- Command moved in obedience to orders of last night, passed through Buckeyestown and encamped beyond the Monocacy, crossing that stream near Dellaplains Mill."

"August 4 -- Day set apart by the President for humiliation and prayer. Religious services held in front of headquarters."

---

[6]Clark correspondence, Pennsylvania Archives.

[7]As cited in Wert, *From Winchester...*, p. 15.

The men of the Sixth Corps were in critical need of rest, if not "humiliation and prayer," as perceptively noted and recorded by Captain John W. Deforest of the Nineteenth Corps when he camped near the Greek Crosses on August 4: "... The Sixth Corps, one of the best in the Army of the Potomac, is lying near us. They seem to be badly demoralized by the severe service and the disastrous battles of the campaigns in Virginia. Their guns are dirty; their camps are disorderly clutters of shelter tents; worst of all the men are disrespectful of their officers. I heard a private say to a lieutenant, 'I'll slap your face if you say that again.'"

"These fellows lurk around our clean, orderly camps and steal our clean, bright rifles. I went over to the nearest brigade to complain about this and to recover lost ordnance stores."

"'Looking for guns, Cap?' drawled a sergeant. 'Well, if you find a clean gun in this camp, you claim it. We hain't had one in our brigade since Cold Harbor.'"

The captain, fresh from the west, continued his rather bemused account of what appeared to him to be clear indications of broken morale amongst the Greek Crosses. "The camp astonished me by its contrast to ours, ... there were no boundary lines between the different regiments, all being tumbled together higgledy-piggledy, officers mixed up anyhow with the men, and the brigade commander in the middle. He was a colonel, a pleasant and gentlemanly young fellow, surrounded by young officers. Their talk about the war and our immediate military future had a tone of depression which astonished me."

"'But don't you believe in Grant at all?'" I finally asked.

"'Yes, we believe in Grant,' replied the colonel. 'But we believe a great deal more in Lee and in that Army of Virginia.'"[8]

"August 5 -- Leave of absence applied for, granted, and we [departed] Buckeyestown Station at 2:30 p.m.

Showing a remarkable degree of magnanimity, on that same date Lt. Colonel Clark was the first to sign (although it does not appear who among the total of twelve signing Regimental officers was the author), a letter addressed to Pennsylvania's Governor Curtin requesting that Captain Goodman be reinstated to his former position as an officer in the

---

[8]DeForest, p. 165.

Regiment. Unfortunately the letter does not address the motivation for the request, whether from forgiveness and reconciliation over the charges filed by Goodman against Clark, or merely from a desperate need for experienced officers. In any case, like wise fathers, both Curtin and President Lincoln approved the request, seemingly putting to an end the spat that had divided the staff of the Regiment in the spring, and Goodman was soon back in command of his former company.[9]

"August 7 -- Went by Doylestown [Pa.] with Pa and Nellie at 3:00 p.m. What a miserably dull and insipid town this has got to be."

While Latta was away on leave, Grant made several significant changes in the organization of the military in the eastern theater. Previously, the backwater areas of Maryland, Pennsylvania, West Virginia, and Washington had been divided into four separate military districts, each with a separate commander. Although this system provided a fine way to employ generals not good enough to fight, but with too much political pull to cashier, it proved to be a nightmare when trying to deal with Early, who kept moving from one district into another. On August seventh, Grant combined all four districts into one, the "Middle Military Division," and placed his trusted young protege, Philip H. Sheridan, in charge of the whole.[10]

Although subsequent events would show this to have been a wise appointment, at the time, Grant's decision was subjected to quite a bit of second-guessing and criticism in the administration and the press, based partly on Sheridan's age and relative lack of experience, and also in part because of the appearance that the younger man obtained the position primarily because of a friend in a high position. In fact, the relationship between Grant and Sheridan was certainly beneficial to the latter, given that early in his military career, Sheridan had served under then Captain David A. Russell, the excellent commander of the First Division of the Sixth Corps; but with the appointment to command of the Middle Military District, Sheridan moved two levels above his former superior.[11]

---

[9]Clark correspondence, Pennsylvania Archives.

[10]Pond, *Campaigns...*, vol. 6, p. 120.

[11]Sheridan, p. 292.

"August 11 -- Left for Harpers Ferry on the 7:45 train, reached that place at 1:00 p.m., found that the entire army had moved in the direction of Winchester and that there was no communication with it."

Not only did Latta miss the reorganization, he also missed some depressing special duty. On August 12, the Grays' brigade was detailed to return to Winchester to escort a train of supply wagons. After the mission was successfully completed, the Brigade entered the city. In building after building, the Yankees discovered the wounded from a heavy skirmish several days earlier -- sixty Confederates and seventy Federals, all in various states of pain and suffering.[12]

"August 13 -- Reached Winchester at sunrise, found the brigade on duty at that place. Quite a Union sentiment prevailed. Met several pretty ladies. Left the town at 12:00 and marched through _____ and Kernstown. Reached the main army ... at 7:00 p.m."

"August 14 -- Remained in position all day ... Firing going on the skirmish line."

"August 15 -- Remained in position taken up yesterday. Took a chance in a raffle for a horse, lost of course. Nineteenth Corps moved off to right, supposed in the direction of Front Royal. The enemy made a demonstration here on the skirmish line."

"August 16 -- Orders came towards evening to the effect that the ordnance would move at 11:00 p.m. At that hour started, marched all night via the Winchester Turnpike and [rested] at that place shortly after daylight, where remained several hours, spending the greater part of the time visiting the Union ladies ..."

"August 17 -- The remarks of yesterday refer to this morning. The ______ brigade left behind to garrison the town. We rather envy them their position, but towards night Breckinridge's entire corps comes down on them and completely cleans them out." [The undecipherable reference was probably to the Jersey Brigade which fought a rear-guard action at Winchester against Early's significantly larger forces on the seventeenth, and was routed.[13]] "We moved on to the Opequon Creek where we encamped for the night."

---

[12]Pond, *Campaigns...*, vol. 6, p. 125.
[13]Pond, *Campaigns...*, vol. 6, p. 130.

"August 18 -- Roused up at 2:00 a.m. to go into position on the banks of the [Opequon]. Moved shortly after daylight, passing through Berryville and halted at Cliffton, expecting to encamp, but the movement continued throughout the day until we arrived within a mile of Charleston, where at 7:00 p.m. the troops encamped. It has rained quite heavily today."

"August 19 -- Remained in camp established last evening during the day. Colonel Edwards and Captain Young received leave of absence for five days."

"August 20 -- In the afternoon rode through Charleston, purchased a gray mare. Everything today appears to be quiet with no prospects of an immediate movement."

"August 21 -- The day opens quietly and matters are such that a quiet Sunday seems to be in prospection. Engaged in writing letters when about 9:00 firing opens briskly on the picket line. Tents are struck immediately and the troops prepared for action, but had the enemy pressed their first attack vigorously, they could certainly have thrown us into confusion and possibly have defeated us. The engagement which opened in the morning continues all day, but is confined to fighting on the skirmish line. The enemy also have some artillery."

"August 22 -- Shortly after midnight abandoned the position held yesterday and moved back towards Halltown occupying the heights in that vicinity shortly after daylight. Occupy a position on the extreme right. Pitch tents and propose to remain comfortable for the day anyhow, but about noon orders received to move to the extreme left to the support of General Crook's command, the enemy having made a demonstration in his front and seemingly threatening. A very severe rainstorm passes over."

"August 23 -- Remained in the same position taken up yesterday on the extreme left ... In the afternoon rode out to the 49th P. V. stationed on Bolivar Heights. The term of service of the 23rd P. V. having expired, they today left the brigade."

"August 24 -- Again announced as Judge Advocate of a general court martial for the trial of Colonel ______ F. Stainton, 67th [Pennsylvania] Regiment commanding 2nd brigade 3rd division. A reconnaissance consisting of troops of the Nineteenth Corps and Crook's command moves out. They developed the enemy in some force in front of our left."

"August 25 -- ... Heavy firing in the direction of Shepherdstown, cavalry force supposed to be engaged, should not be at all surprised if a movement were ordered tonight."

In sharp contrast to the depressing picture of the Sixth Corps painted on August 4, a Colonel Chipman, who was observing the army on behalf of Secretary Stanton, made these observations only three weeks later: "Sheridan's army is in splendid condition, well in hand and manifesting the greatest anxiety for a fight. There is a feeling of entire confidence in their leader, and regiments talk about being able to whip brigades. Sheridan really has a very fine army here, and the universal good spirits that prevail and anxiety to fight manifested would make it a hard army to compete with."[14] Events would soon support the Colonel's observations about the army's fighting prowess, but the report ought to be viewed with a certain amount of skepticism. It is possible that Sheridan's appointment could have improved morale so dramatically within such a short period of time, despite no significant reduction in the physical demands being made upon the troops. It is equally possible, that the report was intended more to curry favor with Sheridan, who obviously had a very influential mentor, than as an objective assessment of the army.

"August 26 -- Quite a sharp skirmish to the left of our immediate front."

"August 27 -- No enemy in front of the Army of Western Virginia today."

"August 28 -- Moved shortly after daylight and marched as far as Flowing Spring, where the command halted a while late in the afternoon, when it again moved on as far as the position held by the troops on Sunday last. Establish headquarters in the yard of Briscoe's House."

"August 31 -- The barn belonging to the house where Advocate General are is fired and burned."

The almost continuous movements up and down the Shenandoah Valley during this period appear virtually inexplicable until the motivations of the two commanders are taken into consideration. Early's primary task was to keep as many Federal soldiers as possible away from

---

[14]O.R.-1-43-1-907.

Petersburg, and, if possible, cause some embarrassment for the Lincoln Administration, which would soon be facing re-election.

For Sheridan, the problem was more complex. First and foremost, he had to protect Washington. Second, it was crucially important that he not suffer a defeat which could further sour Lincoln's chances at the polls. Lastly, he was expected to win a smashing victory, not just an ordinary victory. To resolve those somewhat conflicting goals, Sheridan evolved a strategy somewhat similar to a boxer circling his opponent looking for an opening or mistake, while trying to avoid a knockout punch. The Union army would advance while looking for an opening, hoping to catch Early's army in a dangerous formation or after a portion had been returned to Richmond. Whenever the Confederates, who were reinforced during this period with an extra division, showed any serious aggressive intentions, however, the Union army scurried back up the valley, because the perfect opening for an attack had not yet been discovered.

"September 1 -- A dispatch from headquarters Middle Military District reports the enemy concentrating his forces at Bunker Hill."

"September 3 -- Left at 4:00 a.m. and moved to the position formerly occupied by the Corps near Cliffton. Quite brisk fight takes place toward night to our left. The enemy ... attacked Crook's forces."

Captain DeForest of the Nineteenth Corps described that skirmish in more vivid detail than did his fellow officer from Philadelphia. "Of a sudden, just about sundown, one of his [Early's] columns stumbled upon our left wing and pitched into it at a lively rate, showing first a heavy force of skirmishers and then a line of battle. Some of Crook's regiments were driven out of a wood where they had just begun camping; but they rallied in the open fields, charged back into the timber and recovered it in fine style. There was noisy musketry and cannonading for half an hour, and then the Rebels retired under cover of their artillery."[15]

"September 4 -- Earthworks thrown up along the front, the enemy shows himself and attack from him anticipated at daylight tomorrow."

---

[15]DeForest, pp. 169-170.

If we may assume that the Yankees in the Nineteenth Corps constructed works in a fashion similar to their comrades of the Greek Cross, the Grays' fortifications were built as follows: "... let me instruct you how to make a fieldwork. Steal all the rails that you can find in a township; then build two parallel fences four feet apart and four and a half feet high; fill in with stones, earth, and green timber, and bank up the front with earth laid at an angle of forty-five degrees; then look across it and wish the enemy would come."[16]

"September 5 -- It rained all day heavily. The enemy did not attack this morning as it was expected they would. A few shots fired in the morning along the left of our division's line, but otherwise everything passes off quickly. Passed the day in reading *Very Hard Cash*, a novel of some pretensions, but highly overdrawn in many of its incidents."

Captain Latta and the rest of the Regiment may have had the luxury of reading and relaxation, but for a small contingent of the 119th, this was a time of suffering and death. Throughout the latter part of 1863, and during the Forty Days campaign, a number of Philadelphians had the misfortune to be captured by their adversaries. Of those, twelve were doubly cursed; they were shipped, usually in cattle cars, to the hell hole known as Andersonville Prison. Five, Walter Barnes, Julius Honneger, Joseph Maun, James McGurk, and James Whitehead, died there in late August and early September 1864. They were reunited in the camp's pitiful excuse for a cemetery with their comrades from Philadelphia, Agniola Brunett, Archibald Currie, Phineas Dow, Frank Hanson, and Joseph Robertson, all of whom had been claimed earlier by conditions in the prison.[17]

It is really not surprising that ten of the twelve Grays succumbed to disease while imprisoned at Andersonville. Rather, given the deplorable conditions in the camp, it is a wonder that two of them survived. The following, taken from a report of the Confederate prison

---

[16]DeForest, p. 168.

[17]Andersonville Prison Records. Only two of the twelve Grays known to have been incarcerated at Andersonville Prison survived the ordeal: Benjamin Constantine and Thomas M. Seth. Perhaps Seth owed his survival to the rather limited period of time which he spent in Andersonville, since he was released in Savannah, Ga. on November 31, 1864. Muster Out Rolls, Pennsylvania Archives.

inspector Chandler, provides what is presumably a frank, if not charitable, description of the camp. "'This prison when completed in February, 1864, contained an area of 17 acres. It was afterward enlarged to embrace 24 acres.... There are now [August 1, 1864] 30,000 prisoners in this enclosure, giving somewhat less than six square feet to each man.... A small stream passes through the enclosure from West to East. This furnishes the water for washing purposes. The water in the stream is rendered unfit for drinking before it reaches the enclosure, by refuse matter from the bakery and cook house. Under pressure of necessity, the prisoners have dug numerous wells with spoons and cups from which they obtain water to drink. The space along the stream, used as a sink [latrine], is in shocking condition, and cannot fail to breed pestilence.... There is no material for the prisoners to erect places of protection from inclement weather [or the baking sun]. Each man has been permitted to protect himself as best he can by stretching his blanket, if he has one [most were confiscated either at the front by needy Butternuts, or at processing centers by greedy guards], over him on such sticks as he can procure. Some of the men have dug holes in the ground, to seclude themselves during hot days.... There are no established rules for police consideration, and for the health, comfort and sanitary condition of those within the enclosure.... There is no medical attendance furnished within the stockade. Small quantities of medicine are placed in the hands of certain prisoners, of each squad or division, and the sick are directed to be brought by the sergeants of the squads to the "sick call," to the medical officers who attend at the gate. The crowd, at such times, is so great that only the strongest can get access to the doctor. Twenty or more dead bodies are carted out each day.... The dead are buried without coffins. The Sanitary condition of the prison is wretched. The principal causes of death are scurvy and chronic diarrhoea. No effort is being made to stop this condition of affairs by supplying proper food....'" "'This beats anything I ever saw or heard of; it is indeed a hell on earth.'"[18]

"September 6 -- The position now occupied by the Corps, Cliffton, derives its name from a farm in this vicinity. It is a strong one, being a range of knolls that overlook and command an extended plain in

---

[18]Prowell, pp. 237-239.

front. We are about 3-1/2 miles from Berryville and lay parallel to a road that strikes the Berryville and Winchester turnpike at right angles."

"September 7 -- It has cleared off beautifully this morning. The army holds continually the same relative position in all the points of defense that it takes up. The Sixth Corps on the right, Nineteenth in the center, and Army of Western Virginia on the left. It does not appear from all the movements since General Sheridan assumed command to be designed to bring on a general engagement, unless the enemy attack, the sole object to keep Early in the valley and prevent him either from crossing the Potomac or sending his force to Lee."

"September 8 -- General Sheridan's movements have invariably shown skill, promptness and efficiency, and he has always succeeded in developing the enemy ______ and discovering his position. The day dawns clear and pleasant."

Finally, on September sixteenth, after weeks of probing, marching, and countermarching, Sheridan found his opening, thanks in part to the low esteem in which he was held by his Confederate counterpart: "... if it was [Sheridan's purpose] to convince me that he was not an energetic commander, his strategy was a complete success ..."[19] Based upon the foregoing assessment of the young Union General, and faced with the pressing need for troops at Richmond, Early released General Kershaw's division to return to the trenches around the Southern capital. That departure was observed by a young lady with strong Union sympathies named Rebecca M. Wright, who smuggled a message to Sheridan that the Confederate division had departed.[20]

Sheridan immediately began to formulate final plans for a battle which he hoped would crush his weakened opponent. Coincidentally, Sheridan's mentor was also beginning to have concerns about the young general's willingness to engage the enemy, and as a result, Grant arranged to travel north to meet with his protege. During this meeting, Sheridan laid out his battle plan, which Grant approved without modification; whereupon Sheridan immediately returned to the

---

[19]As cited in Freeman, vol. 3, p. 576.

[20]Sheridan, p. 278.

Shenandoah Valley confident that he would turn his plan into a major triumph.[21]

"September 18 -- Rumors afloat this morning that a movement is anticipated. About 4:00 p.m. orders came to move at once. Everything in a bustle and the camp we have occupied for the past two weeks is suddenly broken up and everything prepared for a movement. The movement is however subsequently suspended."

The movement was not, however, to be suspended for long. Not only had the Confederate forces in the valley been weakened by the loss of Kershaw's division, but Early had also increased his vulnerability when he divided his forces, positioning one division to the east in front of Winchester, and the other two north of the city, toward Martinsburg. Sheridan planned to exploit the opportunity to defeat the enemy in detail with a drive, early on the nineteenth, against the smaller of the two segments of the Confederate army located to the east of Winchester behind the Opequon Creek.

The area at which the attack was aimed had attributes favorable to both the attacking Federals and the defending Confederates. The axis of the assault was to be westward along the Berryville-Winchester Pike, a seemingly positive guide for enhancing unit cohesion. Between the Federals and the enemy lay the Opequon Creek, which did not present a significant obstacle, because it was fordable at the crossing of the pike. Much more troublesome was the Berryville Canyon on the west side of the Opequon; a two-mile long, steep-sided gorge through which the pike passed on its way to Winchester. After exiting the canyon, the pike ran onto a broad plain on which "... clumps of woods and patches of underbrush occurred here and there, but the undulating ground consisted mainly of open fields, many of which were covered with standing corn that had already ripened."[22] Before the enemy could be engaged on this relatively benign battlefield, Rebel earthworks situated at the western end of the canyon would have to be carried, a job assigned to Wilson's cavalry.

The Grays were roused about 1:00 a.m. on September 19, and from their position on the left of the column at the head of the brigade,

---

[21]Grant, vol. 2, p. 328.

[22]Sheridan, p. 286.

commenced the march toward the Berryville Pike ford at 3:00 a.m.[23] While the infantry tramped toward the creek, Wilson's faster moving cavalry splashed across the ford, charged down the canyon, and carried the Southern works at the far end. Once the defenders were scattered from the works, the Union troopers dug in, hoping to be able to hold the emplacements until the more powerful blue-coated infantry could arrive. The arrival of that relief was not imminent, however, since the head of the leading Sixth Corps would not even reach the Opequon until around 8:00 a.m.[24]

The Red Crosses had neither a fast nor easy journey to the ford: "The first division of the Sixth Corps was very much mixed up with the artillery and wagon trains. The troops were pressed upon the sides of the road, and much hindered in making a rapid march. We made frequent short halts, then quick runs to recover what we had lost; so that it was near 9:00 a.m. before our [Jersey] brigade crossed the ford."[25]

Once over the creek, the 119th "... threw out one commissioned officer and twenty men as flankers on the right."[26] As for the rest of the column: "The troops marched on either side of the pike, the artillery, ambulances, and such trains as was carried taking the macadamized road."[27] This procession through the gorge was necessarily slow and ponderous, delaying the passage of the Sixth Corps and bringing the march of the trailing Nineteenth Corps to a dead stop for hours. "[Brigadier General Cuvier] Grover's division [lead Nineteenth Corps division] was greatly delayed by a train of ammunition wagons, and it was not until late in the forenoon that the troops intended for the attack could be got into line ready to advance."[28]

The congestion in the gorge nearly drove Sheridan into a frenzy of frustration and anger. Probably similar, though less intense emotions, were experienced by Clark, his officers, and the rest of the Grays, as they struggled to reach the battlefield. "The scene in this swarming gorge was one not easily forgotten. The road was crowded with wagons,

---

[23]Latta diary; O.R.-1-43-1-189, Clark.
[24]Rhodes, p. 183.
[25]Haines, p. 257.
[26]O.R.-1-43-1-189.
[27]As cited in Stackpole, *Sheridan in the Shenandoah*, p. 157.
[28]Sheridan, p. 288.

ambulances, gun carriages and caissons, getting onward as fast as possible, but so very slowly that one might already divine that we should fight our battle almost without artillery. On the right and on the left endless lines of infantry struggled through the underbrush and stumbled over rocks and gutters. On every knoll and under every thicket gravely watching us pass, sat the hundreds of men who belonged to any army but never fight: the cooks, the officers' servants, the hospital gangs, the quartermasters' people, the 'present sick' and the habitual skulkers."[29] The scene which the Philadelphians encountered as they exited the gorge was even worse for morale than had been the sight of hundreds of blue-coated non-combatants: "Presently we met litters loaded with pallid sufferers [wounded troopers], and passed a hospital tent where I saw surgeons bending over a table, and beneath it amputated limbs lying in pools of blood."[30]

The congestion in the canyon which so frustrated Sheridan also produced a more tangible result, the addition of probably hundreds of extra Union names on the casualty rolls. When Early learned of the Federal attack on his works at the end of the canyon, he recognized that Brigadier General Stephen D. Ramseur's lone division was in serious peril, and immediately summoned his northern two divisions under the command of Major General Robert E. Rodes and Brigadier General John B. Gordon. At approximately 11:00 a.m., as the Sixth and Nineteenth Corps were nearing completion of their battle alignment just beyond the mouth of the canyon, the two Confederate divisions arrived, effectively tripling the size of the Southern forces.[31]

The delay produced a second deadly consequence for the Federal warriors. It took hours for the Sixth and then the Nineteenth Corps troops to file out of the canyon and into position -- Brigadier General George W. Getty's Sixth Corps Second Division to the far left of the front line; the Third Division under Brigadier General James B. Ricketts straddling the Pike to the right of the Second; Brigadier General Cuvier Grover's Division of the Nineteenth Corps with its left on the right of the Blue Crosses; and the Grays' division in reserve three hundred yards to

[29]DeForest, p. 173.
[30]DeForest, p. 173.
[31]Stackpole, *Sheridan in the Shenandoah*, p.159.

the rear of the Third Division.[32] The Southern gunners did not stand idly by as the men in blue neatly filled and dressed their lines; rather, the Rebels made sure that during the entire maneuver the Union "... command suffered severely from a hot and continuous fire from the enemies artillery."[33]

The Grays maintained their line at two different positions on the field for approximately an hour under a galling fire, in each location receiving a heavy dose of hot iron as shells passed over the front line and exploded over and in the midst of the Regiment.[34] One Yankee who shared the Grays' experience of waiting in position under that terrible fire described the ordeal: "That is the time that tries the courage of the bravest. Once in the heat and hurry and inspiration of the battle, the average soldier forgets fear in the excitement of the hour, but to stand ... ready, expectant, every nerve strung, awaiting the word of command to march into a hailstorm of death, that is the crucial test. It is at such a time that all the mental struggle involved in a soldier's death is undergone, leaving nothing but the mere physical pang of sudden dying to complete the sacrifice."[35] Despite nerves screaming for flight, virtually all of the men in those exposed lines displayed that special kind of courage and held their ground. Although discipline and composure were maintained, there were presumably many anxious glances to the right, watching for the last unit to take its position, so that the attack could start and the shelling could be put to an end.

At precisely 11:40 a.m., when the last Federal hustled into position, the blue line surged forward toward the enemy.[36] Seeing the Union attack finally under way, "... the Confederates covered by some heavy woods on their right ... opened fire from their whole front."[37] At first, the Union onslaught appeared irresistible, with the Sixth Corps

---

[32]Stackpole, *Sheridan in the Shenandoah*, p. 203; Sheridan, p. 290. Sheridan, in his memoirs, placed Ricketts' Division entirely to the north of the Pike, but this assertion is in conflict with the other sources. Likewise, Stackpole located Russell's Division entirely to the north of the Pike, a position also in conflict with the other sources.

[33]O.R.-1-43-1-189.

[34]O.R.-1-43-1-189.

[35]As cited in Wert, *From Winchester...*, p. 56.

[36]O.R.-1-43-1-149, Wright.

[37]Sheridan, p. 291.

making steady gains on the left and the Nineteenth Corps breaking the enemy on the right. The Grays were swept along with the front line: "... we [119th] again moved by the left flank (meantime brisk skirmishing going on in our front) with much difficulty through a dense woods of timber and scrub oak. After getting through this piece of woods and again coming out into open country we formed in line in a ravine, fifth regiment from the right; then received orders to advance in line, we being the second line of battle; the enemy being driven by the first line, we did not become engaged until we had advanced probably half a mile or more, taking a diagonal course to the left across a ravine and strip of woods of thick underbrush ..."[38]

Sheridan had earlier ordered General Ricketts to guide his Sixth Corps division along the pike. The Third Division commander followed his orders explicitly, even though a slant in the road caused his division to drift to the left, away from Grover's Division, which at the same time was impetuously pursuing the fleeing Butternuts on the right of the pike.[39] The Southern Commander seized the opportunity presented by the breach in the Federals' line, and sent Brigadier General Cullen Battle's newly arrived brigade headlong into the gap. Both Ricketts' and Grover's already partially disorganized divisions broke under the attack on their separated flanks, and both divisions began to stream to the rear, closely pursued by the Confederate line, which had been retreating only minutes before.[40] Suddenly, what had looked to be an easy victory in the making, began to take on the appearance of a major catastrophe.

When originally posted in reserve, General Russell approached his commander and questioned the deployment, which seemed to indicate a certain lack of confidence in the First Division. Sheridan reassured his former superior that no slight was intended, explaining his thought process as, "... I know what I shall have there in a commanding officer if the line should break at or near that point."[41] Perhaps that comment reverberated in Russell's mind as his reserve division of hard-handed veterans suddenly became the only hope of stanching the eruption of

---

[38]O.R.-1-43-1-189.

[39]Stackpole, *Sheridan in the Shenandoah*, pp. 205-208.

[40]Stackpole, *Sheridan in the Shenandoah*, p. 161.

[41]As cited in Wert, *From Winchester...*, p. 67.

Opequon - September 19, 1864

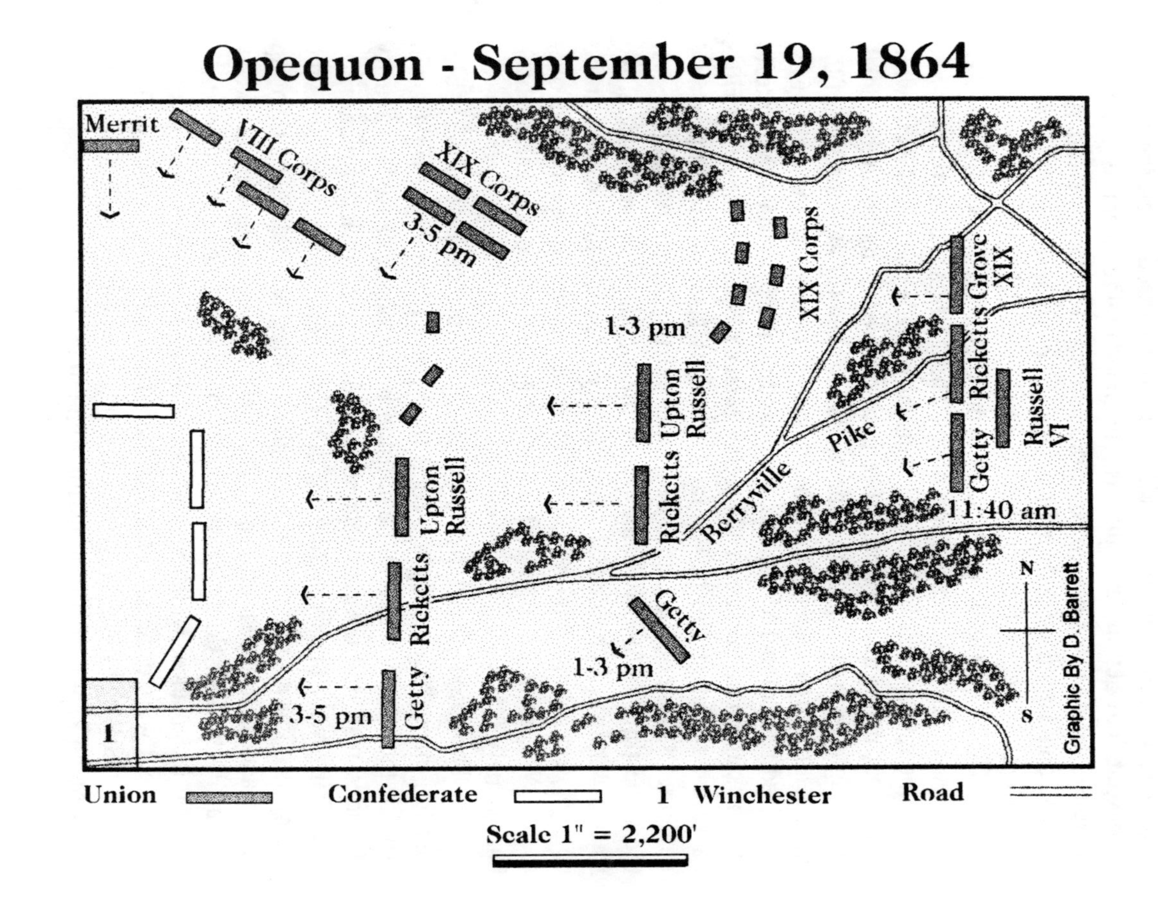

Confederate troops into the Union rear. "As these troops [Ricketts' and Grover's] were retiring I [Sheridan] ordered Russell's reserve division to be put into action, and just as the flank of the enemy's troops in pursuit of Grover was presented, Upton's Brigade, led in person by both Russell and Upton, struck it in a charge so vigorous as to drive the Confederates back in turn to their original ground."[42]

Upton's Brigade could not claim sole credit for saving the day, as Colonel Edwards' description of his Third Brigade's participation in the counterattack clearly shows: "Thus the brigade continued its forward movement under quite a severe fire until ordered to move double-quick to the right of the road, as the enemy had broken through the line of the Nineteenth Corps. Seeing the enemy had got to the rear and right of us, I ordered Lt. Colonel Montague, commanding the 37th Mass. Volunteers to attack them at this point [The Bay Stater's Spencer repeating rifles gave that regiment fire power far beyond its size, but the unit would nevertheless lose about a third of its men during the counterattack]. At the same time the enemy came out of the woods in front of us in two lines of battle and charged. I advanced my brigade with bayonets at the charge, forcing the fugitives in front to lay down as we passed over them. We opened fire at 150 yards range and drove the enemy back handsomely."[43]

The Grays played their part during this critical part of the battle. The Regiment "Moved by the right flank, and filing to the right again crossed the ravine with slight confusion in the ranks, caused by density of underbrush, but the regiment soon again formed in its original line. The firing with the front line by this time became very spirited, the enemy driving it in confusion through our line, and following them up soon made their appearance in a corn field in our front, their musketry and artillery both doing great execution to our line. We were then ordered to advance, which we did, and driving them from their position in the field were ordered to halt behind a fence, at which time the firing became brisk and the enemy fell back into a woods of high timber, the firing being kept up between us for some time."[44]

---

[42]Sheridan, p. 292.
[43]O.R.-1-43-1-184, 185, Edwards.
[44]O.R.-1-43-1-189.

The line was restored and the tide was again turned in favor of the Union, although at an especially high price. While leading his men from the front line, General Russell was hit in the left breast by a bullet. Recognizing the psychological importance of his presence on the field, Russell remained on his horse and carried on as if nothing had happened, despite almost certain knowledge that the wound was mortal. A few moments later, the veteran of so many bloody battles was cut from his horse by a shell fragment through his heart.[45] Many lower-ranking Red Crosses shared the fate of their leader, leaving a monument of corpses on the spot where the breakthrough was halted: "... the two lines of battle must have stood for some time, steadily firing at each other. Between two thickets, probably twenty rods apart there was a row of blue clad dead lying close together, and fairly touching each other; and only a few yards in front of them a similar windrow of gray clad dead, lying as closely and straightly aligned as were their opponents ..."[46]

After the Southerners fled from the area of their earlier breakthrough, a relative calm passed over the battlefield as both sides struggled to regroup and reorganize. Clark's men spent the next two hours waiting in the position which they occupied when the Rebel counterattack was broken, undoubtedly involved in a desultory exchange of sniper fire.[47] The Federals, having a significantly larger force, were better able to put the lull to good use, bringing Crook's Army of Western Virginia [Eighth Corps] to the front and placing it on the far right, to the northeast of the Confederate line.[48] Beyond Crook's men, Union cavalry massed in formation, poised for a charge.

The calm being enjoyed on the front line did not extend to the rear, the direction in which the wounded were either carried, or dragged their torn and bleeding bodies. "Down by the creek where the train stopped, they put up the division hospitals for our corps [Sixth Corps]. Ambulance loads of wounded men were continually coming in, and the surgeons had all they could attend to, and more too. Wounds of every description; some in the head, some in the body, some in the hands,

---

[45]Sheridan, p. 292.
[46]Best, p. 184.
[47]O.R.-1-43-1-189.
[48]OR-1-43-1-150, Wright.

arms, legs or feet were constantly being brought forward for attention. It was impossible to attend to them all at once, and many had to wait and suffer a long time with their savage wounds undressed. Amputations at several tables were being made all the time. As fast as one man was removed from the board another was put on. Many poor fellows had to wait for several hours before their turn came. The surgeons, besmeared with blood, and hardened to their business, looked more like butchers cutting up beef than like professional men, adopting the stern alternative of removing a limb to save the life of a fellow man. A hospital on the battlefield always presents a horrid ghastly sight."[49]

Back at the front, between 4:30 and 5:00 p.m., when all the preparations were completed, the attack was renewed along the entire line. "It was a beautiful sight when the charging army, four miles in breadth from wing to wing moved over the plain."[50] As the Federal infantry pressed forward, the Union troopers on the far right charged into the Southern line, pitting sword and pistol against rifle and bayonet. The entire Rebel front began to slowly contract under the pressure.

At first, the Confederate withdrawal was gradual, as the determined Southern infantry briefly stood their ground and brought the Union line to a halt. "A skirmish line was then thrown out and we [the 119th] were ordered to advance. Moved forward in line of battle, driving the enemy before us, halting at the outer edge of the woods a few moments, thence forward to the crest of a hill. At this point we received a severe enfilading fire from the enemy's guns on our left flank and in our immediate front. We were ordered to about face, moved some fifty paces to the rear, about faced and were ordered to lie down."[51]

Soon, however, "... we [the 119th] pressed forward, driving the enemy in great disorder; advanced some 200 yards under fire of the enemy's artillery planted on redoubt upon a high piece of ground near the town of Winchester."[52] Private Westbrook of the 49th Pennsylvania, only yards from the 119th, described the same shelling: "Soon we

---

[49]Fisk, p. 256.
[50]Haines, p. 260.
[51]O.R.-1-43-1-189.
[52]O.R.-1-43-1-189.

made a left turn, facing the town and the rebel fort. We pause a few moments at a brick house and receive a tremendous shelling from the fort. The limbs and flesh of our boys would fly ten feet in the air ..."[53] Perhaps a few of the Grays, who while panting to catch their breath behind a tree, or hugging the dirt in response to the shriek of an incoming shell, noticed that, "Behind the piling smoke of the guns spread a crimson autumnal sunset, partly veiled by long somber bars of clouds," and wondered if it was to be the last such scene he was ever to witness.[54] Fortunately, before much more of such carnage was inflicted the "... artillery was soon compelled to cease firing and we moved forward ..."[55]

Another member of the Third Brigade, John C. Arnold, also of the 49th Pennsylvania, described this portion of the battle in a letter home to his wife: "... as they were driven out of the woods they had to get. I never seen any men run faster than the rebs run last Monday after we got them driven out in the open plain. It was fun to see them running. I seen the greatest bravery shown by some of our officers ever I have seen specially of one of our brigade staff officers, a young man by the name of John Young. He rode away front of the line sometimes and where he was a raise or any little height he was sure to be there and watching the movements of the rebs and smoking his cigar all the time, sometimes on his horse and sometimes dismounted. General Sheridan rode along the lines several times, the first time he came along when he got up alongside of our colonel he made a short halt and said 'boys the only way we have to do is to kill every son of a bitch off.' He went like a streak of lightning, seemed to be smiling all the time, and such a cheering I never heard. Before if ever the rebs got a nice licking they got it last Monday."[56]

As the pressure along the entire contracting perimeter continued to increase, small groups of the Confederates who had been fighting the Sixth and Nineteenth Corps began to drift away from the front, hastened by the sounds of battle growing ominously louder and closer to their left

---

[53]Westbrook, pp. 219-220.
[54]DeForest, p. 190.
[55]O.R.-1-43-1-189.
[56]Arnold, *Letter*, 9/23/1864.

flank and rear. The trickle soon turned into a flood, and then the entire Southern line buckled and ran for the city. Confederate General Grimes, a commentator unlikely to have exaggerated the wild scene, described the rout of Early's army: "Upon coming into the open field, I perceived everything to be in the most inextricable confusion -- horses dashing over the field, cannon being run to the rear at the top of the horses' speed, men leaving their command, and scattering in confusion."[57]

Arnold was not the only Bluecoat thrilled with the unusual sight of the bottoms of Confederate feet and streaming butternut coat-tails: "After the fight the men were wild with joy. I [Elisha Rhodes] could have knelt and kissed the folds of the old flag that waved in triumph ... I have been in a good many battles but never in such a victory as this."[58] A captured Confederate officer glumly summarized the perspective from his side of the line: "I never saw our troops in such confusion before."

Reminiscent of the Federal rout through the streets of Gettysburg a year earlier, the panicked Butternuts streamed through Winchester on their way south. Nothing could stem the retreat, not even appeals to the chivalry or manhood of the terror stricken men. General Gordon's wife, Fanny, who had come to be almost revered by the Southern soldiers for her devotion to her husband which kept her hovering near the front lines, attempted to halt the flight. At first, from the balcony of the home in which she was staying, she pleaded with the refugees to stand and fight. A few heeded her call and turned toward the front with comments such as, "'Come, boys, let's go back. We might not obey the general, but we can't resist Mrs. Gordon.'" Seeing that the brave souls who tried to stop were being swept along with the rest, Mrs. Gordon rushed out into the street, perhaps hoping that her physical presence would literally dam the flood. It didn't, and her husband, when he found her thus engaged, ordered her into the house, and made arrangements for a carriage to carry her to safety.[59]

The conclusion of the battle was somewhat anti-climactic: "After our forces reached Winchester the enemy made a show of standing on

---

[57]As Cited in Wert, *From Winchester...*, p. 96.
[58]Rhodes, p. 185.
[59]Gordon, p. 323.

the Strasburg Road, and the Sixth and Nineteenth changed front with the design of again attacking, but the opposing line fell back, and the darkness and exhausted condition of the men, who had been on foot since 2 a.m. ... precluded further pursuit for the time."[60] Pursuit of the fleeing Confederates was not immediately abandoned, however, as cavalry under Wilson and some of Crook's infantry followed the Butternuts down the road. The horse-soldiers swept up stragglers until halted by the determined stand of Ramseur's rear guard, who remained unchallenged by the more powerful Union infantry, who because of the darkness, were prevented from mounting a serious assault.[61] As darkness descended, the Philadelphians ended the day by bivouacking in a cemetery.[62]

[As previously, all the following unannotated quotes are from the Latta diary.]

"September 20 -- [I] Employed Negro servant Jake."

"September 21 -- Sheridan still continues his advance up the valley and we remain on this pleasant duty at Winchester."

Perhaps as a reward for exemplary performance at the battle of Opequon, Edward's Third Brigade was assigned to garrison duty in the city of Winchester on the twentieth.[63]

"September 23 -- News arrives of the defeat of the enemy at his stronghold on Fisher's Hill, with the capture of a large number of prisoners and several pieces of artillery, our forces still pursuing."

"September 26 -- The city of Winchester, or town rather as it is called, lays at the foot of a range of hills in its northwestern side and in a sort of a basin. From the fortifications of Millroy a very excellent pleasing view of the place can be obtained ... The gasworks of the city although ... in a state of repair are entirely useless from a want of fuel. A spring without the [necessity] of any machinery situated in the Romney Road supplies the place with water by hydrant and pipes."

"September 27 -- There are no places of particular interest or moment to the stranger. The cemetery was at one time a place of some

---

[60]O.R.-1-43-1-150.

[61]O.R.-1-43-1-190; Sheridan, p. 294.

[62]O.R.-1-43-1-190.

[63]Rhodes, p. 185.

beauty but is now in a sad state of repair. Piccadilly London, Kent Braddock Market are the names of the principal thoroughfares upon some of which are handsome residences, although none of any modern style of architecture. There are churches of every denomination, but every one is now used as a hospital. From the number of stores in ______ quite a trade must have flourished here in time of peace. Taylor House, Virginia House, Union House, are the names of the public houses."

"September 28 -- The courthouse and jail are buildings of mean pretensions, and are now used to stow away prisoners. The better class of society, the first lawyers of the place, are all around secessionists, although there are some families quite wealthy, who are unquestionably staunch Unionists."

"October 1 -- ... we of course avail ourselves of them [idle hours] to ride horseback with some fair damsel, or in some other way relieve the mind from the events, pressure of business, by the enjoyment which the town affords."

"October 2 -- ... Scarce a dispatch that goes to the front but that some of the escort are killed, wounded or taken prisoner. The dispatches that left yesterday never reached their destination, the ... [officer] in command of the party having been taken prisoner with them."

"October 4 -- No one has any idea of the multiplicity of duties at a military post until placed on duty at one for a time, nor have we in the field any idea of the sufferings at hospitals until thrown amongst them immediately after a battle."

In a letter to his wife written on October 17, Private Arnold of the 49th Pennsylvania described the responsibilities undoubtedly shared with Clark's men at the bottom rung of the chain of command: "We have a great deal of duty to do here, such as guarding, picketing, etc. No hard work, most guarding around town."

"October 6 -- A large train with 200 prisoners and a number of ... [wounded] arrive from the front. Also 603 wagons loaded with forage. Subsistence stores from Martinsburg. This post is ... established as a general depot from which the troops in its front will draw direct ..."

"October 7 -- Trains for the front and rear got off in due ... [course] and the terrible rush of business slackens up. Took a horseback ride in the afternoon with _____ out the Romney Road, via the fortifications of Milroy to the battlefield. Returned through the Sheridan hospital."

"October 19 -- Fight at Cedar Creek. Town crowded during the day with various transportation en-route for the ... [front] ..."

On this date Latta was a witness to the beginning of one of the minor mythical events of the war. In an addition to his diary, dated October 19, 1920, Latta recounted the events which occurred immediately before Sheridan began his eulogized ride to the Battle of Cedar Creek, where he, with the assistance of the Sixth Corps' commander, rallied his routed troops and literally snatched victory from the jaws of defeat. "5 or 6 a.m. -- Sheridan and his staff at our headquarters overnight, and when cook came in while at breakfast and announced that there was heavy fighting at the front. S. [Sheridan] responded 'that s. of a b. Rosser, Custer will give him hell directly.' Dining resumed, was in the basement. From the porch after breakfast ... the firing was ... much ... as of a real battle ... Little of any necessity for haste, he mounted and began what subsequently was known as his famous ride."

Curiously, Sheridan's own description of the event indicated that the Union commander was much more concerned about the implications of the firing and the need for haste than Latta's account would indicate. "Toward 6 o'clock the morning of the 19th, the officer on picket duty at Winchester came to my room, I being yet in bed, and reported artillery firing from the direction of Cedar Creek ... I remarked, 'It's all right; Grover has gone out this morning to make a reconnaissance, and he is merely feeling the enemy.' I tried to go to sleep again, but grew so restless that I could not, and soon got up and dressed myself ... I still inferred that the cannonading was caused by Grover's division banging away at the enemy simply to find out what he was up to. However, I went down-stairs and requested that breakfast be hurried up, and at the same time ordered the horses to be saddled and in readiness, for I concluded to go to the front before any further examinations were made in regard to the defensive line ... We mounted our horses between half-past 8 and 9 ..."[64] We will probably never know whether the disparity between the two accounts resulted from a general's vanity or the clouded memory of an eighty-year-old man.

Between the middle of October and the middle of November Latta's diary was uncharacteristically silent, apparently because he found

---

[64]Sheridan, pp. 318-319.

the routine of garrison duty too mundane to record. During this time, however, the Grays' brigade, and particularly its commander Oliver Edwards, were involved on the periphery of one of the most notorious series of atrocities committed during the Civil War.

Colonel Oliver Edwards

(USAMHI-MOLLUS)

On September 25 the Union cavalry stationed in Front Royal became incensed when a mortally wounded Federal lieutenant, Charles McMaster, reported that he had been shot down by one of Mosby's men after the Lieutenant had surrendered. Whether the story was true or not, the Federal troopers retaliated by executing a number of Mosby's partisans who had the misfortune of being prisoners in Front Royal that day. Six weeks later, on November 6, Mosby evened the bloody account by requiring twenty-seven Union captives to draw lots to see which seven of them were to be executed. Three of the seven were hung, two escaped, and two who survived the attempted execution were delivered by locals to Colonel Edwards in Winchester. Along with the two wounded Federals, Edwards received a message from Mosby: "These men have been hung in retaliation for an equal number of Colonel Mosby's men hung by order of General Custer, at Front Royal. Measure for measure."[65] Rather than escalate the situation, the Federals made no additional reprisals, and there were no further officially sanctioned executions of prisoners in the Shenandoah Valley by either side.

"November 13 -- During the entire course of our experience in Winchester it has been one continued scene of business of a character

---

[65]As cited in Wert, *Mosby's Rangers*, pp. 213-214, 248, 249.

entirely different from field operations of a nature not worthy of being recorded, so we have only made casual observations during our sojourn citing its commencement and ending."

On the twenty-first, the Grays, along with the balance of the Sixth Corps, participated in a grand review, vividly described by Private Arnold of the 49th Pennsylvania; "I wish you could've been here to see what a splendid scene it was. About 35,000 troops were present. All the artillery and wagon trains, everything belonging to the 6th Corps was drawn out in line and we all had to have our rifles as bright as a new silver dollar and all shoes and cartridge boxes had to be blackened that they glistened, and no one was allowed to have their overcoat on, even the generals and colonels and all the officers only had their dress coats on. It was the nicest scene ever I witnessed in all my lifetime. All brigade and division generals with their aides and nice flags were all present. The corps general and General Sheridan with their staff officers and the nice large flags, all the drum corps and all bands belonging to the corps were present. Everything so nice and clean it looks splendid."[66]

"November 22 -- Relieved from duty at Winchester, Virginia and ordered to report to headquarters of the 3rd brigade. Rather displeased with the idea but of course compelled to submit. Have two months of a remarkably good time. Upon our arriving at the brigade reportedly found it about to commence a march to Martinsburg to escort a wagon train ... we escaped this job and remained in camp."

"November 24 -- Thanksgiving Day, visited Winchester, where remained during the day visiting our lady friends."

"November 30 -- Orders came about 11:00 p.m. to move at 7:00 a.m. tomorrow ... It is with the great regret that we leave the Shenandoah. Many pleasant associations have been formed which cannot be broken without causing sensations of a character akin to those we experienced upon first leaving home to participate in the rebellion."

"December 1 -- The column moved at the hour named [after putting to the torch huge piles of excess material and their abandoned huts, which created huge bonfires visible for miles].[67] Marched to

---

[66]Arnold Papers, National Archives.

[67]Fisk, p. 284.

Stevens Depot where cars awaited. Our destination is now known to be Petersburg or its vicinity. Spent our last hours in Winchester pleasantly, bade farewell to our lady acquaintances with a spirit of reluctance which usually characterizes our partings upon such occasions, at least such as did in days gone by. Got on board the cars about 3:30 and immediately commenced our journey. At Summit Point met Young, the last of our old friends that we saw."

The Grays knew they were taking a train to a reality which was vastly different from the rural beauty of the Shenandoah Valley. Those train cars were undoubtedly filled with solemn young men who, unlike two years earlier, were not sheltered by ignorance as to the true significance of being ordered to the front. There were no illusions that glory was waiting for them at the end of the line -- only something like Cold Harbor, or worse.

15

PETERSBURG

It was reasonable that those in command would have anticipated that the men of the Sixth Corps would be in a dark mood when they disembarked in Washington from the troop transport train. It is impossible to know whether any of the Greek Crosses were so despondent that desertion into the crowded streets of the capital would have been viewed as a viable option. Taking no chances, however, that possibility was eliminated.

"December 2 -- Arrived in Washington at 10:00 a.m., the cars not stopping until they reached the wharf. The troops were immediately embarked of this brigade on ... [the] City of Albany. On the last mentioned vessel ... [we steamed] down to Alexandria where the entire fleet remaining all night awaiting the arrival of division headquarters on the Idaho."

"December 3 -- Got underway immediately after daylight and continued the voyage during the day arriving at Fortress Monroe at about 9:30 p.m. where remained until the following morning. The most miserable accommodations in the way of eating that have ever to be furnished to a ... [soldier] on board a transport ... The ... idea of exchange the equities and pleasantness of the valley for the wilds and deserts of Petersburg and its vicinity seems to be fully imposed on all."

"December 4 -- Left the neighborhood of the Fortress Monroe at daylight and continued the journey up the James, reaching City Point at about ... 1:00 p.m., having passed almost every boat of the fleet. Massed the troops to await further orders. Just after dark, cars being in readiness, the brigade was shipped and transported as far as Paiks Station where it remained during the night."

"December 5 -- Moved up and occupied the position formerly held by General Crawford's 3rd division 5th corps. It appears to be quite a comfortable place on the line, the firing that we heard last night being all to our right."

"December 6 -- Got into nice comfortable quarters formerly occupied by the headquarters of the 2nd brigade, 3rd division, 5th corps."

War generally produces winners and losers, but in this case both were on the same side. Theodore Lyman, a volunteer officer on General Meade's staff, noticed that upon arrival Wright's men were visibly despondent over the twist of fate which had brought them back to the barren trenches outside Petersburg. "However, they find things better now, and will doubtless get contented in time. What must have gratified them was that they relieved Crawford's division of the Fifth Corps, on the line and took possession of their very nice log huts, which had been carefully constructed uniformly in all the brigades. Crawford's people by no means saw the thing in the same light. They took down their canvas roofs and rolled them up with dudgeon and marched off ... I rode along the breastworks as the Red Crosses marched into the deserted camps and observed the aspect of grim satisfaction with which the new comers went about, looking into the abandoned huts."[1]

"December 7 -- It rained considerably during the morning. Towards evening rumors prevail of an anticipated movement."

"December 8 -- At 2:00 a.m. the order came to hand, designating what troops should remain as a garrison in the enclosed fortifications and dictating that those not so designated should be held in readiness to move at very brief notice ... [and] providing number of rounds of ammunition and number of days rations, etc. Moved at 4:00 p.m. for the left out the Vaughn Road. The night intensely cold and snow and hail fell to a considerable extent. Bivouacked in the vicinity of Hasher's [Hatcher's Run?]."

"December 9 -- At the latter part of the entry of yesterday should have been made today."

"December 10 -- Went into position, the right of the line resting at or near the picket of the main army at the Claypole House. Moved

---

[1]Lyman, p. 299.

back to the old camp at night, the enemy attacking at the three fords just as we left. Instead of remaining quietly in camp as we anticipated, we were taken from our comfortable quarters and moved to the right in the vicinity of Fort Hell. The most fearful night of the season. The snow still on the ground."

"December 11 -- Remained in the position taken up last night until 9:00 p.m. when the troops of the Ninth Corps returning, we returned to our ... [previous] camp. Intensely cold and the wind howls frightfully."

"December 12 -- The cold weather continued but the wind lulled. We are still under orders to move but had hoped to not be moved off again." [This was the last entry in Latta's diary until December 28, 1864.]

Major Rhodes of the 2nd Rhode Island, still with the Grays' Third Brigade, noted in his diary that on the twentieth of December the Brigade was turned out for a dress parade. He also took the opportunity on that date to describe the trenches which his regiment and the Grays, not very far down the line, were occupying: "The forts and batteries, as they are called, are within range of each other and are connected by curtains or rifle pits. In front of our works are deep ditches now filled with water and in front of this an abatis made of limbs and trees driven slanting into the ground and with the points sharpened. Then we have wires stretched about in every direction about six inches or a foot above the ground and still in front of this the trees are slashed and piled up in great confusion. I wish the Rebels would try to take our lines. It would be fun for us."[2]

"December 28 -- Visited Fort Sedgwick (Hell) and mortar batteries to its right where two hours were spent under remarkably heavy shelling. We were amused at the expressions used when referring to the above-mentioned place. An officer when inquiring as to the destination of a ... journey to the front, 'where do you want to go? To Hell?' 'No', replies the driver, 'just to the left of Hell'." [Latta's last diary entry for 1864.]

Private Anderson of the 49th Pennsylvania, still with the Third Brigade which was a fair distance from Fort Sedgwick, described the day

---

[2]Rhodes, p. 202.

somewhat differently in a letter he wrote home to his beloved wife. "Today it is very nice and warm here although it is muddy and unpleasant underfoot. Everything has been very quiet along the line for the last four days, no firing heard, not any more than when salutes were fired when the good news came concerning Sherman's great victory. They was as high as 300 guns fired as a salute for the old hero of the southwestern army. The rebs are coming over into our lines daily. Yesterday there was a brigadier general came over, captains, privates, lieutenants are coming daily. I think this great rebellion will close til spring, at least I hope it may."[3]

"January 1 1865 -- Did not succeed in getting this diary until on or about the 6th. Consequently, events transpiring between the 1st and that date have not been noted."

Time dragged from hour to hour for the men, as they stood watch in the trenches that were probably too strong to be attacked by the beleaguered Confederates but not so secure so as to fully alleviate the pervasive stress of trench warfare. Captain DeForest of the 12th Connecticut, at a different time and location but under similar circumstances, described that tension: "The nuisance of trench duty does not consist in the overwhelming amount of danger at any particular moment, but in the fact that danger is perpetually present. The spring is always bent; the nerves never have a chance to recuperate; the elasticity of the courage is slowly worn out."[4]

Unit commanders had little to do other than fret about potential disasters or devise creative ways to occupy bored or over-stressed privates. On January 5, Brigadier General Frank Wheaton, who had replaced Russell as First Division commander when the latter fell at Opequon, attempted to satisfy both concerns at once when he ordered his men to construct additional slashings and abatis in front of the already impregnable defenses which Rhodes had described.[5] Unfortunately, the fatigue details dreamed up by unit commanders were not always just a nuisance -- sometimes they were dangerous. On January 11, while out

---

[3]Anderson, *Letter*, 12/28/1864. Private Anderson would be killed only three days prior to the surrender at Appomattox which he predicted.

[4]DeForest, p. 116.

[5]O.R.-1-46-2-43.

in front of the emplacements constructing abatis, four Red Crosses (one officer and three enlisted men) were wounded when Confederate pickets unexpectedly unleashed a volley into the toiling Yankees.

Not every day in the trenches was punctuated by the sudden death or injury of some unfortunate who, by order or carelessness, became an easy target for a Southern sniper. Colonel Lyman described several incidents which, although occurring earlier in the siege, undoubtedly were representative of the way the two armies often conducted their original version of trench warfare. "At one part, there was a brook between, and our pickets, or theirs, when they want water, hold up a canteen, and then coolly walk down to the neutral stream."[6]

Although such unofficial truces were most often honored only between the blue and butternut privates, occasional compassion was also shown to an officer. At one point, a Union general came to the very front and stood in full view, surveying the Southern lines with an opera glass. A Rebel private did not appreciate the attention, but rather than pick off the impertinent officer, he wrote the following note, wrapped it around a rock, and threw it into the Federal trench: "Tell the fellow with the spy-glass to clear out, or we shall have to shoot him."[7]

On another occasion, either out of ignorance or youth, a Johnny Reb fired on the Union pickets, who promptly dove for cover. Immediately thereafter, from a nearby Rebel pit, came a shout: "Don't shoot; you'll see how we fix him!" They did. "Then they took the musket from the unfortunate grey-back, put a rail on his shoulder, and made him walk up and down for a great while in front of their rifle pits."[8]

The Greek Crosses also became involved in such unofficial peace accords during the winter of 1865. A short distance down the line from the 119th, an arrangement was worked out between members of the 87th Pennsylvania [Third Division, Sixth Corps] and the "Johnnies" on the other side of the no-man's land. "The month of January, 1865, opened with a cold day. The wood for fuel, to the rear of the Union Army, became scarce. The men were compelled to get wood from timber lands

---

[6]Lyman, p. 181.
[7]Lyman, p. 181.
[8]Lyman, p. 182.

Bartering during unofficial truce - *Leslie's Illustrated Newspaper*

lying between the opposing armies. To accomplish this a truce was ordered, and squads of men of both armies marched toward each other, with axes to cut down the timber. When the 'Yanks' and 'Johnnies' met they shook hands, exchanged articles and questioned one another about the war. Then they all went to work cutting up the trees. After dividing the wood they carried it back to their respective lines."[9]

"January 6 -- Left Warren Station at 7:00 a.m. en route for home on a 15 days' leave of absence. Took the James L. Grady at City Point and left the wharf at 10:30 [a.m.]. Passed Fortress Monroe at 4:30 p.m. and debauched there on the bay all night, it being impossible to get into the mouth of the Potomac on account of the fog."

Captain Latta picked a good day to commence his leave, because later that same day a prisoner from the Jersey Brigade was executed for desertion. The condemned man was first paraded to his gravesite sitting astride his coffin. Then, as he struggled to maintain his composure, the

---

[9]Prowell, p. 218.

prisoner was seated upon his coffin in front of a newly dug grave while the stone-faced members of the Grays' First Division marched into formation to the prisoner's front and on both sides. After the man was blindfolded, the firing squad performed its grim duty, and then the entire division was marched past the riddled and bleeding corpse under orders of "eyes right" so that no one could avoid the full impact of the message.[10]

"January 24 -- Left at 3:00 p.m. on the Daniel Webster for City Point."

"January 25 -- Arrived at Fortress Monroe at 8:00. We heard rumors of the naval engagement that had taken place up the James, resulting in the driving back of the rebel ironclad fleet. Continued the trip up the river past the Atlanta ... Arrived at City Point between 2 and 3 o'clock and reached our destination at Warren Station at about 5:00. Found our quarters in a tolerably comfortable condition and a letter awaiting us from General Upton announcing the fact of his application for our ... [assignment] to him."

"January 26 -- The weather is most intensely cold and ... [the Brigade] suffers severely at night. Jones and Weidersheim have both returned from Winchester."

"January 27 -- General Bassett being corps officer of the day takes me on a tour around the picket line. There has been little or no firing along the Petersburg front during the entire period of our absence. Weather still continues intensely cold."

"January 28 -- Severity of the weather in no wise changed ..."

"January 29 -- ... The Potomac and Patapsko are now almost completely closed by ice and all communication is had by the way of Annapolis."

"January 31 -- ... Brigadier General Joseph E. Hamblin assigned to the command of the Brigade. At division headquarters met a foreign officer recently arrived to report to General Meade. Orders came in the middle of the night to be ready to move at very short notice. It rather startled us as this disturbed our being continued quiet by orders of such a character as this."

---

[10]Rhodes, p. 206.

"February 1 -- General Hamblin assumed command. A very pleasant gentlemanly soldier and under whom we will be pleased to serve. We will expect the orders to move may be carried out and consequently remain about headquarters all day."

On the same day that Hamblin assumed command of the Third Brigade, Major General Wheaton filed a report on the disposition of his division. The Red Crosses occupied Fort Howard, Batteries 25 and 26, two small forts named McMahon and Davison to the rear of the main line, and the rifle pits between them.[11]

"February 2 -- The idea of the movement seems to have been abandoned. Rode to division and army headquarters with the General. Bird on First brigade staff gave us a field desk which we intend to keep, not only for its intrinsic value but for the sake of the donor."

The plan for a movement had not been abandoned, only postponed. Although the Federal lines encircled only about a third of the circumference around Richmond and Petersburg, the Army of the Potomac was nevertheless conducting a siege of its foe. In order to further reduce the meager flow of supplies reaching the Confederate troops and the cities they defended, Grant decided to send the Fifth Corps beyond the Union left towards Hatcher's Run, in hopes of blocking wagon traffic on the Boydton Plank Road.

"February 5 -- At 4:00 a.m. orders came to be prepared to march at an early hour in the morning, thus disturbing a repose which we did not undertake to get until 2:00. The Fifth Corps, [and] two divisions of the Second [Corps], move off towards the left, cannonading sharp and brisk heard during the afternoon. Quite a cold wind springs up. At 8:00 we move, first taking the Vaughn Road, and then turning back, move out the ... Squirrel Level Road, taking pretty much the same position we had here in the last headquarters at Claypole House."

By 11:30 p.m. the Grays had reached their destination in the area of Fort Cummings near the Claypole House. Rather than being permitted to sleep, however, the men spent the next several hours struggling in the dark and cold to dig trenches, an especially obnoxious task for the unfortunate foot soldiers whose portion of the line ran

[11]O.R.-1-46-2-436.

through either of the two swamps over which the line passed.[12] Unlike many previous excursions, the men were able to obtain their rest the following morning, because they were not ordered to move out until 2:30 p.m.

"February 6 -- It turns out that the fight of yesterday resulted from an attack made by the enemy on the Second Corps in which that enemy were badly beaten. Moved from the vicinity of the Claypole to the other side of Hatcher's Run to support an advance by the Fifth Corps. The musketry ... [continued] quite fearfully for a time, but the principal part of the noise seems to come from our side. The troops engaged behaved badly, making completely through our lines. Nothing seemed to stay their rout, and they made for the east bank of the run. Seemed to be the result of a stampede and not forced upon us by any persistent attack of the enemy. At 11:00 our division was withdrawn to the Cummings House."

The troops of the once proud Fifth Corps behaved very badly. In his report, General Wheaton described the rout: "... [a] mass of the troops in front came rushing through the dense woods and quite over us, and it was with the greatest difficulty that the line could be formed, so obstructed was it by the fugitives, who were deaf to every entreaty of myself and staff and refused to rally on the flanks or in support of the brigade there forming."[13]

Fortunately, the veterans of the First Division did not succumb to the infectious panic which often caused troops not yet under fire to join their terrified comrades in a race to the rear. The Second Brigade managed to form in front, pickets were thrown out, and the Jersey and Grays' brigades formed in support. Most of the twenty-seven casualties taken by the First Division during this brief encounter were suffered when the picket line took several volleys to its left and rear. Bowing to the volatile nature of the situation and the fear of "friendly fire" from the terrified soldiers in his rear, Wheaton pulled his men back 300 yards to better ground, where they remained for about an hour until 9:00 p.m., when the Division was withdrawn.[14]

---

[12]O.R.-1-46-1-297, Wheaton.
[13]O.R.-1-46-1-297.
[14]O.R.-1-46-1-297.

Aaron Wick

(courtesy K. Turner collection)

"February 7 -- Rain and snow and hail fell all night, and the rain continued throughout the day. Moved off again in the morning. I report to General Warren who wants us to support General Crawford on their advancing. Quite a lively skirmishing kept up all day, and another advance ... in the afternoon. The enemy ... [send] quite an extensive artillery fire into us, causing a few casualties ..."

The seventh was a truly miserable day for the men in blue. During the night the men had "... built fires, but they were of little avail."[15] The troops woke up shivering under blankets first soaked by rain, then frozen stiff by the plunging temperature, and finally dusted with a thin layer of snow.[16] After turning out, the Grays and their comrades were sent across a river, soaking any fugitive dry spots, and were then made to form up and stand in line of battle for most of the day, while being pelted with a cold, driving rain.[17]

"February 8 -- At 1:00 a.m. our division was withdrawn and after a cold and disagreeable march we reached our old camping ground at 4:00 a.m. ... I do think that I was never so completely used up from the effects of any campaign." Major Rhodes shared Latta's sentiments: "We had a hard march in the darkness and reached camp about daylight, tired, wet, and hungry."[18]

---

[15]As cited in Trudeau, *The Last Citadel*, pp. 320-321.
[16]Haines, p. 293.
[17]Rhodes, p. 212.
[18]Rhodes, p. 212.

"February 9 -- The lines of the army have been changed, the left of it resting at the Armstrong House and Hatcher's Run. The Fifth Corps pickets from that point to the left of the Vaughn Road as it crosses the Run. This has necessitated the movement of many of the troops, but our brigade fortunately has not been disturbed." For the next several weeks, the Grays' lives reverted to the dull, disagreeable and sometimes dangerous routines of trench warfare.

"February 18 -- Application from General Upton requesting my assignment received at our headquarters favorably endorsed and returned. We shall probably be en-route for the Fourth Cavalry Division in the course of ten days."

"February 19 -- There is nothing at present transpiring that is particularly worthy of mention. Deserters in large numbers continually come into our lines telling tales of distress and demoralization."

On the twenty-first, the Grays' brigade was deployed to a new location, this time with orders to occupy Fort Wadsworth and to post at least 300 men in the forward trenches stretching to Battery 26. Gideon Clark's men became responsible for the sector of the line between that battery and the nearest sally port to the left. Each regiment of the Brigade was required to detail 10 percent of its effective force for duty in the forward trenches, and as a result twenty-three Grays rotated in and out of the front line.[19]

The new brigade commander sent out very particular orders on how he expected his men to behave in the new forward positions. "No more than one third of the guard thus formed will be allowed to sleep when on duty. This guard will mount sentinels on the breast-works on their proper front not more than fifty paces apart. A drummer will accompany each detail and the roll will be called every two hours while on duty. The details will be put on duty at retreat and relieved next morning at guard mount ... One wagon will report to-morrow morning to each regiment ... for the purposes of hauling timber to build flooring, rafters, etc. for the shelter tents of the trench guard. Regimental commanders will ... see that they are not destroyed when the details are off duty, by posting guards over them ... Each regiment will be practiced

[19]O.R.-1-46-2-615.

in manning the works, and companies deployed at such intervals as may be necessary to cover the entire front."[20]

"February 22 -- Washington's birthday properly celebrated at 119th in the morning and at headquarters in the evening. Just before dark orders came to hold the troops in readiness to meet an attack in the morning at 5:00. The necessary dispositions made, but the enemy do not attack. One clause of the order stated 'if the enemy are allowed to come through our lines, recollect it is for a purpose'".

"February 23 -- Deserters continually report various movements being and about to be made by the enemy, some of which information is undoubtedly reliable."

Major Rhodes added a bit more detail concerning the proceedings in the Grays' camp that day: "At twelve o'clock noon I was invited to the camp of the 119th Penn. Vols., Lt. Col. Gideon Clark commanding, where we found a fine collation spread to which we did ample justice. Music by the band and a glee club followed. A flag was raised at this camp, and the hour was much enjoyed." As if in honor of the occasion, 100 Southerners deserted to the Brigade that day.[21] At 2:00 p.m. on the next day, the Division put on a parade.[22]

"February 25 -- The routine of camp duties progresses as heretofore during long periods of inactivity interposed now and then however by occasional salvos of artillery in front of the Ninth Corps, and discharges of musketry at some forlorn deserter who may attempt to come in our front. The numbers of these characters who have come in of late is really astonishing. The news of glorious victories elsewhere is frequently [received], Charleston, Wilmington, and now Columbia have all fallen."

"March 4 -- The weather after a long period of rain resulting in a great amount of mud. About twelve today cleared up handsomely. This a.m. about 9:00 we were visited by one of the most severe rainstorms of the season. Nothing in our recollection equaled it, except the storm after crossing the Shenandoah at Snickers' Ferry last summer

---

[20]O.R.-1-46-2-616.
[21]Rhodes, p. 215.
[22]O.R.-1-46-2-676.

when the rain descended in such pelting showers as to actually break that column as if it had been demoralized by fire from the enemy."

"March 5 -- The usual Sunday morning inspection came off, nothing have of any ... interest transpired. Have been anxiously expecting the arrival of the order detailing me from this army but it has not as yet come to hand. Deserters who come in on our front confirm that success of Sheridan over Early at Warrenton."

Brevet Lieutenant Colonel James W. Latta
Post-war

(USAMHI)

"March 6 -- Received an intimation from Army headquarters that the order detaching us had come to Army headquarters and would probably reach the brigade today or tomorrow."

"March 7 -- Orders came to hand, bade goodbye to many old friends who extended great regret at losing us and we can assure them that we never have as yet parted with those to whom we were so much attached."[23]

[23]Latta left the Army of the Potomac to join Upton's Fourth Cavalry Division on the western front, where he participated in the great cavalry raid which ended with the capture and sacking of Selma, Alabama. In the process, Latta received a promotion to lt. colonel for gallantry in the battles of Ebenezer Church, Alabama, and Columbus, Georgia. Because he was assigned to cavalry duty in the Southwest for a number of months after the war, his transfer resulted in a longer term of service than if he had remained with the Grays, but otherwise his luck accompanied him west, and he ended his service without serious injury. After returning home to Philadelphia, Latta remained involved with the First Infantry Regiment of the Pennsylvania National Guard, which ultimately resulted in a commission to the rank of adjutant general. He also wrote a comprehensive history of that unit, gave a presentation on the Grays' involvement at Gettysburg, fathered three children, maintained a substantial law practice, and lived to a distinguished 82 years of age. *Philadelphia North American*, 3/27/1922.

The next week passed without significant military developments, although not without diversions from the monotony of the siege. On the twentieth, the First Division was "honored" as the designated division to perform a full dress parade for Meade, Wright, and the visiting Admiral David Porter. Three days later, out of a cloudless sky, a gale-like wind spawned a sandstorm that ripped the canvas tops off many of the Federal huts and covered the contents with a layer of dirt. It was even worse across the no-man's land, where a fire was whipped into such an inferno that the Butternuts were driven out of their forward emplacements.[24]

It is doubtful that the fire in front of the First Division was brought to the attention of the commander of either army. Both commanders knew, however, that the Confederates could not hold out much longer around Richmond and Petersburg, and that sooner or later the Union forces would sweep over the Southern defenses just like the fire. As a result, during the middle of March, both Grant and Lee were planning -- the latter devising a means to escape from the tightening noose, while the former fretted that the Confederates would escape his grasp. For Lee, the dilemma was exactly how to extricate his forces from the trenches so that his army could move south to join General Joseph E. Johnston in the Carolinas without being cut to pieces in transit; while Grant needed a strategy that would prevent his lighter and faster adversary from accomplishing that goal. Both recognized that the crisis would arrive, probably at month's end, when the roads would finally be dry enough for the armies to move.

Ever the aggressor, Lee decided that he needed a diversion to draw in the left wing of the Union army, thereby affording the Confederates more room to escape, and a longer distance for the Federals to travel in order to catch them. Early on the morning of March 25, Confederate Major General John B. Gordon, Lee's chosen instrument, launched his division in a dawn assault against the Ninth Corps guarding Fort Stedman. Using the subterfuge of pretending to be deserters (at that point the Union was paying a cash bonus to any Rebel deserter who came over with his rifle) the Southerners gained the Federal picket line and then, with a rush, captured the fort. Each phase of the attack progressed like clockwork, until the Confederates were stymied in their

---

[24]Rhodes, pp. 424-431.

attempt to carry several batteries to the rear of the fort. With the momentum of the assault blunted, the Union forces began to apply their overwhelming superiority of numbers in a series of counterattacks which soon regained the fort. In the process, many unfortunate Southerners were cut down trying to recross the killing zone between the lines, and many others surrendered rather than chance the gauntlet.[25]

For the Grays, a veritable storm broke over the camp at 7:00 a.m. when the Brigade received imperative orders to take up arms in preparation for supporting the Ninth Corps on the right.[26] The Philadelphians accompanied their comrades in a rapid four-mile march to the vicinity of Fort Stedman, where they stood in readiness for two hours expecting momentarily to be ordered forward in an attack.[27] After it was determined that the Ninth Corps had salvaged its own situation, the Red Crosses returned to camp, but their day's work had only just begun.

As the events of the morning became clearer, General Wright realized that the Confederates must have significantly weakened their position in his front to support the failed attack on Fort Stedman, and he quickly made preparations to capitalize on that weakness. At 10:50 a.m. Wright announced his intention to press his pickets forward in an attempt to capture the Confederate forward line, but in his next communication to headquarters at 1:15 p.m., he reported: "My first attack on the enemy's picket-line has failed ... The enemy is strong in my front, and I think I may fail."[28] Despite his misgivings, the Sixth Corps' commander ordered another attempt. The Third Brigade was shifted to the left to cover the right flank of Hamblin's Brigade (Edwards had returned to command of the Grays' brigade resulting in Hamblin's reassignment), and the two units renewed the assault. "On the inner edge of the swamp we found the enemy on Hamblin's flank, and quickly drove them out, capturing about 100 prisoners."[29] Having gained the enemy's forward line, the next challenge became to hold it.

Edwards could see that the Confederates were massing for a counterattack on his right flank, and he promptly refused his line in

---

[25]Freeman, vol. 4, p. 671.
[26]O.R.-1-46-1-301, Edwards.
[27]O.R.-1-46-1-301.
[28]O.R.-1-46-3-143.
[29]O.R.-1-46-1-301.

order that the impending attack could be met head on. "The enemy attacked with a double skirmish line, but were handsomely repulsed by our skirmishers [from the 37th Massachusetts and the 5th Wisconsin]."[30] In all, the Federals of the Sixth Corps managed to advance their position a half mile, while taking 547 prisoners in the process.[31] By dusk, the fighting was over for the day; and the Third Brigade, trading rifles for shovels, promptly reversed the enemy emplacements and made the new advanced position so secure that the Union officers confidently returned most of the Brigade to camp, leaving only 250 riflemen to hold the newly-won forward pits.[32]

Wright's men had gained an extremely valuable prize for a relatively small price. The First Division suffered a total of eighty-four casualties, including ten deaths, to which toll the Grays offered four enlisted men wounded; while the balance of the Third Brigade added an additional one enlisted man killed and fourteen wounded.[33] Although the number of casualties was significant, the losses bought the Federals a much narrower killing zone, a concurrently shorter period of time during which the attackers in the inevitable final assault would be exposed to canister and musket volleys, and a reduced time for the Rebels to rally and deploy reinforcements.

The success of the twenty-fifth got Grant's fighting blood up, and orders began to stream from Headquarters in preparation for an all-out offensive. The Sixth Corps was ordered to send all its baggage to the rear, to issue ammunition and four days' ration, and to be under arms and prepared to move out at 4:00 a.m. the next morning.[34] Rather than an order to attack, the Grays and their Brigade received instructions to post one regiment in support of the picket line, and to shift the balance of the Brigade to a location near the Weldon Railroad.[35]

Then, for several days, perhaps because of the snail's pace at which the roads were drying, nothing happened. The Sixth Corps' commander did not squander the lull while the armies waited to get back

---

[30]O.R.-1-46-1-301.
[31]O.R.-1-46-3-181-182, Wright.
[32]O.R.-1-46-1-301.
[33]O.R.-1-46-3-145; O.R.-1-46-1-302.
[34]O.R.-1-46-3-183.
[35]O.R.-1-46-3-203.

at each other. While his men marked time, Wright conducted a personal, detailed reconnaissance of the lines in front of his Corps, and reported to his superiors that he was confident that his men could pierce the enemy defenses.[36]

On March 29, Grant was satisfied that the roads were dry enough to begin the offensive; but then, as if toying with the Union commander, nature sent another deluge so heavy that "It became necessary therefore to build corduroy roads every foot of the way as we advanced to move our artillery ..."[37] The rain "... descended in torrents all night, and continued with but little interruption during the next day. The country was densely wooded, and the ground swampy, and by the evening of the thirtieth whole fields had become beds of quicksand, in which the troops waded in mud above their ankles, horses sank to their bellies, and wagons threatened to disappear altogether ... The roads soon became sheets of water, and it looked as if the saving of that army would require the services, not of a Grant, but of a Noah."[38]

Although the offensive stalled again, the First Division was denied the luxury of remaining in its warm, dry huts until the weather conditions would permit the Union army to take the initiative. Instead, the Confederates unleashed a barrage that night, and in response the entire First Division was turned out into the forward trenches in anticipation of an imminent battle. Rather than sleeping, the Red Crosses spent the night out in the downpour, wallowing in mud-filled rifle pits.[39] Although often a precursor to an attack, that particular Confederate barrage, which initiated so much discomfort for the Grays, was probably only intended to forestall the expected assault by the Federals.

By the morning of the thirtieth, Grant's plans for what he hoped would be the final chapter of the war were complete. The cavalry under General Sheridan was to advance around the Confederate right flank and capture the hamlet of Five Forks, whose name explains its strategic significance, thereby denying the Rebels their best avenue of escape.

---

[36]Trudeau, p. 366.
[37]Grant, p. 439.
[38]Porter, p. 427.
[39]Haines, p. 298.

Sheridan, upon learning of the plan, requested that the Sixth Corps supply the necessary infantry support for his troopers in hopes of re-creating the partnership that had been so successful in the Shenandoah Valley the previous fall.[40] Instead, he was assigned the Fifth Corps because Grant had other plans for Wright's men -- a blitz up the Confederate middle, which was to immediately follow Sheridan's capture of Five Forks.[41]

Orders arrived late on the thirty-first requiring the Sixth Corps to be prepared to strike at 4:00 a.m. the next morning in conjunction with Sheridan's anticipated capture of Five Forks.[42] Instead, plans and reality failed to coincide as Sheridan's capture of the key intersection, a condition precedent to the Sixth Corps' assault, was delayed first by Confederate preemptive strikes, then by determined resistance from Southern skirmishers, and finally by delays in the arrival of the infantry support provided by the Fifth Corps. Every minute of April 1 must have dragged by like an hour, as the Philadelphians stood in position waiting for the dreaded order to go over the top; and hundreds of hearts must have raced each time an officer stirred in such a way as to hint that the attack was about to commence. To add to the anxiety along the trenches, the men could clearly hear the sounds of the fighting off to their left, at first the staccato popping of skirmishing, which slowly grew until 4:00 p.m. when the roar of a full-blown battle washed over them.[43]

What the veterans of the 119th recognized as the sounds of a battle was the Fifth Corps smashing into the division under the command of Confederate Major General George E. Pickett. Without their leader, who was enjoying a shad roast at the time of the attack, Pickett's troops were quickly crushed. By nightfall the Union cavalry held Five Forks, Pickett's troops were routed, and the stage was set for the Sixth Corps to launch itself against the Confederate trenches defending Petersburg.

Despite the eventual capture of Five Forks late in the afternoon, the expected order sending the Grays into the killing zone that day never arrived. Initially, Meade had delayed the order to launch the assault

---

[40]Horn, p. 223.
[41]Grant, pp. 440, 447.
[42]Rhodes, p. 223.
[43]Haines, p. 299.

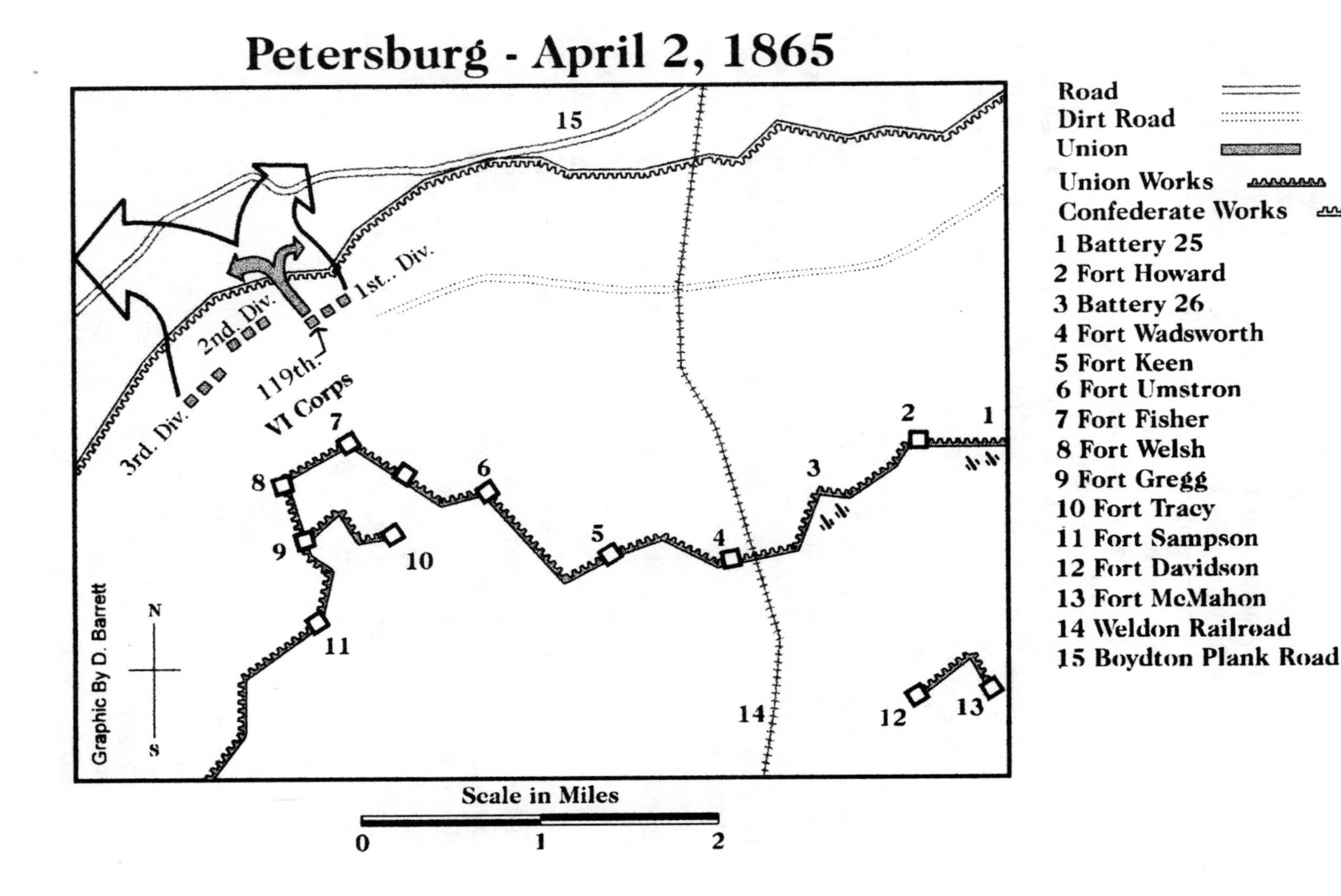
Petersburg - April 2, 1865
Road
Dirt Road
Union
Union Works
Confederate Works
1 Battery 25
2 Fort Howard
3 Battery 26
4 Fort Wadsworth
5 Fort Keen
6 Fort Umstron
7 Fort Fisher
8 Fort Welsh
9 Fort Gregg
10 Fort Tracy
11 Fort Sampson
12 Fort Davidson
13 Fort McMahon
14 Weldon Railroad
15 Boydton Plank Road
1st. Div.
2nd. Div.
3rd. Div.
119th.
VI Corps
N
S
Graphic By D. Barrett
Scale in Miles
0
1
2

because the hamlet had not been captured; but as the day wore on, the cautious Union general became increasingly reluctant to attack due to the steadily dwindling amount of remaining daylight. Finally, acquiescing to Meade's misgivings, which were apparently shared by the other participating corps commanders, Grant postponed the assault until April 2 at 4:30 a.m., and appropriate orders were issued.[44]

At 10:30 p.m., under the cover of a Union artillery barrage that had commenced a half hour earlier, the Sixth Corps began its final maneuvers into attack formation in front of Fort Fisher. By divisions, the Grays' First Division formed on the right of the Corps; the Second Division took a position in the center slightly advanced; and the trailing Third Division massed on the left slightly behind the Second and parallel to the First.[45] By brigades in the First Division, the Third Brigade was on the left; the First was in the middle; and the Second was on the right.[46] Within the Grays' Third Brigade, the regiments were formed into three lines. From left to right: the first line consisted of the 5th Wisconsin and the 37th Massachusetts; the 2nd Rhode Island, the 49th Pennsylvania, and the 119th made up the second line; while the 82nd Pennsylvania took its place in the third. To complete the formation, 20 axe-men and 75 volunteer skirmishers, each armed with a Spencer repeating rifle, were deployed to the front of the Grays' brigade.[47]

A short distance to the right of the Grays, the Second Brigade was also in the process of getting organized when "... the [Federal] pickets began firing, as we supposed, to cover the noise of our forming, and we were treated to the sensation of lying upon a field for a long time exposed to the fire of the enemy's skirmishers without any shelter. Every once in a while some one would get hit with a ball, and we could hear his cry of anguish as the lead tore through. Finally our men, by stopping their fire and crying, 'April Fool, Johnnies,' restored quiet, and for a long time we lay perfectly quiet, waiting for the time to come when we could move forward."[48]

---

[44]Grant, p. 447.
[45]Humphreys, vol. 6, p. 364.
[46]O.R.-1-46-3-427.
[47]O.R.-1-46-1-941, Edwards.
[48]Best, pp. 209-210.

Union Barrage - *Leslie's Illustrated Newspaper*

As the Federals hugged the ground, some certainly attempted to sleep, or if that was impossible, to at least distract themselves from thoughts of the coming ordeal. Across the no-man's land from the Grays, the Confederates probably rested little better than their counterparts in blue, despite the security of their position. The Southern boys of the Third Corps under Wilcox, Davis, McComb, and Lane didn't need the shells exploding over their heads to help them understand that an attack was coming -- if not in the morning, soon.

The stress and anxiety of that seemingly endless night were suddenly replaced by a surge of adrenaline when the order to advance was delivered in hushed tones by the Union officers. "At 4:00 a.m. the line moved forward, taking up the double-quick after passing the ravine in my front ..."[49] Shortly after passing over the barren no-man's land the Federals met and overcame the first obstacle: "Abatis was cut away, and through the openings thus made, and through those made by the enemy for his convenience of access to the front ..." the blue wave swept forward.[50] Next, the Grays and their comrades encountered the enemy's forward position: "Forward we go, and the rebel pickets fall back after firing a few volleys ..."[51] The advance continued, despite the men being exposed to a "... heavy fire of artillery and a more deadly though less noisy fire of musketry from the parapets."[52]

Within minutes, the Union troops reached and huddled beneath the enemy parapets, knowing that failure now almost certainly carried the penalty of death or capture. Improvising under fire, the marksmen of the 37th Massachusetts used their Spencer repeaters to keep the Confederates pinned down beneath the safety of their walls "... so that a handful of men, under protection of their volleys found a standing place under the angle of a parapet, where they could not be reached by artillery or struck by the rifleman. ... [A]fter a volley ... a few more would rush into the place until there was a sufficient number to leap into the fort and carry it by assault."[53] Suddenly, blue-clad soldiers swarmed up and over the wall, the works were carried, and the Third

---

[49]O.R.-1-46-1-941, Edwards.
[50]O.R.-1-46-1-903.
[51]Westbrook, p. 237.
[52]O.R.-1-46-1-903.
[53]Haines, p. 301.

Brigade found itself in possession of a large number of prisoners, ten cannons and three battle flags.[54] At 5:15 a.m., the Grays' brigade became the first Federal unit to breach the Confederate defenses around Petersburg.[55]

Decisive action was required to insure that this incursion would be a repeat of Rappahannock Station, and not of the breakthrough on May 10 at Spotsylvania. Edwards "... directed a fire to be opened on the right and left flanks, for the purpose of sweeping the front of the First and Second Brigades and as much of the Second Division as possible ..."[56] Some of the men of the Third Brigade continued ahead, cut the Confederate telegraph lines, and established a defensive position against a possible counterattack, while most of the rest reformed for a drive to the left.[57]

Although the Third Brigade had pierced the enemy defenses, it appears that the balance of the First Division remained pinned down in front of the enemy emplacements. Colonel Edwards recognized the crisis, and ordered the 119th to clear the right flank and free the balance of the division, thus giving the Grays their first opportunity, and the concurrent responsibility, to act alone without the assistance of the rest of the Brigade.[58] Responding immediately, "... The command [the 119th] formed a line facing to the right. The enemy at this time occupied the forts and batteries on the right, and were shelling the First and Second Brigades vigorously. With that portion of the command that had been previously faced to the right the forts and batteries were charged and captured ..."[59]

It was probably during this charge that the luck of the young Irishman Lewis Dunlap, one of the first men over the parapet that morning despite wounds received at Salem Church and the Wilderness, finally ran out. As he rushed forward, a minie ball smashed into his left leg and spun him to the ground with a shattered knee joint.[60] His

---

[54]O.R.-1-46-1-941.
[55]Porter, p. 445.
[56]O.R.-1-46-1-941.
[57]O.R.-1-46-1-941.
[58]O.R.-1-46-1-941.
[59]O.R.-1-46-1-950, Gray.
[60]National Archives, Dunlap Pension Records.

comrades continued the rush and captured, "... in all, seven pieces of artillery and a large number of prisoners." Then, "After holding the captured works for an hour and a half our ammunition gave out. The command was ordered to rejoin the brigade ..."[61]

Major William C. Gray

(courtesy K. Turner collection)

By the time the 119th rejoined its Brigade, command of the Regiment had devolved to Major William C. Gray, thanks to a gunshot wound to the leg which forced Lt. Colonel Clark off the field. Although the wound cost Clark the command of the Regiment, and a portion of his thigh bone, it probably erased any questions about the Lt. Colonel's courage which may have lingered from the incident in the woods outside of Rappahannock Station.[62]

Another more significant casualty occurred in the confused area of the breakthrough, when Lieutenant General A. P. Hill, who was valiantly attempting to reach his troops of the Confederate Third Corps, which he had commanded since before Gettysburg, was cut down by two stray Sixth Corps soldiers.[63] For all practical purposes, Lee's Third Corps died the same morning as its commander.

While the Grays were clearing the defenses in front of the rest of their division, and holding the newly acquired lines against counterattack, "Wright swung around to his left and moved to Hatcher's Run,

---

[61]O.R.-1-46-1-950.
[62]National Archives, Clark Military Records.
[63]Freeman, vol. 4, p. 679.

sweeping everything before him."[64] "On reaching Hatcher's Run (a small portion of the force crossed it) I [Wright] learned from staff officers of the Lieutenant General that the Second and Fifth Corps and the cavalry were sweeping down in that direction, and that it was not necessary to proceed farther. I therefore turned and moved toward Petersburg."[65]

As the Sixth Corps returned from the south and began to press toward the city, the Grays were reunited with their comrades. In a terse narrative, Major Gray described the Philadelphians' role for the balance of the day: "[we] ... rejoined the brigade on its return from the left, marched to the right, formed line on the left of Second Division; advanced in line to near the enemy's interior works; formed line in a road on the right of the brigade. During this movement the command was exposed to a severe artillery fire. We were relieved at 5 p.m. by troops from the Second Corps ..."[66]

Colonel Edwards provided a somewhat more detailed account of the balance of the day: "I was then ordered to move back in the direction of Petersburg. My brigade skirmished toward the city for a distance of two miles, where we formed a connected line with the First Brigade, on my left, and the Second Division of the Second Corps, on my right. During this advance, and while forming my lines, the command was exposed to a severe and at times to an enfilading fire from the enemy's batteries, advantageously posted. As soon as my lines were formed I received orders to throw up a rifle-pit, covering my front, which was completed before dark."[67]

With his main defensive line ruptured, and with Federal troopers in control of his right flank, Lee knew that the time had finally arrived to evacuate the Confederate capital and its rail link to the South. As soon as darkness fell, the Southern forces began a desperate attempt to escape from the Union trap that was about to snap shut. Longstreet's Corps, the contingent farthest north, abandoned Richmond and crossed behind the lines at Petersburg, and was soon followed by Ewell's men

[64]Grant, vol. 2, p. 448.
[65]O.R.-1-46-1-904.
[66]O.R.-1-46-1-950.
[67]O.R.-1-46-1-941.

who drew the assignment of rear guard. As the cities were abandoned, bridges and military structures were blown up; and the resulting fires, together with the fires set by Southern looters, caused much of Richmond and some of Petersburg to be consumed. To the men in blue, those fires shone as beacons of hope and triumph: "A happier night I never have seen, as the fires which lit up the whole country were burning and the city we had fought for four years was ours. The boys would wake each other up to see the fires burn."[68]

At 5:30 a.m. on the morning of the third, skirmishers from the Sixth Corps entered Petersburg and verified that their adversaries had departed.[69] Spared from house-to-house fighting, the Grays were able to savor their accomplishments for a while longer, especially the formal surrender of the city, by the Mayor of Petersburg, to their brigade commander, Colonel Edwards.[70] Soon thereafter, the Union army began the earnest business of attempting to intercept the remainder of the Confederate army before it could effect a juncture with General Johnston.

---

[68]As cited in Trudeau, *The Last Citadel* ..., p. 378.

[69]O.R.-1-46-3-520.

[70]Rhodes, p. 227. It appears from similar claims asserted by other units, that several delegations from the city surrendered to different Union commanders.

16

SAILOR'S CREEK

By 7:30 a.m. on April 3, the Sixth Corps was on the River Road in pursuit of the Rebels, and would continue marching all day until finally permitted to rest for the evening at Sotherland Station on the Southside Railroad.[1] Each mile the men would cover over the next several days would present the paradox of difficulties sufficient to sap the resolve of the men, and signs of impending victory adequate to restore it. "The roads in places were horrible, the terrible rain of Thursday & Friday before having covered the level land & the road was badly cut up by the enemy's train; in many of the low bad places the enemy had been obliged to abandon wagon, caisson, forges, &c, while the roadside was thickly strewn by ammunition of every kind and sort ..."[2]

On April 4, the race commenced again before dawn, and soon became, at least for the Confederates, even more desperate because of hunger and fatigue. The Southern army had only limited provisions in the city, and a significant portion of those were abandoned during the evacuation. Believing that supplies awaited their arrival, the ragged and undernourished Butternuts pressed on toward Amelia Court House as fast as their weakened bodies could carry them. They suffered severely from the effects of months of relative inactivity, limited rations, and from the psychological impact of the crushing defeat on April 2. "Drowsiness and nervousness were worse than were hunger and exhaustion. Men staggered as if they were drunk. When some of them tried to talk, they were incoherent."[3]

---

[1]O.R.-1-46-3-520; Haines, p. 304.

[2]Hannaford, *Reminiscences*, as cited in Starr, vol. 2, p. 460.

[3]As cited in Freeman, p. 692.

Almost like the victims of a cruel hoax, when the Southerners finally dragged themselves to the Court House they discovered that no such supplies existed, reducing the once proud Confederates to foraging and begging for food amongst the local farmers.[4] If the Butternuts "... got anything to eat at all, they begged it from citizens in passing by or stole it, and the great trouble was there was so little left to steal. The country was stripped."[5] As a result of having managed to out-pace the supply wagons, the Federals in the Sixth Corps also suffered from hunger that day, although to a much more limited degree.[6] For the Union men who had previously been well-fed, the situation created just another of the innumerable irritations to which they had almost become accustomed. For their antagonists, however, who faced the very real possibility of physical collapse or even death by starvation, the time was fast approaching when the ongoing physical deprivations could render the Southern army virtually helpless.

The armies resumed their respective flight and pursuit early on the morning of the fifth, and continued the race throughout the day. Most of the Butternuts were able to draw upon their seemingly bottomless reservoir of dedication and fortitude to continue the march to the southwest. For some, though, the psychological and/or physiological effects of the situation caused them to straggle behind their comrades, where they were eventually scooped up by the pursuing Federals. Despite his pathetic circumstances, at least one such weary Butternut was able to maintain a wry sense of humor. When approached by Union soldiers who claimed to have gotten him as their prisoner, the Southerner responded, "Yes, ... you've got me, and the hell of a git you got."[7]

Later in the afternoon, the Sixth Corps rolled into Jetersville on the right flank of the Union front, where the Grays, on the right of the First Division, bivouacked for the night in the vicinity of Amelia Court House.[8] The new Union position blocked Lee's route to his intended

---

[4]Freeman, p. 692.
[5]Peck, *Reminiscences*, as cited in Starr, vol. 2, p. 457.
[6]Grant, vol. 2, p. 464.
[7]As cited in Freeman, p. 718.
[8]O.R.-1-46-1-950.

destination of Burkville, forcing the Confederate commander to shift his course to the northwest -- through Rice, toward Farmville.[9]

On the morning of April 6, the Philadelphians joined in a maneuver which they expected would develop into a battle: "[the 119th] ... formed on the left of front line of the brigade, supporting the Second Division; moved by left of regiment to the front through the woods and thicket for about an hour; finding no enemy, returned to original camp ..."[10] While the Federal troops were beating the bushes searching for the departed Rebels, their commanders were struggling over power and prestige.

Sheridan, believing that Meade's disposition would result in a repeat of the latter's performance after Gettysburg, lobbied Grant to adopt a plan that would cut Lee's army off rather than merely chase it. Meade, who was very ill at the time, either chose not to press the issue, or was unaware of Sheridan's actions. In any case, Grant sided with his protege from the western theater, and according to Sheridan stated, "The Sixth Corps will go in with a vim any place you may dictate ..."[11] Whether Meade was aware at the time that he had been stripped of control over the Sixth Corps is not clear, making the issue one of the innumerable topics of debate after the war. Grant confirmed the change when he wrote in his memoirs, "The Sixth Corps now remained with the cavalry and under Sheridan's direct command until after the surrender."[12]

Back in the field, the Federals came up empty-handed in the thicket outside of Amelia Court House, because Lee had already gotten his men on the road and out of reach. At 9:30 a.m., as the Grays were returning to camp and the true situation became clear, Sheridan began to exercise his newly won authority. In hopes of blocking the Southern retreat, he ordered the Sixth Corps to swing behind the Second Corps and to assume a position on the left of the Union army.[13]

All afternoon the Southern column and the Sixth Corps marched on basically parallel courses, with the Confederates somewhat in the lead

---

[9]Freeman, pp. 692-693, 699.
[10]O.R.-1-46-1-951.
[11]Sheridan, p. 384.
[12]Grant, vol. 2, p. 473.
[13]O.R.-1-46-3-596.

due to their earlier start. Lee's column was led by his First Corps under the command of James Longstreet; next in line was a small corps under the command of Lieutenant General Richard H. Anderson; third in line was a contingent of approximately 3,000 troops under General Ewell; and in the rear trudged the Confederate Second Corps under the command of John B. Gordon.[14] The geometry of the situation dictated that the two columns would meet somewhere near where the Rice's Station Road crossed over Sailor's Creek, in an area that neither side would probably have chosen for a confrontation, consisting as it did, of "Long, frowning ridges [which] ran for several miles toward the Appomattox, as if they guarded deep, swift streams. Instead, the two branches of the creek, except in rainy weather, were small, sluggish and heavily bogged."[15]

As the Confederates neared the creek, their column separated into fragments; and instead of Butternuts in his front, Anderson discovered that his path was blocked by Union cavalry. Aware that a quick response was essential to prevent the Sixth Corps from falling upon the rear of the Confederate column, Anderson brought the news of his discovery to Ewell, the ranking officer, and the two quickly evaluated the limited options available. Discarding the option of abandoning the road and sending the Confederate troops north through the woods, Ewell resolved to send Anderson westward against the cavalry, in hopes that the road ahead could be quickly cleared; while in the meantime, Ewell planned to personally supervise a holding action in the rear of the command.[16]

Perhaps had he known the true proximity of his adversaries, Ewell's decision might have been different. Unfortunately for the Confederates, while still waiting for Anderson's attack to begin, the Southerners discovered Sixth Corps troops under Brigadier General Truman Seymour closing in on their rear. Ewell immediately began to deploy his troops onto a naturally strong defensive position on a ridge overlooking the point where Rice's Station Road passed through the Sailor's Creek -- positioning Major General Custis Lee's men on the

---

[14]Freeman, p. 699.
[15]As cited in Freeman, p. 702.
[16]Davis, p. 249.

right, the Naval Battalion in the center, and Kershaw's Division on the left. All the while, Federal artillerymen made the Rebel deployment as hot as possible by lobbing shells into the formation, to which the Confederates were unable to respond because they had no artillery with them.[17]

Sheridan, perhaps having been with the cavalry that cut off Anderson, claimed that he was quickly on the scene and in charge. "... I directed General Wright to put it [Seymour's Division] on the right of the road, while Wheaton's men [of the First Division] coming up all hot and out of breath, promptly formed on Seymour's left."[18] As the Grays arrived on the scene at around 5:00 p.m., it must have been clear that something big was in the works, because they saw Sheridan, Wright, Wheaton, and Edwards huddled together in conference.[19] While the brass conferred, the Philadelphians and their comrades formed up approximately 300 yards away from the Rebel line, and then waited for the death-bearing command to advance.[20]

Presumably Edwards was doing much more listening than talking, although when Sheridan gave the order "The enemy are there ... I want you to form your brigade in one line, cross the creek and carry the heights," the Colonel supposedly raised a question about the safety of his flanks. To this Sheridan was reported to have responded, "Never mind your flanks! Go through them. They're as demoralized as hell."[21] According to one member of the 49th Pennsylvania, Edwards was not the only inquisitive member of the Third Brigade. "While forming Major Gray [the new Regimental commander] of the One hundred and nineteenth asked the general [presumably Sheridan] of the situation. He replied aloud, 'Boys, Custer is across there (pointing) about two miles with his cavalry and fourteen pieces of artillery and we're here, and Ewell with his corps is between us and if we press them they will be in a _ _ _ _ tight fix.'"[22] Events would soon prove Sheridan to be a better tactician than judge of Confederate morale.

---

[17]Davis, p. 249.
[18]Sheridan, p. 384.
[19]O.R.-1-46-1-950, Gray; Rhodes, p. 227.
[20]Freeman, p. 703.
[21]As cited in Davis, p. 268.
[22]Downing, *Pennsylvania at Gettysburg*, vol. 1, pp. 298-299.

Sailor's Creek - April 6, 1865

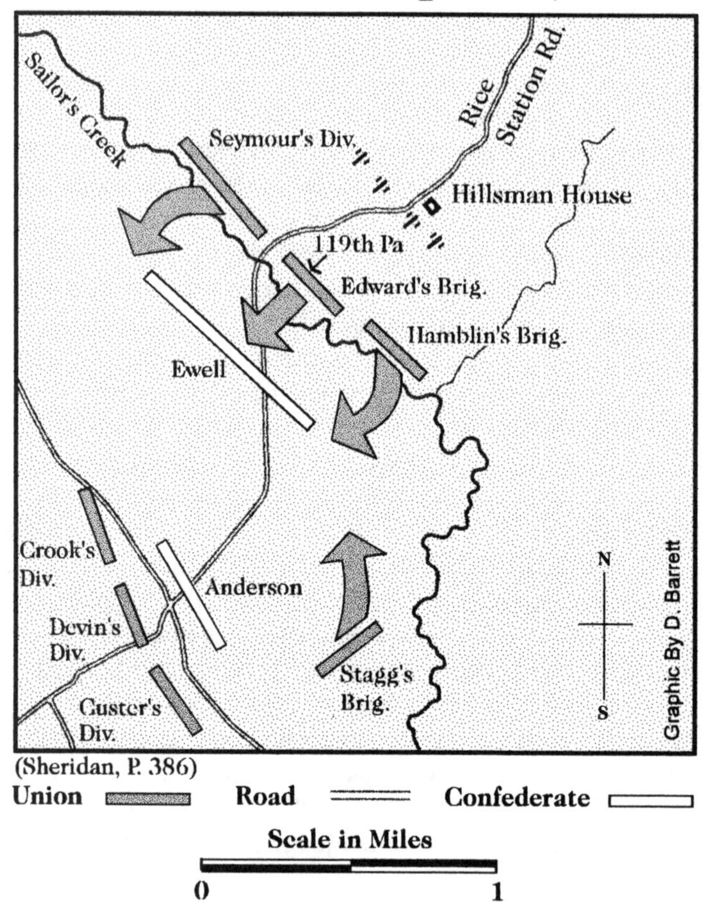

With the question and answer session completed, Edwards began to make preparations for an assault, but for reasons that are now unclear, rather than cross the creek in one line as ordered, Edwards sent his charges across in four lines -- the first manned by the 82nd Pennsylvania and the 5th Wisconsin; the second by the 49th Pennsylvania; the third by the Grays and the 2nd Rhode Island; and the last by the 37th Massachusetts.[23] The crossing was difficult and perilous: "I will here state that the water and mud in the creek was waist deep, and the crossing was made under a very severe musketry fire."[24] "At the foot of the hill we [the 49th Pennsylvania] came to a quicksand swamp. As soon as I put my foot on it I knew what it was. I immediately stepped out in front and, jumping from one bunch of grass to another, I reached the other side dry shod, while many of the Company got in mire so deep that they could not get out without assistance."[25] "The Rebels opened upon us as soon as we reached the river, but we jumped in with the water up to our waists and soon reached the other side."[26]

Once across, Edwards carried out his orders, forming the Third Brigade in one line under the protection of a small knoll, which formation when completed, from left to right, consisted of the 37th Massachusetts, 2nd Rhode Island, 49th Pennsylvania, 119th, 82nd Pennsylvania, and the 5th Wisconsin.[27] Rather than attack immediately, however, it appears that a Union officer, perhaps acting on his own, crossed the 150 yards of open ground separating the combatants under a white flag, and offered the Confederates the opportunity to surrender. The Rebels signaled their rejection of the offer with a volley.[28]

Then, "... the [Grays'] brigade moved rapidly forward and soon became heavily engaged with the enemy. At this time I [Edwards] was deprived of the Thirty-seventh Massachusetts, on which I depended for holding my left; the Second Rhode Island Volunteers, losing its connection with the Thirty-seventh and being exposed to a severe fire from the left flank and our own batteries, were thrown into disorder and

---

[23]O.R.-1-46-1-942, Edwards.

[24]O.R.-1-46-1-950, Gray.

[25]Cpl. B. J. Jones as cited in Korn, p. 123.

[26]Rhodes, p. 228.

[27]O.R.-1-46-1-942; Downing, *Pennsylvania at Gettysburg*, vol. 1, p. 299.

[28]Davis, p. 253; Downing, *Pennsylvania at Gettysburg*, vol. 1, p. 299.

obliged to fall back, and by so doing partially exposing the left flank of the Forty-ninth, which was also thrown into disorder, but soon rallied. The Fifth, Eighty-second, and One hundred and nineteenth, though exposed to a heavy flank fire from the enemy, posted not thirty yards from them, maintained their ground, and after a severe contest, and losing heavily, drove the enemy from their position ... The Thirty-seventh Massachusetts advanced at the same time with the brigade, driving the enemy slowly, but soon found both flanks exposed and a column of the enemy coming in on their left. Their left was thrown back to meet this attack, which they admirably repulsed. By this time they discovered the enemy on their right flank and some 100 yards in the rear. The regiment faced about, and a desperate hand-to-hand fight ensued."[29]

Contrary to Sheridan's earlier assessment, the Rebels were still full of fight and, without orders, impetuously launched a ferocious counterattack down the hill, and pitched into the blue line. Becoming fierce and personal, "... the battle degenerated into a butchery and a confused melee of brutal personal conflicts. I saw numbers of men kill each other with bayonets and the butts of muskets, and even bite each other's throats and ears and noses, rolling on the ground like wild beasts. I saw one of my officers and a Federal officer fighting with swords over the battalion colors ... Near the end of the 37th Massachusetts had the fiercest literally savage encounter of the war ... They clubbed muskets, fired pistols into each others faces and used bayonets savagely."[30]

The Philadelphians were apparently spared most of the hand-to-hand combat, suffering instead from an impersonal, but deadly, enfilading fire which temporarily threw the left portion of the Regiment into a panic.[31] The Rebel onslaught was sufficient to push some of the Union troops, particularly the 2nd Rhode Island, back across the creek; but order amongst the Federal troops was quickly restored, and soon the blue line surged back up the hill, where the 49th Pennsylvania and

[29]O.R.-1-46-1-942.
[30]As cited in Davis, p. 255.
[31]O.R.-1-46-1-951.

probably the 119th on their right became engaged with "... a regiment of marines from Richmond [probably the Naval Battalion]."[32]

This time the Confederate forces, already disorganized and depleted from the earlier encounter, and assailed on the flanks by Yankee cavalry, succumbed to the Union forces closing in from three sides. The collapse of the Southern defense was sudden and complete. Lt. General Ewell surrendered to a soldier of the 5th Wisconsin, and within a short time was joined in captivity by Generals Kershaw, Custis Lee, Hunter, and Corse.[33] Within a week, the Third Brigade had either eliminated or captured two of the three corps commanders that led the Confederate army at Gettysburg.

After the fighting ceased, a curious and almost incredible event occurred. Confederate Captain Blake, sounding somewhat incredulous, even though a witness, related that: "The infantry we had so recently repulsed came up with smiling faces. They showed no resentment, but opened their haversacks and offered to share their hard tack with us saying, 'you Johnnies sure put up a good fight.'"[34] It may be difficult for modern readers, raised in the era of "total war," to comprehend how men who recently bit at each other's throats, could so quickly change from killers to benefactors; but the incident goes a long way toward explaining how this country was able to mend from the effects of the war.

Unfortunately, the Battle of Sailor's Creek did not end the war, it only helped to further seal the fate of the Confederacy. The next morning at 5:00 a.m. the Grays were up and on the road, where perhaps in recognition of their accomplishments of the previous evening, they would spend the day marching along with and guarding the wagon train. The visage of war, due to the obvious deterioration of the Confederate forces, had lost some of its grimness for the Yankees, who were "already on the move, singing, laughing, joking and apparently happy as they marched along, though a little inclined to growl at being obliged to let the cavalry have the road, while they took the rougher, harder-to-march-over ground at the side. Along the side were evidences of the

---

[32]Rhodes, p. 229; Downing, *Pennsylvania at Gettysburg*, vol 1, p. 299.

[33]Rhodes, p. 228; Humphreys, p. 383.

[34]As cited in Davis, p. 256.

rapid retreat of the enemy -- all sorts of munitions of war laying around in loose profusion, -- a dead rebel soldier lying on the road where he halted his last time, with every appearance of having died from hunger and exhaustion, -- dead horses, the infallible army guideboards, lying where they dropped, and others abandoned because unable longer to carry their riders, -- all informed the men that the men ahead of them were in a great hurry, and had an exhilarating effect upon their spirits."[35] One must wonder whether mixed in with the jubilation over the impending victory were fears of becoming one of the last to die in the war. Whether exultant or pensive, the tired men were certainly very grateful when the day's march ended at Farmville and the Regiment bivouacked for the night.[36]

The Grays spent April 8 much the same way as they had the seventh, trudging after the fleeing Confederates, until allowed to camp for the night at Buckingham. Up again at 5:00 a.m. on the ninth, the men marched for about six hours until suddenly orders came to deploy for battle. Instead of immediately pitching into the enemy as they had at Sailor's Creek, the Federals held their position in line of battle in hopes that negotiations, rather than muskets, would settle the matter. At 5:00 p.m. those hopes were answered with news that Lee had finally surrendered.[37] "The batteries began to fire blank cartridges, while the infantry fired their muskets in the air. The men threw their knapsacks and canteens in the air and howled like mad."[38]

The next day the surrender was formally announced, and the scenes of jubilation were repeated. "There was every demonstration of joy imaginable -- the men were shaking hands and shedding tears of gladness at the thought of no more bloodshed and a speedy return to their homes." Repeating the generosity shown to the Southerners at Sailor's Creek, "Our boys opened their haversacks to give to the hungry rebels, and soon full rations were distributed to them."[39] For the Grays the fighting was over, and for the nation the healing process had begun.

---

[35]Tobie, *First Maine Cavalry*, as cited in Starr, vol. 2, p. 475.
[36]O.R.-1-46-1-951.
[37]O.R.-1-46-1-951; Humphreys, p. 393.
[38]Rhodes, p. 228.
[39]Haines, p. 309.

EPILOGUE

The last week of the war was, for the Grays, a time of tragedy, heroism, and glory. The raw statistics show that the Regiment suffered a significant, although not the highest, number of casualties in the Brigade which did suffer the greatest number of casualties in the Sixth Corps that week. According to the *Official Record*, forty members of the 119th became casualties, with one officer and four enlisted men killed; four officers and twenty-nine enlisted men wounded; and two men reported missing in action -- a total almost equal to twenty percent of the Regiment at the time. The Third Brigade as a whole suffered 538 casualties, as compared to the First Brigade with 76 and the Second Brigade with 106. In the Grays' brigade, the warriors from Wisconsin accounted for 172 casualties, a third of the total.[1]

On a more personal level, any death or serious injury at the very end of a conflict was especially poignant. Adjutant John D. Mercer was the only officer from the 119th to lose his life during the final week, one of only two staff officers from the Regiment to lose his life during the entire war. John H. Millard of Company I was killed in action at Sailor's Creek, leaving behind a wife and a four-year-old daughter. Perhaps Millard shouldn't have tempted fate when he wrote to his convalescent brother James shortly before the battle "... of his surprise that no bullet had found him out thus far."[2]

Joshua Fisher of Company E and Lewis Dunlap of Company F simply ran out of luck during the attack against Petersburg. Fisher, who lost a forefinger to a minie ball in the Wilderness and survived

---

[1]O.R.-1-46-1-582.
[2]*Philadelphia Sunday Press*, 12/28/1890.

Adjutant John D. Mercer

(1st Regiment Museum)

pneumonia in the winter of 1863, took a nasty shot in the left forearm while on the picket line. He was left with an ugly scar and a fifty percent disability. His disability would not, however, interfere with fathering nine children after the war.[3] Lewis Dunlap was wounded at Salem Church and again in the Wilderness. Although he lost his leg from the third wound he received at Fort Fisher, he would go on to serve for decades as a sergeant on the Philadelphia police force, perhaps helping to perpetuate the image of the tough Irish cop.[4]

The last casualty of the Regiment seems to have been George C. Booze, the fiercely patriotic nurse with the soul of an artist. Despite having been spared most of the risks of combat while helping the wounded and dying at the Regimental hospital, Booze succumbed to jaundice at the City Point, Virginia hospital on May 20, 1865. Besides the usual gear, Booze left behind a Bible, a grooming set, a memo book, a satchel, and a portfolio, perhaps containing other sketches or poems. He also left behind a pension for his impoverished mother.[5]

In all, 1,200 men served with the 119th Regiment, Gray Reserves, during the war. Of those 136 died in combat, 300 were wounded, and 68 died from other causes, mostly disease, during the rebellion.[6] Typically, a different total was provided in Fox's compilation, according to which the Regiment suffered a total of 141 men killed,

---

[3]National Archives, Fisher Pension Records.

[4]National Archives, Dunlap Pension Records.

[5]National Archives, Booze Pension and Military Records.

[6]Monument to the 119th at the Gettysburg National Park.

of which 9 were officers and the rest were enlisted or noncommissioned. Thus, the Regiment suffered a killed-in-action ratio of 11.5 percent. Fox put the total figure of killed and wounded in the Regiment at 519, with another 21 men having died in captivity.[7] Of the thirteen "compositors" (twelve according to another source) who originally enlisted with the Regiment, Sergeant Rowan Foulke was the sole survivor.[8] Only 316 Grays were present in Philadelphia to be mustered out with their comrades-in-arms on June 19, 1865.[9]

Captain William A. Wiedersheim

(USAMHI)

In contrast to those grim statistics, there was also glory of sorts flowing from the final week of the war. Colonel Edwards, the commander of the Grays' Third Brigade, was ordered to recommend officers who, because of their performance, deserved a brevet promotion. From the seven regiments that comprised the brigade, thirty officers were nominated, eight of whom were from the 119th. Gideon Clark, William C. Gray, William A. Wiedersheim, Henry C. Warner, D. S. Hassinger, James Dutton, and Thomas Morris, were all recognized for "... gallantry and meritorious service ..." on either the second, the sixth, or both. In

[7]The combat mortality rate for the Grays was lower than that of the 6th Maine, 5th Wisconsin, and 49th Pennsylvania, who suffered a loss rate of 153-12.6%, 165-12.5%, and 195-14.6% respectively. However, those three regiments also participated in the Peninsular Campaign and at Antietam. Fox, p. 294.

[8]*Bucks County Intelligencer*, 6/20/1865.

[9] In an incredible coincidence, Fox also maintained that the Grays' sister regiment, the 118th Pennsylvania (Corn Exchange Regiment), suffered an identical number of killed, with exactly the same number of officers and non-officers as in the 119th losing their lives in combat. Fox, p. 294; Bates, *History...*, vol. 4, 119th.

addition, Edwin A. Landell received special commendation "... for meritorious services in being one of the first in the enemy's works April 2 ...", and for conspicuous gallantry on the sixth.

Samuel Winterbottom

(USAMHI)

It was not only the officers of the 119th who earned praise for their conduct. Sergeants George W. Johnson and William Ployd, and Privates Samuel Winterbottom and Lewis Dunlap, were commended "... for being the first to enter the enemy's works and securing two pieces of artillery April 2, 1865."[10] The accolade must have brought at least some consolation to Private Dunlap during the lonely hours in the hospital, as he contemplated his loss and his future.

In summary, the 119th was more than "... just another regiment from Philadelphia ..." although having to consider the question provides more honor to the other Philadelphia regiments than disrespect for the Grays. Certainly the 119th was not a 20th Maine or a 1st Minnesota, but there were only a handful of such renowned regiments. The 119th was, however, an integral part of a brigade that had one of the most prestigious records for valor and achievement in the Army of the Potomac. For daring, there was the amphibious crossing of the Rappahannock in front of Fredericksburg; for elan, the capture of the fortress at Rappahannock Station and the breakthrough at Spotsylvania on May 10, 1864; for determination, the twelve hours at the "Bloody Angle"; and in addition the battles of Opequon, Petersburg, and Sailor's Creek provided an honor roll of stunning victories.

---

[10]O.R.-1-46-1-943-944.

For the men in the Gray Reserves, the soldier's life had indeed been "rough" and the suffering had been "regular." As the survivors raised families, pursued careers, convalesced, or relived the war with comrades at countless G.A.R. meetings, First Infantry Regimental functions, or Washington Grays' banquets, all those who persevered had the satisfaction of knowing that they responded to the call of their nation, and that they had done their duty.

APPENDIX A

Roster - 119th Regiment Pennsylvania Volunteer Infantry

Name	Rank	Co.	Enlistment or Draft Date	Exit Date	Remarks
Abbott, William	Pvt.	A	E-08/12/62	06/19/65	Mustered Out
Abertson, William H.	Pvt.	I	E-08/13/62	07/02/64	Died
Able, John P.	Corp.	G	E-08/13/62	10/12/62	Discharged-Surgeon's Certificate
Acheson, Alex	Pvt.	K	E-11/11/64	06/19/65	Mustered Out
Achuff, Samuel	Pvt.	D	E-08/13/62	07/02/63	Deserted
Acker, Henry S.	Pvt.	H	E-08/25/62	06/19/65	Mustered Out
Adams, Albert	Pvt.	A	E-08/12/62	11/07/63	Died of Wounds-Rappahannock St.
Adams, George	Pvt.	A	08/12/62	05/15/65	Disch. Surg. Cert.
Adams, Hamilton	Pvt.	K	E-08/15/62	06/19/65	Mustered Out
Adams, James	Pvt.	G	E-08/15/62	06/19/65	Mustered Out
Adams, Samuel	Pvt.	H	E-08/18/62	unk.	Not on Muster Out Roll
Adams, Samuel	Pvt.	I	E-08/18/62	04/02/65	Died Wounds Rec. at Petersburg
Adams, Theodore	Pvt.	I	D-09/07/64	06/19/65	Deserted, Returned, Mustered Out
Adams, Thomas	Pvt.	A	E-08/12/62	unk	Dishonorably Discharged
Adams, William	Corp.	I	E-06/23/63	06/04/65	Transferred to 82nd P.V.
Aimon, Edwin	Pvt.	F	E-08/19/62	07/08/63	Discharged-Surgeon's Certificate
Aitkin, William	Sgt.	F	E-08/18/62	06/19/65	Mustered Out
Albertson, Enoch	Pvt.	K	E-11/09/62	06/19/65	Mustered Out
Alexander, Thomas	Pvt.	B	E-08/18/62	06/19/65	Mustered Out
Allen, Charles	Pvt.	C	D-08/22/63	09/15/63	Deserted
Allen, Howard	Sgt.	G	E-08/07/62	11/14/63	Lost Leg from Wound Rec. in Action
Allen, Samuel	Pvt.	B	E-08/15/62	06/19/65	Mustered Out
Amon, Jacob H.	Pvt.	B	E-08/15/62	06/19/65	Mustered Out
Anderson, Alex	Pvt.	E	D-07/17/63	unk.	Discharged by General Order
Andress, John	Pvt.	F	E-08/23/62	11/01/62	Deserted
Andrews, Adam	Pvt.	F	E-08/29/62	12/01/63	Wd. Salem Church, Trans. Vet. Res.
Antis, Jacob	Pvt.	H	E-08/30/62	08/09/63	Discharged-Surgeon's Certificate
Armbruster, Clement	Pvt.	H	D-08/30/63	06/19/65	Deserted, Returned, Mustered Out
Arnold, Daniel S.	Pvt.	G	D-08/31/63	03/31/65	Lost Arm in Action, Discharged
Arnold, George	Pvt.	H	D-08/29/63	unk.	Wd. Spotsyl. 5/10/64, Disch. G.O.
Arthur, Rudolph	Pvt.	H	D-09/01/63	09/15/63	Deserted
Arthur, William	Pvt.	G	E-08/15/62	05/12/64	Killed at Spotsylvania
Ash, George	Pvt.	D	E-08/15/62	06/19/65	Mustered Out
Auchy, Joseph G.	Pvt.	H	E-08/25/62	06/19/65	Mustered Out
Aull, Henry	Pvt.	E	E-08/19/62	06/19/65	Mustered Out
Ayers, Henry	Pvt.	C	D-09/01/63	unk.	Deserted
Baker, Henry	Pvt.	C	D-08/31/63	07/29/64	Deserted
Baker, John	Pvt.	E	E-08/29/62	12/12/64	Trans. Veteran Reserve
Paldwin, William H.	Pvt.	F	E-08/08/62	11/01/62	Deserted
Bales, John E.	Pvt.	I	E-08/11/62	05/14/64	Killed at Spotsylvania
Ballinger, William H.	Sgt.	H	E-08/19/62	12/05/62	Discharged by Special Order
Bantle, Augustus	Pvt.	I	E-08/21/62	05/10/64	Killed at Spotsylvania
Barber, James	Pvt.	D	D-07/17/63	06/04/65	Transferred to 82nd P.V.
Bardman, Daniel	Pvt.	H	E-08/23/62	06/19/65	Mustered Out
Bardsley, Jacob	1st Sgt.	E	E-08/11/62	06/19/65	Mustered Out
Barker, Richard	Pvt.	D	E-08/13/62	03/09/64	Discharged by Special Order

Name	Rank	Co.	Enlistment or Draft Date	Exit Date	Remarks
Barnes, Walter	Pvt.	G	D-08/29/63	09/01/64	Capt'd 11/9/63, Died Andersonville
Barnett, Alfred	Corp.	F	E-08/18/62	05/03/63	Missing in Action at Salem Church
Baroux, Charles T.	1st Lt.	D	E-08/05/62	06/21/64	Discharged
Baroux, James R.	Pvt.	D	E-08/15/62	05/15/65	Discharged by General Order
Barr, John	Pvt.	A	E-08/12/62	05/12/64	M.I.A.-Spotsylvania
Barrell, Henry	Pvt.	B	E-08/13/62	11/14/62	Died
Barrett, Heston	Pvt.	A	08/12/62	07/13/65	Transferred to Vet. Res.
Barrett, James W.	Pvt.	C	E-08/22/62	05/--/65	Discharged by Special Order
Barry, Charles	Pvt.	G	E-08/07/62	05/15/65	Disch.-Wd. Rec. Wilderness 5/5/64
Barry, John L.	Pvt.	I	E-08/19/62	06/19/65	Mustered Out
Barry, Thomas	Pvt.	A	D-09/01/63	09/63	Deserted
Barwis, Howard	Pvt.	G	E-08/15/62	06/19/65	Mustered Out
Basler, Henry	Pvt.	H	E-08/23/62	11/29/62	Died at Stafford Court House, Va.
Bastian, Daniel	Sgt.	D	E-08/11/62	05/15/65	Discharged by General Order
Bastobol, Patrick	Pvt.	B	E-08/16/62	08/29/62	Deserted
Batran, John	Pvt.	E	E-08/30/62	unk.	Not on Muster Out Roll
Batty, John	Pvt.	C	E-08/21/62	unk.	Deserted
Batzel, Jacob	Pvt.	H	E-08/23/62	06/09/63	Died at Belle Plain, Va.
Beagley, James	Pvt.	C	D-07/17/63	11/05/64	Deserted
Beans, Howard	Pvt.	E	E-08/22/62	unk.	Not on Muster Out Roll
Beauregard, Peter	Pvt.	F	D-08/29/63	06/04/65	Transferred to 82nd P.V.
Beidleman, Daniel	Pvt.	C	E-08/23/62	unk.	Discharged-Surgeon's Certificate
Belcher, Charles E.	Pvt.	C	E-08/22/62	10/--/62	Deserted
Bell, William	Pvt.	A	E-07/22/63	06/04/65	Transferred to 82nd P.V.
Bender, Thomas	Pvt.	F	D-07/17/63	10/--/63	Deserted, Rtd., Trans. Navy
Bendinagle, John	Pvt.	C	E-08/16/62	08/--/62	Deserted
Bennett, James M.	Sgt.	G	E-08/09/62	02/13/63	Discharged-Surgeon's Certificate
Bern, Jacob	Pvt.	H	E-07/23/64	06/04/65	Transferred to 82nd P.V.
Berrell, Charles	Pvt.	B	E-08/16/62	06/19/65	Mustered Out
Berry, Albert J.	Pvt.	C	E-01/12/65	06/04/65	Transferred to 82nd P.V.
Birmingham, Francis	Pvt.	C	E-08/30/62	unk.	Transferred to Veteran Reserve
Bittenbender, J. W.	Pvt.	E	D-09/02/63	07/25/64	Deserted
Blackburn, John B.	Pvt.	C	E-08/21/62	unk.	Transferred to Veteran Reserve
Blair, James	Pvt.	C	D-07/15/63	unk.	Absent sick at Muster Out
Blake, Henry	Pvt.	B	E-08/15/62	09/01/62	Deserted
Blake, Samuel	Pvt.	A	E-08/13/62	04/14/65	Died of Wounds-Petersburg
Blakey, Edward H.	Pvt.	B	E-08/16/62	10/05/62	Died at Camp Addicks
Blakey, James W.	Pvt.	B	E-08/22/62	06/19/65	Mustered Out
Blakey, Thomas	Pvt.	B	E-06/09/63	06/02/65	Discharged by General Order
Blakey, William T.	Pvt.	B	E-08/15/62	06/19/65	Wd.-Wilderness 5/5/64, Mustered O.
Blaney, Daniel	Corp.	G	E-08/13/62	12/08/62	Discharged-Surgeon's Certificate
Blessing, Peter	Pvt.	I	E-08/23/62	11/01/63	Transferred to Veteran Reserve
Blundin, Richard	Pvt.	A	E-08/13/62	11/07/63	Died of Wounds-Rappahannock St.
Bodder, Stephen	Pvt.	I	E-08/12/62	unk.	Discharged by General Order
Bole, Kennedy	Pvt.	B	E-08/14/62	06/26/65	Wd.-Wilderness 5/5/64, Disch. G.O.
Bole, William	Pvt.	B	E-08/14/62	06/19/65	Mustered Out
Boner, Stephen	Pvt.	D	E-08/20/62	12/16/63	Discharged-Surgeon's Certificate
Boon, William J.	Pvt.	A	E-08/12/62	06/19/65	Mustered Out
Boot, William	Pvt.	C	D-08/31/63	09/15/63	Deserted
Booth, Henry	Pvt.	G	E-08/15/62	07/11/64	Died of Wds. Rec. in Action at Phila.
Booze, George C.	Pvt.	G	E-08/13/62	05/20/65	Died at City Point, Va.
Boozer, John	Corp.	K	E-08/22/62	06/19/65	Mustered Out

Name	Rank	Co.	Enlistment or Draft Date	Exit Date	Remarks
Bostick, William	Pvt.	A	E-08/12/62	06/19/65	Mustered Out
Boulter, David	Pvt.	E	E-08/20/62	06/10/63	Deserted
Boulter, Henry	Pvt.	A	E-08/13/65	06/19/65	Mustered Out
Bowen, George E.	Sgt.	G	E-08/11/62	07/22/63	Died at Frederick M.D.
Bowman, Samuel H.	Pvt.	H	E-08/28/62	08/15/65	Discharged by General Order
Bowman, William	Pvt.	A	E-08/12/65	06/19/65	Mustered Out
Boyd, Thomas	Pvt.	B	E-08/22/62	01/07/63	Died
Boyer, Jonas	Sgt.	H	E-08/23/62	06/19/65	Mustered Out
Boyer, Peter S.	Pvt.	H	E-08/23/62	06/19/65	Mustered Out
Braden, Samuel	Pvt.	E	E-08/25/62	06/19/65	Mustered Out
Bradley, Hugh	Pvt.	E	E-08/28/62	10/20/62	Deserted
Bradley, James B.	Pvt.	G	E-08/12/62	01/30/63	Died at Washington D.C.
Brady, William	Pvt.	C	D-09/17/63	12/29/63	Deserted
Brady, William H.	1st Lt.	G	E-08/16/62	06/19/65	Capt'd Salem Church, Mustered Out
Branin, Mordicai	Pvt.	B	E-08/16/62	06/19/65	Wd.-Wilderness 5/6/64, Mustered O.
Branin, Samuel	Pvt.	B	D-09/11/63	09/30/64	Deserted
Branson, William H.	Pvt.	F	E-08/23/62	12/02/62	Deserted
Brash, George	Pvt.	A	E-08/07/62	11/11/62	Disch. Surg. Cert.
Brazer, William P.	Sgt.	B	E-08/07/62	05/10/64	Killed- Spotsylvania C.H.
Breen, John	Sgt.	D	E-08/18/62	06/19/65	Wd'd-Opequon 9/19/64, Mustered O.
Bremer, Charles F. C.	Pvt.	C	D-09/01/63	10/22/64	Deserted
Bressillian, John	Corp.	K	E-08/14/62	05/05/64	Killed at Wilderness
Brewer, George	Pvt.	K	E-08/22/62	unk.	Not on Muster Out Roll
Brewer, Robert	Pvt.	K	E-08/30/62	09/31/64	Transferred to Veteran Reserve
Brightman, W. W.	Pvt.	E	E-08/22/62	unk.	Not on Muster Out Roll
Brittain, Joseph	Pvt.	D	E-08/22/62	07/08/63	Deserted
Broadbelt, Franklin	Corp.	H	E-08/23/62	06/19/65	Mustered Out
Broadhead, Francis	Pvt.	C	D-08/29/63	unk.	Deserted
Brodigan, James	Pvt.	D	E-08/18/62	07/08/63	Deserted
Brondenberg, Peter	Pvt.	C	D-09/01/63	unk.	A.W.O.L. at Muster Out
Brooks, Edwin W.	Pvt.	K	E-09/01/62	06/19/65	Mustered Out
Brooks, John	Pvt.	D	E-08/14/62	02/09/63	Discharged-Surgeon's Certificate
Brown, Francis	Pvt.	H	E-08/28/62	08/28/65	Wd. Spotsyl. 5/10/64, Expired Term
Brown, George C.	Capt.	A	E-08/11/62	06/19/65	Mustered Out
Brown, William	Pvt.	D	D-07/17/63	unk.	Wd.-Cold Harbor 6/4/64, Disch.G.O.
Brown, William H.	Pvt.	D	E-04/05/65	06/17/65	Discharged by General Order
Brunett, Agniola	Pvt.	K	D-09/01/63	07/10/64	Capt'd 5/10/64, Died, Andersonville
Brunett, Charles	Pvt.	K	D-09/01/63	03/28/64	Discharged-Surgeon's Certificate
Brunner, Thomas	Corp.	E	E-08/20/62	unk.	Absent with Leave at Muster Out
Brunson, Charles	Corp.	F	E-08/27/62	12/14/62	Deserted
Bryan, Charles	Pvt.	H	E-08/28/62	06/23/64	Died Wds. Rec. Spotsyl. 5/10/64
Bryan, Samuel	Pvt.	H	E-08/29/62	unk.	Transferred to Veterans Reserve
Bryson, James	Pvt.	C	E-08/18/62	unk.	Deserted
Buchanan, James	Pvt.	E	E-08/29/62	unk.	Not on Muster Out Roll
Buddy, William M.	Pvt.	D	E-12/29/63	03/30/65	Promoted to Adjutant-214th P.V.
Buffington, J. M.	Pvt.	G	E-08/11/62	12/10/62	Discharged-Surgeon's Certificate
Bulmer, Henry	Pvt.	D	E-08/15/62	05/10/64	Missing in Action-Spotsylvania
Bulmer, Richard	Pvt.	D	E-08/13/62	06/19/65	Mustered Out
Burk, Charles	Corp.	G	E-08/16/62	06/19/65	Mustered Out
Burk, James	Pvt.	F	D-08/21/63	09/20/63	Deserted
Burke, Michael	Pvt.	E	D-09/03/63	10/31/63	Discharged-Surgeon's Certificate
Burns, James	Pvt.	E	E-08/20/62	10/--/64	Capt'd & Died at Charleston S.C.

Name	Rank	Co.	Enlistment or Draft Date	Exit Date	Remarks
Busby, William	Pvt.	A	E-08/07/62	06/19/65	Mustered Out
Butler, Lyell	Pvt.	F	E-08/28/62	11/18/62	Died at Washington
Buzzard, John H.	Pvt.	I	E-08/19/62	06/01/64	Killed at Cold Harbor
Buzzard, Jonas T.	Pvt.	I	E-08/20/62	06/19/65	Mustered Out
Byers, Thomas B.	Pvt.	G	D-07/17/63	06/04/65	Transferred to 82nd P.V.
Byington, W. C.	A. Surg.	Stf.	E-10/01/62	03/06/64	Transferred 183rd P.V.
Calian, Robert	Pvt.	G	E-08/12/62	08/13/62	Deserted
Calimane, Jeremiah	Pvt.	C	E-08/18/62	06/19/65	Mustered Out
Camody, John	Pvt.	C	E-08/21/62	08/--/62	Deserted
Campbell, Robert	Pvt.	F	D-08/31/63	06/04/65	Transferred to 82nd P.V.
Campbell, Walter	Pvt.	D	E-08/19/62	11/07/63	Killed at Rappahannock Station
Campion, Stacy B.	Capt.	H	E-08/10/62	11/20/63	Resigned
Canouse, Samuel	Pvt.	B	E-08/15/62	07/11/63	Deserted
Carbine, John	Pvt.	E	D-09/03/63	06/04/65	Transferred to 82nd P.V.
Care, William S.	Corp.	D	E-08/14/62	06/19/65	Mustered Out
Carlin, Francis	Pvt.	D	E-08/12/62	06/19/65	Mustered Out
Carnathan, Davis	Pvt.	K	E-08/15/62	05/15/65	Discharged by General Order
Carr, Francis H.	Pvt.	A	E-08/12/62	06/19/65	Mustered Out
Carr, Rush B.	Pvt.	H	E-08/28/62	06/19/65	Mustered Out
Carroll, James	Pvt.	G	D-08/31/63	06/04/65	Transferred to 82nd P.V.
Carroll, William	Corp.	F	E-08/14/62	01/08/63	Deserted
Carter, William	Pvt.	A	D-08/31/63	10/63	Deserted
Casey, John	Pvt.	C	D-08/14/63	08/--/63	Deserted
Cassidy, John B.	Musc.	I	E-08/10/62	05/15/65	Discharged by General Order
Chandler, Amos M.	Pvt.	B	E-08/04/62	05/17/65	Discharged-Surgeon's Certificate
Chappell, John	Pvt.	G	E-08/13/62	03/15/64	Transferred to Veteran Reserve
Charles, Joseph	Pvt.	C	E-08/18/62	09/--/62	Deserted
Cheek, Joseph	Pvt.	--	E-08/18/64	unk.	Not on Muster Out Roll
Christ, William H.	Pvt.	B	E-08/04/62	12/08/62	Discharged-Surgeon's Certificate
Clark, Charles	Pvt.	C	E-08/14/62	unk.	Deserted
Clark, Gideon	Lt. Col.	Stf.	E-09/01-62	06/19/65	Mustered Out
Clark, Isaac	Pvt.	C	D-09/02/63	05/15/64	Died at Winchester of Wounds rec.
Clark, John G.	Pvt.	D	E-08/16/62	06/19/65	Wd.-Petersburg 4/2/65, Mustered O.
Clary, Dennis	Pvt.	D	D-07/20/63	07/12/64	Deserted
Clayton, Samuel	Pvt.	E	E-08/30/62	unk.	Not on Muster Out Roll
Clayton, Samuel R.	Pvt.	G	E-08/16/62	06/12/65	Discharged by General Order
Clayton, William D.	Pvt.	C	E-09/01/62	unk.	Deserted
Cleavenstein, John	Pvt.	I	E-08/14/62	05/29/63	Died Wds. Rec. Banks Ford 5/5/63
Clegg, Thomas	Pvt.	K	E-08/30/62	10/11/62	Deserted
Clewell, Frank	Pvt.	F	E-08/29/62	01/01/64	Promoted to Principal Musician
Clewell, Frank A.	Pl-Muc	Stf.	E-08/29/62	06/19/65	Mustered Out
Cliff, James	Capt.	E	E-08/20/62	06/19/65	Mustered Out
Closson, Caleb H.	Pvt.	G	D-07/17/63	04/08/64	Discharged by General Order
Clowdon, Charles	Pvt.	C	E-08/23/62	05/17/65	Disch.- Wds. rec. Rappahannock St.
Cobourn, Thomas	Pvt.	C	E-08/23/62	unk.	Transferred to Veteran Reserve
Coleman, Charles	Sgt.	D	E-08/19/62	06/19/65	Mustered Out
Coles, George	Pvt.	D	E-08/18/62	08/27/63	Transferred to Signal Corps
Collins, James	Pvt.	G	E-08/15/62	11/01/63	Transferred to Veteran Reserve
Collins, Stephen	Pvt.	B	D-08/26/63	12/03/64	Wd.-Spotsylvania 5/11/64, Deserted
Collison, Isaac	Pvt.	E	E-08/25/62	06/19/65	Prisoner 6/1/64-5/14/65, Must. Out.
Collom, Charles B.	Pvt.	G	E-08/11/62	06/19/65	Mustered Out
Commerford, Arthur	Pvt.	F	E-08/21/62	06/19/65	Wd. Spotsylvania 5/10/64, Must. Out

Name	Rank	Co.	Enlistment or Draft Date	Exit Date	Remarks
Congleton, David P.	Pvt.	E	E-08/22/62	06/19/65	Mustered Out
Conrad, John	Pvt.	D	E-08/19/62	06/19/65	Mustered Out
Conrad, Thomas	Pvt.	D	E-08/16/62	06/19/65	Mustered Out
Conrow, George	1st Lt.	I	E-08/11/62	06/19/65	Wd. Petersburg 4/2/65, Muster. Out
Constantine, Banjamin	Pvt.	A	E-08/11/62	06/19/65	Mustered Out
Conway, James	Pvt.	F	D-08/29/63	11/20/63	Deserted
Cook, John M.	2nd Lt.	E	E-08/11/62	08/14/63	Discharged
Cook, William	Pvt.	B	D-08/22/63	01/31/64	Wd.-Rappahannock St., Deserted
Cook, Zephaniah	Pvt.	A	E-08/13/62	05/12/64	Killed-Spotsylvania
Cooper, George W. P.	Pvt.	C	E-05/09/64	06/04/65	Transferred to 82nd P.V.
Cooper, John	Pvt.	C	E-08/16/62	unk.	Discharged- Surgeon's Certificate
Cooper, Michael	Pvt.	C	E-08/27/62	01/--/63	Deserted
Cooper, William E.	Corp.	C	E-08/19/62	09/19/64	Killed at Opequon
Corkery, William	Pvt.	H	E-08/28/62	05/12/64	Missing in Action-Spotsylvania
Coughlin, James	Pvt.	F	E-08/19/62	08/04/63	Deserted
Cowan, Gilbert	Pvt.	B	E-08/19/62	06/19/65	Wd.-Spotsylvania 5/10/64, Must. O.
Cowperthwait, A. D.	Pvt.	F	E-08/08/62	05/19/65	Des., Rtd., Wd. 4/1/65, Disch. G.O.
Coxe, Edward E.	2nd Lt.	D	E-08/15/62	11/22/63	Died Wds. Rec.-Rappahannock St.
Coyle, Samuel	Pvt.	K	D-09/01/63	12/02/63	Captured, Died at Richmond
Coyne, William	Pvt.	I	E-08/15/62	unk.	Discharged by General Order
Craig, Joseph	Pvt.	A	E-08/09/62	05/10/64	Died
Crater, Sylvester	Pvt.	I	E-08/12/62	06/19/65	Mustered Out
Crooks, James	Pvt.	K	E-08/15/62	05/05/63	Killed at Wilderness
Crooks, John	Pvt.	K	E-08/15/62	11/10/63	Died Wds. Rec. Brandy Station, Va.
Crosby, Thomas	Pvt.	I	E-08/11/62	06/19/65	Mustered Out
Crossett, James	Pvt.	C	E-08/19/62	06/19/65	Mustered Out
Crowthers, John	Pvt.	I	D-08/31/62	09/12/63	Deserted
Crozier, Alexander	Pvt.	C	E-08/23/62	06/19/65	Mustered Out
Cubler, George	Pvt.	I	E-08/27/62	06/19/65	Mustered Out
Culbert, James	Corp.	K	E-08/09/62	05/25/65	Discharged by General Order
Culbert, Jonathan	Pvt.	E	E-08/20/62	05/20/64	Died Wds. Rec. Spotsyl. 5/10/64
Cullen, Francis	Pvt.	C	E-08/27/62	09/--/62	Deserted
Cummings, John	Pvt.	C	E-11/17/64	06/04/65	Transferred to 82nd P.V.
Cunningham, W. H.	Pvt.	E	E-08/23/62	unk.	Not on Muster Out Roll
Curran, David	Pvt.	F	E-08/21/62	06/28/65	Wd. Wilderness 5/5/64, Disch. G.O.
Currie, Archibald	Pvt.	E	D-09/03/63	04/--/64	Capt'd, Died at Andersonville
Curtison, Charles	Corp.	K	E-08/15/62	02/10/63	Discharged-Surgeon's Certificate
Cuskaden, Robert E.	Sgt.	E	E-08/30/62	12/06/62	Transferred to 88th P.V.
Cuthbert, John P.	Pvt.	D	E-08/15/62	03/--/65	Deserted
Cutler, Elias	Pvt.	I	E-08/13/62	06/19/65	Mustered Out
Dager, John M.	Pvt.	F	E-08/20/62	12/08/62	Discharged-Surgeon's Certificate
Daily, John	Pvt.	C	D-09/02/63	08/11/65	Discharged by General Order
Dalton, George	Pvt.	C	E-08/14/62	unk.	Not on Muster Out Roll
Danenhower, G.B.	Pvt.	A	E-08/12/62	06/01/64	Died of Wounds- Cold Harbor
Dannielly, John W.	Pvt.	F	E-08/14/62	03/20/64	Discharged-Surgeon's Certificate
Danzeglocke, H.	Pvt.	K	E-08/27/62	01/08/63	Discharged-Surgeon's Certificate
Davenport, E. E.	Pvt.	A	E-08/09/62	06/19/65	Capt'd & Mustered Out
Davis, Edmund W.	Pvt.	B	E-08/11/62	05/17/65	Discharged-Surgeon's Certificate
Davis, James H.	Pvt.	F	D-07/17/63	03/20/64	Deserted
Davis, John	Pvt.	I	D-09/01/63	unk.	Absent with Leave at Muster Out
Davis, William H.	Pvt.	B	E-08/15/62	04/02/65	Killed at Petersburg
Deal, James	Pvt.	I	E-08/15/62	02/07/63	Discharged-Surgeon's Certificate

Name	Rank	Co.	Enlistment or Draft Date	Exit Date	Remarks
Deal, Samuel H.	1st Lt.	A	E-08/12/62	06/19/65	Mustered Out
Dearolf, William	Pvt.	H	E-08/23/62	05/10/64	Killed at Spotsylvania
Deetz, Henry C.	Pvt.	I	E-08/16/62	06/19/65	Mustered Out
DeHaven, Francis	Pvt.	D	E-08/14/62	01/08/63	Discharged-Surgeon 's Certificate
Dempsey, James	Pvt.	G	E-08/16/62	08/31/62	Deserted
Dempsey, Stephen	Pvt.	K	D-09/01/63	01/18/64	Died at Brandy Station, Va.
Denight, Joseph	Pvt.	E	E-08/27/62	06/19/65	Mustered Out
Dennis, Ebenezer H.	Pvt.	G	E-08/13/62	04/30/63	Discharged for Wds. Rec. 12/11/62
Dessalate, John R.	Hos-St	Stf.	E-08/11/62	06/19/65	Mustered Out
Duell, Seymour	Pvt.	K	E-08/19/62	01/16/63	Discharged-Surgeon 's Certificate
Devereaux, James	Pvt.	K	E-08/15/62	06/19/65	Mustered Out
Devine, James C.	Pvt.	H	E-08/22/62	unk.	Never Joined Company
Dickey, Hiram C.	Sgt.	A	E-08/11/62	12/28/63	Disc.-Surg. Cert.
Dickson, George	Pvt.	F	E-08/29/63	unk.	Wd'd Spotsyl. 5/10/64, Disch. G.O.
Dickson, George R.	1st Lt.	C	E-08/22/62	06/19/65	Mustered Out
Dill, Alexander	Sgt.	A	E-08/12/62	06/19/65	Mustered Out
Doan, Joshua	Sgt.	C	E-08/14/62	06/19/65	Mustered Out
Donahue, Daniel	Pvt.	A	D-09/01/63	11/19/63	Deserted
Donaldson, Joseph	Corp.	G	E-08/11/62	07/16/63	Transferred to Veteran Reserve
Donaldson, LeGrand	Corp.	F	E-08/30/62	06/19/65	Capt'd Salem Church, Mustered Out
Donaldson, William J.	Corp.	D	E-08/14/62	09/24/63	Discharged-Surgeon 's Certificate
Donehow, George	Pvt.	C	E-12/15/64	06/04/65	Transferred to 82nd P.V.
Dott, Charles	Sgt.	G	E-08/13/62	05/03/63	Killed at Salem Church
Dougherty, Edward	Pvt.	D	E-08/19/62	06/13/65	Wd.-Petersburg 4/2/65, Disch. G.O.
Dougherty, George	Pvt.	C	E-08/--/62	09/--/62	Deserted
Dougherty, John	Pvt.	I	E-08/14/62	05/17/65	Discharged-Surgeon 's Certificate
Dougherty, William	Pvt.	C	E-08/19/62	unk.	Absent in Hospital at Muster Out
Dow, Christopher C.	Pvt.	K	E-08/11/62	04/15/63	Discharged-Surgeon 's Certificate
Dow, Phineas A.	Pvt.	K	E-08/11/62	05/03/64	Capt'd 10/11/63, Died Andersonville
Dowling, James	Musc.	G	E-08/15/62	06/19/65	Mustered Out
Dowrey, Benjamin F.	Pvt.	F	E-08/29/62	06/19/65	Mustered Out
Duckett, Thomas P.	Pvt.	I	E-08/23/62	06/19/65	Mustered Out
Dudrow, George W.	Musc.	B	E-08/16/62	03/25/63	Transferred- 1st Md. Vol.
Duffee, William	Pvt.	B	E-08/23/62	07/06/63	Discharged-Surgeon 's Certificate
Duffey, Bernard	Pvt.	F	D-08/29/63	06/19/65	Capt'd, Desert. & Rtd., Must. Out
Duffy, Patrick	Pvt.	K	D-09/01/63	05/12/64	Killed at Spotsylvania
Dugan, John	Pvt.	F	E-08/18/62	06/19/65	Mustered Out
Duncan, Alexander	Pvt.	G	D-08/31/63	unk.	Transferred to Navy
Dungan, Daniel	Pvt.	F	E-08/22/62	06/19/65	Capt'd Salem Church, Mustered Out
Dunlap, Lewis J.	Pvt.	F	E-08/18/62	06/03/65	Wd. 5/13/63, 5/5/64, 4/2/64, D.G.O.
Duplaine, Benjamin C.	Corp.	F	E-08/18/62	12/13/62	Discharged-Surgeon 's Certificate
Dutcher, George	Pvt.	A	E-08/11/62	08/10/63	Died
Dutton, James	1st Lt.	E	E-08/20/62	06/19/65	Brev. Capt. 4/6/65, Mustered Out
Dwyer, William	Pvt.	B	D-08/03/63	10/10/63	Deserted
Dykes, James	Capt.	A	E-08/15/62	02/12/64	Discharged
Earb, Michael	Pvt.	C	D-01/17/63	05/05/64	Deserted
Easton, Henry	Pvt.	F	D-08/31/63	03/07/64	Deserted
Easton, Jesse	Pvt.	A	E-09/01/63	06/04/65	Transferred- 82nd P.V.
Eckert, Christian	Pvt.	I	E-08/16/62	09/01/62	Deserted
Eckstein, H.C.	A. Srg.	Stf.	E-08/07/62	n/a	Never Joined Regiment
Eckstein, John G.	Pvt.	G	E-08/15/62	05/12/64	Killed at Spotsylvania
Edwards, Joseph	Pvt.	E	E-08/22/62	unk.	Not on Muster Out Roll

Name	Rank	Co.	Enlistment or Draft Date	Exit Date	Remarks
Egner, Robert H.	Pvt.	D	E-08/20/62	06/15/65	Wd.5/3/63,5/5/64, Capt'd 5/8/64
Elder, James	Pvt.	--	E-08/18/64	unk.	Not on Muster Out Roll
Elkin, John	Pvt.	K	E-08/30/62	06/19/65	Mustered Out
Elkin, William	Pvt.	K	E-08/29/62	06/19/65	Mustered Out
Eller, George	Corp.	K	E-08/10/62	06/19/65	Mustered Out
Ellinger, John	Pvt.	C	E-08/27/62	1863	Deserted
Elliot, Armstrong	Pvt.	E	E-08/27/62	12/08/62	Discharged-Surgeon 's Certificate
Elliot, James	Corp.	E	E-08/22/62	unk.	Discharged by General Order
Elliot, Robert	Pvt.	E	E-08/22/62	unk.	Wd. Wilderness 5/5/64, Disch. G.O.
Elliot, Timothy	Corp.	A	E-08/12/62	unknown	Wounded Spotsylvania 5/12/64
Ellis, Edward	Pvt.	F	E-08/29/62	06/19/65	Mustered Out
Ellison, James	Pvt.	A	E-04/12/65	06/04/65	Transferred- 82nd P.V.
Ellmaker, Peter C.	Col.	Stf.	E-09/01/62	01/12/64	Resigned
Emeneker, Charles	Pvt.	B	E-08/14/62	unk.	Wd-Wilderness 5/6/64, Disch. G.O.
Emory, Edwin T.	Pvt.	K	E-08/28/62	06/19/65	Mustered Out
Emory, Enos R.	Pvt.	I	E-08/23/62	07/07/63	Deserted
Enli, Henry	Pvt.	H	E-08/23/62	unk.	Never Joined Company
Erhart, Joseph	Pvt.	H	D-08/31/63	04/04/65	Died Wds. Rec. Petersburg 4/2/65
Erisman, Jacob	Pvt.	D	E-08/12/62	06/19/65	Mustered Out
Ewing, Nathaniel	Pvt.	E	E-08/20/62	12/12/64	Transferred to Veterans Reserve
Ewing, Theodore	Pvt.	D	E-08/15/62	12/15/62	Died at White Oak Church
Ewing, William	Pvt.	E	E-08/20/62	unk.	Wd. Spot. 5/10/64, In Hos. at M.O.
Farley, James	Pvt.	C	E-12/15/64	04/02/65	Deserted
Farrell, Thomas	Pvt.	K	D-08/31/63	11/26/63	Deserted
Faust, Aaron	Pvt.	H	E-08/23/62	05/03/63	Missing in Action at Salem Church
Faust, Francis R.	1st Lt.	G	E-08/04/62	01/27/64	Resigned
Faust, John E.	Pvt.	H	E-08/23/62	05/19/63	Died of Wounds Rec.-Salem Church
Fawn, George B.	Pvt.	C	D-09/01/63	10/18/63	Deserted
Fay, Patrick	Pvt.	B	D-08/25/62	03/07/64	Deserted
Ferber, Julius	Sgt.	K	E-08/19/62	06/19/65	Mustered Out
Ferris, Daniel	Corp.	C	E-08/18/62	01/--/63	Discharged by Special Order
Fesmire, Horace B.	Pvt.	G	E-08/15/62	06/19/65	Mustered Out
Fetterolf, John	Pvt.	H	E-08/13/62	05/16/65	Discharged by General Order
Fink, Daniel	Pvt.	I	E-09/07/64	06/19/65	Mustered Out
Fink, Samuel	Pvt.	I	E-09/16/64	06/19/65	Mustered Out
Fisher, Henry	Pvt.	H	D-08/31/63	06/04/65	Transferred to 82nd P.V.
Fisher, John	Corp	A	E-08/12/62	06/19/65	Mustered Out
Fisher, Joshua J.	Pvt.	E	E-08/21/62	unk.	Wd. Petersburg 4/2/65, Disch. G.O.
Fisher, William	Pvt.	I	E-08/15/62	unk.	Discharged by General Order
Fitzgerald, John	Pvt.	E	D-09/03/63	05/09/65	Transferred to Veteran Reserve
Fleming, John	Pvt.	F	E-08/19/62	06/19/65	Wd. Wilderness 5/5/64, Mustered O.
Flicker, William E.	Pvt.	G	E-08/09/62	unk.	Not on Muster Out Roll
Flockhart, David S.	Corp.	D	E-08/28/62	unk.	Wd.-Rappahannock St., Disch. G.O.
Fly, Reuben	Pvt.	B	E-08/18/62	06/19/65	Wd.-Petersburg 4/2/65, Disch. G.O.
Flynn, James M.	Pvt.	D	E-08/30/62	05/15/65	Discharged by General Order
Flynn, John	Pvt.	B	E-08/19/62	06/19/65	Mustered Out
Follwell, David C.	Pvt.	D	E-08/18/62	09/12/62	Discharged-Surgeon 's Certificate
Ford, Edward	2nd Lt.	I	E-05/01/63	05/10/64	Killed at Spotsylvania
Fornaman, Mahlon	Pvt.	B	E-08/12/62	06/19/65	Mustered Out
Fornman, John	Corp.	B	E-08/12/62	05/10/64	Killed at Spotsylvania C.H.
Foster, Wilfred	Pvt.	C	E-08/18/62	unk.	Discharged-Surgeon 's Certificate
Foulke, Rowan	Sgt.	F	E-08/23/62	06/19/65	Mustered Out

Name	Rank	Co.	Enlistment or Draft Date	Exit Date	Remarks
Fox, Peter	Pvt.	C	D-09/02/63	09/15/63	Deserted
Fox, Thomas	Pvt.	C	D-09/01/63	07/09/64	Dishonorably Discharged
Fox, William	Pvt.	E	D-08/31/63	06/04/65	Transferred to 82nd P.V.
Frank, Christian	Pvt.	H	D-09/01/63	05/05/64	Deserted
Frazier, R. M.	Pvt.	I	E-09/01/63	04/15/64	Transferred to Veteran Reserve
Freed, Edward	Pvt.	I	E-08/23/62	06/19/65	Mustered Out
Freeman, Charles R.	Pvt.	F	E-08/14/62	06/05/65	Wd. Wilderness 5/8/64, Disch. G.O.
Freese, Isaac	Sgt.	H	E-08/23/62	05/12/64	Killed at Spotsylvania
Freese, John H.	Pvt.	H	E-08/25/62	11/15/63	Transferred to Veteran Reserve
French, Eli	Pvt.	E	D-09/03/63	unk.	Wd. Spotsyl. 5/12/64, Disch. G. O.
Frick, George L.	Sgt.	I	E-08/27/62	06/19/65	Mustered Out
Fulmer, Samuel	Corp.	F	E-08/19/62	01/11/64	Deserted
Gagus, John	Pvt.	A	E-08/11/62	Unk.	Discharged- Surg. Cert.
Gallagher, Hugh	Pvt.	C	D-09/01/63	unk.	Absent with Leave at Muster Out
Gallagher, John	Pvt.	C	D-09/02/63	10/18/63	Deserted
Gallagher, John	Pvt.	E	D-09/03/63	unk.	Capt'd, ret'd, Discharged G. O.
Garth, James	Pvt.	A	E-08/14/62	02/25/63	Discharged- Surg. Cert.
Garton, Benjamin	Pvt.	I	E-08/23/62	07/16/63	Discharged-Surgeon's Certificate
Garwood, George W.	Pvt.	F	E-08/27/62	11/11/63	Died of Wds. Rec. Rappahannock St.
Gastinger, Leopold	Pvt.	H	E-08/25/62	06/19/65	Mustered Out
Gaw, Robert H.	Sgt.	C	E-08/18/62	11/18/63	Capt. and Died at Richmond
Getz, Edward H.	Pvt.	F	E-08/29/62	05/03/63	Missing in Action at Salem Church
Gibbs, Robert	Pvt.	G	E-08/15/62	06/19/65	Mustered Out
Gifford, Anthony	Sgt.	K	E-08/21/62	02/27/65	Discharged- loss of arm in Action
Gillan, William	Pvt.	K	D-09/01/63	unk.	Absent-Detached Service at M. Out
Gillingham, F. D.	1st Lt.	K	E-08/07/62	06/04/63	Discharged-Surgeon's Certificate
Gilligan, Patrick	Pvt.	B	E-08/22/62	05/03/63	Killed at Salem Church
Gold, Miles	Pvt.	D	E-08/15/62	06/19/65	Mustered Out
Golden, John K.	Corp.	D	E-08/27/62	02/09/65	Capt. Berryville 9/3/64, Died captive
Goldey, Charles	Pvt.	D	E-08/27/62	unk.	Wd.11/7/63, Abst. w/Leave at M.O.
Goodall, Samuel L.	Pvt.	K	E-08/18/62	11/11/62	Discharged-Surgeon's Certificate
Goodman, Andrew T.	Capt.	C	E-08/05/62	04/21/65	Promoted to Major of 215th P.V.
Goodwin, Edward	Pvt.	G	E-08/13/62	06/19/65	Mustered Out
Gordon, William H.	Corp.	F	E-08/18/62	11/14/62	Deserted
Gorman, James	Pvt.	A	D-09/01/63	11/07/64	Deserted
Gorman, Thomas	Pvt.	C	E-08/30/62	04/29/64	Died of Wounds rec.-Fredericksburg
Goud, William H.	Pvt.	F	E-08/15/62	11/27/63	Discharged-Surgeon's Certificate
Gow, Robert C.	Pvt.	I	E-08/20/62	06/19/65	Mustered Out
Grafe, Jacob	Pvt.	F	E-08/14/62	01/08/63	Discharged-Surgeon's Certificate
Grafe, William	Pvt.	D	E-08/15/62	06/19/65	Mustered Out
Graham, John	Pvt.	B	E-08/15/62	06/19/65	Wd.-Opequon 9/19/64, Mustered Out
Graham, Joseph	Pvt.	I	E-08/27/62	06/19/65	Mustered Out
Gravener, Joseph H.	Sgt.	I	E-08/12/62	06/19/65	Mustered Out
Gray, Josiah	Pvt.	G	E-08/15/62	unk.	Wd. Spotsyl. 5/10/64, Discharged
Gray, William C.	Maj.	Stf.	E-08/10/62	06/19/65	Promoted from Capt. 6/29/64
Green, Edward	Pvt.	K	D-09/02/63	08/03/64	Discharged-Surgeon's Certificate
Green, Joseph	Pvt.	G	E-08/15/62	09/01/63	Transferred to Veteran Reserve
Green, William	Pvt.	K	D-09/02/63	unk.	Absent-Detached Service at M. Out
Gregg, Fenton	Pvt.	E	E-08/21/62	unk.	Not on Muster Out Roll
Grier, Lewis	Pvt.	A	E-08/12/62	unk.	Not on Muster Out Roll
Grimes, Charles	Pvt.	D	E-08/15/62	06/15/65	Mustered Out
Grimes, Oliver	Sgt.	F	E-08/15/62	05/26/64	Capt'd, Died Wds. at Richmond

Name	Rank	Co.	Enlistment or Draft Date	Exit Date	Remarks
Groom, Benjamin	Pvt.	C	E-08/29/62	06/19/65	Mustered Out
Groves, Andrew J.	Pvt.	C	E-09/01/62	11/07/63	Killed at Rappahannock Station
Grow, Jacob	Pvt.	G	E-08/15/62	08/01/64	Died of Wounds Received in Action
Haines, Rush T.	Pvt.	D	E-08/22/62	05/10/64	Missing in Action at Spotsylvania
Hairland, William	Pvt.	A	E-08/13/62	08/--/62	Deserted
Hall, Francis	Pvt.	E	E-08/20/62	10/20/62	Deserted
Hall, Henry	Pvt.	E	E-08/21/62	06/19/65	Mustered Out
Hall, John M.	Pvt.	K	E-08/22/62	11/24/62	Died at Washington, D.C.
Hall, William	Pvt.	H	E-08/22/62	02/28/63	Deserted
Hallan, William	Pvt.	C	E-08/29/62	05/--/65	Discharged for Wounds rec. 5/5/64
Hallman, William	Pvt.	I	E-08/14/62	06/19/65	Mustered Out
Halzinger, Jacob	Pvt.	C	E-08/23/62	unk.	Deserted
Hamilton, William	Pvt.	E	E-08/20/62	06/13/65	Discharged by General Order
Hance, Alfred L.	2nd Lt.	K	E-08/13/62	08/05/63	Resigned
Haney, William	Pvt.	D	E-08/13/62	06/19/65	Mustered Out
Hanline, DeWitt C.	Q.M.	Stf	E-08/09/62	06/19/65	Mustered out
Hanna, William	Pvt.	K	E-03/08/65	06/04/65	Transferred to 82nd P. V.
Hannings, Alfred	2nd Lt.	F	E-08/08/62	unk.	Not Accounted For
Hannon, John P.	Pvt.	E	E-08/09/62	06/05/64	Transferred to 82nd P.V.
Hansberry, George	Pvt.	D	E-08/30/62	unk.	Capt'd-Salem Church, Disch. G.O.
Hansell, Nicholas	Pvt.	G	D-08/29/63	10/27/63	Deserted
Hanson, Frank	Pvt.	E	D-09/03/62	04/05/64	Capt'd & Died at Andersonville
Harbour, Lewis, Jr.	Pvt.	F	E-08/15/62	06/19/65	Mustered Out
Hardy, William	Pvt.	C	D-09/01/63	unk.	Deserted
Haring, Joseph	Pvt.	G	E-08/14/62	06/19/65	Mustered Out
Harkins, George	Pvt.	K	E-08/15/62	06/19/65	Mustered Out
Harkins, James	Pvt.	K	E-08/15/62	03/19/63	Dis. Wds. Rec. Fred'burg 12/13/62
Harkins, William	Pvt.	K	E-08/15/62	06/19/65	Mustered Out
Harned, Charles C.	Pvt.	E	E-08/19/62	09/02/63	Discharged- Surgeon's Certificate
Harney, Joseph	Pvt.	C	D-09/01/63	05/10/64	Deserted
Harris, Henry	Pvt.	E	E-08/28/62	unk.	Not on Muster Out Roll
Hart, John	Pvt.	C	E-08/16/62	09/--/62	Deserted
Hart, John W.	Pvt.	F	E-08/18/62	06/19/65	Mustered Out
Hartranft, John	Pvt.	H	E-08/30/62	03/02/63	Transferred to Veteran Reserve
Haslam, Joseph	Pvt.	G	E-08/14/62	08/16/65	Wd. Spotsyl. 5/10/64, Disch. G.O.
Hassinger, David S.	1st Lt.	F	E-08/18/62	06/19/65	Wd. Spotsyl. 5/10/64, Mustered Out
Haverstick, Patrick	Pvt.	B	E-08/13/62	06/19/65	Wd.-Spotsylvania 5/11/64, Must. O.
Hayes, James H.	Pvt.	F	D-08/29/63	03/20/64	Deserted
Hayhurst, James	Pvt.	F	D-08/29/63	09/20/63	Deserted
Hazlett, William	Pvt.	C	E-08/23/62	unk	Absent in Arrest at Muster Out
Hazlett, William H.	Pvt.	F	E-08/19/62	12/02/64	Wd. Spotsyl. 5/12/64, Trans. Vet. R.
Heacock, Nathan	Sgt.	E	E-08/22/62	10/04/64	Died of Wds. Rec. Opequon, 9/19/64
Heck, Martin	Pvt.	B	E-08/14/62	06/13/65	Discharged-Surgeon's Certificate
Heffner, John J.	Pvt.	A	E-08/12/62	06/19/65	Mustered Out
Hein, Nicholas	Corp.	I	E-08/22/62	06/19/65	Mustered Out
Heiser, William H.	Corp.	B	E-08/16/62	05/03/63	Killed at Salem Church
Heitman, Charles	Pvt.	I	E-08/23/62	12/09/63	Discharged-Surgeon's Certificate
Heizer, William	Pvt.	C	D-09/01/63	unk.	Deserted
Hellings, John P.	Sgt.	G	E-08/15/62	06/24/65	Wd. Petersburg 4/2/65, Disch. G.O.
Helm, Charles	Sgt.	G	E-08/11/62	06/19/65	Mustered Out
Helm, Theodore	Sgt.	K	E-08/18/62	06/19/65	Mustered Out
Henderson, William	Pvt.	B	E-08/14/62	05/12/64	Killed at Spotsylvania C.H.

Name	Rank	Co.	Enlistment or Draft Date	Exit Date	Remarks
Hendricks, Aaron	Pvt.	I	E-08/18/62	06/19/65	Mustered Out
Henry, Jesse	Pvt	A	E-08/13/62	11/07/63	Killed- Rappahannock Station
Henry, Joseph B.	Pvt.	D	E-08/15/62	06/19/65	Mustered Out
Herbert, John	Pvt.	A	E-08/12/65	unk.	Transferred- Vet. Res.
Heritage, John F.	Capt.	B	E-08/08/62	06/19/65	Wd.-Opequon, Mustered Out
Herpst, Henry	Sgt.	H	E-08/30/62	06/16/64	Died Wds. Rec. Wilderness 5/5/64
Herpst, Mahlon	Pvt.	H	E-08/25/62	10/30/62	Died in Montgomery County, Pa.
Herse, Samuel	Pvt.	K	E-08/22/62	06/19/65	Mustered Out
Hess, John J.	Q.M.	Stf.	E-08/08/62	02/27/64	Discharged
Hettler, Gottleib	Pvt.	K	D-08/31/63	06/04/65	Transferred to 82nd P. V.
Hewes, William T.	1st Sgt.	K	E-08/09/62	05/06/64	Transferred to Veteran Reserve
Hibbs, Joseph R.	Corp.	B	E-08/14/62	06/19/65	Mustered Out
Hickey, Alexander	Pvt.	K	D-08/16/62	08/16/62	Deserted
Hicks, Aaron	Pvt.	H	E-08/23/62	unk.	Not on Muster Out Roll
Higgins, Joshua S.	Pvt.	D	E-08/14/62	10/16/62	Deserted
Hilt, Allen	Pvt.	B	E-08/16/62	06/19/65	Mustered Out
Hilton, George H.	Corp.	F	E-08/15/62	02/10/63	Deserted
Hipple, John H.	Pvt.	F	E-08/20/62	06/19/65	Mustered Out
Hirons, Edward G.	2nd Lt.	D	E-08/05/62	01/07/63	Resigned
Hodgson, Cephas M.	Capt.	B	E-08/26/62	11/07/63	Killed at Rappahannock Station
Hodgson, William M.	Pvt.	F	E-08/18/62	01/28/63	Died at Belle Plain, Va.
Hoffman, Francis J.	Pvt.	F	E-08/22/62	04/13/65	Deserted 10/30/62, Rtd. Disch. S.C.
Hoffman, Isaac	Pvt.	B	E-08/15/62	06/19/65	Mustered Out
Hoffman, James	Pvt.	G	E-08/14/62	06/19/65	Mustered Out
Hogg, Robert	Pvt.	H	E-08/25/62	unk.	Never Joined Company
Holroyd, Joseph	Pvt.	I	E-08/23/62	06/19/65	Wd. Wilderness 5/5/64, Mustered O.
Honnegger, Julius	Pvt.	H	D-09/01/63	09/02/64	Capt'd 9/15/63, died Andersonville.[1]
Hoover, William	Pvt.	E	E-08/19/62	unk.	Not on Muster Out Roll
Hopkins, William M.	Corp.	K	E-08/21/62	04/02/65	Died of Wounds Rec. at Petersburg
Hoy, Martin	Pvt.	I	E-08/14/62	06/19/65	Mustered Out
Huff, William F.	Pvt.	G	E-08/13/62	06/06/64	Died at Wash. from Wds. in Action
Hughes, Charles S.	Pvt.	D	E-08/13/62	08/27/63	Transferred to Signal Corps
Hughes, James C.	Pvt.	E	E-09/28/62	06/19/65	Mustered Out
Hughes, Joseph B.	Pvt.	B	E-08/15/62	unk.	Absent on detached service at M.O.
Humes, George	1st Lt.	B	E-08/15/62	06/03/64	Killed at Cold Harbor
Hunsworth, Thomas	Pvt.	G	E-08/16/62	05/06/63	Accidentally Killed Banks Ford, Va.
Hunter, Joseph R.	Pvt.	G	E-08/13/62	06/19/65	Mustered Out
Hurbell, George	Pvt.	G	E-08/15/62	06/19/65	Mustered Out
Hurel, William	Pvt.	H	E-08/15/62	07/31/63	Deserted
Hutchinson, John	Pvt.	I	E-02/29/64	06/04/65	Transferred to 82nd P. V.
Hyneman, Isaac	Pvt.	B	E-08/18/62	06/19/65	Mustered Out
Hyneman, Jacob E.	Pvt.	G	E-08/14/62	08/17/63	Transferred to Signal Corps
Ingham, James	Pvt.	A	E-08/12/62	08/07/63	Died- Warrenton, Va.

[1]Apparently Private Honnegger disappeared, perhaps as a deserter, but just as likely he was captured by a partisan while on picket duty or while straggling behind the marching column. In any case, he was listed on the muster rolls and later in Bates as having deserted. In fairness to him, the Andersonville prisoner records indicate that he was a prisoner there, and died of "scorbutus."

Name	Rank	Co.	Enlistment or Draft Date	Exit Date	Remarks
Irwin, Alexander	Pvt.	D	E-08/14/62	06/19/65	Wd.5/3/63, Capt'd. Berryville 9/3/64
Jackson, George	Pvt.	B	E-08/22/62	06/19/65	Mustered Out
Jackson, William H.	Pvt.	A	E-08/12/62	12/09/62	Discharged- Surg. Cer.
Janney, Francis	Pvt.	A	E-08/12/62	04/28/65	Deserted & returned, Disch. by G.O.
Jarrett, Richard	Pvt.	B	E-08/23/62	06/19/65	Mustered Out
Johnson, Andrew	Pvt.	D	E-08/16/62	11/07/63	Killed at Rappahannock Station
Johnson, George W.	1st Sgt.	K	E-08/18/62	06/19/65	Mustered Out
Johnson, Henry	Corp.	E	D-09/01/62	05/31/65	Discharged-Surgeon 's Certificate
Johnson, Henry	Pvt.	F	D-07/17/63	07/26/64	Deserted
Johnson, Henry	Pvt.	H	E-08/23/62	unk.	Not on Muster Out Roll
Johnson, Jacob	Capt.	H	E-08/25/62	06/19/65	Mustered Out
Johnson, James	Pvt.	B	D-08/31/63	11/30/64	Wd.-Spotsylvania 5/10/64, Deserted
Johnson, Randall H.	Corp.	C	E-08/22/62	unk.	Discharged- Surgeon's Certificate
Jones, Ashton H.	Pvt.	I	E-08/19/62	05/20/65	Discharged-Surgeon 's Certificate
Jones, Charles	Pvt.	G	E-08/15/62	05/03/63	Killed at Salem Church
Jones, Daniel	Pvt.	D	E-08/16/62	01/08/63	Discharged-Surgeon 's Certificate
Jones, Francis	Pvt.	C	D-09/01/63	1864	Deserted
Jones, John F.	Pvt.	I	E-08/12/62	01/09/63	Discharged-Surgeon 's Certificate
Jones, Robert	Pvt.	I	E-08/31/63	05/14/64	Killed at Stopsylvania
Jones, Thomas	Pvt.	D	D-09/05/63	05/05/64	Deserted
Jones, William H.	Pvt.	F	E-08/22/62	05/10/64	Missing in Action at Spotsylvania
Keck, Harry T.	Pvt.	F	E-08/28/62	06/08/65	Wd. Wilderness 5/5/64, Disch. G.O.
Keers, William	Pvt.	E	E-08/19/62	04/15/63	Discharged by Special Order
Keller, William	Pvt.	I	E-08/14/62	10/01/62	Deserted
Kelly, Daniel	Pvt.	C	E-08/20/62	05/03/63	Died of Wounds rec.-Fredericksburg
Kelly, Edwin A.	Corp.	B	E-08/23/62	06/19/65	Mustered Out
Kelly, John W.	Pvt.	C	E-09/01/62	11/--/62	Deserted
Kelly, Patrick S.	Pvt.	E	E-08/20/62	unk.	Not on Muster Out Roll
Kelly, William	Pvt.	I	E-08/14/62	06/19/65	Mustered Out
Keltcher, Thomas	Pvt.	E	D-09/03/63	06/11/64	Deserted
Kendricks, Daniel	Pvt.	C	E-08/20/62	01/01/63	Died at White Oak Church
Kennedy, David C.	Pvt.	I	D-09/01/63	unk.	Discharged by General Order
Kent, John W.	Pvt.	C	E-08/27/62	unk.	discharged- Surgeon's Certificate
Kepp, Edward	Pvt.	H	E-08/23/62	06/19/65	Mustered Out
Kershaw, Edmund	Pvt.	A	E-08/12/62	05/24/65	Wounded 5/6/64-Disch. Surg. Cert.
Keyser, Augustus	Pvt.	H	E-08/23/62	06/19/65	Mustered Out
Keyser, Thomas S.	Pvt.	F	E-08/13/62	10/01/63	Wd. Salem Church, Trans. Vet. Res.
Kincaide, John	Pvt.	E	E-08/30/62	06/19/65	Mustered Out
Kinder, Edwards	Corp.	A	E-08/12/62	06/19/65	Mustered Out
King, Edward	Corp.	G	E-08/07/62	06/04/63	Deserted
King, James	Pvt.	E	D-09/03/63	09/20/63	Deserted
King, John	Pvt.	A	E-11/12/64	unk.	Not on Muster Out Roll
Kingkade, David	Pvt.	K	E-08/15/62	06/19/65	Discharged-Surgeon 's Certificate
Kite, Robert	Pvt.	G	E-08/14/62	12/08/62	Discharged-Surgeon 's Certificate
Kleinhaus, Augustus	Pvt.	H	D-09/01/63	07/11/65	Discharged by General Order
Kline, Nathan	Pvt.	K	E-08/30/62	06/19/65	Mustered Out
Knause, Benjamin	Pvt.	I	E-08/23/62	05/15/64	Missing in Action- Spotsylvania
Knight, Charles C.	Maj.	Stf.	E-09/01/62	08/04/63	Wounded Fredericksburg 12/13/62
Knight, Thomas W.	Corp.	K	E-08/09/62	unk.	Died Wounds Rec. Spotsyl. 5/10/64
Knox, John	Pvt.	K	D-08/31/63	06/04/65	Transferred to 82nd P. V.
Kohl, John	Pvt.	H	E-08/25/62	01/07/64	Discharged-Surgeon 's Certificate
Koockogg, F. M.	Pvt.	D	E-08/15/62	06/19/65	Mustered Out

Name	Rank	Co.	Enlistment or Draft Date	Exit Date	Remarks
Koons, Abraham P.	1st Sgt.	H	E-08/23/62	10/26/63	Died at Warrenton, Va.
Koons, Frederick P.	Sgt.	H	E-08/30/62	06/19/65	Mustered Out
Koons, John	Pvt.	H	E-08/30/62	08/12/63	Deserted
Krause, Milton	Pvt.	H	E-08/23/62	06/19/65	Mustered Out
Kreche, Ernest	Pvt.	H	D-09/01/63	06/04/65	Transferred to 82nd P.V.
Kreer, Lewis	Pvt.	A	E-08/12/62	06/19/65	Mustered Out
Kurtz, Israel A.	Pvt.	F	E-08/22/62	03/29/64	Discharged by Special Order
Kurtz, Ross B.	Pvt.	G	E-08/16/62	12/18/62	Died at White Oak Church Va.
Kyle, Frederick	Pvt.	E	E-08/18/62	06/19/65	Mustered Out
Labold, John	Pvt.	I	E-08/13/62	08/11/65	Wd. Wilderness 5/5/64, Disch. G.O.
Lacher, William	Pvt.	E	D-09/03/63	09/20/63	Deserted
Lackman, Charles	Pvt.	A	E-08/13/62	06/19/65	Mustered Out
Lafferty, John	Pvt.	D	E-08/14/62	01/08/63	Discharged-Surgeon's Certificate
Landell, Edwin A.	Capt.	I	E-08/22/62	06/19/65	Mustered Out
Lare, George	Pvt.	D	E-08/15/62	06/04/64	Died of Wds. Rec. at Wilderness
Lare, Peter	Corp.	D	E-08/12/62	unk.	Wd.-Spottsyl. 5/12/64, Disch. G.O.
Latta, James W.	Capt.	B	E-09/01/62	01/20/66	Mustered Out
Latta, Joseph	Pvt.	I	E-08/12/62	06/19/65	Mustered Out
Laurens, John R.	1st Sgt.	C	E-08/17/62	05/10/64	Died of Wounds rec. Spotsylvania
Lawton, John	Pvt.	A	E-08/11/62	04/06/65	Died of Wounds-Sailor's Creek
Lazarus, Henry	Pvt.	C	E-05/09/64	07/22/65	Transferred to Veteran Reserve
Leaffey, Michael	Pvt.	F	E-08/16/62	unk.	Discharged by General Order
Leap, Dennis J.	Pvt.	A	E-08/11/62	06/19/65	Mustered Out
Learmont, Andrew	Pvt.	F	D-08/29/63	03/25/65	Disch.- Wds. Rec. Spotsyl. 5/12/64
Lee, Charles S.	Pvt.	C	E-08/18/62	05/10/64	Died of Wds. rec.-Spotsylvania
Lee, Thomas G.	Pvt.	E	E-08/27/62	06/19/65	Mustered Out
Leech, James	Corp.	A	E-08/11/62	06/19/65	Mustered Out
Lees, Thomas	Pvt.	G	E-08/13/62	06/19/65	Mustered Out
Leidig, Samuel	Pvt.	H	E-08/23/62	10/10/62	Died at White Oak Church
Leidy, Albert	1st Lt.	H	E-08/30/62	06/19/65	Mustered Out
Leidy, Philip	Surg.	Stf.	E-09/16/62	06/19/65	Mustered Out
Lentz, Benjamin T.	Sgt.	G	E-08/15/62	06/19/65	Mustered Out
Levering, Allen F.	Pvt.	A	E-08/13/62	03/12/65	Transferred- Vet. Reserve
Levering, Benjamin	Pvt.	A	E-08/13/62	06/19/65	Mustered Out
Levezey, Theodore	Pvt.	B	E-08/23/62	05/05/65	Wd.-Spots. 5/10/64, Disch. S. Crt.
Lewis, Alfred	Pvt.	G	D-08/31/63	05/16/64	Died Washington-Wds. Rec. Spotsyl.
Lewis, George	Pvt.	C	E-08/23/62	unk.	Not on Muster Out Roll
Lewis, Henry	Pvt.	E	D-09/02/63	05/--/64	Capt'd, Died at Richmond
Lewis, Ranson R.	Sgt.	B	E-08/14/62	01/12/63	Discharged-Surgeon's Certificate
Lightcap, Charles	Pvt.	A	E-08/13/62	03/12/65	Transferred- Vet. Reserve
Lilley, Alfred	Pvt.	C	E-08/19/62	06/19/65	Mustered Out
Lilley, Edward J.	Corp.	C	E-09/01/62	unk.	Wd.-Spotsyl. 5/10/64, Disch. G.O.
Lilley, Jacob G.	Pvt.	A	E-08/12/62	06/19/65	Mustered Out
Lilley, Joseph	Pvt.	C	E-01/26/64	03/14/64	Died at Philadelphia
Lilley, William	Pvt.	C	E-08/18/62	unk.	Deserted
Lindsay, James	Pvt.	I	D-09/31/63	unk.	Absent with Leave at Muster Out
Lindsay, John	Pvt.	C	D-09/01/63	unk.	Deserted
Lineaweaver, Albert	Hos-St	Stf.	E-08/20/62	01/20/63	Discharged
Linker, John S.	Pvt.	B	E-08/12/62	07/02/63	Deserted
Linker, William A.	Pvt.	F	E-08/16/62	05/12/64	Killed at Spotsylvania
Linton, Matthew	Pvt.	E	E-08/20/62	06/19/65	Mustered Out
Lippard, John	Pvt.	H	D-08/31/63	09/19/64	Killed at Opequon

Name	Rank	Co.	Enlistment or Draft Date	Exit Date	Remarks
Lister, Charles B.	Pvt.	A	E-08/12/62	05/06/64	Killed at Wilderness
Little, Josiah B.	Pvt.	E	D-09/03/63	09/24/63	Deserted
Lloyd, Wood	Pvt.	F	E-08/30/62	unk.	Captured Salem Church, Disch. G.O.
Lodge, Samuel	Pvt.	D	E-08/15/62	06/19/65	Mustered Out
Logan, William	Pvt.	E	E-08/29/62	unk.	Not on Muster Out Roll
Logo, Frank	1st Lt.	C	E-08/05/62	10/03/64	Discharged- Surgeon's Certificate
Long, Adam D.	Pvt.	A	E-08/09/62	06/19/65	Mustered Out
Long, Henry	Pvt.	B	D-09/01/63	06/05/65	Discharged-Surgeon 's Certificate
Long, Jacob	Pvt.	A	E-08/11/62	11/03/63	Deserted
Longaker, Henry S.	Pvt.	H	E-08/30/62	08/21/65	Wd. Rappahannock St. Expired Term
Longdon, Alex	Corp.	I	E-08/15/62	10/--/62	Deserted
Lord, Adam	Pvt.	E	E-08/22/62	11/09/64	Discharged-Surgeon 's Certificate
Lorenz, Henry	Pvt.	E	D-08/03/63	unk.	Discharged by General Order
Loudenslager, G. W.	Pvt.	I	E-08/13/62	05/03/63	Killed at Salem Church
Loughley, James	Pvt.	K	D-09/02/63	05/15/65	Discharged by General Order
Loughlin, William	Pvt.	I	E-10/03/62	unk.	Wd. Cold Harbor 6/30/64, Dis. G.O.
Louther, James	Pvt.	E	E-08/20/62	06/05/65	Wd. Wilderness 5/5/64, Disch. G.O.
Lovett, George G.	2nd Lt.	G	E-08/15/62	05/30/64	Died Wds. Rec. Wilderness 5/5/64
Lowe, Lewis	Pvt.	D	E-08/11/62	10/17/62	Deserted
Lower, Joseph B	Sgt.	C	E-08/20/62	05/15/64	Died of Wounds rec.-Spotsylvania
Lowrey, Benjamin F.	Pvt.	F	E-08/23/62	06/19/65	Mustered Out
Luby, James B.	Corp.	K	E-08/27/62	05/09/65	Discharged by General Order
Ludwig, Walter K.	1st Lt.	I	E-08/07/62	03/13/63	Resigned
Luther, Barney	Pvt.	F	D-09/01/63	09/20/63	Deserted
Lutz, Stimmel	Corp.	K	E-08/11/62	01/08/63	Discharged-Surgeon 's Certificate
Lynch, Peter	Pvt.	C	D-09/01/63	11/05/64	Deserted
Lyndall, David	Pvt.	G	E-08/13/62	05/15/65	Wd. Spotsyl. 5/12/64, Disch. G.O.
M'Allester, Charles	Pvt.	K	E-08/30/62	04/28/64	Transferred to Veteran Reserve
M'Allister, Charles	Pvt.	G	E-08/13/62	06/19/65	Wounded Opequon, Mustered Out
M'Allister, Robert	Pvt.	A	E-08/12/62	06/19/65	Mustered Out
M'Avoy, Daniel	Pvt.	G	E-08/07/62	07/20/63	Deserted
M'Bride, Daniel	Pvt.	D	E-08/22/62	06/30/63	Deserted
M'Bride, Henry	Pvt.	E	E-08/18/62	10/28/62	Died at Frederick, Md.
M'Bride, James	Pvt.	K	D-09/01/63	11/04/64	Deserted
M'Bride, William H.	Pvt.	F	E-08/18/62	08/23/62	Discharged- Writ of Habeas Corpus
M'Cartey, H.C.C.	Pl-Muc	Stf	E-08/12/62	06/19/65	Mustered Out
M'Carty, Alexander H.	Pvt.	D	E-08/28/62	06/19/65	Mustered Out
M'Carty, Frank	Pvt.	G	D-07/17/63	unk.	Absent/Sick at Muster Out
M'Carty, Joseph	Pvt.	E	E-09/03/63	11/04/63	Transferred to Navy
M'Cauley, William	Pvt.	C	E-08/18/62	07/20/64	Deserted
M'Clay, Samuel	Pvt.	C	E-08/19/62	06/--/63	Died of Wounds rec.-Fredericksburg
M'Clellan, Hugh	Pvt.	K	D-09/11/63	unk.	Wd. Wilderness 5/5/64, Disch. G.O.
M'Clintock, George	Sgt.	E	E-08/20/62	06/19/65	Mustered Out
M'Cloud, Hugh	Pvt.	C	D-09/02/63	06/04/65	Transferred to 82nd P.V.
M'Cloy, William B.	Pvt.	F	E-08/22/62	unk.	Captured at Salem Church
M'Cluskey, James	Pvt.	B	D-08/15/63	03/31/65	Wd.-Cold Harbor 6/1/64, Disch.
M'Cone, William	Pvt.	E	E-08/29/62	06/19/65	Mustered Out
M'Connell, James	Corp.	K	E-08/19/62	01/08/63	Discharged-Surgeon 's Certificate
M'Crossin, John	Pvt.	D	D-08/29/62	07/16/63	Deserted
M'Dowell, Harry S.	Sgt.	A	E-08/09/62	02/13/63	Disc.-Surg. Cert.
M'Dowell, John F.	Pvt.	A	E-08/13/62	unk.	Transferred- Vet. Reserve
M'Elroy, George	Corp.	G	E-08/15/62	06/19/65	Mustered Out

Name	Rank	Co.	Enlistment or Draft Date	Exit Date	Remarks
M'Elwee, John	Pvt.	H	E-08/29/62	unk.	Wd. Spotsyl. 5/10/64, Disch. G. O.
M'Fadyen, James	Pvt.	E	E-08/19/62	06/19/65	Deserted, Rtd. & Mustered Out
M'Gee, James	Pvt.	E	E-08/25/62	unk.	Wd. Wilderness 5/5/64, Disch. G.O.
M'Ginley, Edward	Pvt.	D	E-08/19/62	06/19/65	Mustered Out
M'Graves, David	Pvt.	C	E-12/15/64	03/14/65	Deserted
M'Gurk, James	Pvt.	E	E-09/01/63	09/--/64	Capt'd, Died at Andersonville
M'Kain, John H.	Pvt.	D	E-08/20/62	06/30/64	Dd. Wds. Rec.-Hanover C.H. 6/4/64
M'Kee, Robert	1st Sgt.	C	E-08/22/62	06/19/65	Mustered Out
M'Kinley, J. W. F.	Pvt.	D	E-08/12/62	unk.	Wd.& Captured at Wilderness 5/5/64
M'Laughlin, Patrick	Pvt.	G	E-08/15/62	06/19/65	Mustered Out
M'Laughlin, William	Capt.	G	E-08/09/62	06/19/65	Mustered Out
M'Manus, James	Pvt.	C	D-09/02/63	unk.	A.W.O.L. at Muster Out
M'Michael, Andrew	Pvt.	C	E-08/19/62	05/03/63	Died of Wounds rec.-Fredericksburg
M'Mullen, John H.	Pvt.	B	E-08/19/62	05/26/65	Wd.-Spotsyl. 5/18/64, Disch. G. O.
M'Vaugh, John	Pvt.	H	E-08/28/62	02/22/64	Transferred to Veteran Reserve
Mack, Patrick	Pvt.	G	E-10/05/64	unk.	Not on Muster Out Roll
Maguire, William	Pvt.	D	E-08/15/62	06/19/65	Mustered Out
Mallen, James W.	Sgt.	B	E-08/08/62	12/19/63	Discharged- Surgeon's Certificate
Malony, Edward	Pvt.	B	E-08/13/62	09/01/62	Deserted
Manere, William	Pvt.	I	E-08/20/62	04/02/64	Died at Washington, D.C.
Mansfield, Samuel D.	Pvt.	D	E-08/16/62	03/15/64	Wd.-Salem Church, Trans.-Vet. Res.
Maree, Lewis	Sgt.	A	E-08/13/62	06/19/65	Mustered Out
Marker, Edwin N.	Corp.	G	E-08/15/62	unk.	Wd. Rappahannock St., Disch. G. O.
Marple, Nathan R.	Pvt.	K	E-08/18/62	unk.	Died Wds. Rec. Spotsyl. 5/10/64
Marsh, Samuel M.	Sgt.	C	E-08/18/62	11/15/63	Transferred to Veteran Reserve
Marshall, John	Pvt.	G	E-08/15/62	unk.	Capt. Salem C., Wd. 4/2/65, D.G.O.
Marshall, Thomas	Pvt.	I	E-08/11/62	09/09/62	Discharged-Surgeon's Certificate
Marshall, William	Pvt.	D	E-08/16/62	05/26/65	Discharged by General Order
Martin, James	Pvt.	H	E-07/06/64	06/04/65	Transferred to 82nd P.V.
Martindell, William N.	Pvt.	B	E-08/22/62	06/19/65	Mustered Out
Matthews, Thomas	Pvt.	F	E-03/16/64	09/12/65	Discharged by General Order
Mattis, Isaac E.	Pvt.	F	E-08/18/62	09/21/64	Discharged-loss of arm in action
Mattis, William H.	Sgt.	A	E-08/11/62	06/19/65	Mustered Out
Maull, John J.	Pvt.	A	E-08/12/62	06/19/65	Mustered Out
Maum, Joseph	Corp.	G	E-08/15/62	08/17/64	Capt'd 5/10/64, Died Andersonville
Maxwell, Allen	Pvt.	C	E-08/18/62	unk.	Transferred to Verteran Reserve
May, William	Pvt.	F	D-08/29/63	09/20/63	Deserted
Maybrey, William E.	Corp.	B	E-08/14/62	06/19/65	Mustered Out
Meehan, Cornelius	Pvt.	F	E-08/21/62	10/28/63	Des., Rtd.10/63, Dishonorable Dis.
Memminger, Charles	Pvt.	I	E-03/14/64	unk.	Wd. Wilderness 5/5/64, Disch. G.O.
Mentz, John	Pvt.	I	E-08/21/62	06/19/65	Mustered Out
Merch, John	Pvt.	I	D-08/31/63	04/13/64	Deserted
Mercer, John D.	Adj.	Stf.	E-09/01/62	04/02/65	Killed at Petersburg
Merrick, James	Pvt.	D	E-08/14/62	06/19/65	Mustered Out
Meyer, Frank H.	Pvt.	H	D-09/01/63	09/13/63	Deserted
Miles, Thomas	Pvt.	B	E-08/15/62	05/10/64	Missing in Action-Spotsylvania
Millard, James B.	Pvt.	I	E-08/21/62	unk.	Wd. Salem Church, Disch. G.O.
Millard, James T.	Pvt.	I	E-08/22/62	09/01/63	Transferred to Veteran Reserve
Millard, John H.	Pvt.	I	E-08/22/62	04/06/65	Killed at Sailor's Creek
Miller, Alexander	Corp.	B	E-08/16/62	06/19/65	Wd. Opequon 9/19/64, Mustered Out
Miller, Benjamin R.	Chap.	Stf.	E-09/19/62	09/26/64	Discharged
Miller, Daniel	Pvt.	E	E-08/30/62	09/03/64	Promoted Quartermaster, 200th P.V.

Name	Rank	Co.	Enlistment or Draft Date	Exit Date	Remarks
Miller, Dorey	1st Sgt.	K	E-08/14/62	09/19/64	Died of Wounds Rec. at Opequon
Miller, Frank	Pvt.	H	D-08/31/63	11/07/64	Deserted
Miller, George	Pvt.	C	E-08/27/62	unk.	Deserted
Miller, James	Pvt.	K	E-08/29/62	06/19/65	Mustered Out
Miller, John	Pvt.	F	E-08/27/62	06/19/65	Mustered Out
Miller, John G.	Sgt.	H	E-08/30/62	06/19/65	Mustered Out
Miller, John R.	1st Sgt.	B	E-08/12/62	05/31/65	Wd.-Petersburg 4/2/65, Disch. G.O.
Miller, Joseph	Pvt.	F	E-08/27/62	06/30/64	Deserted
Miller, Lewis D.	Pvt.	H	E-08/23/62	03/05/64	Discharged-Surgeon 's Certificate
Miller, Robert	Pvt.	C	E-08/18/62	06/19/65	Mustered Out
Miller, Robert	Musc.	K	E-08/15/62	03/16/64	Transferred to Veteran Reserve
Mills, George	Pvt.	E	E-08/25/62	unk.	Not on Muster Out Roll
Miser, Lewis	Corp.	D	E-08/16/62	05/16/64	Died of Wds. Rec. Spotsyl. 5/12/64
Mitchell, David K.	1st Lt.	I	E-08/09/62	01/02/65	Discharged
Mitchell, George W.	A. Srg.	Stf.	E-02/14/63	06/19/65	Mustered out
Mitchell, Thomas	Pvt.	K	D-09/02/63	09/27/63	Deserted
Mock, Lewis	Pvt.	I	E-08/30/62	12/31/63	Died Wounds Rec. Rappahannock St.
Monroe, Charles	Pvt.	D	D-09/02/63	01/01/64	Transferred to Navy
Montgomery, William	Pvt.	B	E-08/20/62	06/19/65	Mustered Out
Moore, David	Pvt.	G	E-08/15/62	07/20/63	Deserted
Moore, James	Pvt.	F	D-07/17/63	08/28/64	Wd. Rappahannock St., Disch. S.C.
Moore, William	Pvt.	F	E-08/22/62	03/30/63	Wd. Rappahannock St., Disch. S.C.
Moreau, George D.	Pvt.	F	E-08/22/62	unk.	Deserted, Rtd. 12/28/64, Disch. G.O.
Moreau, Joseph N.	Pvt.	F	E-08/13/62	05/03/63	Killed at Salem Church
Morgan, Edward J.	Pvt.	D	E-08/27/62	06/19/65	Mustered Out
Morgan, James	Pvt.	I	D-08/31/63	unk.	Wd. Wilderness 5/6/64, Disch. G.O.
Morgan, Newton H.	Pvt.	E	E-08/20/62	01/24/65	Transferred to Veteran Reserve
Morris, James	Pvt.	B	E-08/14/62	09/01/62	Deserted
Morris, Joseph R.	Pvt.	A	E-08/12/62	12/22/63	Died- Brandy Station, Va.
Morris, Thomas	1st Lt.	K	E-08/15/62	06/19/65	Mustered Out
Morris, William	Pvt.	K	E-08/15/62	01/15/65	Transferred to Veteran Reserve
Moss, Jacob R.	Corp.	D	E-09/01/62	06/19/65	Wd.-Sailor's Cr. 4/6/65, Must. Out.
Moss, William C	Capt.	D	E-08/05/62	02/11/64	Died at Washington D.C.
Moulton, James	Pvt.	I	E-08/31/63	unk.	Wd. Rappahannock St., Disch. G.O.
Mount, Barney	Pvt.	D	D-09/02/63	05/25/65	Discharged-Surgeon 's Certificate
Moutz, John	Pvt.	K	D-08/31/63	11/24/63	Discharged-Surgeon 's Certificate
Moyer, Adam	Corp.	H	E-08/25/62	06/19/65	Mustered Out
Muir, William	Pvt.	K	E-08/22/62	05/03/63	Deserted
Muldoon, James	Pvt.	D	E-08/18/62	05/03/63	Killed at Salem Church
Mullen, John	Pvt.	E	D-09/03/63	unk.	Wd. Wilderness 5/7/64, Disch. G.O.
Mullen, Robert	Pvt.	C	E-08/18/62	unk.	Not on Muster Out Roll
Murphy, John	Pvt.	E	D-08/31/62	05/29/64	Deserted
Murphy, Patrick	Pvt.	D	E-08/29/62	08/29/62	Deserted
Murray, Samuel T.	Pvt.	F	E-08/13/62	02/13/64	Discharged by Special Order
Murry, George	Pvt.	A	E-10/24/64	06/04/65	Transferred- 82nd P.V.
Myers, Casper	Pvt.	F	D-07/17/63	06/04/65	Transferred to 82nd P.V.
Myers, Conrad	Pvt.	I	E-08/30/62	06/19/65	Wd. Wilderness 5/5/64. Mustered O.
Myers, Frederick	Pvt.	G	E-08/16/62	05/10/64	Killed at Spotsylvania
Myers, Henry	Pvt.	F	E-08/19/62	06/27/64	Discharged-Loss of Leg in Action
Myers, William H.	Pvt.	K	E-08/21/62	06/19/65	Mustered Out
Naber, William	Pvt.	G	E-08/15/62	06/19/65	Mustered Out
Neall, William M.	Sgt.	K	E-08/09/62	06/19/65	Mustered Out

Name	Rank	Co.	Enlistment or Draft Date	Exit Date	Remarks
Neely, Richard	Pvt.	E	D-09/03/63	07/20/64	Discharged-Surgeon's Certificate
Neff, Edward	Pvt.	D	E-08/30/62	02/14/63	Discharged-Surgeon's Certificate
Neiffer, John	Sgt.	H	E-08/23/62	05/05/64	Killed at Wilderness
Neild, Thomas	Pvt.	A	E-08/11/62	unk.	Not on Muster Out Roll
Neiman, John	Pvt.	H	E-08/25/62	06/19/65	Mustered Out
Nelson, Edwin	2nd. Lt.	B	E-08/26/62	06/04/64	Discharged- Surgeon's Certificate
Nelson, Robert	Pvt.	B	E-08/14/62	12/09/64	Wd.-Salem Ch., Disch. Surg. Cert.
Nesbit, William	Pvt.	B	E-08/14/62	09/01/62	Deserted
Nesley, William	Corp.	F	E-08/16/62	04/08/63	Discharged-Surgeon's Certificate
Newcomb, Charles	Pvt.	D	E-08/19/62	05/12/64	Killed at Spotsylvania
Newman, Thomas	A. Srg.	Stf.	E-08/11/62	12/03/62	Resigned
Newton, Isaac	Pvt.	K	E-08/11/62	05/31/64	Died Wds. Rec. Wilderness 5/5/64
Nice, Edward S.	Sgt.	B	E-08/14/62	05/10/64	Killed at Spotsylvania C.H.
Nice, George T.	Pvt.	B	E-08/14/62	06/19/65	Mustered Out
Nicholls, John	Capt.	D	E-08/12/62	06/19/65	Captured 7/24/64, Mustered Out
Nickel, William	Pvt.	D	E-08/19/62	06/19/65	Mustered Out
Nipperd, Henry C.	Pvt.	C	E-08/12/62	05/30/64	Died of Wounds rec.-Spotsylvania
Noble, Charles Jr.	Capt.	G	E-08/19/62	10/29/64	Discharged
Noble, Thomas R.	Corp.	F	E-08/23/62	5/5/64	Killed at Wilderness
Noll, Phillip	Pvt.	A	E-08/13/62	05/03/65	Discharged- Surg. Cert.
O'Brian, William	Pvt.	F	E-08/15/62	10/03/62	Deserted
O'Donnell Bernard	Pvt.	K	E-08/13/62	06/19/65	Mustered Out
O'Donnell, Roger	Pvt.	C	D-09/01/63	09/15/63	Deserted
O'Donnell, Thomas	Pvt.	B	E-08/29/62	unk.	Wounded 6/21/64, Trans. Vet. Res.
O'Kane, Edward	Pvt.	A	E-07/23/64	04/02/65	Deserted
O'Leary, Jeremiah	Sgt.	E	E-08/11/62	06/19/65	Capt'd - rtd. 3/17/65, Mustered O.
O'Neal, James	Pvt.	E	D-09/01/63	06/04/65	Transferred to 82nd P.V.
O'Neill, John	Pvt.	B	D-09/01/63	10/10/63	Deserted
O'Neill, Thomas	Sgt.	F	E-08/10/62	05/22/65	Wd'd. Spotsyl. 5/12/64, Disch. G.O.
Obert, Marcus	Pvt.	A	E-08/07/62	06/19/65	Mustered Out
Oliver, William B.	Pvt.	A	E-08/13/62	unk.	Dishcarged- Surg. Cert.
Osborn, Charles P.	Sgt.	D	E-08/12/62	05/10/64	Missing in Action-Spotsylvania
Osborn, Edward	Pvt.	C	E-08/18/62	12/14/64	Died of Wounds rec. in Action
Osborne, Charles	Pvt.	E	D-07/17/63	09/24/63	Deserted
Osborne, George	Pvt.	E	D-09/03/63	09/24/63	Deserted
Ott, Harkus	Pvt.	A	E-08/11/62	01/04/63	Died
Ottey, Philip	Pvt.	A	E-08/13/62	01/07/65	Discharged- Surg. Cert.
Owens, Richard	Pvt.	B	D-08/31/63	10/10/63	Deserted
Painter, Edward M.	Pvt.	C	E-08/22/62	06/19/65	Mustered Out
Palmer, Richard	Pvt.	B	E-08/22/62	02/21/63	Deserted
Parker, Charles F.	Pvt.	K	D-07/17/63	09/17/63	Deserted
Parkin, Joseph	Pvt.	C	E-08/21/62	unk.	Deserted
Patterson, John	Pvt.	E	E-09/03/63	07/24/65	Trans. Vet. Res., Disch. G. O.
Pedlow, Edward	Corp.	F	E-08/16/62	08/14/63	Deserted
Pedrick, Alfred L.	Sgt.	D	E-08/11/62	06/19/65	Wd'd-5/3/63, 6/1/64, 4/6/65, M.O.
Pepper, Joseph	Pvt.	B	E-08/14/62	07/11/63	Deserted
Peterman, Dallas	Pvt.	E	E-08/19/62	unk.	Not on Muster Out Roll
Peterman, Jacob M.	Pvt.	I	E-08/15/62	unk.	Not on Muster Out Roll
Peterman, John A.	Pvt.	E	E-08/20/62	unk.	Capt'd, Rtd., Discharged by G. O.
Peterson, Charles	Pvt.	K	D-08/31/63	04/15/64	Transferred to Veteran Reserve
Phares, John	Corp.	B	E-08/13/62	06/19/65	Mustered Out
Phelps, Lewis	Pvt.	A	E-11/12/64	06/04/65	Transferred- 82nd. P.V.

Name	Rank	Co.	Enlistment or Draft Date	Exit Date	Remarks
Phillips, Jacob S.	Pvt.	G	E-08/15/62	06/19/65	Mustered Out
Pierce, Ephraim T.	Sgt.	I	E-08/19/62	06/19/65	Mustered Out
Pierce, Marmaduke L.	Pvt.	K	E-08/23/62	06/19/65	Mustered Out
Pike, Isaac	Pvt.	E	E-08/20/62	08/15/64	Died Wds. Rec. Wilderness 5/5/64
Platt, Alfred	Pvt.	K	E-08/15/62	06/19/65	Mustered Out
Platt, John	Pvt.	K	E-08/15/62	05/10/64	Killed at Spotsylvania
Ployd, Naaman K.	Musc.	B	E-08/15/62	03/04/63	Discharged-Surgeon 's Certificate
Ployd, William	1st Sgt.	B	E-08/15/62	06/19/65	Wd.-Petersburg 4/2/65, Must. Out
Ployed, Tennis	Pvt.	A	E-08/12/62	03/13/65	Transferred- Vet. Reserve
Pollard, John	Sgt.	G	E-08/13/62	06/19/65	Mustered Out
Pool, John	Pvt.	H	E-08/23/62	04/27/64	Died of Wds. Rec. Rappahannock St.
Porter, John	Pvt.	E	E-08/20/62	unk.	Not on Muster Out Roll
Potts, Albert	Pvt.	D	E-08/16/62	06/19/65	Mustered Out
Potts, William	Pvt.	B	E-08/09/62	06/19/65	Mustered Out
Pratt, George	Pvt.	A	E-11/11/64	unk.	Not on Muster Out Roll
Preston, John E.	Corp.	G	E-08/15/62	05/05/64	Killed at Wilderness
Price, Richard	Pvt.	D	E-08/20/62	10/17/62	Deserted
Price, Thomas	Pvt.	E	E-09/03/63	09/20/63	Deserted
Priest, Isaac	Pvt.	E	E-08/19/62	12/15/64	Died near Petersburg
Prinzing, William	Pvt.	F	E-08/27/62	04/04/65	Wd. Spotsyl. 5/12/64, Disch. S. C.
Pritchard, Robert	Pvt.	K	D-08/31/63	unk.	Wd. Wilderness 5/5/64, Disch. G.O.
Puhl, Daniel	Corp.	H	E-08/25/62	05/05/64	Died of Wounds Rec. Wilderness
Pyott, William	Pvt.	A	E-08/07/62	05/03/63	M.I.A.- Salem Church
Quigg, William D.	Pvt.	H	E-08/23/62	06/19/65	Mustered Out
Quiggley, Daniel	Pvt.	F	E-08/18/62	11/01/62	Deserted
Raab, Barclay W.	Pvt.	B	E-01/29/64	unk.	Not on Muster Out Roll-Vet.
Raab, Lykens P.	Pvt.	B	E-08/13/62	06/19/65	Mustered Out
Rankin, William A.	Corp.	C	E-08/18/62	05/05/64	Killed at Wilderness
Rapine, William	Pvt.	E	E-08/28/62	05/03/63	Died of Wds. Rec. Salem Church
Rapp, John G.	1st Lt.	I	E-08/12/62	07/01/64	Discharged
Ratican, Peter	Pvt.	B	E-08/21/62	07/16/63	Deserted
Ray, Thomas	Pvt.	C	E-08/18/62	unk.	Wd'd-Spotsyl. 5/10/64, Disch. G.O.
Reaney, Robert	Pvt.	E	E-08/20/62	11/07/63	Killed at Rappahannock Station
Reaves, William	Pvt.	E	E-08/19/62	unk.	Not on Muster Out Roll
Redgate, Andrew	Pvt.	D	E-08/16/62	07/16/63	Deserted
Reed, John	Pvt.	D	E-08/15/62	09/22/62	Deserted
Reed, John	Pvt.	F	E-08/27/62	02/19/65	Wd. Cold Harbor 6/1/64, Dis. S.C.
Reeves, John N.	Pvt.	F	E-08/21/62	06/19/65	Mustered Out
Reimel, Joseph	Pvt.	D	E-08/19/62	06/19/65	Mustered Out
Reimel, Nicholas	Pvt.	D	E-08/21/62	06/19/65	Mustered Out
Repsher, William B.	Pvt.	D	E-08/15/62	05/10/64	Killed at Spotsylvania
Rice, Edward	Pvt.	G	E-10/05/64	unk.	Not on Muster Out Roll
Rice, George W.	Sgt.	G	E-08/11/62	12/08/64	Transferred to Veteran Reserve
Rice, Justice	Pvt.	B	E-08/22/62	11/19/62	Deserted
Richards, George W.	Sgt.	F	E-08/30/62	03/24/64	Capt'd Salem Church, Disch. Sp. O.
Richards, Thomas	Pvt.	E	D-09/02/63	unk.	Wd. Spotsyl. 5/10/64, Disch. G.O.
Richards, Will	Pvt.	G	E-08/13/62	11/01/64	Discharged by Special Order
Richardson, James S.	Pvt.	I	E-08/16/62	04/10/63	Discharged-Surgeon 's Certificate
Richardson, John	1st Lt.	D	E-08/11/62	06/19/65	Mustered Out
Richardson, John H.	Pvt.	I	E-08/16/62	01/29/63	Discharged-Surgeon 's Certificate
Richardson, W. H.	Pvt.	E	E-08/27/62	05/26/65	Discharged by General Order
Richmond, Cornelius	Pvt.	F	E-08/18/62	05/03/63	Missing in Action at Salem Church

Name	Rank	Co.	Enlistment or Draft Date	Exit Date	Remarks
Ricot, Leopold	Pvt.	B	E-08/12/62	10/13/62	Discharged by special order
Ridgway, Jacob	Capt.	I	E-08/05/62	12/30/62	Resigned
Ridgway, Richard S.	1st Sgt.	I	E-08/30/62	05/12/64	Killed at Spotsylvania
Righter, Daniel	Pvt.	A	E-08/12/62	11/07/64	Disch. Wds. rec. Rappahannock St.
Righter, Richard	Pvt.	A	E-08/13/62	06/30/65	Wd.- Sailor's Creek, Disch. G.O.
Righter, William	Pvt.	A	E-08/13/62	06/19/65	Mustered Out
Riley, Francis	Pvt.	E	D-09/02/63	06/04/65	Transferred to 82nd P.V.
Riley, George W.	Pvt.	E	E-unk.	08/19/65	Discharged by General Order
Riley, John	Pvt.	D	D-07/24/63	05/13/64	Discharged-Surgeon's Certificate
Riley, Martin	Pvt.	B	E-08/12/62	06/19/65	Wd.-Cold Harbor 6/1/64, Must. Out
Riley, Patrick	Pvt.	B	E-08/14/62	06/19/65	Mustered Out
Rink, John	Pvt.	I	E-08/12/62	06/19/65	Mustered Out
Ripka, Andrew A.	Capt.	A	E-08/15/62	03/03/63	Discharged-Surgeon's Certificate
Ritchie, John	Pvt.	C	E-08/30/62	06/19/65	Mustered Out
Ritenhouse, John M.	Pvt.	G	E-08/14/62	06/19/65	Mustered Out
Roat, John C.	Pvt.	C	D-08/31/63	05/25/65	Discharged-Surgeon's Certificate
Robbins, Jonathan	Pvt.	G	E-03/02/64	01/30/65	Deserted
Roberts, Charles F.	Pvt.	C	E-12/15/64	04/02/65	Deserted
Roberts, Lewis E.	Pvt.	G	E-08/15/62	08/22/62	Discharged
Roberts, Peter B.	Pvt.	A	E-08/09/62	06/19/65	Mustered Out
Roberts, William	Pvt.	E	E-08/28/62	01/21/63	Died at Belle Plain, Va.
Robertson, Joseph	Pvt.	K	D-09/01/63	03/23/64	Captured, died Andersonville
Robinson, Edwin	Pvt.	G	E-08/15/62	01/03/63	Died Near White Oak Church, Va.
Robinson, James	Pvt.	C	E-08/28/62	05/--/65	Discharged by Special Order
Robinson, Joseph	Pvt.	G	D-07/17/63	06/04/65	Transferred to 82nd P.V.
Rodgers, John	Corp.	C	E-08/18/62	06/19/65	Mustered Out
Rodgers, Peter W.	Capt.	B	E-08/26/62	05/03/63	Killed at Salem Church
Rogan, Edward L.	Pvt.	C	E-08/28/62	unk.	Deserted
Rogan, Joseph	Pvt.	C	E-02/15/65	06/04/65	Transferred to 82nd P.V.
Rogers, George H.	Pvt.	D	E-08/30/62	01/20/63	Deserted
Rose, Theodore C.	Pvt.	K	E-08/23/62	12/01/62	Discharged-Surgeon's Certificate
Roshow, Oliver	Pvt.	H	E-08/23/62	11/07/63	Killed at Rappahannock Station
Rousher, John F.	Pvt.	A	E-08/13/62	06/19/65	Mustered Out
Rousher, Martin	Pvt.	A	E-01/06/65	06/04/65	Transferred- 82nd P.V.
Rowan, Charles G.	1st Sgt.	F	E-08/15/62	unk.	Wd. & Capt'd Salem C., Wd.4/2/65
Rowland, Samuel	Pvt.	B	E-08/14/62	06/19/65	Mustered Out
Rubican, Coleman F.	Corp.	D	E-08/11/62	10/16/62	Deserted
Ruckstool, Samuel P.	Pvt.	E	E-06/10/64	06/04/65	Transferred to 82nd P.V.
Rugan, James	Pvt.	C	E-08/18/62	05/--/65	Discharged by Special Order
Rumley, Alfred	Pvt.	A	E-08/11/62	06/19/65	Capt'd & Ret'd- Mustered Out
Russell, Alexander	2nd Lt.	H	E-09/30/62	03/12/63	Resigned
Ruth, Henry P.	Pvt.	I	E-08/19/62	05/12/64	Killed at Spotsylvania
Rutter, David	Pvt.	C	D-08/31/63	05/30/64	Died Wounds rec. at Spotsylvania
Ryan, Dennis	Pvt.	K	D-09/01/63	10/22/63	Deserted
Sage, Henry	Pvt.	C	E-09/12/64	unk.	Not on Muster Out Roll
Sailor, William	Pvt.	E	D-09/03/63	11/07/63	Died Wds. Rec. at Rappahannock St.
Sample, Jesse	Pvt.	G	E-08/15/62	06/19/65	Mustered Out
Sample, William	Pvt.	F	E-08/30/62	06/19/65	Mustered Out
Sanders, William H.	Pvt.	F	E-08/27/62	12/30/63	Transferred to Veteran Reserve
Sargeant, Edward L.	Pvt.	G	E-08/16/62	06/19/65	Mustered Out
Satterthwait, J. W.	Sgt.	I	E-08/16/62	04/10/63	Discharged-Surgeon's Certificate
Sauerland, John H.	Pvt	C	E-08/22/62	unk.	Absent in arrest at Muster Out

Name	Rank	Co.	Enlistment or Draft Date	Exit Date	Remarks
Saylor, Benjamin	Capt.	H	E-08/04/62	08/10/65	Mustered Out
Schaffer, John	Pvt.	E	E-08/20/62	unk.	Not on Muster Out Roll
Schelley, Henry	1st Sgt.	I	E-08/14/62	06/19/65	Mustered Out
Schlotterer, Samuel	1st Sgt.	H	E-08/23/62	06/19/65	Mustered Out
Scholdgen, Peter J.	Pvt.	H	D-09/03/63	04/12/64	Deserted
Schuler, Franklin	Pvt.	H	E-08/23/62	03/19/63	Died near White Oak Church, Va.
Schwenk, John	Pvt.	H	E-08/25/62	02/13/63	Died at Windmill Point, Va.
Scott, G. W.	Pvt.	E	E-unk.	unk.	Wd. Petersburg 3/25/65, Disch. G.O.
Scott, James	Pvt.	B	E-08/16/62	04/03/63	Deserted
Scott, Walker	Pvt.	C	E-08/21/62	11/--/62	Deserted
Scull, George	Pvt.	G	E-08/13/62	06/19/65	Mustered Out
Searl, John	Sgt.	B	E-08/16/62	09/27/62	Deserted
Seek, Henry	Pvt.	H	D-08/29/63	07/14/65	Discharged by General Order
Seeper, William R.	Pvt.	C	E-08/21/62	unk.	Deserted
Seffarlen, Joseph A.	2nd Lt.	E	E-08/08/62	12/27/63	Dismissed
Seiberling, Walter P.	Pvt.	I	E-08/22/62	06/19/65	Mustered Out
Seigfried, John	Pvt.	K	E-08/13/62	08/08/63	Transferred to Veteran Reserve
Seiser, Charles	Com Sr.	Stf.	E-08/13/62	06/19/65	Mustered Out
Seizer, Thaddeus	Pvt.	H	D-08/31/63	10/12/63	Deserted
Semple, James	Pvt.	H	E-08/23/62	06/19/65	Mustered Out
Sendos, John D.	Pvt.	I	E-08/22/62	unk.	Discharged by General Order
Seringhouse, Peter	Pvt.	H	D-09/03/63	02/26/64	Capt'd, Died at Richmond, Va.
Seth, Thomas M.	Corp.	E	E-08/25/62	06/08/65	Discharged by General Order
Seull, John	Pvt.	E	E-08/25/62	06/19/65	Mustered Out
Seymour, Thomas	Pvt.	B	D-08/31/63	10/10/63	Deserted
Shaffer, Benjamin	Pvt.	D	E-08/13/62	05/03/63	Killed at Salem Church
Shaffer, Benjamin M.	Pvt.	B	E-08/16/62	12/06/64	Died at Montgomery County, Pa.
Sharpley, Daniel	Pvt.	A	E-08/07/65	unk.	Disch.- Surgeon's Certificate
Sharpley, Joseph	Pvt.	A	E-08/12/62	06/19/65	Mustered Out
Shaw, George	Pvt.	C	E-08/21/62	unk.	Deserted
Shaw, Nicholas A	Pvt.	K	E-03/06/65	06/04/65	Transferred to 82nd P. V.
Shea, James	Pvt.	K	D-09/01/63	04/13/64	Deserted
Sheard, John	Pvt.	D	D-09/03/63	05/05/64	Deserted
Sheets, George	Pvt.	D	E-08/14/62	06/19/65	Mustered Out
Sheetz, Charles N.	Corp.	A	E-08/09/62	01/09/63	Discharged
Sheetz, Thomas	Pvt.	I	E-08/27/62	01/16/64	Died near Brandy Station, Va.
Sheffer, Lewis	Pvt.	I	D-07/17/63	04/14/64	Deserted
Sheldrake, Horace	Corp.	G	E-08/15/62	unk.	Discharged by General Order
Shervon, James	Pvt.	F	E-08/22/62	06/04/65	Transferred to 82nd P.V.
Shick, Josiah	Corp.	G	E-08/15/62	06/15/65	Mustered Out
Shiedt, Jacob E.	Pvt.	F	E-08/12/62	unk.	Wd. Salem Church, Discharged G.O.
Shields, Henry C.	Pvt.	F	E-08/23/62	10/19/63	Died at Philadelphia
Shields, John	Pvt.	A	E-08/11/62	06/15/65	Discharged- General Order
Shimpfe, Frank	Pvt.	F	E-08/30/62	01/08/63	Discharged-Surgeon's Certificate
Shriver, George A.	Pvt.	F	E-08/22/62	01/13/64	Discharged by General Order
Shriver, George W.	1st Lt.	B	E-08/15/62	05/28/65	Wd.-Petersburg 4/2/65, Disch. G.O.
Shronk, Peter	Pvt.	A	E-08/12/62	06/19/65	Mustered Out
Shubert, Davenport	Pvt.	K	E-08/19/62	08/20/62	Deserted
Shuster, Miles	Corp.	A	E-08/09/62	06/19/65	Mustered Out
Shutteworth, William	Pvt.	D	E-09/02/63	10/26/64	Died at Martinsburg, Va.
Sigafoos, Leonard	Pvt.	F	E-08/19/62	06/19/65	Wd. Wilderness 5/5/64, Mustered O.
Signs, Henry	Pvt.	I	E-08/23/62	06/19/65	Mustered Out

Name	Rank	Co.	Enlistment or Draft Date	Exit Date	Remarks
Silvers, Addison	Pvt.	K	E-08/22/62	02/04/63	Discharged-Surgeon's Certificate
Silverthorne, Charles	Pvt.	A	E-08/12/62	06/19/65	Mustered Out
Simon, William H.	Corp.	D	E-08/13/62	06/19/65	Mustered Out
Simpson, James	Corp.	H	E-08/19/62	05/19/64	Died of Wds. Rec. Spotsyl. 5/10/64
Simpson, William R.	Corp.	B	E-08/12/62	05/10/64	Wd.-5/3/63, M.I.A.-Spotsylvania
Sines, Abram L	Pvt.	A	E-08/09/62	01/05/64	Disch. for wounds rec. in action
Sinex, Charles	Pvt.	K	E-09/01/62	09/02/62	Deserted
Singer, Bernard	Pvt.	H	D-09/01/63	05/12/64	Killed at Spotsylvania
Sithens, Richard B.	Pvt.	I	E-08/11/62	06/19/65	POW 8/14/64-5/2/65, Mustered Out
Skinner, Theodore	Pvt.	F	E-08/09/62	07/20/65	Wd. Spotsyl. 5/12/64, Disch. G.O.
Sleeper, Edward	Pvt.	E	E-10/16/62	unk.	Transferred to Veteran Reserve
Sloan, David	Pvt.	E	E-08/19/62	05/12/64	Killed at Spotsylvania
Sloop, John	Corp.	H	E-08/23/62	05/12/64	Missing in Action-Spotsylvania
Smallwood, Thomas	Pvt.	E	D-09/03/63	unk.	Discharged by General Order
Smiley, William	Pvt.	I	E-08/15/62	09/01/63	Transferred to Veteran Reserve
Smith, Charles	Pvt.	H	E-08/21/62	01/08/63	Discharged by Special Order
Smith, Charles	Pvt.	H	D-09/03/63	04/03/64	Deserted
Smith, Charles J.	Pvt.	I	E-08/27/62	06/19/65	Mustered Out
Smith, Charles P.	Pvt.	C	E-08/22/62	06/19/65	Mustered Out
Smith, Charles S.	Pvt.	K	E-08/21/62	unk.	Wd. Spotsyl. 5/10/64, Disch. G.O.
Smith, Edward	Pvt.	H	D-08/31/63	05/29/65	Discharged-Surgeon's Certificate
Smith, Elias	Pvt.	H	E-08/23/62	06/19/65	Mustered Out
Smith, George S.	Pvt.	E	E-09/28/62	unk.	Wounded at Fredericksburg 12/13/62
Smith, Henry	Pvt.	G	D-08/29/63	unk.	Transferred to Navy
Smith, Jacob	Sgt.	H	E-08/23/62	05/20/64	Died Wds. Rec. Spotsylvania 5/10/64
Smith, James	Pvt.	G	E-10/05/64	unk.	Not on Muster Out Roll
Smith, John	Pvt.	C	D-09/02/63	unk.	Wd'd-Wilderness 5/5/64, Disch. G.O.
Smith, John	Pvt.	G	D-08/31/63	03/17/64	Discharged-Surgeon's Certificate
Smith, John	Pvt.	K	D-08/31/63	11/07/63	Missing in Action-Rappahannock St.
Smith, Joseph	Pvt.	K	D-08/28/63	unk.	Wd. Rappahannock St., Disch. G.O.
Smith, William	Pvt.	H	E-08/25/62	06/19/65	Wd. at Sailor's Creek, Must. Out
Smyth, George W. A.	Pvt.	D	E-08/19/62	06/19/65	Mustered Out
Snow, Edward	Pvt.	D	D-07/20/63	04/10/64	Deserted
Snow, George W.	Sgt.	C	E-08/21/62	06/19/65	Mustered Out
Sorber, Jacob	Pvt.	I	E-08/21/62	unk.	Wd. Salem Church, Discharged G.O.
Souder, Benjamin	Pvt.	B	E-08/15/62	05/03/63	Killed at Salem Church
Souder, Charles A.	Pvt.	I	E-08/12/62	06/19/65	Mustered Out
Souder, Harvey	Pvt.	B	E-08/19/62	06/19/65	Mustered Out
South, Henry	Pvt.	G	E-08/15/62	10/03/62	Deserted
Southwick, Jon	Pvt.	C	D-08/22/63	unk.	Discharged by General Order
Spangler, Stephen	Pvt.	I	E-03/14/64	04/20/64	Discharged by Special Order
Spangler, Thomas B.F.	Pvt.	I	E-08/13/62	09/01/63	Transferred to Veteran Reserve
Sparks, Edward	Pvt.	D	E-08/23/62	06/19/65	Wd.-Spotsyl. 5/10/64, Mustered O.
Sparks, Joseph F.	1st Sgt.	F	E-08/08/62	unk.	Killed at Spotsylvania
Spear, William J.	Pvt.	A	E-08/11/62	06/19/65	Mustered Out
Spicer, Isaac	Pvt.	C	E-08/20/62	05/10/64	Died of Wounds rec.-Spotsylvania
Spicer, Joseph G.	Pvt.	C	E-08/21/62	05/--/65	Discharged by Special Order
Spicer, William M.	Pvt.	C	E-08/20/62	06/29/65	Wd.-Fred. 12/13/62, Disch. G.O.
Springer, James P.	Corp.	I	E-08/16/62	unk.	Discharged-Surgeon's Certificate
Stackhouse, George	Pvt.	B	E-08/14/62	06/29/65	Wd.Wilderness 5/5/64, Disch. G.O.
Stackhouse, William	Pvt.	B	E-08/22/62	06/19/65	Mustered Out
Stapler, Thomas W.	Sgt.	B	E-08/23/62	06/19/65	Mustered Out

Name	Rank	Co.	Enlistment or Draft Date	Exit Date	Remarks
Starratt, John W.	Pvt.	B	E-08/13/62	07/16/63	Deserted
Steel, John	Pvt.	E	E-08/20/62	12/08/63	Died at Annapolis
Steel, John C.	Pvt.	E	E-08/23/62	06/19/65	Mustered Out
Steel, Josiah J.	Pvt.	B	E-08/18/62	05/03/63	Killed at Salem Church
Steever, Samuel G.	Pvt.	I	E-08/19/62	06/19/65	Mustered Out
Stein, Henry	Pvt.	H	D-09/03/63	04/12/64	Deserted
Stephens, Joseph, Jr.	Pvt.	K	E-08/29/62	unk.	Not on Muster Out Roll
Sterritt, James	Pvt.	C	E-08/21/62	unk.	Discharged by General Order
Stevens, Henry	Pvt.	K	D-08/31/63	09/17/63	Deserted
Stevens, Joseph	Pvt.	E	E-08/22/62	02/24/63	Deserted
Stevenson, Newbold	Pvt.	F	E-08/22/62	06/30/64	Wd. Salem Church, Disch. Sur. Cert.
Stever, Charles L.	Corp.	B	E-08/16/62	09/27/62	Deserted
Stewart, William	Pvt.	B	E-01/09/65	unk.	Not on Muster Out Roll
Stewart, William	Pvt.	E	E-08/19/62	unk.	Died Wds. Rec. at Rappahannock St.
Stief, Frederick	Pvt.	K	E-08/12/62	01/10/65	Transferred to Veteran Reserve
Stillewagon, William	Pvt.	K	E-08/15/62	05/03/63	Killed at Salem Church
Stratton, John	Pvt.	I	E-08/29/63	04/20/64	Discharged-Surgeon's Certificate
Stratton, Oliver	Pvt.	K	D-09/01/63	06/04/65	Transferred to 82nd P. V.
Streeter, Charles	Pvt.	F	D-09/01/63	03/20/64	Deserted
Stribig, Roney	Pvt.	G	E-08/15/62	06/19/65	Mustered Out
Strine, Charles	Sgt.	F	E-08/13/62	02/13/63	Discharged-Surgeon's Certificate
Stull, George	Pvt.	K	E-08/15/62	02/15/64	Transferred to Veteran Reserve
Styer, Henry	Pvt.	H	E-08/23/62	05/12/64	Killed at Spotsylvania
Sullivan, Eugene	Pvt.	H	E-08/13/62	10/09/62	Deserted
Sullivan, William	Pvt.	C	E-08/--/64	09/15/64	Deserted
Swanson, Peter	Pvt.	I	D-08/31/63	unk.	Wd. Rappahannock St., Disch. G.O.
Swope, Simpson T.	Pvt.	B	E-08/19/62	11/10/62	Died at Acquia Creek
Tams, George Y.	2nd Lt.	A	E-08/15/62	03/17/63	Discharged
Tappen, George	Pvt.	G	E-08/16/62	03/04/63	Deserted
Tappan, Oscar	Pvt.	K	E-08/20/62	10/26/62	Deserted
Taylor, Amos	1st Sgt.	A	08/12/62	06/19/65	Mustered Out
Teller, Michael	Pvt.	K	E-08/27/62	06/19/65	Mustered Out
Templeton, John	Pvt.	F	E-08/16/62	06/19/65	Mustered Out
Tetlow, John B.	Pvt.	E	E-08/20/62	05/03/63	Killed at Salem Church
Tevis, James H.	Pvt.	F	E-08/08/62	01/08/63	Deserted
Thomas, Charles A.	1st Lt.	H	E-09/30/62	03/11/63	Resigned
Thomas, David	Pvt.	F	D-08/29/63	09/20/63	Deserted
Thomas, Joseph	Pvt.	D	E-08/11/62	06/19/65	Mustered Out
Thomas, Henry	Pvt.	B	D-08/25/63	02/20/65	Wd.-Spotsyl. 5/10/64, Deserted
Thomas, Henry	Pvt.	D	E-08/28/62	unk.	Discharged by General Order
Thomas, John	Corp.	A	E-08/12/62	11/24/63	Disch. Surg. Cert.
Thomas, John J.	Pvt.	A	E-08/12/62	04/16/63	Disch.- Surgeon's Certificate
Thomas, William	Pvt.	A	E-08/12/62	1863	Disch.- Writ of Habeas Corpus
Thomas, William G.	Pvt.	D	D-09/02/63	unk.	Absent with Leave at Muster Out
Thompson, Benj. F.	Pvt.	B	E-08/11/62	07/15/63	Deserted
Tindall, Benjamin T.	Sgt.	E	E-08/22/62	06/19/65	Mustered Out
Tobias, E. S.	Pvt.	G	E-08/16/62	08/24/62	Discharged-Surgeon's Certificate
Torley, Robert	Pvt.	C	D-08/31/63	unk.	A.W.O.L. at Muster Out
Townsend, Charles	Pvt.	I	E-08/14/62	12/09/62	Discharged-Surgeon's Certificate
Townsend, John H.	Pvt.	B	E-08/12/62	06/19/65	Mustered Out
Toy, George	Pvt.	G	E-10/04/64	unk.	Not on Muster Out Roll
Trefts, William	Pvt.	G	E-08/12/62	06/19/65	Wd. Petersburg 4/2/65, Mustered O.

Name	Rank	Co.	Enlistment or Draft Date	Exit Date	Remarks
Trexler, John	Pvt.	I	E-08/15/62	06/19/65	Mustered Out
Trimber, John	Pvt.	A	E-08/12/62	07/13/63	Missing in Action
Troupe, Cornelius	Pvt.	F	D-08/29/63	unk.	Wd. N. Anna 5/24/64, Disch. G.O.
Truefitt, H.P. Jr.	Maj.	Stf.	E-08/19/62	05/12/64	Killed Spotsylvania
Trysbock, Daniel	Pvt.	G	E-08/14/62	05/17/65	Wd. Spotsyl. 5/12/64, Disch. S.C.
Tucker, George E.	Pvt.	D	E-08/30/62	12/24/62	Discharged-Surgeon's Certificate
Tucker, William Ellis	QM. Sr.	Stf.	E-09/09/62	06/19/65	Mustered Out
Turner, Robert	Pvt.	C	E-08/21/62	05/03/63	Died of Wounds Rec.-Fredericksburg
Turner, Thaddeaus B.	Pvt.	I	E-08/27/62	01/14/63	Discharged-Surgeon's Certificate
Tyson, David P.	Sgt.	H	E-08/25/62	10/04/64	Died of Wounds Rec. at Opequon
Uffelman, Henry	Pvt.	H	D-09/01/63	05/10/64	Killed at Spotsylvania
Ulmer, Arnold	Pvt.	H	E-08/23/62	12/09/62	Died near White Oak Church, Va.
Underkoffer, Abel	Pvt.	K	E-08/27/62	06/19/65	Mustered Out
Undercoffer, Joseph	Pvt.	H	E-08/25/62	05/10/64	Missing in Action- Spotsylvania
Vandegrift, Charles M.	Pvt.	G	E-08/13/62	unk.	Discharged by General Order
Vesbist, August	Pvt.	D	D-07/17/63	06/04/65	Transferred to 82nd P.V.
Vincent, Daniel	Pvt.	K	E-08/28/62	06/19/65	Mustered Out
Vinson, George	Pvt.	D	E-08/15/62	09/02/62	Deserted
Wachtler, George	Pvt.	H	D-07/17/63	01/17/65	Discharged-Surgeon's Certificate
Wagner, Joseph	2nd Lt.	G	E-08/07/62	09/01/63	Discharged by Special Order
Wagner, William W.	Capt.	F	E-08/04/62	03/09/63	Discharged-Surgeon's Certificate
Wainwright, Joshua	Corp.	A	E-08/13/62	06/19/65	Mustered Out
Walker, Richard	Pvt.	I	E-08/29/62	09/01/63	Transferred to Veteran Reserve
Walker, Robert	Pvt.	E	E-08/28/62	unk.	Not on Muster Out Roll
Walsh, John	Pvt.	–	E-02/24/64	unk.	Not on Muster Out Roll
Walters, Jacob	Pvt.	A	E-08/12/62	06/19/65	Mustered Out
Walton, Charles	Corp.	F	E-08/19/62	06/19/65	Mustered Out
Walton, James	Pvt.	A	E-08/09/62	06/01/64	Died
Walton, John	Corp.	I	E-08/28/62	unk.	Deserted
Walton, John J.	Pvt.	A	E-08/12/62	01/09/63	Disch.- Surgeon's Certificate
Walton, Thomas B.	Pvt.	B	E-08/14/62	05/03/63	Died of Wounds rec. Salem Church
Ward, Charles	Pvt.	E	D-09/03/63	11/05/64	Deserted
Ward, James	Pvt.	E	D-09/03/63	04/13/65	Discharged-Surgeon's Certificate
Ward, Samuel L. Jr.	2nd Lt.	H	E-08/09/62	04/30/64	Resigned
Ward, Thomas	Pvt.	A	E-08/09/62	05/17/65	Disch.- Surgeon's Certificate
Ward, Thomas	Pvt.	C	E-12/15/64	06/19/65	Dishonorably Discharged
Warner, Charles P.	Capt.	K	E-08/04/62	05/12/64	Killed at Spotsylvania
Warner, Henry C.	Capt.	K	E-08/05/62	06/19/65	Mustered Out
Wartman, John	Pvt.	G	E-08/15/62	05/05/64	Killed at Wilderness
Watson, Edwin J.	Pvt.	K	E-08/27/62	06/19/65	Mustered Out
Watt, William	Pvt.	I	E-08/13/62	06/19/65	Mustered Out
Watterson, W. F.	Pvt.	F	E-08/21/62	08/24/62	Deserted
Weaver, George	Pvt.	D	E-08/15/62	11/13/64	Died at Philadelphia
Weirman, Henry	Pvt.	A	E-08/12/62	09/08/64	Deserted
Weller, Adam	Pvt.	F	E-08/23/62	unk.	Capt'd Salem Church/Absent at M.O.
Wells, Joseph W.	Pvt.	K	E-08/23/62	06/19/65	Mustered Out
Welser, Ebenezer C.	Pvt.	E	E-08/20/62	unk.	Discharged by General Order
Welsh, John	Pvt.	C	E-08/21/62	unk.	Transferred to 2d U.S. Artillery
Welsh, Peter	Pvt.	H	E-08/14/62	06/19/65	Mustered Out
Welsh, William	Pvt.	B	E-08/19/62	06/09/65	Discharged by General Order
Welsh, William B.	Pvt.	B	D-09/01/63	10/10/63	Deserted
West, William R. Jr.	Sr. Mjr.	Stf.	E-09/15/62	06/19/65	Mustered Out

Name	Rank	Co.	Enlistment or Draft Date	Exit Date	Remarks
Wharton, William	Pvt.	G	E-08/15/62	06/19/65	Mustered Out
Whitby, Daniel F.	Pvt.	F	E-08/18/62	09/22/64	Wd. Spotsyl. 5/12/64, Disch. S.C.
White, Benjamin	Pvt.	I	E-08/15/62	06/19/65	Mustered Out
White, Edward	Pvt.	C	E-08/23/62	05/03/63	Died of Wounds Rec.-Fredericksburg
White, Frank	Pvt.	G	D-09/01/63	10/25/64	Wd. Wilderness 5/5/64, Disch. S.C.
White, Samuel	Pvt.	G	E-08/15/63	06/19/65	Capt'd Salem Church, Mustered Out
Whitehead, James	Pvt.	G	E-08/14/62	09/04/64	Captured, Died at Andersonville
Whitmer, John	Pvt.	K	E-08/22/62	05/05/64	Killed at Wilderness
Whitmier, John	Pvt.	H	D-07/17/63	04/29/65	Discharged-Surgeon 's Certificate
Wick, Aaron	Corp.	H	E-08/23/62	06/19/65	Mustered Out
Wick, Christian	Pvt.	H	E-08/23/62	06/19/65	Mustered Out
Widner, Benjamin	Pvt.	B	E-08/14/62	02/09/63	Discharged-Surgeon 's Certificate
Wiedersheim, J. H.	Pvt.	F	E-08/08/62	12/20/64	Discharged by Special Order
Wiedersheim, W. A.	Capt.	F	E-08/04/62	06/19/65	Mustered Out
Wiegand, Casper P.	Corp.	F	E-08/16/62	06/19/65	Mustered Out
Wiggins, Rufus	Pvt.	B	E-08/14/62	06/04/64	Died Wds. Spotsylvania 5/10/64
Wigle, Adolph	Pvt.	H	D-09/02/63	05/10/64	Missing in Action- Spotsylvania
Wild, George	Pvt.	C	D-09/01/63	10/18/63	Deserted
Wildman, Benj. A.	Sgt.	B	E-08/15/62	06/19/65	Wd.-Wilderness 5/5/64, Must. Out
Wiley, James	Pvt.	I	E-08/16/62	unk.	Captured at Cold Harbor 6/1/64
Wilgus, Robert G.	Pvt.	K	E-08/14/62	04/03/65	Discharged-Surgeon 's Certificate
Wilkins, George	Pvt.	A	E-08/12/62	06/19/65	Mustered Out
Wilkinson, Anthony	Pvt.	I	E-08/23/62	06/19/65	Mustered Out
Williams, Beverly	Pvt.	C	D-09/17/63	06/04/65	Transferred to 82nd P.V.
Williams, Charles A.	Pvt.	B	D-09/03/63	06/04/65	Transferred to 82nd P.V.
Williams, Charles A.	Pvt.	E	D-09/03/63	06/12/65	Wd. Petersburg 4/2/65, Disch. G. O.
Williams, Frederick	Sgt.	E	E-08/11/62	07/05/65	Wd.Ft. Stedman 3/25/65, Dish. G.O.
Williams, John	Pvt.	G	E-08/15/62	06/19/65	Mustered Out
Williams, John J.	1st Sgt.	G	E-08/17/62	05/25/65	Wd. Sailor's Creek, Disch. S.O.
Williams, Joseph R.	Pvt.	I	E-08/23/62	11/15/63	Transferred to Veteran Reserve
Williamson, Samuel	Pvt.	G	E-08/16/62	01/15/65	Transferred to Veteran Reserve
Williams, Thomas	Corp.	G	E-08/15/62	05/10/64	Killed at Spotsylvania
Williamson, Charles	Pvt.	H	E-08/29/62	06/19/65	Mustered Out
Wilson, Ebenezer	Pvt.	E	E-08/22/62	unk.	Not on Muster Out Roll
Wilson, George	Pvt.	C	E-08/22/62	unk.	Deserted
Wilson, George	Pvt.	G	E-10/05/64	unk.	Not on Muster Out Roll
Wilson, James	Pvt.	B	D-09/03/63	05/26/64	Wd.-Spotsylvania 5/10/64, Deserted
Wilson, James	Pvt.	F	E-08/17/62	06/24/65	Wd. Spotsyl. 5/12/64, Disch. G.O.
Wilson, John B.	Pvt.	G	E-08/15/62	06/19/65	Mustered Out
Wilson, Robert	Pvt.	G	E-08/15/62	05/10/64	Killed at Spotsylvania
Wilson, Thomas G.	Pvt.	G	E-08/11/62	06/04/65	Transferred to 82nd P.V.
Wilson, William	Pvt.	A	E-08/07/62	03/13/64	Transferred to Vet. Reserve
Wilson, William	Pvt.	I	E-08/13/62	06/19/65	Mustered Out
Wilson, William	Pvt.	K	D-08/31/63	06/18/64	Transferred to Veteran Reserve
Winebrenner, D. C.	Corp.	D	E-08/13/62	01/28/63	Promoted to 2d. Lt.- 99th P.V.
Winterbottom, S.	Pvt.	A	E-08/11/62	06/19/65	Mustered Out
Winton, William J.	Pvt.	E	E-08/25/62	06/19/65	Mustered Out
Wise, Howell	Pvt.	G	E-08/15/62	06/19/65	Mustered Out
Witcraft, William	Corp.	B	E-08/15/62	12/09/64	Discharged-Surgeon 's Certificate
Witt, Addis	Pvt.	I	E-08/30/62	06/19/65	Mustered Out
Woerner, Rudolph	1st Sgt.	D	E-08/21/62	06/19/65	Wd'd-Wilderness 5/5/64, Must.Out
Wolf, Henry	Pvt.	H	E-08/30/62	05/26/65	Discharged by General Order

Name	Rank	Co.	Enlistment or Draft Date	Exit Date	Remarks
Wolf, John	Pvt.	B	D-08/25/63	01/31/64	Wd.- Rappahannock St., Deserted
Wolf, Martin	Pvt.	E	E-08/30/62	unk.	Not on Muster Out Roll
Wolfinger, Elias	Corp.	I	E-08/18/62	06/19/65	Mustered Out
Wood, George	Corp.	C	E-08/22/62	06/19/65	Mustered Out
Wood, Jacob	Pvt.	G	E-08/15/62	05/05/64	Killed at Wilderness
Wood, Michael F.	Pvt.	K	E-08/19/62	unk.	Never Joined Company
Wood, Thomas B. H.	Pvt.	A	E-08/07/62	06/19/65	Mustered Out
Wood, William	Pvt.	C	E-08/21/62	06/19/65	Mustered Out
Wood, William	Pvt.	K	D-07/24/63	04/02/65	Killed at Petersburg
Woodfall, Richard	Pvt.	D	E-09/16/62	05/12/64	Died of Wounds Rec. Spotsylvania
Woods, Samuel	Pvt.	K	E-08/15/62	08/15/62	Deserted
Wright, Elwood	Pvt.	F	E-03/10/64	05/28/64	Died-Wounds Rec. Wilderness 5/5/64
Wright, James	Pvt.	A	E-08/11/62	04/06/65	Disch.-Wds. Rec'd Sailor's Creek
Wright, Nathan	Pvt.	F	E-08/15/62	04/03/63	Died near White Oak Church, Va.
Wright, Robert	Pvt.	E	D-08/25/63	03/24/64	Discharged by Special Order
Wunder, Jacob N.	Sgt.	A	E-08/07/62	09/25/62	Disc.-Surg. Cert.
Wyncoop, George H.	Corp.	K	E-08/22/62	12/06/63	Deserted
Yapp, Richard	Pvt.	D	D-09/02/63	06/04/65	Transferred to 82nd P.V.
Yarnall, Griffith	Pvt.	A	E-08/09/62	06/19/65	Mustered Out
Yeager, Charles	Pvt.	D	E-08/11/62	12/29/62	Discharged-Surgeon's Certificate
Yemmer, Stephen	Pvt.	H	D-09/03/63	06/04/65	Transferred to 82nd P. V.
Yeo, John	Corp.	I	E-08/13/62	06/19/65	Mustered Out
Yocum, Edward P.G.	Pvt.	–	D-07/15/63	06/02/65	Discharged by General Order
Young, Charles E.	Pvt.	K	E-08/22/62	unk.	Never Joined Company
Young, David	Pvt.	E	E-08/20/62	unk.	Not on Muster Out Roll
Young, Edward H.	Corp.	D	E-08/19/62	07/18/65	Wd.-Sailor's Cr. 4/6/65, Disch. G.O.
Young, William	Pvt.	F	E-08/27/62	01/08/63	Discharged-Surgeon's Certificate
Zeigler, James	Pvt.	K	E-08/31/64	07/17/65	Discharged by General Order
Zimmerman, G. W.	2nd Lt.	H	E-08/04/62	08/04/62	Missing[2]

[2]Bates, *History*..., vol. 4, 119th Pa.

APPENDIX B

Historical Outline
First Regiment Infantry, N.G.P.
"The Dandy First"

by Colonel J. Craig Nannos

7 December 1747	Constituted through recognition of Associators, founded 21 November 1747 in Philadelphia by Benjamin Franklin
29 December 1747	Organized as Artillery Companies of the Associated Philadelphia
18 June 1748	Captain John Siebold, commissioned as an artillery officer in command of fortifications
15 October 1754	Records cite a "Train of Artillery" indicating more than one company in existence
1 January 1756	Identified Artillery Companies The Artillery Company at the Fort Association Battery at Wiccocoe Cpt. Samuel Mifflin, Lt. Oswald Eve, Ensign William Moore Artillery Company of the City (a newly established command) Cpt. George Noarth, Lt. Benjamin Loxley, Lt. John Goodwin
18 March 1756	Captain Jehu Eyre appointed as chief engineer and director of artillery
May 1756	Captain Jehu Eyre's Company, Associator Artillery of Northern Liberties, mustered into Crown service for French and Indian War
2 October 1760	Records indicate Captain Eyre's Company saw service at Fort Pitt and Presque Isle (Erie)
1775	Reorganized as Associators of the City and Liberties of Philadelphia, consisting of six battalions (one of which was artillery) Identified Artillery Companies Cpt. Jehu Eyre, Cpt. James Biddle, Cpt. Benjamin Loxley, Cpt. Thomas Proctor, Cpt. Joseph Moulder
1775-1776	Reorganized as Philadelphia Artillery Battalion Commanded by Col. Samuel Mifflin

Annex

27 October 1775	Captain Thomas Proctor's company designated as the Pennsylvania State Artillery Company and placed in full time service
14 August 1776	Company expanded and designated the Pennsylvania Artillery Battalion
23 September 1776	Mustered into service as Proctor's Continental Artillery
15 November 1783	Demobilized at Philadelphia following Continental Service. Personnel enter artillery battalion, Pennsylvania Militia

19 June 1777	Constituted in the Pennsylvania Militia as The Artillery Battalion (Colonel Jehu Eyre Commanding)
16 August 1777	Organized at Philadelphia, Pennsylvania comprising 1st Company, Captain Samuel Massey 2d Company, Captain John McCullough 3d Company, Captain Peter Browne (Cpt. Eyre's Company) 4th Company, Captain William Prowell 5th Company, Captain Andrew Summers (Cpt. Loxley's Company) 6th Company, Captain John Ruper (Cpt. Moulder's Company)
1794	Expanded into the Regiment of Artillery of the City of Philadelphia (Colonel Thomas Proctor Commanding)
August 1814	Mustered into Federal service for War of 1812 as the Regiment of Artillery, LTC Andrew M. Prevost, commanding, comprising the following companies: Junior Artillerists Company of Independent Artillerists 2d Company of Independent Artillerists Northern Liberty Artillerists Frankford Volunteer Artillerists Captain Landis Company of Volunteer Artillery
January 1815	Mustered out of Federal service
2 April 1822	Reorganized as the Artillery Battalion, 1st Brigade, 1st Division, Pennsylvania Militia
1828	Redesignated as the 1st Artillery Regiment, Pennsylvania Militia comprising: Junior Artillerist Jackson Artillery Pennsylvania Artillery State Artillery Phalanx Artillery Artillery Corps, Washington Grays
19 April 1861	Reorganized in part as the 3d (later 1st) Regiment Infantry, Gray Reserves
25 April 1861	While remaining in state service for Civil War, the former 1st Artillery Regiment (also known as the Gray Artillery Battalion) 1st Brigade, 1st Division formed the following units for Federal service for Civil War
25 April 1861	1st Artillery Regiment (also known as Gray Artillery Battalion), 1st Brigade, 1st Division, mustered into Federal service for Civil War at Philadelphia, Pennsylvania, to consist of the following companies: Washington Grays (2 companies) Cadwalader Grays Philadelphia Grays West Philadelphia Grays Independent Grays State Guards National Artillery
15 May 1861	Redesignated as 17th Regiment, Pennsylvania Volunteer Infantry
2 August 1861	Mustered out of Federal service at Philadelphia, Pennsylvania

15-30 August 1862	118th Regiment (Corn Exchange Regiment) Pennsylvania Volunteer Infantry Mustered into Federal service for Civil War at Philadelphia, Pennsylvania
15-17 Sept. 1862	119th Regiment (Gray Reserves), Pennsylvania Volunteer Infantry, mustered into Federal service for Civil War at Philadelphia, Pennsylvania
1 June 1865	118th Regiment (Corn Exchange Regiment) Pennsylvania Volunteer Infantry mustered out of Federal service at Alexandria, Virginia
19 June 1865	119th Regiment (Gray Reserves), Pennsylvania Volunteer Infantry, mustered out of Federal service at Philadelphia, Pennsylvania
18 September 1866	Reorganized as 1st Regiment Infantry, Gray Reserves, Reserve Brigade, Pennsylvania Militia (consolidation of 118th and 119th Pennsylvania Volunteer Infantry)
1870	Pennsylvania Militia redesignated as the National Guard of Pennsylvania
10-11 May 1898	Mustered into Federal service for War with Spain at Mount Gretna, Pennsylvania, as the 1st Pennsylvania Volunteer Infantry
26 October 1898	Mustered out of Federal service at Philadelphia, Pennsylvania
30 June 1916	Mustered into Federal service at Mount Gretna, Pennsylvania, for Mexican border service
23 October 1916	Mustered out of Federal service at Mount Gretna, Pennsylvania
5 August 1917	Drafted into Federal service for World War I at Philadelphia, Pennsylvania
11 October 1917	Consolidated with the 13th Infantry, Pennsylvania National Guard (organized 1877); consolidated unit reorganized and redesignated 109th Infantry, an element of the 28th Division
17-20 May 1919	Mustered out at Camp Dix, New Jersey
16 October 1919	1st Infantry reorganized in the Pennsylvania National Guard at Philadelphia, Pennsylvania
1 April 1921	Converted and redesignated 103d Engineer Regiment, an element of the 28th Division
18 July 1921	Organized and Federally recognized at Philadelphia, Pennsylvania
17 February 1941	Inducted into Federal service for World War II at Philadelphia, Pennsylvania
17 February 1942	Regiment broken up and its elements reorganized and redesignated as follows: Regiment (less 2d Battalion) as the 103d Engineer Battalion, an element of the 28th Infantry Division 2d Battalion redesignated as 180th Engineer Battalion and relieved from assignment to the 28th infantry Division
1 August 1942	180th Engineer Battalion redesignated as the 180 Engineer Heavy Pontoon Battalion
9 March 1943	103d Engineer Battalion redesignated 103d Engineer Combat Battalion
27 October 1945	Inactivated 103d Engineer Combat Battalion at Camp Shelby, Mississippi
27 November 1945	Inactivated 108th Engineer Heavy Pontoon Battalion at Camp Miles, Standish, Mass.
24 May 1946	103d Engineer Combat Battalion and the 180th Engineer Heavy Pontoon Battalion consolidated and designated 103d Engineer Combat Battalion
8 April 1947	Reorganized and Federally recognized at Philadelphia, Pennsylvania
5 September 1950	Ordered into active Federal service for Korean War at Philadelphia, Pennsylvania
5 June 1953	Redesignated 103d Engineer Battalion
17 August 1953	103d Engineer Battalion [NGUS] organized and Federally recognized with Headquarters in Philadelphia, Pennsylvania

15 June 1954	Released from active Federal service and reverted to state control; Federal recognition concurrently withdrawn from 103d Engineer Battalion [NGUS]
21 January 1968	Company C, allotted to the MDARNG
1 February 1968	Company D, allotted to the VAARNG
1 April 1975	Companies C, and D, reallotted to the PAARNG

Campaign Participation Credits

Revolutionary War (Proctor's 4th Continental Artillery and Phila. Artillery Battalion)

Trenton	
Monmouth	4th Continental
Princeton	
Yorktown	4th Continental
Brandywine	
Pennsylvania 1776	4th Continental
New Jersey 1776	
New York 1776	
Germantown	
New Jersey 1777	4th Continental & Phila. Bn
New Jersey 1778	4th Continental
New York 1779	4th Continental

War of 1812

Streamer without Inscription

Civil War	(State recognized)
Antietam	
Shenandoah	(119th Regiment)
Fredericksburg	
Maryland 1863	(32d Regiment)
Chancellorsville	

Pennsylvania 1863	(32d Regiment)
Gettysburg	
Wilderness	
Spotsylvania	
Cold Harbor	
Petersburg	
Appomattox	
Maryland 1862	
Virginia 1863	
Maryland 1864	
Virginia 1864	

World War I

- Champagne-Marne
- Aisne-Marne
- Oise-Aisne
- Meuse-Argonne
- Champagne 1918
- Lorraine 1918

World War II

- Normandy
- Northern France
- Rhineland
- Ardennes-Alsace
- Central Europe

Decorations:

Luxembourg Croix de Guerre, Streamer embroidered LUXEMBOURG

BIBLIOGRAPHY

BOOKS -- Primary Sources

Allen, William. *Stonewall Jackson, Robert E. Lee, and the Army of Northern Virginia, 1862*. New York: First Da Word Capo Press, 1995.

Anderson, James S. *Fifth Wisconsin Reunion Pamphlets: Report of Proceedings of the 5th Wisconsin Volunteer Association Annual Reunions*. ________, 1900, 1901, 1903.

Best, Isaac O. *History of the 121st New York State Infantry*, reprint Baltimore, Maryland: Butternut & Blue, 1996.

Billings, John D. *Hardtack & Coffee, The Unwritten Story of Army Life*. Lincoln, Nebraska: University of Nebraska, 1993.

Chamberlain, Joshua Lawrence. *The Passing of the Armies. An Account of the Final Campaign of the Army of the Potomac, Based Upon Personal Reminiscences of the Fifth Army Corps*. New York: Bantam Books, 1993.

DeForest, John William. *A Volunteer's Adventures: A Union Captain's Record of the Civil War*. Edited by James H. Croushore. Baton Rouge: Louisiana State University Press, 1996.

Fisk, Wilbur. *Hard Marching Every Day, The Civil War Letters of Private Wilbur Fisk, 1861-1865*. Edited by Emil and Ruth Rosenblatt. Lawrence, Kansas: University Press of Kansas, 1992.

Gordon, John B. *Reminiscences of the Civil War*. Baton Rouge: Louisiana State University Press, (reprint) 1993.

Grant, Ulysses S. *Personal Memoirs of U. S. Grant*. New York: Charles L. Webster & Company, 1885.

Haines, Alanson A. *History of the Fifteenth Regiment New Jersey Volunteers*. New York: Jenkins & Thomas, Printers, reprint Olde Soldier Books, Inc., 1883.

Humphreys, Andrew H. *Campaigns of the Civil War: The Virginia Campaign of 1864 and 1865, vol. 6*. Thomas Yoseloff, Ed. New York: A. S. Barnes & Co., 1993.

Hyde, Thomas W. *Following the Greek Cross or Memories of the Sixth Army Corps*. New York: Houghton, Mifflin & Comp., 1894.

LaFantasie, Glenn (Editor). *Gettysburg, Colonel William C. Oates and Lieutenant Frank A. Haskell*. New York: Bantam Books, 1992.

Latta, James W. *History of the First Regiment Infantry N.G.P.* Philadelphia: J. B. Lippencott, 1912.

Lyman, Theodore. *With Grant & Meade From the Wilderness To Appomattox*. Lincoln, Nebraska: University of Nebraska Press, reprint, 1994.

Pennsylvania, Gettysburg Battlefield Commission. *Pennsylvania at Gettysburg. Ceremonies at the Dedication of the Monuments Erected by the Commonwealth of Pennsylvania*. Vol. 1 (49th Pa. Vol., Joseph P. Downing), (61st Pa. Vol., A. P. Brewer); (93rd Pa. Vol., Chaplain J. S. Lame), Vol. 2 (119th Pa. Vol., James W. Latta). Harrisburg, Pennsylvania: E. K. Myers, State Printers, 1893.

Porter, Horace. *Campaigning With Grant*. Edited by Wayne C. Temple. New York: Bonanza Books, 1961.

Prowell, George R. *History of the Eighty-seventh Regiment, Pennsylvania Volunteers, Prepared From Official Records, Diaries, and Other Authentic Sources of Information*. Press of the York Daily, reprint. Mt. Vernon, Indiana: Windmill Publications, Inc., 1994.

Rhodes, Robert Hunt. *All For the Union, The Civil War Diary and Letters of Elisha Hunt Rhodes*. New York: Orion Books, 1985.

Sheridan, Philip H. *The Personal Memoirs of P. H. Sheridan*. New York: Da Capo Press, 1992.

Stevens, George T. *Three Years in the Sixth Corps*. Albany, New York: S.R. Gray, Publisher, 1866.

United States War Department. *The War of the Rebellion: A Compilation of the Official Records of the Union and Confederate Armies*. 70

vols. in 128 parts. Washington, D.C.: Government Printing Office, 1880-1901.

Watkins, Samuel R. *Co. Aytch, A Side Show of the Big Show.* New York: McMillan Publishing Company, reprint 1962.

Westbrook, Robert S. *History of the 49th Pennsylvania Volunteers.* Altoona, Pennsylvania: Altoona Times Print, 1898.

BOOKS -- Secondary Sources

Baquet, Camille. *History of the First Brigade New Jersey Volunteers from 1861 to 1865.* Trenton, New Jersey: State of New Jersey, 1910.

Bates, Samuel P. *History of the Pennsylvania Volunteers - 1861-1865.* Vol. 4, Philadelphia: B. Singerly, 1870.

--------. *Martial Deeds of Pennsylvania.* Philadelphia: T. H. Davis & Co., 1875.

Beyer, W. F. & Keydel (Ed.). *Deeds of Valor, How America's Civil War Heroes Won the Congressional Medal of Honor.* Stamford, Connecticut: Longmeadow Press, 1994.

Bilby, Joseph G. *Three Rousing Cheers, A History of the Fifteenth New Jersey From Flemington to Appomattox.* Highstown, New Jersey: Longstreet House, 1993.

Coddington, Edwin B. *The Gettysburg Campaign, A Study in Command.* New York: Charles Scribner's Sons, 1968.

Cozzens, Peter. *This Terrible Sound, The Battle of Chickamauga.* Chicago: University of Illinois Press, 1992.

Davis, Burke. *To Appomattox, Nine April Days in 1865.* New York: Rinehart & Company, Inc., 1959.

Faust, Patricia L. (Ed.). *Historical Times Illustrated Encyclopedia of the Civil War.* New York: Harper Perennial, 1986.

Foote, Shelby. *The Civil War, a Narrative.* New York: Vintage Books, 1986.

Fox, William F. *Regimental Losses in the Americal Civil War 1861-1865.* _______: _____________, 1889.

Freeman, Douglas Southall. *Lee's Lieutenants, vol. 3*. New York: Charles Scribner's Sons, 1944.

Furgurson, Ernest B. *Chancellorsville 1863, The Souls of the Brave*. New York: Alfred A. Knopf, 1992.

Gordon, Harmon Y. *History of the First Regiment of Pennsylvania and Antecedent and Successor Echelons to the 103d Engineer Battalion (Infantry Division)*. Pennsylvania Army National Guard (The Dandy First), 1777-1961. Philadelphia: Legal Intelligencer, 1961.

Hassler, Warren W. *Crisis At the Crossroads, The First Day at Gettysburg*. Gettysburg, Pennsylvania: Stan Clark Military Books, reprint 1991.

Henderson, William D. *The Road to Bristow Station, Campaigning With Lee and Meade, August 1 - October 20, 1863*. Lynchburg, Virginia: H. E. Howard, Inc., 1987.

Hennessey, John J. *Return to Bull Run, The Campaign and Battle of Second Manassas*. New York: Simon & Schuster, 1993.

Horn, John. *The Petersburg Campaign, June 1864-April 1865*. Conshohocken, Pennsylvania: Combined Books, Inc., 1993.

Jordan, David M. *Winfield Scott Hancock, A Soldier's Life*. Bloomington: Indiana University Press, 1996.

Korn, Jerry. *Pursuit to Appomattox*. Alexandria, Virginia: Time Life Books, 1987.

Lewis, Thomas A. *The Guns of Cedar Creek*. New York: Harper & Rowe, Publishers, 1988.

Longacre, Edward G. *The Cavalry at Gettysburg, A Tactical Study of Mounted Operations During the Civil War's Pivotal Campaign, No. 9 June - 14 July 1863*. Lincoln, Nebraska: University of Nebraska Press, 1993.

Lord, Francis A. *Civil War Sutlers and Their Wares*. Cranbury, New Jersey: Thomas Yoseloff Ltd., 1969.

Maney, R. Wayne. *Marching to Cold Harbor, Victory and Failure, 1864*. Shippensburg, Pennsylvania: White Mane Publishing Co., Inc., 1995.

Matter, William D. *If It Takes All Summer, The Battle of Spotsylvania*. Chapel Gate North Carolina: The University of North Carolina Press, 1988.

McPherson, James M. *Battle Cry of Freedom, The Civil War Era*. New York: Ballentine Books, 1989.

Mundy, James H. *No Rich Men's Sons, The Sixth Maine Volunteer Infantry*. Cape Elizabeth, Maine: Harp Publications, 1994.

Pfanz, Harry W. *Gettysburg - Culp's Hill and Cemetery Hill*. Chapel Hill, North Carolina: The University of North Carolina Press, 1993.

--------, *Gettysburg - The Second Day*. Chapel Hill, North Carolina: The University of North Carolina Press, 1987.

Pond, George E. *Campaigns of the Civil War: The Shenandoah Valley*. Thomas Yoseloff Ed. vol. VI. New York: A. S. Barnes & Co., 1963.

Priest, John Michael. *Antietam, the Soldiers' Battle*. Shippensburg, Pennsylvania: White Mane Publishing Co., Inc., reprint Oxford Press, 1989.

--------. *Nowhere to Run, The Wilderness, May 4th and 5th, 1864*. Shippensburg, Pennsylvania: White Mane Publishing Co., Inc., 1995.

Rhea, Gordon C. *The Battle of the Wilderness, May 5-6, 1864*. Baton Rouge, Louisiana: Louisiana State University, 1994.

Sears, Stephen W. *Chancellorsville*. New York: Houghton Mifflin Company, 1996.

Slade, A. D. *That Sterling Soldier, The Life of David A. Russell*. Dayton: Morningside, 1995.

Stackpole, Edward J. *Chancellorsville, 2nd Edition*. Harrisburg, Pennsylvania: Stackpole Books, 1988.

--------. *The Fredericksburg Campaign, 2nd Edition*. Harrisburg, Pennsylvania: Stackpole Books, 1991.

--------. *Sheridan In the Shenandoah, Jubal Early's Nemesis, 2nd Edition*. Harrisburg, Pennsylvania: Stackpole Books, 1992.

Starr, Stephen Z. *The Union Cavalry in the Civil War. Vol. 1 & 3*. Baton Rouge, Louisiana: Louisiana State University Press, 1981.

Steere, Edward. *The Wilderness Campaign*. Harrisburg, Pennsylvania: The Stackpole Company, Olde Soldier Books, Inc., reprint 1987.

Stewart, George R. *Pickett's Charge, A Microhistory of the Final Attack at Gettysburg, July 3, 1863*. Boston, Massachusetts: Houghton Mifflin Company, 1959.

Symonds, Craig L. *Gettysburg, A Battlefield Atlas*. Baltimore, Maryland: The Nautical & Aviation Publishing Company of America, 1992.

Taylor, Frank H. *Philadelphia in the Civil War*. Philadelphia, 1913, reprint J. M. Santarelli, 1991.

Trask, Kerry K. *Fire Within; A Civil War Narrative from Wisconsin*. Kent, Ohio: The Kent State University Press, 1995.

Trudeau, Noah Andre. *Bloody Roads South, The Wilderness to Cold Harbor, May-June 1864*. Boston, Massachusetts: Little, Brown & Company Ltd., 1989.

--------. *The Last Citadel, Petersburg, Virginia*. Boston, Massachusetts: Little, Brown and Company, 1991.

United States War Department. *Atlas to Accompany the Official Records of the Union & Confederate Armies*. Board of Publication: George B. Davis, Leslie J. Perry, Joseph W. Kirkley. Compiled by Capt. Calvin D. Cowles, Washington, D.C., 1891-1895.

Wert, Jeffrey D. *General James Longstreet, The Confederacy's Most Controversial Soldier*. New York: Simon & Schuster, 1993.

--------. *Mosby's Rangers*. New York: A Touchstone Book, 1990.

--------. *From Winchester to Cedar Creek: The Shenandoah Campaign of 1864*. Carlisle, Pennsylvania: South Mountain Press, Inc., 1987.

Wheeler, Richard. *Witness to Gettysburg*. New York: Meridian, 1989.

--------. *On Fields of Fury, From the Wilderness to the Crater, An Eyewitness History*. New York: Harper Collins, 1991.

Winslow, Richard Elliot III. *General John Sedgwick, The Story of a Union Corps Commander*. Novato, California: Presidio Press, 1982.

MANUSCRIPTS

John Carvel Arnold Letters, Library of Congress, May 1864 - March 28, 1865.

Michael R. Benson, M.A. Paper, The Early History of the Artillery Battalion of Philadelphia, 1760-1777 (1976).

George C. Booze, enlisted man's letters and sketch, United States Army Military and Historical Institute, Sep. 14, 1863 - March 14, 1865.
Gideon Clark Correspondence, Pennsylvania Archives, 119th Pa. Vol., Harrisburg, Pennsylvania.
Peter C. Ellmaker Correspondence, Pennsylvania Archives, 119th Pa. Vol., Harrisburg, Pennsylvania.
G. Norton Galloway extract from an historical paper by Galloway of Company "A" 95th Pennsylvania Volunteers. *Gosline's Pennsylvania Zouaves in the Sixth Corps*. U.S. Army Military History Institute, Pennsylvania Infantry - 95th Regiment Papers, 1961.
Andrew T. Goodman Correspondence. Pennsylvania Archives, 119th Pa. Vol., Harrisburg, Pennsylvania.
Edmund Halsey Diary, 15th New Jersey Regiment, USAMHI, Carlisle, Pennsylvania.
Henry Keiser Papers, Harrisburg Civil War Round Table Collection, Pennsylvania Infantry - 95th Regiment, Pa. Volunteers, USAMHI, Carlisle, Pennsylvania.
James W. Latta Diary, Library of Congress, vol. 1862 - 1865
J. Craig Nannos, Outline of History of the 103d Engineer Battalion, 28th Infantry Division (MECH), Philadelphia, Pennsylvania.
Henry T. Peck, Wartime Letters. First Regiment Corp., 103rd Engineer Museum, Philadelphia, Pennsylvania.
Pennsylvania Dept. of Military Affairs, Outlines of Organizations, 103d Engineers, Harrisburg, Pennsylvania 1937.

Military Records, National Archives, Washington, D.C.:

Booze, George C.
Cassady, John G.
Clark, Gideon
Coxe, Edward E.
Dunlap, Lewis J.
Ellmaker, Peter C.
Faust, Aaron
Faust, Francis

Faust, John E.
Fisher, Joshua
Millard, James B.
Millard, John H.
Morris, Thomas
Moss, William C.
Rodgers, Peter W.
Warner, Charles P.

NEWSPAPERS

Bucks County Intelligencer, Doylestown, Pennsylvania, September 30, 1862.

Bucks County Intelligencer, Doylestown, Pennsylvania, October 14, 1862.

Bucks County Intelligencer, (Stapler, T. W.), Doylestown, Pennsylvania, October 14, 1862.

Bucks County Intelligencer, (W., T. B.), Doylestown, Pennsylvania, March 31, 1863.

Bucks County Intelligencer, (W., B. A.), Doylestown, Pennsylvania, May 26, 1863.

The Philadelphia Inquirer, December 27, 1862.

The Philadelphia Inquirer, May 10, 1863.

The Philadelphia Inquirer, May 19, 1863.

The Philadelphia Inquirer, March 27, 1922.

Philadelphia Public Ledger, July 30, 1862.

Philadelphia Sunday Press, December 28, 1890.

The Press, Philadelphia, October 9, 1862.

The Press, Philadelphia, May 5, 1863.

INDEX